ON THE FRINGE

FRINGE

FRINGE

ON THE

Gays

and

Lesbians

in Politics

DAVID RAYSIDE

CORNELL UNIVERSITY PRESS   Ithaca and London

First published 1998 by Cornell University Press.
First printing, Cornell Paperbacks, 1998.

Library of Congress Cataloging-in-Publication Data

Rayside, Morton David, 1947–
    On the fringe : gays and lesbians in politics / David Rayside.
        p. cm.
    Includes index.
    ISBN 0-8014-3321-5 (cloth : alk. paper). — ISBN 0-8014-8374-3
    (paper : alk. paper)
        1. Gay liberation movement—Great Britain.   2. Gay liberation
    movement—Canada.   3. Gay liberation movement—United States.
    4. Gays—Great Britain—Political activity.   5. Gays—Canada—
    Political activity.   6. Gays—United States—Political activity
    I. Title.
    HQ76.8.G7R39   1998
    305.9'0664—DC21   97-35245

Printed in the United States of America.

Cornell University Press strives to utilize environmentally responsible suppliers and materials to the fullest extent possible in the publishing of its books. Such materials include vegetable-based, low-VOC inks and acid-free papers that are also either recycled, totally chlorine-free, or partly composed of nonwood fibers.

Cloth printing   10 9 8 7 6 5 4 3 2 1
Paperback printing   10 9 8 7 6 5 4 3 2 1

Once again,
with enduring love
to

    Gerry Hunt

    Ron Rayside

    Judi Stevenson

Contents

Illustrations

Tables

Preface

This book is an assessment of the relevance of legislative politics for achieving gay and lesbian equality. It is motivated in part by a recognition of how little analytical work has been undertaken on contemporary lesbian/gay/bisexual activism and its political impact. Most scholarly literature on state policy and social movements avoids more than the slightest mention of sexual diversity. This project springs also from a belief in the importance of contributing to our understanding of how members of sexual minorities can help provoke changes that improve the quality of people's lives—gay and straight. The book combines, I hope, the thoroughness of rigorous scholarship and the engagement of activist intent.

In some respects, my research has been rooted in an autobiographical interest in the consequences of immersion in established political processes, whether in a provincial legislature or a large and equally complex university. I originally came to be interested in such questions from activist experience that began in the late 1970s with *The Body Politic*, at the time Canada's best-known gay magazine. I was then taken up with legal defense work in the Right to Privacy Committee, which emerged in response to Toronto police raids against gay bathhouses. In 1986 I coordinated a coalition to press (successfully) for the addition of sexual orientation to the Ontario Human Rights Code. It was at the conclusion of this campaign that I came to realize the importance of that political process, not only to social scientists but to activists themselves. Since that time I have retained a particular interest in discovering what creates opportunities for progress within mainstream processes.

As both activist and analyst, I bring to this inquiry a heterodox framework and an increasing aversion to certainty. I draw from analytical traditions born of class and feminist analysis, blended with liberal and social democratic traditions that rest on conceptions of individual and group agency. More than ever, I react against the surety with which many observers and participants interpret the long-term effects of processes and decisions just past. If, with the benefit of hindsight, skilled historians can disagree honestly about the significance of events in the past, how can we as analysts of the present claim we truly understand?

There is no more vivid demonstration of the difficulty we face in taking the temperature of our times than trying to make sense of public opinion toward sexual diversity. In most democracies, strong support for the principle of equal treatment exists alongside strong moral disapproval of homosexuality. Even within each of these categories of belief, there are wide variations on particulars and considerable volatility over time. I say this not to denigrate social scientific analysis of polls and surveys, but to signal my wariness of taking their data as indicative of a fixed attitude or cultural context.

In my analysis of lesbian and gay activism, I react against two strong currents I detect in the academic literature on social movements in general, and the lesbian/gay movement in particular. One tends to romanticize the movement and imagine that all failings are a result of factors external to it. The other tends to treat movement activists in the political mainstream as unwitting dupes easily assimilated and drawn into unprincipled compromise. The former fails to differentiate between furthering a cause and understanding it; the latter understates the strategic complexities facing activists, while patronizing them as incapable of a broader or more reflective view.

There is an equally strong tendency among activists to attack one another more fiercely than their opponents, particularly in the face of defeat or pressure to compromise. At one point in the debate over the ban on lesbians and gays in the U.S. military, Barney Frank, an openly gay member of Congress, proposed a compromise that provoked angry denunciation among many who sought nothing less than a full lifting of the ban. In sorting out such difficult moments in the profiles and case studies presented here, I have mentally tried to walk a mile or two in the shoes of my various protagonists. In particular, I have tried to take account of the highly constrained roles of politicians, and of those who seek to influence them. I bring to that effort not a naive belief that all politicians are honorable, but an honest conviction that many work hard at complex roles that few on the outside would abide.

I began the project by focusing on the most prominent openly gay politicians in Britain, Canada, and the United States, believing that an analysis of their roles would provide a lens for assessing the impact of gay and lesbian entry into mainstream politics. In 1992 there were only four openly gay politicians in the national legislatures of these three countries, Labour MP Chris Smith in Britain, New Democratic MP Svend Robinson in Canada, and Democratic members of Congress Barney Frank and Gerry Studds. Smith, Robinson, and Frank agreed to be interviewed; Studds, who did not run for reelection in 1996, did not.

By late 1994, events were outpacing my research design. Major issues were acquiring national prominence, at times moved by complex partisan and activist forces. While openly gay politicians were once routinely at the center of the maneuvers designed to thrust sexual orientation issues forward, in the mid-1990s that was becoming less uniformly the case. Understanding the complex roles of politicians such as Frank, Robinson, and Smith was still important to me, but that project had to run in parallel with legislative case studies.

During the course of my research, gay rights issues provoked front-page national debate—in the United States over the ban on homosexuals serving in the military, in Britain over the age of consent for homosexual activity, and in Canada by both anti-discrimination legislation and same-sex relationship recognition. The legislative struggles over each of these issues formed the core of a case study.

In compiling these case studies, I have retained my preference for unstructured interviews, allowing those I talked to as much room as possible to offer their own interpretations of events and their own role in them. I have, in other words, tried to avoid creating an artificial division of labor between the analysis I was asking others to engage in and the analysis I have undertaken myself, though I impose on myself the daunting challenge of making sense of each case as a whole, and situating each in wider questions of political process.

The style of analysis is unashamedly inductive. Though the material is undoubtedly shaped by my prior views about structured inequality, I have built up each case study from the ground, rather than starting my inquiry with clear hypotheses set up in competitive relationship to other theoretical views laid out in scholarly literature. I am not driven by the need to establish generalizable "laws" about the success of social movements or about the patterns of relations between movements and mainstream politics. Activists and policy makers in one political setting can learn from what has taken place in other systems, but no one can simply apply a successful strategy developed in one system to another without recognizing the differences created by the cultural environment and institutional setting. This comparative analysis is less driven by a need to formulate generalization than it is meant to help those in each setting learn lessons for specific application.

I have interviewed about 350 people, in sessions lasting from ten minutes to three hours. The largest categories of interview subjects were those who work inside legislative or administrative political institutions—either as legislative aides, elected politicians, or officials—and those who are engaged in activism aimed at effecting change within those institutions. In neither case did I intend to construct representative cross-sections. Instead I sought out those who I believed would best understand the particular case studies at hand, including their process and outcomes. I make substantial use of direct quotation, sometimes from participants with unusual insight into the issues at hand, sometimes from those representing an important perspective. With a very few exceptions, my interviews were based on firm pledges of confidentiality. I have taken those pledges extremely seriously, in many cases providing only vague descriptions of role or position in order to minimize the risk of recognition. That may frustrate readers whose research designs, interviewing styles, and ethical demands differ from my own.

My case studies are asymmetric in several ways. First, I had differential access in the various sites of my research. Of the national capitals and major cities that I worked in, Washington, D.C., provided the most challenges and frustrations in making contacts and securing interviews. I benefited from enormous cooperation and honesty from those I did talk to, but there were many more I wished to interview who were unreachable or unavailable. In London and Ottawa I enjoyed considerable access to the majority of politicians, aides, and activists I sought out. The provincial legislature at the doorstep of my university provided me with the richest array of contacts, permitting an especially detailed look at the debate over same-sex benefits in Ontario.

The case studies are also asymmetrical in that there are two major legislative case studies on Canada, one at the federal level and one in the province of Ontario. Each in my view had national significance, the Ontario case mostly because of the sweeping nature of the changes being proposed, and also because the province is Canada's largest.

The cases are obviously asymmetrical, too, in that they do not cover the same issues in the three countries. The U.S. military ban, the British age of consent, the Canadian Human Rights Act, and the recognition of same-sex relationships in Ontario each has a very particular character, posing distinct challenges to both activists and politicians. That may make the formulation of generalizations across cases and countries more difficult. But they called out for examination because they constituted the major struggles over gay and lesbian equality in their time. In all their peculiarity and distinctiveness, then, these are the windows through which we have an opportunity to observe and assess the current status of gays and lesbians in mainstream politics.

In both the case studies and the analysis of openly gay politicians, the unrepresentativeness of political institutions themselves has to be addressed. Legislatures and governmental institutions are populated disproportionately by those who are privileged along gender, race, and class lines. The fact that all of the openly gay politicians at the national level in Britain, Canada, and the United States were Caucasian men was no coincidence. The fact reflects the makeup of the legislative chambers in which they sit. In Canada and Britain, only a handful of gays and few lesbians, none of them people of color, have won legislative office even at local or regional levels. The ranks of sexual minority politicians in the United States includes some women, and the merest handful of African Americans, none at the national level.

I have responded to these questions of representation and diversity by interviewing a wider range of openly gay and lesbian politicians at the state and local level. I have also raised questions about gender and race in interviews with non-gay politicians at the national level, and have taken up some of the analytical literature that speaks to the experience of women and minorities in legislative politics. I have also tried to recognize that the experience of male Caucasian politicians and activists does not stand for a universal lesbian and gay existence.

The terms by which groups or communities are known vary within them and change over time. From the late 1960s on, the term "homosexual" was increasingly rejected as signaling the clinical language of oppression in favor of the word "gay," appropriated from historical colloquialism for a variety of people on the social margins. "Lesbian" was soon widely used to balance the male connotations frequently attached to "gay." By the end of the 1980s, as a bisexual identity became more visible, writers and activists began incorporating specific mention of bisexuality in discussing the political movement or the issues pressed by it. In the 1990s, the growth in visibility and assertiveness of those who cross-dress or in other ways transcend gender boundaries has been reflected in the common incorporation of "transgendered" in the inclusive designation of the movement addressing sexual orientation issues. The word "queer" has also been taken up as an affirmative identifier, as part of an attempt at a global term crossing the boundaries implied in the other terms, and as part of a more confrontational political strategy.

I believe deeply in an inclusive vocabulary, one that is adaptable to changes in the way people most affected by it wish to be known. The challenge is to write as inclusively as possible and still retain fluidity and variety in language. I tend to use "lesbian and gay" or the reverse, with the occasional addition of "bisexual" and "transgendered," purely for the sake of simplicity. I sometimes use the word "gay" on its own in adjectival or adverbial form, especially if a more complex form would make an already cumbersome sentence worse. I frequently use the phrase "sexual minorities" to take in all variations in sexual orientation, as well as the term "sexual diversity."

Earlier versions of two chapters of this book have appeared in published form. Chapter 1, on Britain, evolved from an article titled "Homophobia, Class, and Party in England," first published in 1992 by the *Canadian Journal of Political Science*. Chapter 7, on the United States, is an expansion of my chapter in a volume edited by Craig Rimmerman, *Gay Rights, Military Wrongs: Political Perspectives on Lesbians and Gays in the Military*, published in 1996 by Garland.

I am grateful to the Social Sciences and Humanities Research Council of Canada, which provided the major grant that allowed me to inaugurate this research and cover most of its expenses. I am also grateful to my own Political Science Department at the University of Toronto for providing smaller grants (using SSHRC funds). A number of my departmental colleagues offered comments on drafts or presentations related to this project, or inquired about its progress in encouraging ways. The University of Toronto granted me a sabbatical leave in 1994–95 which was indispensable for making progress on this project amidst administrative and teaching responsibilities.

Before and during my term as vice principal, University College provided me a supportive home for my scholarly interest in sexual diversity, and my advocacy on behalf of gay/lesbian and other issues. UC-based academics from disciplines across the humanities and social sciences read drafts of my first attempts to understand the British case. Substantial numbers of college members from the professorate, the administrative staff, and the student body have supportively attended talks and seminars on sexual orientation themes, and have in their own day-to-day activity contributed to the creation of a lively, good-humored, and supportive community. Program directors and fellow college officers, including former principal Lynd Forguson, helped in all kinds of ways to create an environment encouraging of my academic, administrative, and political work. My assistant Audrey Dennie simply kept the vice principal's office running, and made it possible for me to steal time for writing, especially in the final crucial months.

The following organizations provided essential documentation about themselves or the issues with which I was most concerned, and in some cases access to files and meetings: in Britain, Stonewall, OutRage, Liberal Democrats for Lesbian and Gay Action (DELGA), the Tory Campaign for Homosexual Equality, the Labour Campaign for Lesbian and Gay Rights, and the Labour Party itself; in Canada, Equality for Gays and Lesbians Everywhere (EGALE), the Campaign for Equal Families, and the Coalition for Lesbian and Gay Rights in Ontario; in the United States, the National Gay and Lesbian Task Force, the Human Rights Campaign, the Victory Fund, the International Network of Gay and Lesbian Officials, the Campaign for Military Service, and the National Resource Center at People for the American Way. Environics provided public opinion poll data for Canada. Broadview Press, Ashgate Publishing, and Yale University Press permitted use of data in books published by them.

David Smith, editor of *Gay Times*, was particularly helpful in providing photographic illustrations and permission for their use. Gordon Rainsford (London), Brandon Matheson (Ottawa), and Wayne Shimabukuro (Los Angeles) permitted the use of their photographs, as did the *Toronto Star*, AP/Wide World Photos, Archive Photos, *Congressional Quarterly*, and the White House. The *Guardian* permitted the use of extensive quotation from a Chris Smith "Diary" published in 1994. Del Carroll provided access to her "Robinson" archive.

I owe incalculable intellectual debts to those independent researchers and academics in whose pathways I now follow, who were writing in the 1970s and early 1980s, when the risks were greater and the audiences smaller. I mention only one to represent them all. Dennis Altman is a political scientist who has long stood as a model of the balance I have sought between intellectual rigor and political engagement. He has also been one of the few to venture into comparative analysis, and has done so with striking clarity and sensitivity to local and national context.

I could not have begun this work without Chris Smith, Svend Robinson, and Barney Frank having agreed to participate. To each of them, and to members of their staffs, I owe enormous debts. Aides to Frank and Robinson were especially helpful in responding to my numerous requests for information and documentation, despite mountains of work on legislative or constituency matters.

I am also grateful to the many activists, legislative assistants, parliamentarians, and other "insiders" who agreed to confidential interviews, often in the midst of pressing schedules. Many received me with patience and answered questions with great insight. Some helped by suggesting the names of others I should talk to, and assisted me in making contact with them. New York State Representative Deborah Glick, former Seattle City Council member Sherry Harris, and Vancouver activist Betty Baxter kindly allowed me to quote them on the record.

A number of colleagues and friends provided advice, assistance, encouragement, and comment on draft material. They include, in Britain, Christina Baron, Bernard Greaves, Alan Butt Philip, Peter Caldwell, Kevan Horne, the household at 16 Pyrland Road in Islington, Annis May Timson, John Wayman, Jeffrey Weeks; in the United States, Martha Ackelsberg, Mark Blasius, Tim Cook, Kristian Fauchald, Leonard Hirsch, Doug Mitchell, Shane Phelan, Craig Rimmerman, Ken Sherrill, Jack Yeager; and in Canada, Sylvia Bashevkin, Terry Farley, Dennis Findlay, Dan Mahoney, Brian Pronger, Barb Stevenson, Robert Vipond, Joseph Wearing, Graham White, David Wolfe, and Lisa Young. Other friends and family helped simply by understanding my preoccupations and absences, occasionally asking "How's the book?" and patiently enduring the response.

I was supported by graduate students in transcribing interviews and scheduling research trips: Ben Davidson, Elizabeth Lorenzin, James Murray, Karen Murray, and Neil Thomlinson. Further transcription was provided by Jean Smith at University College. Invaluable assistance in the final stages was provided by Michael Johnson.

At Cornell University Press, Alison Shonkwiler fought for this book and nurtured it once she had it. She was supportive, good-humored, direct, and immensely perceptive. Carol Betsch and Amanda Heller added their editorial intelligence in refining the manuscript.

Judi Stevenson read almost all of the manuscript in draft form, and offered the kind of detailed commentary and insightful overview, alongside supportive encouragement, that only she could provide. This she has done more than once over the thirty years of our warm friendship. Gerry Hunt read large sections of manuscript, also offering both critical comment and essential encouragement. He lived with this project from beginning to end, and held on tightly during the intellectual and emotional roller coaster ride that it produced. He knew when to leave me alone with this work, and when to hug.

A great many of these informants, assistants, colleagues, and friends believed in this book, and by so doing helped ensure its completion. Whatever shortcomings remain are my responsibility alone.

DAVID M. RAYSIDE

Toronto, Ontario

ON THE FRINGE

Introduction:
Activist Influence
and Political
Context

In the state of virtual equality, gay and lesbian people are at

once insiders, involved openly in government and public af-

fairs to a degree never before achieved, and outsiders,

shunned by our elected officials unless they need our money

or votes in close elections. We are at once marginal and

mainstream, at once assimilated and irreconcilably queer.

Urvashi Vaid, activist and writer

What is clear is that activist voices articulating gay and lesbian concerns have entered mainstream politics. Less certain, however, is the extent of the gains made in legislative and partisan politics, and the role of sexual minority networks in effecting those gains. Equally uncertain is the effect of engagement with such institutionalized politics on the gay, lesbian, bisexual, and transgendered movement itself. Such are the questions that underlie this book. This detailed exploration demonstrates that becoming a player in mainstream political processes is necessary, though costly; that making gains through them is possible, though only under very particular circumstances; and that maintaining links between political insiders and outsiders in the gay and lesbian movement is both difficult and essential.

The visibility of sexual minorities has increased beyond the wildest imaginings of activists caught up in the surge of liberationist politics that began in the late 1960s. Literary, theatrical, film, and television productions commonly take up issues of sexual diversity, and the mass media frequently cover gay-related stories. Growing numbers of corporations pitch advertising to what they see as an important market, and adopt non-discriminatory employment policies. Even with the sickness and death accompanying the spread of AIDS, gay and lesbian communities themselves have grown in size, institutional diversity, and strength. Annual lesbian and gay pride celebrations have mushroomed in size, attracting several hundred thousand in cities such as Toronto, Sydney, New York, and San Francisco.

By the late 1980s and 1990s, a social movement that in the recent past had been relegated to protesting from the outside was spawning organizations that focused on inside politics. Gay and lesbian activists began participating visibly in the nomination and policy conventions of political parties. They were contesting elections, and sometimes winning. They were meeting openly with cabinet members and senior officials, and occasionally with presidents and prime ministers. Activists operating both inside and outside mainstream political institutions have also pushed their issues onto the political agenda. In the middle and late 1980s, issues involving HIV and AIDS constituted a policy wedge, augmented by pressure built up in other areas.[1] In the 1990s, legislative and legal gains became numerous and significant, with prohibitions of discrimination on the grounds of sexual orientation more common, oppressive patterns of policing modified, and first steps taken toward the recognition of same-sex relationships.[2]

But this period in which the political access of lesbian, gay, and bisexual activists was most noticeably improving was also one in which the limits of their influence was most apparent. Legislation was far more often pondered than delivered, even when promising only the most basic right to equal treatment. Proposals acknowledging sexual diversity were greeted with massive protests and expressions of raw hatred normally beyond the limits of public acceptability. Political parties claiming allegiance to principles of equality found themselves more riven by angry division on sexual orientation issues than on any others. The forces arrayed against demands for full citizenship by gays and lesbians include the religious right, especially powerful in the United States. Highly influential sectors of the media have given free rein to these and other extremist voices treating gay and lesbian visibility as symptomatic of all that is corrupting in the modern world. The public response to these messages has been contradictory. Although strong majority support for the principle of gay civil rights has emerged since the mid-1980s, "moral" disapproval and a powerful impulse to avoid the subject persists among equally strong majorities.[3] Politicians are reluctant to take unequivocal stands on sexual orientation even when favorably disposed.

Gains are still being made, and with increasing frequency, but they require unusual combinations of institutional openings, partisan alignments, and skill in marshaling support within and outside the political mainstream. Activist organizations that take up sexual orientation issues are often at a disadvantage in entering mainstream political processes: they lack the resources of most interest groups, and they often form part of a social movement that is itself divided over how such engagement should be organized, and to what ends. Lesbian and gay activists have gained unprecedented access, but often have little say in policy deliberations and little influence over outcomes. They have found themselves in governmental and legislative arenas with little of the leverage thought to count. Their principled arguments for equality have been buffeted by partisan and electoralist considerations, or simply overwhelmed by the resources of groups opposed to sexual diversity.

Disengagement from mainstream politics, however, is no longer an option. The opening up of opportunities in courts, parties, and legislatures demands participation, even if only for preventing setbacks. Opponents are always ready to avail themselves of similar openings, and require constant vigilance. But such engagement reveals pulls and tensions within the gay and lesbian movement, as in other movements. There is an unavoidable conflict between activist networks that work primarily inside mainstream processes and those that do not, manifested in the contradictory demands made on openly gay politicians. The range of roles such politicians play also demonstrates how difficult it is to represent social movements inside legislatures governed by strong norms of compromise and partisan loyalty.

Engagement with the political mainstream has not led the gay and lesbian movement in a uniformly less radical and more bureaucratic direction.[4] It coexists with other strands of activism more wary of or antagonistic to that mainstream. One strategy can as easily provoke as supplant others; each depends on the others. In that sense, mainstreaming can never wholly coopt a social movement, for a movement is always more than a single organization, a single set of political networks, or a uniform strategy. It is, as William Gamson put it, a field of action, encompassing an enormous range of cultural, social, and political work.[5]

Social Movement Challenge to Mainstream Politics

Social movements are not necessarily preoccupied with public policy, or even with state action in the broader sense. They are made up of loosely connected individuals, networks, and associations, often operating primarily at the local level, sharing an identity, a belief, or a political objective. Their adherents usually want to see a change in the policies or behavior of state institutions, but may be at least as interested in building their own communities, securing their identities, or legitimizing themselves in public opinion. Some of the networks and organizations that emerge out of a social movement may focus on cultural or social activity; some on political action. Among those that concentrate on politics, the ideology, strategic repertoire, degree of institutionalization, and issue focus will vary both across groups and within them.

Some writers conceive of social movements as mounting disruptive challenges to the state on the part of people tied by feelings of deep-seated solidarity and political marginality.[6] Movements that emerged in the 1960s and 1970s are seen as having mobilized populations largely excluded from the political mainstream, challenged ordinary politics, rejected traditional processes. In fact, several of the social movements that arose in that period did mount challenges to the postwar "consensus" based on the Keynesian welfare state.[7] Some challenged norms associated with the industrial system itself—the environmental movement being the most obvious. Others emerged from identities based on culture or ethnicity or gender, and were seen as challenging the homogenization implicit in "fordist" production and politics. The spontaneity and localism of such movements contrasted with the institutionalized and often highly centralized processes of mainstream politics.

This does not mean that the kind of politics represented by the social movements of the 1960s and 1970s were in any comprehensive way "new," as many writers have claimed. Such a claim ignores similarities in strategy and in relationship to existing political processes with much earlier movements such as "first wave" feminism and the anti-slavery movement.[8] In any event, generalizing about the social movements of the period since the 1960s is hazardous. Neither social movements as a whole nor the organizations that they spawn are unified in ideology or strategy. They also undergo changes over time in the balance of forces either opposed to or drawn to the political mainstream. Political groups will often experience a "life cycle" shift from radicalism and unstructuredness toward institutionalization. In addition to these "short waves," there are also "long waves" of protest that entail the radicalization of entire social movements—at least for a time.[9] Layered on top of such cycles are the changes that groups sometimes go through as they are pressured to mold themselves to the shape of the political environment in which they operate.

In some respects, too, the groups and associations that emerge from social movements operate like other organized interests. Even those social movements born of a widespread rejection of established processes may include groups that work inside the political mainstream. What differentiates them from most interest groups is that they see themselves, and are seen by others, as representing a broader set of loosely bound activist networks. Groups based on the assertion of a particular identity have a still larger constituency, most of which is uninvolved politically, but parts of which can in certain circumstances be mobilized.

There is a recurrent tension in the relationship between social movements and mainstream institutions. The difficulty facing movement activists is that proximity to complex rule-bound institutions can alienate them from important components of the broader social movement sustaining them. Lobbying in legislative and administrative arenas immerses activists in a culture of incrementalism and compromise—one that is at odds with the transformative impatience of some of the activists who provide energy for the movement at the grass roots, and foreign to many constituents who are simply alienated or otherwise quiescent.

The exercise of influence in the political mainstream requires the development of permanent institutions with specialized expertise, and this too opens up distances between those on the inside and on the outside.[10] Another factor emphasizing the gulf between those who work within mainstream political processes and those who are outside is the tendency of those movement activists closest to the inside to mirror the unrepresentative demographics of political institutions. The broader social movement is likely to be unrepresentative enough, shaped by unequal access and participation across social class, race, gender, and geographic lines. Those parts of it closest to state institutions, particularly electoral institutions, will tend to be even more unrepresentative.

And yet because of the role ascribed to lobbying organizations by politicians, officials, and the media, activists on the inside are often construed as leaders of the movement. Activists themselves will usually deny playing that role, but they cannot avoid being seen to represent the whole movement. Those who are not on the inside, who are skeptical of the dangers of absorption into it, or who feel themselves left out of the political process in general and social movement politics in particular, will object. In some social movements, too, concerns about process lead to distrust of leadership itself.

An added difficulty is that movement activists are often only on the fringes of the political order, bit players in a game dominated by much more powerful interests, partisan considerations, and political circumstances. Social movements may have acquired prominence and importance in civil society, in part as a function of the weakness of political parties and their slowness in taking up new issues. But inside legislative and governmental arenas, the parties remain central players, allying themselves with movement causes in substantial measure as a function of calculations of electoral advantage.[11]

GAY/LESBIAN/BISEXUAL ENGAGEMENT WITH THE STATE. From its very beginnings, the modern lesbian/gay movement has contained divergent views on strategy, organization, and the scope of its political agenda. There has been disagreement, and sometimes tension, opposing those who seek a radical undercutting of social constructions of sexuality and gender against those who seek entry into the existing political and economic order. There are also differences of view between those who believe that gays and lesbians are as ''normal'' as heterosexuals, and deserve acceptance precisely because they are like everyone else, and those who assert that they are and have a right to be different, perhaps subversively so. And then there are those who wish to undermine the boundaries that distinguish gay or lesbian or queer from straight.

Debates over organization pit those who emphasize democratic process and distrust leadership against those who privilege expertise and argue that effectiveness requires hierarchical structure. Debates over strategy have centerd on the merits of direct action and confrontational strategies on the one hand, and tactics for working within existing political and legal structures on the other. There are also those who believe that the movement should focus on gay/lesbian issues alone, and those who believe, on strategic as well as ideological grounds, that coalitions with other causes are indispensable.

Some would write the modern history of gay activism in terms of the tension between "liberation" on the one hand and "legitimation" on the other.[12] This is a view that sees the various polarities over strategy, organization, and ideology as coinciding. But even the most radical of gay activist networks had from the beginning a political agenda that included as many calls for legislative reform as for transformative change. The total exclusion of sexual minorities from full political citizenship gave prominence to demands for civil rights that were couched in the traditional language of liberal democracy. There were those who sought quite conventional ends by unconventional means, and those who used tactics that fit very comfortably with existing political norms, but with radical objectives. If, from the late 1960s through the 1970s, working inside parties, legislatures, and government bureaucracies was unusual, this was based not on principled rejection of the existing political system but on the unlikelihood that mainstream strategies would bear fruit. Politicians were reluctant to identify with issues arising from sexual diversity, and public opinion offered little encouragement to think of the electorate as a potential impetus to change. The oppressiveness of state institutions, so visible in police raids, court judgments, and other forms of officially endorsed discrimination, made working within established political channels suspect even among those ill disposed to radical objectives.

For gays and lesbians, widespread openings into mainstream political processes appeared in the mid to late 1980s in parties, local elections, legislatures, executive bodies, and the courts. The increased visibility of gays and lesbians, and their concentration (especially of gay men) in identifiable urban areas, contributed to the development of a distinct sense of identity and belief in the importance of direct political representation.[13] The devastation of AIDS, and the gay community's response to the epidemic, added to the visibility of sexual minorities and to their mainstream political assertiveness.

The shift toward the mainstream was not simply a function of new openings. It also reflected an activist agenda that moved from simply wanting state institutions to "keep out," toward a politics that sought more positive engagement with gay-related issues. The AIDS epidemic led activists to recognize the indispensability of government intervention and public funding, without necessarily abandoning their wariness of state regulation of sexuality. At the same time, the ongoing development of gay and lesbian communities produced a discontent over the absence of the most basic of civil rights accorded other citizens in liberal democratic societies. The existence of a radical right in some countries prepared to target gay issues added to the urgency of working with mainstream political institutions. In the United States especially, the declaration of "cultural war" threatened the few legislative gains that had been achieved and removed what little choice there was to remain above the partisan fray.

By the 1990s, gay and lesbian activists were being seen as legitimate players inside political arenas to which they had had only partial and sporadic access before. A number of centrist and left parties were taking their first steps toward more expansive views on equity issues, in part because they were searching for new electoral constituencies in a period of major political realignment. In several countries, caucuses and committees were taking up sexual orientation issues within parties and autonomous groups were established for influencing governments. Such developments, though more advanced in the United States than elsewhere, were evident in countries with very different political systems. In a few instances, gay men and lesbians themselves had become legislators or appointed officials, or had come out as such after having entered the political arena. Mass media reports increasingly talked of the power of gays and lesbians to exercise political muscle.

The increased attention to mainstream politics in the gay/lesbian movement did not eliminate confrontational styles or radical visions. It was precisely during a period of increased engagement with institutionalized politics that oppositionist direct action revived, in the form of groups such as ACT UP, Queer Nation, AIDS Action Now, and OutRage.[14] What the recurrence of direct action demonstrates is the wariness of assimilation that is widespread in the lesbian and gay social movement, although the aims of these groups often do not reflect the radical oppositionism suggested by their tactics.

Tensions along class, race, and gender lines, between direct action and lobbying, and between national lobbying groups and local or regional networks are common in this as in other social movements. Substantial lesbian involvement in AIDS work, and the expansion of the gay agenda to include relationship recognition, helped increase the numbers of women working alongside gay men and inside the political system. Gay/lesbian movements have also begun to reflect cultural and racial diversity, though the unevenness of such development is still evident in those networks and groups most closely linked to governments, legislatures, parties, and the courts—not least because of the correlation of race and class and the tendency for political access to be highly structured along social class lines.

In a social movement representing people so long disparaged and marginalized, and so long denied political access, there can at times be an unusual activist unity. The utter centrality of visibility to the lesbian and gay movement also gives importance to measures that would be dismissed in other movements as purely symbolic—for example, legislation formally prohibiting discrimination. But conflict may open up as a result of tension between the culture of respectability on the inside and the culture of the outrageous and flamboyant that so permeates lesbian and gay communities. The still-widespread invisibility of sexual difference, and the struggles that most individual lesbians, gays, bisexuals, and transsexuals have in growing up in heterosexual families, give community life quite a different character than that among women, racial minorities, the disabled, and so on. These factors generate a culture of challenge to the bounds of respectability.[15]

Legislatures and parties, however, are permeated by historically laden norms of proper form and "reasonableness." The expectations of conformity imposed on those speaking to new or controversial issues is potentially much greater. Claimants to political legitimacy will often accentuate the normality of the constituency they speak for, highlighting gays and lesbians who appear and sound "respectable," and same-sex relationships that are recognizable by heterosexual standards. This tactic risks marginalizing those who differ by race, by class, by relational patterns, and by sexual practice from that public image.

Pressures to play by the rules are especially pronounced for those who are actually elected to legislative assemblies. They and others who are active within political parties are also expected to demonstrate a degree of partisan loyalty that inevitably separates them from much, if not most, of a broader social movement tending to skepticism toward all parties. Politicians are often subjected to implicit pressures to disconnect themselves from radical and disruptive elements of the social movements that support them. The failure to conform, especially for those who are represented in very small numbers within legislatures, can well mean complete loss of influence.

But assimilation is not inevitable, in part because gays and lesbians are located on the fringe of the political mainstream. They do not have the kind of political leverage that would allow them to be absorbed into institutionalized "policy communities." They are also linked to a social movement that still incorporates wariness of engagement and often generates criticism of those preoccupied by it. Many who participate in traditional politics recognize the importance of mobilization on the streets, and are fully aware of the distance between the small victories they win and the goals they seek.

DETERMINANTS OF ACTIVIST INFLUENCE. There are major theoretical differences of view over the susceptibility of liberal democratic regimes to the pressure of organized social movements. Liberal or pluralist analysis tends toward a view of the political decision-making arena as a relatively level playing field where success or failure is largely dependent on the resources available to a group or movement and the skill applied to mobilizing them. Socialist and radical analyses, by contrast, see the state as an interlocking array of governments, courts, parties, and administrative structures firmly enmeshed in and defensive of dominant interests. Some see the regulation of sexuality as tied to the needs of capitalism, others to the maintenance of the gendered heterosexual family, others to a larger pattern of domination and marginalization of all those who are different. Still others may argue that issues raised by gay and lesbian activists are not fundamentally threatening to the existing political and economic order, but that attempts at reform encounter elaborate legal and administrative impediments reflecting traditional conceptions of gender, sexuality, and family.

I attach some credence to critiques of liberal democratic regimes that see the state as upholding deeply structured patterns of inequality, but that also see contradictory roles in the functioning of state institutions that create openings for challenge. Even the rightward swings of centrist and social democratic governments abandoning elements of the Keynesian welfare state do not in themselves close down the possibility of progressive reforms on gay-related issues. In seeking to place issues of sexual diversity on the agendas of parties and legislatures, activists do not face the barriers that women and racial minorities confront in trying to increase social spending or modify the play of the free market.

To accept the view that social movement activists can become political players who exercise influence over governmental and legal outcomes leads naturally to the question of what factors make a difference. The resources that social movement groups can summon are of obvious importance. The number of group members, the size of the larger politicizable constituency, financial resources, technical networks, access to information and expertise, media facilities and the skills required to deploy them—these all count.[16] A group's internal cohesion and the unity of purpose in the broader movement are also important.

Resources are not countable in absolute terms, of course, since their weight must be calculated in relation to the resources of the other side, factoring in whatever biases are entrenched in the existing legal and political system. The resources that can be marshaled by an American gay and lesbian movement are hugely more impressive than those available to virtually any other sexual minority movement in the world, even on a per capita basis. But any analysis of the political significance of such resources must take into account the extraordinary power of the American Christian right. (Some interests, too, are so powerful that they can shape the policy process in a wide variety of political circumstances, regardless of the resources available to the groups representing them. The weight of a large automobile manufacturer or financial institution in the United States, Canada, Britain, Germany, or Italy can ensure that its policy preferences prevail most of the time.)

Social movements operate within an "opportunity structure"—one shaped by factors such as the openness or permeability of the political system, the extent of centralization or decentralization of the regime, the relationship between executive and legislature, the pattern of party opposition and cohesion, the nature of the electoral system, the capacity of the courts to challenge governmental action, the support for rights claims in the existing legal environment, and the array of media voices.[17] These are not simply fixed elements, for there can be important shifts in party composition and leadership, and changes in judicial interpretation, some of which are of course subject to influence from the activity of social movements themselves.

Particular characteristics of the political structure within which a movement mobilizes can work sometimes favorably and at other times unfavorably. A centralized regime with power highly concentrated in the leadership of the governing party can be enormously advantageous in the event of that leadership's being disposed to proceed with a pro-gay/lesbian measure. In the absence of such preparedness, structural fragmentation and decentralization may allow activist entry into parts of the political system under more progressive or flexible control. Social movements will often benefit from the support of a particular party, but even that kind of opportunity can have a double edge. The unequivocal support of a small party might do little except provide occasional visibility for the group's demands inside the legislative arena. Similar support from a larger party may be more useful, but can also induce other major parties to exploit that issue among the electorate.

Favorable public opinion is an obvious asset for any movement seeking political change. There have been positive shifts in public attention to homosexuality over the last decade, but opinions are often contradictory and substantially influenced by media coverage and by the way protagonists shape the debate. In many circumstances overall public opinion will matter less than those beliefs that are actually translated into letters, phone calls, and visits to politicians. The opinions promoted by the media are of obvious importance for social movements.

The right setting, timing, and circumstance can provide a political movement of only modest resources with an opportunity to exercise considerable influence on political outcomes. In other environments or at other times, social movement organizations need all the resources traditionally associated with interest group leverage.[18] In some circumstances access and influence will depend on a group's representatives' fitting in with the legislative or legal environment and playing mainstream politics by its rules; in others influence will depend on confrontation.

Political Contexts

This book is a comparative inquiry into the extent to which mainstream openings allow for significant change in policy outcomes. Comparison helps differentiate common challenges facing social movements from those that are distinctive to a single political system. It helps to display variation in patterns of activist mobilization, and to discern the impact of distinctive political and social environments on policy. Comparison is particularly important in the case of the American movement. The development of gay visibility and political activism in the United States has had enormous international reverberation, even if learned and adapted in ways that are shaped by domestic cultural and political norms.[19] That gives the American case unusual importance in any understanding of the status of sexual minorities and the pattern of activism in other countries. But the United States is an exceptional system, its social and political structures distinctive in ways that have a profound impact on social movement organization.

Britain, Canada, and the United States have common roots in cultural and political heritage; similar legal frameworks, government structures, popular attitudes, and institutional practices; and a history of similarities in the regulation of gender and sexuality. But in all these respects American exceptionalism is still pronounced, creating a gay and lesbian political movement unlike any other, with an equally unusual pattern of success and failure. Americans need to understand the peculiarities of sexual diversity politics in their own country. Britons too need to look abroad for comparative lessons, though activists and academics in the United Kingdom are less closed than their American counterparts to goings on in other countries. Canadians are constantly and unavoidably exposed to American influence, so they need in particular to recognize that lessons can be learned from European comparisons as well.

BRITAIN. Political authority in Britain is highly centralized, with government institutions concentrated in a capital city that is overwhelmingly dominant in economic and cultural importance. Power is also highly concentrated in the hands of the political executive; the prime minister and cabinet control the legislative agenda, leaving little room for the policy entrepreneurship available in the more fragmented U.S. system. British courts have much less capacity than their North American counterparts to challenge legislative or administrative actions, leaving social movements comparatively modest capacity to use litigation to overcome parliamentary or governmental resistance.[20] The notion of parliamentary sovereignty lies at the heart of Britain's largely unwritten constitution. The jurisdiction of the national legislature is unconstrained by either autonomous regional assemblies or a charter of rights comparable to the American or Canadian ones, though of course there are constitutional conventions, treaty obligations, and political realities establishing limits.

The party system has offered little encouragement for equity-seeking groups until recently. Britain's politics have been dominated by the Conservative and Labour Parties for most of the twentieth century, with the Liberals and then Liberal Democrats holding third place. The Conservatives under Margaret Thatcher moved toward a firm embrace of free market liberalism, though with elements of moral conservatism remaining. Since the mid-1980s, the Labour Party has moved toward the center left, and toward a loosening of connections to the labor movement, though tackling some sexual diversity issues in the late 1980s and 1990s. The Liberal Democrats have embraced sexual orientation more assertively than the Labour Party, though hesitantly at times, and in any event their third-party status gives them only modest leverage.

This is a political order, then, with relatively few points of access for social movement activists. Gay and lesbian groups have important allies outside parliamentary politics, and to some extent inside, but they face a political order heavily slanted against change, with few opportunities for favorable legal or legislative decisions. If the party in government is not positively disposed, there are few other places to go—even fewer with the erosion of local authority during the Thatcher years.

Such activism as is directed at mainstream political processes is under enormous pressure to accommodate to the norms and rituals of a highly tradition-bound legislative system. Lobbying work is therefore easily separated from more confrontational extraparliamentary forms of activism, antagonistic to working with the existing system on both strategic and ideological grounds. This division is often exacerbated by social class differences between those who move comfortably within the halls and committee rooms of Westminster and those who do not.

CANADA. Canadian decentralization is in stark contrast to the U.K. pattern from which "British North America" inherited so many institutional characteristics in the nineteenth century. The ten provinces have almost complete control over education, health policy, and social welfare, and their regulatory control is at least as extensive as that of the government in Ottawa. Provincial power is reinforced by very strong regional attachments, intensified by the vast distances and forbidding terrain separating regions from one another, as well as by a linguistic duality that separates the French-dominated province of Quebec from the others.

Within each level of government, the parliamentary system concentrates authority in executive hands, as in Britain. Political parties are highly disciplined, and their leaders exert as much power over their legislative caucuses and extraparliamentary parties as any of their counterparts in the liberal democratic world. Three parties dominated the federal political landscape until recently. The center-right Progressive Conservatives and the centrist Liberals between them have held government office since Confederation in 1867. For most of the postwar period, the moderately social democratic New Democratic Party held third place. The 1993 election decimated the Conservatives, reduced the NDP, and increased representation for the right-wing Reform Party and the sovereigntist Bloc Québécois. The 1997 election reelected a Liberal government, but also gave each of the four opposition parties at least twenty parliamentary seats.

This creates a complex institutional framework for social movement activists. Maintaining a national presence is difficult for any movement because so much of what concerns social movements is under provincial or local jurisdiction. Ot tawa, the country's capital, is a medium-sized city without a substantial industrial or commercial base outside government, a situation that diminishes the local pool of activist energy. Yet decentralization and regional differentiation create opportunities in some jurisdictions which may be unavailable in others. With the enactment of the 1982 Charter of Rights and Freedoms, lesbian/gay/bisexual organizations, like those in other movements, were given substantial incentive to wage political struggles in the courts. Overall, the Canadian political system offers more opportunities than the British for mainstream political entry, and more opportunities to make gains.

UNITED STATES. The American political system is the most fragmented of the three. The states do not have as much jurisdictional room as Canadian provinces, but local governments have more power than municipalities in either Canada or Britain. Washington retains enormous control, in part because of its role in funding state and local programs, though power within the capital is itself fragmented. Congress is able to control its own agenda and act independently of the president, and the courts have long been able to challenge the acts of either on constitutional grounds.

The two parties that dominate the political landscape are decentralized, with virtually no permanent organization at the national level and considerable permeability at state and local levels. The Republicans have become more solidly right-wing since the early 1980s, combining free enterprise liberalism with a moral conservatism substantially infused with the anti-gay sentiment of the religious right. (The power of the religious right in U.S. politics is enormous, reflecting unusually high levels of churchgoing and fundamentalist Christian belief.)[21] The Democrats remained a broad formation in the 1990s, moving toward the center on socioeconomic policy under the leadership of President Bill Clinton, though staking out pro-gay positions on selective issues.

The American system creates more openings for social movements to intervene in the policy process than any other liberal democratic political system, and more incentives for even the most skeptical of activists to participate in the mainstream. In all branches of government, and at three jurisdiction levels, opportunities abound for equity-seeking groups to make at least modest gains, and abandoning such fields risks leaving the way clear for opponents. Sexual minorities are not as favorably positioned in law as their Canadian counterparts, though some success has been won on the basis of the Bill of Rights.

American politics is permeated with unusual optimism about the possibility of individual and institutional change. This translates into an in intense political energy that de Tocqueville noticed a century and a half ago. Gay and lesbian presence in Washington reflects this energy, with large permanent organizations established to lobby politicians and support electoral candidacies. And yet for the lesbian and gay movement, along with other social movements drawn to the political mainstream, the strength of American individualism and the anti-state sentiments so prominent in American political history generate distrust of the institutions of that mainstream, and of the activists and politicos who get too absorbed by them. The national government's headquartering in a purely government town simply accentuates distrust, particularly of that level of government farthest away and most inaccessibly large. It is therefore precisely in that political system where the inducements to mainstream engagement are greatest that conflicts over strategy are most intense.

Despite their dramatically increased visibility, gay and lesbian movements are minor players at the fringes of mainstream political processes, occasionally given access to political institutions but without corresponding power. Those instances in which issues of sexual diversity have been brought to the legislative table demonstrate that social movement activists are entirely dependent on a complex array of favorable circumstances, even when parties in power are ostensibly supportive. Access to the political mainstream can pull activists together, but it can also create tensions. The demands of party loyalty can easily split those inside parties from those whose lobbying work remains outside.[22] Activists wrapped up in the minutiae of the existing political system are often perceived to be isolated from grassroots activism.

The chapters that follow illustrate the indispensability to sexual minorities of forcibly entering into mainstream politics. Each chronicles at least one major legislative battle in Britain, Canada, and the United States in which sexual orientation was at issue. I begin with Britain, and with a historical examination of a social class system and a party system in which legislative moves toward equality have been difficult to achieve. There are elements of British political tradition highly relevant for the United States and especially for Canada.

The legislative struggles detailed here include more defeats than victories. The difficulty of removing even obviously discriminatory practices in all three countries is a sobering reminder of the gap between political access and power. These case studies show, particularly in the United States, how opponents of gay and lesbian rights have been able to mobilize grassroots support on a scale unimaginable for gay activist organizations, But what each of these examples also reveals is the development of considerable activist sophistication, along with the ability to place the issue of sexual diversity and equality firmly on the political agenda.

The analyses of the roles played by openly gay politicians remind us of the importance of representation inside legislative arenas, even where those arenas are dominated by the executive and by norms of party discipline that reduce the significance of individual legislators in making policy. The presence of such politicians acts as a constant reminder to allies and potential supporters that sexual orientation issues will not easily be swept under the carpet, and that anti-gay sentiments will not go unanswered. The paucity of voices taking up sexual diversity with firm resolve gives special significance to those few les-

bian and gay politicians who are open about their sexuality and speak forcefully of their experience. This is not to denigrate the work that others have
done, but only to highlight the importance of public figures who can take up an
issue so marked by historical invisibility with the capacity to talk of "we" and
"us."

BRITAIN

Demonstration against Section 28, near prime minister's residence on Downing Street (January 1988). Photo: *Gay Times Magazine*, U.K./Bill Short

Michael Cashman (actor), Chris Smith (Labour MP), and Peter Tatchell (Organization for Lesbian and Gay Action) at second London march against Section 28 (April 1988). Photo: Gordon Rainsford

1

Promoting Heterosexuality
in the Thatcher Years

We understand as does no other party that the defence of

freedom involves a defence of the values which make free-

dom possible without its degeneration into violence.

Norman Tebbit, Conservative Party chair, 1985

In the spring of 1988, the British Parliament enacted a Local Government Bill, to which an amendment, known as Section 28, had been added prohibiting local authorities from "promoting" homosexuality as a "pretend" family relationship.[1] Despite considerable protest in the streets of London and other major cities, and widespread condemnation of the legislation as repressive in general and anti-gay in particular, the Conservative majorities in the House of Commons and the Lords, spurred by the imposition of tight party discipline, passed the amendment essentially intact.

In some ways this was one more episode in a three hundred year history of political measures designed to preserve the respectability of the realm by suppressing homosexual behavior or denying it visibility. It was also the latest attempt to shore up a peculiarly postwar pattern of legal regulation that had tolerated homosexuality in private but had secured heterosexual public space. Until the passage of Section 28, such regulation was only halfheartedly resisted by centrist and left political parties, and enthusiastically bolstered by the police, the courts, influential segments of the mass media, and the Conservative Party. The events of 1988 demonstrated the continuing strength of those forces, though this was also a period in which forces undermining such regulation were building strength. The same long-term socioeconomic changes that were generating anxiety about the stability of social structures were also creating the ingredients for cultural and political challenges to them.

In some respects Britain exemplifies the contradictory tendencies of the 1980s.

19

This was a decade of increased visibility for sexual minorities and of their first entry into mainstream political processes. But it was also a period in which sexual equality had few defenders among national legislators. Here and elsewhere, influential right-wing politicians were preoccupied with both reducing the role of governments and shoring up so-called traditional family values—or at the very least using anti-gay strategies for electoral purposes. The British political system, and the strength of Margaret Thatcher's hold on the prime ministership during this decade, prevented significant challenge to the statutory inequality facing lesbians and gays, though by the end of the 1980s, some aspects of that inequality were appearing anachronistic.

To understand such persistent inequality one must focus on party politics, and in Britain that means exploring the development of attitudes toward homosexuality within the core class constituencies of each party. This treatment of party politics, and of the institutional factors reinforcing heterosexism throughout the 1980s, will have familiar strains for those interested in sexual diversity issues in other countries, while at the same time illustrating peculiarly British sources of resistance to gay and lesbian equality.

The British Political Context

Party politics lie at the very core of the British system, not least because governmental authority is founded on maintaining a majority in a legislature that is entirely structured around the confrontation of disciplined parties. Elections are fought by parties as unified blocs, and local voting is very much a function of preferences for national parties and their leaders. Political power in Britain is concentrated in the hands of the leader of the party in command of majority support in the House of Commons, and is reinforced by governmental centralization. There are no regional governments with sovereign authority, and local autonomy is severely circumscribed by national legislation and regulation.

Parties combat one another in the legislature as unified blocs, with strong norms of discipline imposed on those who represent their party in the House of Commons. The parliamentary leadership of each party (the cabinet on the government side, the shadow cabinet in the leading opposition party, and their equivalents in other opposition parties) has considerable influence over other MPs (backbenchers). Within each front bench, the leader also has considerable leverage. The party system in Britain has been remarkably stable over time, and remains so even in the face of growing cynicism about traditional partisanship.

Analyzing the lead-up to Section 28 requires an understanding of the ideological traditions of the two largest parties in particular, and of the social class foundations of each. The British party system has been dominated by the Conservative and Labour parties for most of the twentieth century. (The average vote for the two parties from the 1940s to the mid-1970s was 90 percent, and thereafter 75–80 percent.) The Conservatives were in power for most of that time, and held government office from 1979 to 1990 under the leadership of Margaret Thatcher, then subsequently under her chosen successor, John Major. The Labour Party, since its turn-of-the-century founding and through the Thatcher period, was strongly linked to the industrial working class, in both its policies and its structural links to unions. From 1983 to 1992 Neil Kinnock was its leader, and from the mid-1980s he led a process of "modernization," distancing the party from its historical commitments to policies such as nuclear disarmament and public ownership. The Liberal Party, a major party in the last quarter of the nineteenth century but supplanted in the twentieth by Labour, occupied third place throughout the postwar period. In the early 1980s it formed an alliance with centrist social democratic politicians who had defected from Labour, and by the end of the decade the two sides had merged to form the Liberal Democrats.

The Conservative Party and Thatcherite New Right Politics

Under Margaret Thatcher, most of the Conservative front bench avoided the moralistic fanaticism of right-wing American Republicans, although most of the party's MPs and activists were opposed to even the most basic equality for gays and lesbians, and were willing to play on anti-gay sentiments in the electorate. Conservatives believed that the heterosexual family constituted an indispensable and irreplaceable unit for raising children and securing social stability.[2] As John Pratt argues, the party had articulated an "authoritarian populism" establishing clear boundaries between "worthy" and "unworthy" recipients of the "fruits of permissiveness" in the postwar period.[3] In the words of an obviously sympathetic observer, "Conservative politicians proclaim that they are the party of the family and respect the solid domestic aspirations of ordinary citizens—as against the rainbow coalition of eccentric life-styles that comprise the Labour Party."[4] Some MPs held extreme views. About thirty were associated with the Conservative Family Campaign during the 1980s, which called for stepped-up policing and a re-criminalization of all homosexual activity.[5] Those in the Campaign based their arguments to some extent on what they purported to be Christian teaching.

Members of the Thatcherite Conservative Party more clearly influenced by laissez-faire liberalism were less likely to marshal the language of religion and morality, but they saw claims for the rights of gay people as an example of excessive demands being placed on state authority. They imagined a zone of tolerance in private relations, accompanied by heightened vigilance over public space. This was the formula adopted by law reformers in the 1950s, and encoded in the 1967 parliamentary act that partially decriminalized homosexuality for people twenty-one and older. The 1957 report of a government-appointed committee chaired by Sir John Wolfenden argued that tolerance of homosexuality should be extended to private acts, but it held to the view that law had a role: "to protect the citizen from what is offensive and injurious, and to provide sufficient safeguards against exploitation and corruption of others."[6] Margaret Thatcher herself was one of the minority of Conservatives who voted for the 1967 bill, and as early as 1960 was one of the very few who supported a Labour MP's resolution calling on the Conservative government of the day to introduce legislation reforming the criminal code on homosexuality. The individual freedom which she and other Conservatives sought to broaden had to be counterbalanced by responsibility and discipline; and because some people would inevitably not understand that, freedom had to be policed. As Anna Marie Smith has noted, Conservatives defended Section 28 in terms of toleration for the "law-abiding, disease-free, self-closeting homosexual figure who knew her or his proper place on the secret fringes of mainstream society."[7]

Thatcher was also prepared to argue in favor of "family values" when it was advantageous to do so, and to prop them up with the authority of the state. In response to a questionnaire sent out prior to the 1979 election, she had promised to fight pornography and talked of basing sex education on Christian values.[8] In February 1990, responding to a parliamentary question, she argued that lowering the age of consent for homosexual activity "would give offence to many people and worry many more."[9] Her onetime ministerial colleague Edwina Currie later commented, "We could never make any progress [on the age of consent] when Margaret was Prime Minister. Absolutely dead against it. Different generation. Most of her life it was illegal."[10] The attitudes of the rest of the parliamentary party seemed little different. A 1990 poll revealed that 68 percent of them favored retaining the existing age of consent for homosexual activity—twenty-one—and only 1.4 percent favored lowering it to sixteen, the age of consent for heterosexual activity.[11]

The invocation of "family values" issues found receptive audiences. As John Pratt argues, such language appealed to "the man left out"—"the man who saw traditional structures of order . . . being undermined; the man who was told that the courts were no longer strong enough and that the prisons were too soft; the man who listened to the experts speaking ineffectively about the growing number of social problems; the man who saw new groups springing up, claiming rights for themselves, but none for himself; the man who in his own life *had* to 'live up to the hilt of his income' to maintain his meagre, unglamorous standard of comfort; the man who saw himself as paying for everyone else's welfare benefits when none ever came his way."[12]

The 1982 Falklands War stiffened resistance to the social change associated with the period since the 1960s. As John Dearlove and Peter Saunders suggest: "Coupled with the Falklands hysteria (ably whipped up by most of the popular press) went a new emphasis on traditional values stressing the family, individual self-help and self-reliance and discipline, all of which was contrasted with the shallow trendiness of permissiveness and the sloppy and easy assumption that the world owed you a living."[13] This kind of sentiment is particularly prominent within two constituencies crucial to the strength of the modern Conservative Party—the lower middle-class and the working class aspiring to middle-class respectability. In such sectors status is integrally tied to traditional gender roles.

AIDS, for a time, fed the moralistic backlash. The epidemic reinforced one of the dominant images of homosexuality, as a "contagious condition, invisible and always threatening to reveal itself where least expected."[14] The government did devote substantial resources to public education and research on AIDS, and officials were given some latitude to mount policies that reflected public health concerns, with some consequent success in slowing the increase of infection.[15] But open discussion of such topics as extramarital sex continued to make some Conservative leaders, including Prime Minister Thatcher, uneasy. And, according to more than one observer, Thatcher and her party recognized a political opportunity to play the anti-gay card once the tabloid press began exploiting the fear of AIDS.[16]

Adding to the Conservative government's temptation to mobilize homophobia were the actions, or supposed actions, of left-wing Labour-controlled metropolitan councils. The tabloid press followed the Thatcher government's lead in characterizing such authorities as the "loony left," citing examples that were sometimes simply invented out of whole cloth. The affirmative action policies of some left-wing councils allowed for the characterization of Labour as the "gay party." As Stuart Weir of the *New Statesman* remarked at the time, "The Conservatives are now positively coming out as the anti-gay party to milk for all it's worth the great and growing hostility towards homosexuals felt by the majority of people in this country."[17]

In the Conservatives' 1985 annual conference, one platform speaker was loudly cheered when she suggested as an election slogan, "If you want a queer for a neighbour, vote Labour."[18] Soon after that, party chairman Norman Tebbit began playing on the backlash against the "poisoned legacy of the permissive society," specifically targeting homosexuality by saying: "Toleration of sexual deviation has generated demands for deviance to be treated as the norm. . . . Love of the sinner has slipped into love of the sin."[19] In the early autumn of 1986, a Conservative minister denounced the Labour Party as campaigning "for a more perverted society."[20] In the 1987 election, Conservative posters showed a row of books, prominently featuring a title, *Young, Gay and Proud*, with the caption "LABOUR'S IDEA OF A COMPREHENSIVE EDUCATION?" A 1988 television ad for the party zeroed in on a "gay seminar" as an example of local council misspending.

Thatcherite policy largely sidestepped issues of sexuality and morality, but did not ignore them altogether. For example, the government maintained the heavy censorship of gay sexual imagery and did nothing to curtail the high rate of arrests for homosexual activity. The government bolstered the traditional elements of the school curriculum, and in its 1986 Education Act required sex education to uphold the values of "normal family life." Section 28 of the Local Government Bill was in part an element in the broad attack on the supposed decline of standards in schools. It was also aimed at local affirmative action policies that had provided a form of gay and lesbian visibility that directly confronted the behavioral norm acceptable to Conservatives, that of the safely closeted homosexual. For that reason the linkage of an anti-gay measure to legislation curtailing local autonomy was not coincidental.[21]

THE FORMATION OF A MORALLY CONSERVATIVE IDEOLOGY. The use of anti-gay rhetoric by the Thatcherites was not entirely a traditional form of moral conservatism. In fact, the government was criticized by its own "family caucus" for not doing enough to shore up traditional values. But it did play into the social and moral anxieties of its electoral and activist constituencies—anxieties that have parallels in the historical moralism of England's middle class.[22] The development in the eighteenth and nineteenth centuries of a middle-class ideology which opposed moral laxity, and sought to contain sexual practice within a marital relationship in which gender roles were sharply demarcated, was not unique to England. What was distinctive was the strength of the social class fostering such views, the assertiveness with which these norms were imposed on all classes in society, the resistance of this moral scheme to radical challenges which emerged in middle-class circles elsewhere, and the prominence given homosexuality. Despite important changes in patterns of thinking about sexuality in the postwar period, what persisted into the Thatcher era was the widely held belief in the importance of defending a respectable public space against sexual practices that challenge community norms, a belief held with special intensity in the lower middle class, to which the Conservatives appealed so strongly.

Social anxieties over gender and sexuality that were apparent in moral crusades in the late seventeenth and eighteenth centuries were intensified in the nineteenth century by the partial erosion of traditional patriarchal morality. The stability of the realm and the continuity of its moral regime came to be associated with the family, particularly as other communal ties and traditional religious institutions declined. The point is not that the middle class always adhered rigidly to these norms, for many did not, particularly in the upper middle classes. But there was an increasingly widespread view that people *should* adhere to such norms, and that criticism of those who acted outside these bounds was legitimate, whether the transgressors be members of the working class, the aristocracy, or the middle classes themselves.

Attacks on homosexuality continued unabated throughout the second half of the nineteenth century, a period when other European countries were relaxing penalties for homosexual acts and legal reformism was softening punishments for a number of crimes, even in England. In 1870 the British attorney general was pleased to declare that there was "very little learning or knowledge upon this subject [homosexuality] in this country," and in 1885 Parliament passed legislation reaffirming the criminalization of all homosexual activity, including that undertaken in private. Oscar Wilde's prosecution and conviction for homosexual offenses in 1895 was greeted with condemnation and incomprehension in upper- and middle-class circles on the Continent, while being widely upheld by "respectable" opinion at home. Concerns about popular corruption and moral decay were particularly strong at the end of the century, and homosexuality was popularly linked to the decline of earlier empires.

Some toleration for discreet homosexual activity became apparent during this same period within the upper middle class. Those who sent their children to prestigious public or private schools were sometimes willing to turn a blind eye to a limited form of schoolboy homosexuality, though vigilance was required to avoid the stigma of homosexual identity. In a sense, one historian notes, schoolboy behavior revealed "a constant homosexual potential which could be expressed when circumstances and the collapse of social restraints indicated."[23]

The 1920s were a period of some liberalization of sexual attitudes and practices among elements of the upper middle class and aristocracy. Certain fashionability became associated with homosexuality, though less so in England than in Berlin, Paris, and even New York, and it never much dented the moral codes of the lower middle class. English publications of all sorts were highly discreet even in the reporting of marital breakdowns, let alone in talking of homosexuality. E. M. Forster could not conceive of publishing *Maurice* during the 1920s, and *The Well of Loneliness* by Radcliffe Hall was banned in England after its 1928 publication in the United States.

POSTWAR CONTRADICTIONS. The world wars brought unprecedented numbers of women into the manufacturing labor force to replace men away in combat, jarring traditional gender conceptions. Both wars brought men and women into close same-sex contact, allowing for unprecedented expression of homoerotic feelings. There was in fact a certain uneven tolerance of homosexuality during World War II. But the aftermath of war revived concern in Britain about the breakdown of sexual restraint and gender boundaries, no doubt intensified by fears of imperial decline in the face of American ascendancy and colonial independence movements. The attention devoted to homosexuality after the war was accentuated by the 1950 defection to the Soviet Union of Guy Burgess and Donald Maclean, which increased the domestic fears of corrupting enemies within. Yearly arrests for homosexual offenses increased from prewar averages of eight hundred to three thousand in 1952.[24]

Still, there were changes in the postwar period—the reverberations of wartime disruption, the decrease in religious practice, the reduction in family size—that made room for questioning traditional values about sexuality and family. As Martin Durham argues, other trends also tended toward liberalization: "The rise of a consumer society and the improvement in living standards inevitably changed both expectations and forms of leisure. Films, books and magazines which emphasized sexual themes became more easily available. . . . And, perhaps above all, there was the ubiquitous television set, bringing into millions of homes argument over religion and 'the new morality,' the work of controversial dramatists and satirical attacks on authority figures."[25]

From the 1960s on, the better-educated middle class shifted to a progressive view of homosexuality and gender, supporting the production of a number of positive portrayals of gay and lesbian characters in British film and theater. During much of the subsequent two decades, however, such cultural development was contingent on discretion, described by a gay activist in these terms: "There's an experience of homosexuality, male homosexuality certainly, amongst the traditional elite which makes it not quite so grotesque, you know, as propaganda might have it. But as long as you don't make a song and dance about it, nobody's going to be terribly fussed. You will not get to absolute high office; you will not get to the absolute pinnacle of your chosen career, but you probably will get a fair way up without causing too many problems.''[26]

The liberalization of the 1960s and 1970s, such as it was, left relatively untouched the intolerance of the lower middle classes, who retained the view that homosexuality was intolerable under any circumstances. It was often they who joined with Roman Catholic and evangelical zealots to form the solid core of support for moral rearmament organizations such as the National Viewers' and Listeners' Association, and it is they who provided the pressure and audience for the Conservative Party's right-wing moralism.

Working-Class Culture and the Contemporary Labour Party

In the 1980s the Labour Party's formal decision-making institutions were the sites of significant lesbian and gay activism. By mid-decade the work of such activists had secured important gains in pro-gay convention resolutions. But much of the party, especially inside its legislative ranks, shared an unease about homosexuality that was still widespread in its traditional working-class constituency. The party's reluctance to appear pro-gay was evident in its leadership over this period, and particularly during election campaigns.

The dominant working-class culture which had coalesced by the end of the nineteenth century incorporated little tolerance for sexual deviation.[27] Early in the nineteenth century, norms antithetical to sexual libertinism emerged within the most influential sectors of the working class itself. Nonconformist religion reinforced the severe morality in this culture, particularly among the ''aristocracy'' of the working class and its leadership. Such influence was evident in nineteenth-century campaigns against alcoholism and licentiousness, which linked these working-class elements to middle-class reformers. It was as true in most worker milieux as it was in middle-class circles that political radicalism did not typically challenge traditional morality. The abhorrence of homosexuality in the dominant working-class culture was exaggerated by the association of homosexual practices with the upper classes and the clergy (both Church of England and Roman Catholic).[28] Adding bite to the working-class critique of upper-class homosexuality was that it was routinely perceived to be predatory on working-class youths, at times a well-founded perception. Whereas in large parts of Continental Europe the prosecution of homosexuality was widely believed in radical circles to represent the kind of oppression characteristic of *anciens régimes*, in England it was thought to be a justifiable attack on the vice of the dominant class.

The working-class culture formed by the turn of the century remained essentially in place until after World War II. In the period following the war, in fact, the publicity surrounding arrests and prosecution for sexual offenses reinforced the sense of homosexuality as a growing problem. When the subject of law reform was raised in the Labour Party during the 1950s, many working-class party members saw homosexuality as symptomatic of "the decadence of those upper echelons of society to which they were so implacably opposed."[29]

THE LABOUR PARTY FROM THE 1960S TO THE LATE 1980S. Social and economic changes during the postwar years began eating away at traditional working-class culture, but it remained strongest in the unionized manufacturing industries and in the North of England, precisely the areas of most significance to the Labour Party. Writing in the 1980s, Ann Tobin could still argue: "[The] Labour Party and the trade union movement is in essence a movement devoted to protecting and upholding the purely sectional and rather limited interests of the white working-class male who is unionised and who works in the manufacturing industries. Those of us who do not fit into that rather narrow spectrum . . . are not of any real interest to the majority of trade unionists who still rule the Labour Party. . . . Nor, of course, are the needs of the gay and lesbian community of particular concern."[30]

There was some change in the late 1960s and 1970s. In 1967 Harold Wilson's Labour government had introduced equal rights legislation for women and racial minorities and had offered support for a bill that partially decriminalized homosexuality. During the late 1970s and early 1980s, official party policy changed significantly on a number of fronts as the party shifted briefly to the left, at just the time when the Conservative Party was shifting right. A large number of feminists, members of visible minorities, and lesbians and gay men became active in the Labour Party, particularly at the local level. Some politicians identified with Labour's left began expressing clear support for new social movement causes. Ken Livingston, who had just been elected leader of the Greater London Council, came to embody the support for lesbian and gay equality in left-controlled local authorities. Tony Benn, the MP most closely identified with the left of the Parliamentary Labour Party, called on his party and its affiliated trade unions to support full legal equality early in 1981. In March the party issued a discussion document, "The Rights of Gay Men and Women," expressing support for equality on a number of fronts, including the age of consent.

But even during the years of the most obvious opening to the left, the early 1980s, the Labour Party as a whole was still heavily influenced by traditional male working-class culture, in which there was widespread suspicion that the party was being taken over by "graduates in dungarees with posh accents and dangling earrings."[31] The 1981 discussion document on gay rights went nowhere, and the party was perceived by activists as backing away from the issue in its major 1982 policy statement.[32] Around that time, London Labour MP Reg Race presented a parliamentary motion on gay rights but, in the words of a colleague, "found it difficult to get support for it."[33]

The conduct of the party's leadership during the 1983 Bermondsey by-election (a special election forced by the resignation of the sitting MP) reflected their discomfort over the issue.[34] On the advice of the local Labour Party, the candidate Peter Tatchell had avoided openly declaring that he was gay, though he had been sufficiently engaged in activist politics that this was widely known to be so. The party's leadership tried unsuccessfully to block his candidacy, and offered no help once he got the nomination. The Liberal campaign courted anti-gay sentiment, and the tabloid press were unremitting in their use of the sexual orientation issue. Although some observers have argued that it was Tatchell's association with the hard left in the Labour Party, or his reluctance to declare his sexual orientation openly, that created the conditions for whipping up homophobic sentiment in the campaign, the exploitation of Tatchell's sexuality was for much of the political class a marker of the danger of being identified as the pro-gay party.

The election of Neil Kinnock to the Party's leadership in October 1983 gave little encouragement for those pressing for a more progressive position on gender and sexual orientation issues. Kinnock was married to a woman unhesitant in her feminism, and was known to be comfortable with gays in his circle of front bench colleagues and close advisers. But he also came from a Welsh mining background characterized by a strong "macho" culture, which no doubt had a continuing influence. Asked to comment on the media treatment of Tatchell in the Bermondsey by-election, Kinnock replied, "I'm not in favour of witch-hunts, but I do not mistake bloody witches for fairies."[35] Later in the decade he seemed to be moving in a progressive direction on such issues, but he was still of a generation that saw sexuality as a personal issue, and not a political one.

In early 1983 the Labour Campaign for Lesbian and Gay Rights emerged as a major campaigning group inside the party, replacing a smaller and more cautious group formed in the 1970s. At the 1982 party conference it organized a large fringe meeting, which garnered considerable national publicity and soon had a membership of about 250. It then began the long march toward changing official party policy, requiring a detailed knowledge of the way party machinery worked, which only an activist group operating inside it could develop. As one MP observed years later: "The Labour Campaign for Lesbian and Gay Rights isn't one of the world's largest pressure groups, but it does understand the way the Labour Party works. . . . [They] performed a very vital task in translating—which is important, because you know they've done a lot of good work through the unions, particularly in taking equal rights policies through the union conferences."[36] The effectiveness of the group was most evident in 1985–86. At the party's 1985 conference a resolution on gay rights had enough support to generate serious consideration. The preparatory work in trade unions was particularly important, and even more arduous than that in constituency parties. The Labour Campaign's union work was eased by visible lesbian and gay support for miners during the strike of 1984–85. One Labour MP recalls: "By the end of the strike, I remember [Arthur] Scargill [miners' union leader] sort of proudly saying all the work that the lesbian and gay community had done for the miners—at a miners' rally. Imagine that! . . . So when it came to party conference decisions in '84–85, the miners were usually the delegation with their hands up first in support of progressive policy on lesbian and gay issues."[37]

In 1985, the Trades Union Congress (TUC) passed a motion supporting equal rights for lesbians and gay men, and called on affiliated unions to campaign for legislation offering protections against discrimination. Later the same year the Labour Party Conference passed a similar motion, with little in the way of vocal opposition but with a majority of only 53 percent.[38] Then in 1986 the annual conference approved a wide-ranging gay rights motion by a 79 percent majority—enough to ensure inclusion in the party's election manifesto. A resolution favoring lowering the age of consent for homosexual activity to the same age as for heterosexual activity was specifically included in the resolution.

It was in just this period, however, that the Labour Party's leadership and parliamentary membership were becoming most anxious about being associated with causes perceived to be extreme. Many Labour politicians had never been fully committed to the issues around sexual orientation, and the activity in Labour-controlled local governments intensified fears among many more that over-identification with gay issues risked alienating voters. By this time a number of authorities, particularly Ken Livingston's Greater London Council, were establishing policies and programs promoting equality and providing services for lesbians and gays. Such anxiety was more visible than ever after the loss of the Greenwich by-election in March 1987. A left-Labour candidate had been selected against the wishes of the parliamentary leadership, who feared that the radicalism of her campaign would cost votes.[39]

The caution of the party's leadership on issues related to sexual orientation was evident in the tepid approach adopted in Labour's manifesto for the 1987 general election. There had long been disputes within the party about the gap between party conference resolutions and election manifestos. Party reforms in the early 1980s had sought to impose more controls on the development of election campaign platforms, but in fact the party leader and advisers reporting to him remained central to a process that still remained mysterious even to party insiders.[40] The identification of gay and lesbian causes with the left, and the Conservatives' success in associating such policies with "loonyism" during the 1980s, remained part of the cautious memory of Labour modernizers as well as a wide range of Labourites cast in a more traditional mold.

The Labour Party's manifesto included some progressive commitments on gender, and part of the campaign was directed specifically at women, thus recognizing the existence of a distinct constituency outside the normal class framework.[41] A confidential memorandum issued in September by the party's Home Policy Directorate, however, speaks volumes about the concern at Party headquarters over seeming too outspoken on lesbian and gay issues: "We were pressed hard by the Labour Campaign for Lesbian and Gay Rights to fulfil our commitment to a clear Party Statement on lesbian and gay rights. But election preparations—and the desire not to divert attention from our central message during the campaign—prevented the NEC [National Executive Committee] from setting up the agreed working party and producing the statement we promised. We did, however, commit ourselves in Labour's manifesto to take steps to ensure that lesbians and gay men were not discriminated against."[42]

"The family" was a sometimes explicit, more often implicit issue in the general election that year, and Labour was intent on appearing on the respectable side of it. This was reflected in the party's presentation of its leader and his wife. Although Glenys Kinnock was a political activist in her own right, "her official role in the Labour Party was firmly established as that of wife and mother, symbolizing traditional family values."[43] The campaign literature evoked stereotypical conceptions of women's roles and female issues, and the visual imagery was explicitly that of the white family.[44]

The loss of the 1987 general election was deeply traumatic for Labour, since much effort had gone into changing the party to make it more electable. For some the defeat was a vote of no confidence in this new image-conscious direction, but for most of the leadership it was a sign that they had to go even farther in the same direction. According to Sarah Roelofs, writing in the late 1980s, "with Third Term Thatcherism staring it in the face, Labour did, in a sense, revert to type. But that "type" was not so much anti-lesbian and gay as pro-family. The Family, the bourgeois, white, patriarchal, heterosexual family, wins elections—or so Labour believes."[45]

LABOUR RESPONSE TO SECTION 28. The embarrassment over gay/lesbian issues, and the concern to distance the national party from the so-called loony left, was evident in the first front bench reactions to Section 28 of the Local Government Bill. Despite the obviously anti-gay sentiment behind the amendment, Labour's senior representative on the committee examining the legislation in detail was quick to add his party's support: "I speak on behalf of the Labour Party when I say that it is not, and never has been, the duty or responsibility of either a local or education authority to promote homosexuality. . . . I hope that no-one in the Committee has any doubt about that."[46] A Labour MP opposed to such accommodation felt that Section 28 "opened the door to all kinds of other prejudices." He blamed this on the fear of electoral backlash. "The word was put around that the front bench was not going to oppose [Section 28] for fear of offending the homophobic vote." But beyond that he noted "a personal thing—sort of a macho mood in the Labour Party in some areas. They rather like the idea of strong, tough men who are not going to get too involved in that kind of stuff . . . [I]t's possibly personal prejudice in some cases—possibly a fear of their personal virility being damaged in some way."[47]

The onslaught of internal criticism that met front bench prevarication on the first introduction of the amendment stung many inside the party and emboldened those who already had allegiance to gay and lesbian causes. Although Jack Cunningham, shadow environment secretary, continued to defend the clause, by late January 1988 Neil Kinnock had come around to condemning it in unequivocal terms, describing as "crude in its concept, slanderous in its drafting, vicious in its purpose . . . this pink triangle clause produced and supported by a bunch of bigots."[48] In the fall of 1988, the Trades Union Congress conference called for the repeal of Section 28 and for the establishment of comprehensive protections for lesbian and gay rights. The Labour Party's own conference backed a motion to repeal by an over-whelming majority and reaffirmed support for full equality. According to MP Jo Richardson, the vote meant that "there will never again be any suggestion of the Labour Party backing off from its support for lesbian and gay rights."[49]

Nevertheless, the major policy review spearheaded by Kinnock produced rec-ommendations in 1989 that distanced the party from its commitment on the cru-cial issue of the equal age of consent. The following year a statement from shadow home secretary Roy Hattersley indicated that any legislative proposal to lower the age of consent would be the subject of a free vote—one that releases members from party discipline.[50] One source of resistance or timidity lay in the Labour Party's continuing preoccupation with respectability. In the late 1980s as much as ever, the party's leadership was seeking an expansion of the electorate beyond its traditional industrial working-class core. As in earlier periods, its sense of how to achieve this goal was to soften its position on a number of issues traditionally associated with the party—for example, nationalization and disar-mament—and to avoid "controversial" stances on new fronts. The fact that the left of the party was blamed for the disastrous electoral defeat of 1983 increased the willingness of mainstream elements to step up the ferocity of their attack on all leftists, including the "loony left" in some municipal councils, the proponents of black sections or caucuses within the party, lesbian/gay activists, and so on.

Within the Labour Party, gay-related issues continued to provoke more polar-ized attitudes than any other, reinforcing wariness among party leaders intent on conveying a unified image to the public. Opinion surveys indicated that the party's core constituency of unionized blue-collar workers retained a deeply em-bedded moral conservatism, particularly on gay-related issues (see Table 1). Labour had lost some of that constituency to the Conservatives during the Thatcher period, and regaining a hold on it would certainly not be eased by talk of gay rights. Among middle-class voters, those who were most progressive on issues such as this were already largely within the Labour fold, and those who remained outside were un-likely to be attracted by more assertive defense of lesbians and gay men.

Divisions on this issue within both the parliamentary and the extraparliamen-tary Labour Party did not neatly correspond to the left-right divisions that were so pronounced at the time. As the historian Jeffrey Weeks noted in 1992: "Some of the Labour MPs from Liverpool and places [with strong left tendencies] often have very large Catholic, working-class constituencies, and are cautious with adopting policies which are too far out of line with their constituents. They can't see what is the least socialist about gay rights or women's rights. . . . And there are others on what is called the revisionist right of the party who are liberal on these issues and see it largely as a case of individual choice. What doesn't exist in the Labour Party is any of the social movement agenda of the '70s and '80s—that doesn't seem to have really influenced the party at a top level."[51]

By the end of the 1980s, the Labour Party had fewer extraparliamentary activ-ists and MPs reflecting conservative perspectives than there were in the govern-ment party, and far more reflecting assertively pro-gay positions. A 1990 survey

Table 1. Britons' support for "left-wing" position on homosexuality, 1987

	Working-class respondents	Salariat respondents
Conservative	9%	9%
Labour	7	43
Alliance	15	29

Source: Anthony Heath and Geoff Evans, "Working-class Conservatives and Middle-class Socialists," in *British Social Attitudes: The Fifth Report*, ed. Roger Jowell et al. (London: Gower, 1988), pp. 56, 58.

Note: The salariat includes professionals and semi-professionals, managers, administrators, and large employers. The working class here means rank-and-file manual employees in industry and agriculture. The "left-wing" position is imputed to those who respond that sexual relations between two adults of the same age are rarely wrong or not wrong at all.

of MPs showed that 83 percent of Labour's parliamentarians favored protecting gays and lesbians against discrimination in employment and the provision of services, as compared to only 18 percent of Conservative MPs.[52] Three quarters of the Labourites favored repealing Section 28, in contrast to only 8 percent of Tories. Yet only 30 percent favored an equal age of consent (at sixteen), and almost a quarter would not lower it at all from the extraordinarily high age of twenty-one.[53] Electoral fears continued to produce caution in the public pronouncements of party leaders through the late 1980s and into the next decade, and most were in any event more comfortable with tolerantly liberal views of sexual diversity than with fully inclusive views.

The Liberals, Social Democrats, and Liberal-Democrats

Through much of the period from the early 1960s to the late 1980s, the Liberal Party had the most progressive official record on gay rights. The support for rights policies, however, was always stronger in the extra-parliamentary party than in the House of Commons, and the small number of MPs diminished their influence on national political debate. Even if some elections in the mid-1970s gave the party significant voting support, the single-member district system consistently gave the two major parties over 90 percent of parliamentary seats. At the time of debate over Section 28, the potential for a dissenting voice was weakened by the process of allying and merging with Social Democrats recently broken away from the Labour Party.

The leadership of Jo Grimmond from 1956 through the next decade reflected a progressive shift in policy on a number of fronts. In 1965, the party council passed a resolution calling for the implementation of the Wolfenden Report's recommendations on homosexuality, the first commitment on such law reform by any major British party.[54] Jeremy Thorpe's leadership from 1967 coincided with the development of community-based activist politics within the party and a push to the left by young Liberals. A party council meeting in July 1975 approved a draft bill on law reform prepared by the Campaign for Homosexual Equality (CHE), one that included reference to an equal age of consent. The full assembly that fall approved an internal educational campaign on gay rights, which had already been discussed and widely supported in the party leadership.[55]

But then in January 1976 a scandal and subsequent criminal trial implicating Thorpe in a homosexual relationship and a conspiracy to murder frightened many Liberals and slowed progress. By the end of the year, Thorpe was forced to resign. He was replaced by David Steele, who was a reformer in some respects (having introduced a bill liberalizing access to abortion in 1967), but not obviously sympathetic to gay rights reform. A party council meeting in mid-1977 retreated from the resolution of two years before, most notably by agreeing to a reduction in the age of consent only to eighteen years.

The party manifesto prepared for the 1979 general election seemed to signal a return to pro-gay assertiveness, with explicit commitment to removing all legal discrimination based on sexual orientation. Even more progress was being made in those party circles focused on local affairs; their influence was evident at the party's 1982 assembly, which confirmed Liberal support for setting an equal age of consent at sixteen. But in 1983 the Liberals in Bermondsey watched contentedly as as the anti-gay smear campaign directed at Peter Tatchell boosted their own fortunes and won them the election.[56]

The 1983 general election represented a setback at the national level. It was the first of two general elections fought in alliance with the Social Democratic Party, a grouping largely of Labourites who had rejected that party's move to the left. The manifesto prepared for the election was negotiated by the Liberals and the SDP, and the result was a dropping of all references to sexual orientation.[57] Although many Social Democratic activists were supportive of strong policies in this area, there were more dominant voices, the leader David Owen most prominent among them, who identified gay rights with the sort of Labour leftism they sought to leave behind.[58] Shortly before the 1987 election, Owen described as a ''devastating blow'' the revelation that a senior security official was gay, and criticized security services for not screening staff more carefully. David Steele was less conservative on the issues, but he had said in 1986 that he would rather treat gay equality issues as a matter of individual conscience and would therefore prefer the private-member's-bill route to reform.[59] (A private member's bill is one introduced on the initiative of an individual MP rather than the cabinet, and only rarely succeeds.)

In the mid-1980s even those who were favorably disposed toward sexual minorities routinely colluded with the tabloid press and the Conservative government in their talk of ''loony left'' local councils having gone too far. The 1987 British Social Attitudes Survey (Table 1) showed less support for progressive policy on homosexuality than party resolutions would have suggested.

By the time of the lead-up to the 1987 election, even if the Liberal extraparliamentary backing of gay rights was as firm as ever, the SDP remained resistant. In the 1987 negotiations over a district council election manifesto, the most difficult sticking points were sections on minority rights in employment and gay/lesbian rights. In fact, the pro-gay stance taken by Liberals in those district council negotiations received at best only modest backing in the parliamentary Liberal Party. One observer reported that the parliamentarians were "queuing up" to join David Owen in criticizing the document first agreed on by a joint working group.[60] The difference between Liberal MPs and local party members had existed for some time, of course. One long-time activist comments: "In the Liberal Party, most of its key activists and most radical people got involved in local government. When you wanted a parliamentary candidate, you looked for a nice respectable-looking barrister from London. . . . When it came to lesbian and gay issues, that meant that . . . the policy commitments of the party were not reflected in the thinking and the actions of the parliamentary party."[61]

Some caution was rooted in widespread middle-class preoccupation with a narrowly construed civility and a deeply embedded resistance to public talk of private life. It was also rooted, though, in religiously based reformism, reflecting the fact that English Liberalism has been more tied to than rejecting of religious belief. As one MP reflected as late as 1992: "I don't think religious *ideas* play a role at all, but I think the link between the nonconformist religious groups and our party remains extremely strong. If you look at where we are strong—Devon and Cornwall, for example—there is a great element of Methodism. . . . In some constituencies, the backbone of constituency activists are and almost always have been Methodists. The deputy leader of the party, Alan Beith, is a leading Methodist lay preacher."[62] There were individuals prepared to speak on behalf of gay rights, but their voices were often weak and highly circumspect, especially in the parliamentary party. At the end of 1987, when Section 28 was first being debated and voted on in committee, there was no more opposition from the Liberal–Social Democratic camp than there initially was from Labour's representatives.

Institutional Reinforcements

A number of institutional forces played a role in marginalizing lesbians and gays, including law enforcement agencies, the churches, and the mass media.

POLICE, JUDICIAL, AND RELIGIOUS AUTHORITIES. The police and judiciary were powerful reinforcers of homophobia in the 1980s, and in some ways helped secure working-class association of sexual deviation with the upper classes. From the nineteenth century through the 1980s, prowling for homosexuals became easy sport for the police, "an almost recreational duty distinct from the difficult or dangerous task of catching thieves or preventing violence," and an easy way to chalk up convictions for the record book.[63] This focus on homosexual offenses, though localized and spasmodic, regularly swept up suspects from the privileged as well as the unprivileged classes. The popular press was eager to publicize the pressing of sex-related charges against the well known. The fact that the law still discriminated against gay people reinforced the impression among law enforcement officers that homosexuality and heterosexuality were to be judged according to different standards. The age of consent was clearly discriminatory, no less so when the voting age was lowered to eighteen (see Chapter 2). The laws on soliciting and importuning were (and remain) stricter in their treatment of gay men than heterosexual men.[64] Until the 1990s, and even later in some jurisdictions, homosexuals were conceived of as a category of criminal suspect and policed as such.

The judiciary reinforced the marginalization of gays and lesbians. Right up to the 1967 revisions of the criminal code, judges were passing harsh sentences up to the limits of the law for consensual homosexual activity. After legal reform, judges continued to make speeches in their courtrooms about community norms, holding to the notion of universally held moral values which the state was bound to uphold. In 1983, for example, Lord Chief Justice Lane criticized the fact that society "deliberately blurs those very boundaries which ought above all to be clearly defined. . . . The men who, by today's jargon are described as gay, are not gay, they are homosexual and/or buggers and it is a pity that they are not called that."[65] These norms were applied in order to keep gay sexuality and imagery out of the public eye. Gay materials were still more routinely censored in Britain than in most other Western countries, and lesbian and gay couples were still successfully brought before the courts, even for kissing in public.

British religious leaders have played much less of a role in reinforcing homophobia than their counterparts in most of western Europe and North America. Religious belief did play a historical role in the development of middle- and working-class cultures with strong anti-gay components. But in the twentieth century, religious participation has been at a relatively low level, and political intervention by religious leaders has also been low-key in comparison to Roman Catholic Europe, Canada, and especially the United States. Britain has little of the religious fundamentalism that began playing such a critical role in U.S. politics in the 1980s. Its Christian leaders have generally argued that homosexual activity falls short of the ideal, and some have been blunter in their condemnation of it, but over the years a number of prominent clerics have argued on the side of limited reform.

MASS MEDIA. Of all the institutions that, in the period leading up to the late 1980s, shored up the homophobia so deeply embedded in English history, the mass media, and in particular the tabloid newspapers, were the most powerful. There have been times, it is true, when British media outlets demonstrated considerable openness and progressivism about gay-related cultural products and political issues. From the 1960s on, a number of television dramas and documentaries treated gay and lesbian themes with considerable sensitivity, and in the late 1980s the Channel 4 television network began a particularly distinguished record in broadcasting gay-positive material in prime time. But it was not until the 1990s that the amount of such cultural production and the diversity of its audience were sufficient to challenge the pervasive messages marginalizing sexual difference.

The affirmative signs that did surface in the media were overwhelmed by the daily vituperative barrage from the tabloids, whose circulation dominates the print media. In the 1980s the *Daily Mirror* sold 2.5 million copies each day, and the *Sun* more than 4 million. (By contrast, the *Times*, the *Independent*, and the *Guardian* each had half a million daily readers or fewer.) All but one of the tabloids were energetic in their support of Thatcherite Conservatism and of its most right-wing policies. And even though the *Daily Mirror* was technically supportive of Labour, it represented a right-wing and moralistically conservative variant of Labourism.

The tabloids were feeding off sensationalist probes into private lives, just as their predecessors had before them. As early as the nineteenth century, there were popular newspapers that dwelled on scandal and the sordid details of criminal cases before the courts, and this sort of coverage carried into the next century with several of the evening papers and weekend pictorials. In the tabloid press of the 1980s, homosexuality received regular play, always with overtones of sordidness, criminality, and disease. In the 1980s the AIDS crisis broadened the scope of tabloid coverage and intensified its open homophobia. Coverage of the "gay plague" consistently drew a sharp divide between the gay male population, which by virtue of its promiscuous and unnatural practices had brought illness and death on itself, and other categories of people who had contracted the disease, invariably characterized as "innocent" victims. Stephen Jeffery-Poulter is far from alone in pointing to AIDS as an important contributor to a public backlash against gays and lesbians: "The appearance of AIDS was the single most important factor in allowing the majority of the British press to unleash an unrelenting torrent of unabashed homophobia which reversed the trend towards greater understanding and sympathy towards gay men and lesbians among the general public, and paved the way for Section 28."[66]

While running in the 1983 Bermondsey by-election, Peter Tatchell got a close-up view of the tactics employed by the tabloids. The *Daily Mail*, for example, linked him to gay rights no matter what the substantive focus of the news item. the *Sun* headlined one story "MY FIGHT FOR THE GAYS—BY RED PETE," and touched up a photograph to make Tatchell look as if he were wearing eyeliner and lipstick. Tatchell himself recalls:

> Occasionally, I was surreptitiously trailed on foot, by car and even on the underground. Periodically, the rubbish chute outside my flat was blocked by journalists so they could sift through the contents of my garbage in the hope of finding some incriminating letters. . . . Those neighbours who consistently refused to speak to the press were subject to obscene and racist abuse. . . .
>
> But the papers did not stop there. Two of them are said to have put a £3,000 "bounty" on my head for a good scandal story, "preferably with photographs." They set a dragnet through the gay bars of London to find someone who would "reveal all." . . . At a cost of tens of thousands of pounds, reporters were dispatched to Australia. Local journalists at that end were also hired as full-time "Tatchell-hunters" to "dig up everything you have ever said or done from the day you were born," to quote one journalist.[67]

At the end of the decade, front-page headlines such as "MUMS FIGHT GAYS IN PLANE BRAWL AT 30,000 FT.: FURY AS KIDS SEE KISSING" were still common.[68] After the 1988 trial of a gay man convicted of murdering a newspaper delivery boy, the *Sun* editorialized: "There are vital lessons to be learned from the awful fate of Stuart Gough. Those who preach that homosexuality is 'normal' should remember Stuart. Those who try to corrupt children at school with gay propaganda should remember Stuart. Those who pour public money into gay and lesbian 'action groups' should remember Stuart."[69]

Some commentators point to the reluctance of most readers to believe much of what they read in the print media, but this grossly understates the influence of the tabloids in creating a long-term climate of opinion. The tabloid campaign against left-wing municipal councils in the 1980s was in the end so successful that the expression "loony left" was ubiquitous even in many Labour Party circles. Some of the tales on the basis of which this reputation was built were virtually fabricated by the tabloids, but so widespread were these stories that they were reported as "controversies" even in some of the non-conservative "quality" papers, and thereby given even more credibility.

As with the Conservative Party, the morality of the tabloids was not a replay of Victorian prudery. Women's bare breasts stared out from page 3 of some tabloids every day, and female sexual imagery regularly appeared in ads and stories in all of the newspapers. As Peter Wildeblood wrote of the popular press of his day, in the 1950s, "[Fleet Street's] morality was that of the saloon bar; every sexual excess was talked about and tolerated, provided it was 'normal.' "[70]

If there was a parallel between the politics of the tabloids and the ruling Conservative Party, there was also a parallel between the timidity of the Labour Party and the reaction of most of the "quality" media on the subject of homosexuality until the late 1980s. In the mid-1960s, at the time of public debate over the Wolfenden proposals, even the otherwise progressive *Guardian* was remarkably restrained: "A sexual act committed in public clearly offends against public decency. But it was argued by the sole dissentient in the Wolfenden Committee, Mr. Adair, that not only the act itself but also 'the presence in a district of adult male lovers living openly and notoriously under the approval of the law is bound to have a regrettable and pernicious effect on the young people of the community.' This is not a negligible point. Could it perhaps be met by adding a proviso to the effect that the parties concerned would forfeit the defence that they had acted in private if their conduct was such as to advertise their relations to the public at large?"[71]

Until the early 1980s at least, the *Guardian* continued to refuse ads from gay organizations, even those offering counseling services. During the debate over Section 28, this *Independent* editorial implied total acceptance of the tabloid-inspired critique of the "loony left": "There is a handful of local authorities who, for whatever reason, would wish to campaign to create propagandistic 'positive images' of homosexuality—and to do so with an unbalanced enthusiasm which Neil Kinnock and many of those who vote for his party find intolerable.

Such authorities are increasingly isolated, are in a chastened mood and now have rather less cash for such frivolities than hitherto.''[72]

The very existence of a gay community went almost unnoticed by the "quality" media, press and most television alike. Even the huge demonstrations organized in opposition to Section 28 (one in Manchester, for example, drew twenty thousand participants) went virtually unreported in the British media. A climate such as this, in a political system dominated for more than a decade by Thatcherite politics, is not conducive to a favorable shift in public opinion.

European and North American Contrasts

At the time of Section 28's passage, Britain had a legal apparatus more oppressive of gays and lesbians than most other liberal democracies. Not only were there few legal remedies for discrimination on the basis of sexual orientation, but also stark discrimination was still encoded in statutes and regulations. The military still barred homosexuals and criminalized homosexuality; the recognition of same-sex relationships was barely being talked about; and the age of consent for homosexuality was not only higher than that for heterosexuality, but the highest in Europe. Discriminatory law was not a dead-letter holdover from some earlier era; it was actively enforced by police and courts and strongly defended in the press. The persistence of such legal regulation positioned Britain nearer the conservative end of a spectrum of sexual regulation, and the passage of Section 28 only reinforced resistance to the legal liberalization building momentum elsewhere.

There were indications that public opinion in Britain was unusually disapproving of homosexuality during the 1980s. One 1981 survey of Europeans and North Americans showed Britons slightly less accepting of homosexuality than most Europeans, but more accepting than either Canadians or Americans. The same questioning in 1990 revealed that Britain was one of only two countries in which attitudes toward homosexuality had become more negative over the preceeding decade, to a point substantially below all other European and North American countries except Ireland and the United States (see Table 2). Other surveys also indicate that disapproval of homosexual relationships increased from 62 percent in 1983 to 74 percent in 1987, falling slightly in the next few years, though not to the 1983 level. The rejection of the idea of gays or lesbians adopting children is even more widespread (see Table 3).[73]

At the same time, the scale of early 1970s gay liberationist activism in Britain's largest cities, the development of gay and lesbian cultural production during the years that followed, and the growth of community visibility in the 1980s all attested to the potential for an energetic challenge to prevailing repressiveness. In the face of legal discrimination and public disapproval, there was space for cultural and social development in gay and lesbian networks and motivation for political development. To some extent, the very repressiveness of the legal system and of the legislative arena helped to prepare the ground for gay and lesbian challenges to it.

Table 2. Attitudes to homosexuality in Europe and North America, 1981–90

	1981	*1990*	*Change*
Homosexuality always justified			
Britain	21.1%	15.4%	− 5.7%
European average	22.5	27.9	+ 5.4
Canada	12.9	24.0	+11.1
United States	7.1	12.9	+ 5.8

Source: Neil Nevitte, *The Decline of Deference: Canadian Value Change in Cross-National Perspective* (Toronto: Broadview Press, 1996), p. 218.

Note: Question asked was: "Please tell me for each of the following statements whether you think it can 'always be justified,' 'never be justified,' or 'something in between'—'homosexuality.' "

CONTINENTAL EUROPE. In the nineteenth and early twentieth centuries particularly, there were reformist elements on parts of the Continent that had only modest counterparts in Britain. Lord Byron (himself ostracized and forced into exile once rumors about his homosexuality were spread in 1816) wrote from Ravenna noting how much more liberal the Italians were than the English.[74] At the end of the century, Oscar Wilde commented that in countries such as France, Italy, and Austria, homosexuality was thought of more as an illness than a sin.[75] These perceptions may have been applicable only to the privileged classes, but they had an impact beyond such circles. Even religiously based social and political movements in Catholic Europe seemed less preoccupied by homosexuality than the moral crusaders of England.

Delayed commercial and industrial development in Europe resulted in slower urbanization, and therefore in smaller and less visible homosexual subcultures. The middle classes that did emerge were generally not in the position of their English counterparts to assert their own legitimacy and to develop their own moral and social codes independently of other classes. The Continental middle classes were also much more likely than their English counterparts to be influenced by radical Enlightenment ideas, many eventually turning to an anti-clerical rejection of traditional values. By the second half of the nineteenth century, scientific and legal reformism had led to even more widespread discussions of homosexuality. In the nineteenth century and to some extent in the twentieth, Continental socialism was also more influenced by anti-clericalism and more open to a rejection of the moral order sustained jointly by the church and state in *anciens régimes*. On the Continent, too, there were fewer middle-class crusades leading to the sort of "scandals" that kept upper- and middle-class homosexuality before the public eye.

Germany provides some of the most striking contrasts with Britain. From the end of the nineteenth century to the early 1930s, a large and highly visible movement led by Magnus Hirschfeld called for law reform and public education on the subject of homosexuality.[76] This was a movement evident only in miniature form in Britain and North America. What then followed, of course, contrasted with Britain in the

Table 3. British attitudes to homosexuality, 1983–90

		1983	1985	1987	1989
"Homosexual relations always or mostly wrong"		62%	69%	74%	68%
"Acceptable for homosexual to be teacher"	Yes	41	36	43	45
	No	53	54	50	47
"Acceptable for homosexual to hold responsible position in public"	Yes	53	50	55	58
	No	42	41	39	37
"Lesbian couples able to adopt"	Yes	—	13	11	18
	No	—	82	86	78
"Gay male couples able to adopt"	Yes	—	6	5	10
	No	—	91	93	87

Source: Lindsay Brook et al., *British Social Attitudes Cumulative Sourcebook* (London: Gower, 1992), pp. M1–3, M1–4, M1–5, M1–6, M1–7; and Roger Jowell et al., eds., *British Social Attitudes: The 8th Report* (London: Dartmouth, 1991, p. 7.)

Notes: Questions asked were:

"What about sexual relations between two adults of the same sex? (Always wrong: mostly wrong; sometimes wrong; rarely wrong; not wrong at all)."

"Now I would like you to tell me whether, in your opinion, it is acceptable for a homosexual person: to be a teacher in a school; to hold a responsible position in public life (Yes; no; depends)."

"Do you think female homosexual couples—that is, lesbians—should be allowed to adopt a baby under the same conditions as other couples?; Do you think male homosexual couples . . .? (Yes; no; depends)."

opposite direction, as the Nazis destroyed the movement and swept up thousands of homosexuals into the concentration camps. In other European countries, right-wing movements sought authoritarian moral rearmament at the same time.

After World War II, however, Britain once again stood out in the extent to which public anxieties about homosexuality were fanned and legal regulation of homosexual activity policed. Popular antipathy to homosexuality and social control by family and community may have been no less restrictive on parts of the Continent than in Britain, but even with the significant reforms recommended by Wolfenden in 1957 and enacted in 1967, British authorities were especially preoccupied with the condemnation and strict containment of homosexuality.

The policy record on AIDS did not fit neatly into this pattern of regulation. In comparison to other national governments, the British developed large-scale public education programs early on. Public health officials were given considerable room to marshal both traditional and adaptive health policy instruments to slow the spread of HIV, at the behest of political masters who had witnessed the devastation being worked in the United States. Few European countries did more in response to AIDS; most did much less, much later. That said, British AIDS policy was silent around the issue of homosexuality, and the national government was reluctant to provide the funding required by AIDS service organizations. Officials relied heavily on gay expertise at first, but then quickly returned to more traditional consultative routes after the early years of policy development.

CANADA. Historically, Canadian policy responses to moral and sexual issues borrowed much from England. The pre-Confederation British colonies used English common law, and subsequent statutory development generally followed the English lead.[77] Moral regulation in Canada, however, has not particularly highlighted homosexuality. Few prosecutions resulted from Canadian sodomy laws, and when they did, the penalties were generally mild by comparison to what was meted out in England. At the end of the nineteenth century and the beginning of the twentieth, when the strains of industrialization helped generate a social purity movement with a substantial following in the middle-class and "respectable" working-class, relatively little attention was focused on homosexuality.

The 1950s saw an increase in the visibility of same-sex networks in Canada's largest cities, and an increase in persecution by local police forces. The Royal Canadian Mounted Police (RCMP) was stepping up surveillance of national civil servants suspected of homosexuality, and a 1952 amendment to the Immigration Act categorized homosexuals as "subversive." Canada's McCarthyism, though, never had the public face of the security scare in the United States, and arrests for homosexual activity were still not as frequent as in Britain.

Reformist sentiment culminated in the 1969 amendment of the criminal code along the same lines as the British amendment of 1967, decriminalizing private consensual homosexual activity for those over twenty-one. More strikingly than in British debates over reform, the "sickness" model of homosexuality prevailed over moralistic condemnation, and the amendment aroused only modest opposition. The measure was also included in a government bill, rather than relegated to a private member's bill.

Although the 1984 federal election brought to power a Progressive Conservative government claiming affinity to the policies of Margaret Thatcher and Ronald Reagan, its right-wing moral agenda was never very fully developed.[78] In fact, a Conservative-dominated legislative committee recommended in 1985 that discrimination on the grounds of sexual orientation be formally prohibited. Although the Conservative governments in power through the rest of the decade did not act on the recommendation, various justice ministers persisted in saying that they would (see Chapter 5). From the late 1970s to the late 1980s, several provincial and territorial governments explicitly added sexual orientation to their human rights codes. Only in British Columbia was there a provincial government controlled by a political party eager to portray itself as anti-gay. Even more than in the United States, governmental decentralization in Canada has prevented any one party from exerting as much influence as the British Conservatives have over the public agenda.

The enactment of a new Charter of Rights in 1982 expanded rights discourse at a time when the idea was under seige elsewhere. Sexual orientation was not explicitly included, but there was growing legal opinion that the courts would interpret the provisions as implicitly including it. The relatively well organized gay and lesbian communities of Canada's major cities were increasingly portrayed as representing the rights claims of legitimate communities. The sex-and-scandal-centered coverage of gay and lesbian issues typical of British tabloids was almost wholly absent from Canada's print and electronic media, and the AIDS-generated hysteria of the British and to some extent the American media was less common.

UNITED STATES. It was the United States that came closest to Britain in having a powerful New Right combining contradictory strains of laissez-faire liberalism and moral conservatism during the 1980s. Even more strongly for the New Right and its supporters, homosexuality came to be a symbol for all of the permissiveness of the decades just past. The fact that the gay subculture was more visible than ever doubled the anxieties of people wanting to shield their children from knowledge that homosexuality even existed. The AIDS crisis simply exacerbated the fears among those already fearful, since it led to expanded and frank discussions of wide-ranging sexual practices. Anti-gay political organizing and public opinion in the United States was also bolstered by the enormous power of the religious right—a force without parallel in either Canada or Britain, or for that matter most other countries of the industrialized West. The religious right as a political force was built on a higher level of religious belief and a more specific adherence to fundamentalist concepts than in most other Western countries, and far exceeding that in Britain and Canada.

The historical record prior to the 1950s shows less preoccupation with homosexuality in the United States than in Britain. Until then, homosexual subcultures were less visible, and consequently less threatening and less targeted for condemnation, even among adherents to puritanical forms of Christianity. More important, the American Revolution legitimized more radical Enlightenment thinking about morality than prevailed in England. There was more emphasis on the pursuit of individual happiness, and more acceptance of all that was related to nature, including sexuality.[79] The individualism enshrined in American constitutionalism made any pretense to moral uniformity difficult, except that based on ideological liberalism.

The puritanical moral codes around sexuality that existed in the United States seemed more fundamentally undermined than their counterparts in Britain by social and economic change from the 1920s onward. While early industrialization had called for saving and restraint, the consumer capitalism and the advertising that grew alongside it so rapidly during the 1920s called for the opposite. As John D'Emilio and Estelle Freedman put it, ''An ethic that encouraged the purchase of consumer products also fostered an acceptance of pleasure, self-gratification, and personal satisfaction, a perspective that easily translated into the province of sex. Such notions would gradually replace the nineteenth-century preoccupation with the control of sexual impulses through individual self-management.''[80] In the post–World War II period, sexuality was increasingly exploited, and sexual imagery became more visible—much more so than in Britain. The changes accelerated by the war were seen by many Americans as part of an ongoing process of social change, whereas Britons were more likely to see wartime changes as threats to social stability and signs of imperial decline.[81]

The forces of reaction were strengthened in the early postwar decades by anticommunism. The Wolfenden reformism that was developing during the late 1950s in Britain had little resonance outside a few progressive states in the United States. Law enforcement agencies may have expended less energy than their British counterparts in applying sodomy laws, but at least as much raiding bars and other establishments serving a gay clientele. In the late 1970s and 1980s, conservative moralism was still being supported by elements of the secular right, but also, more significantly, by the Protestant revivalism and fundamentalism of the postwar period. Court challenges had loosened government censorship of sexual imagery, but the self-censorship of Hollywood film and TV studios on gay-related subjects remained firmly in place. Legal changes and policy progress at the national level and in many states were slowed to a crawl by the growing power of the religious right inside the Republican Party, and the considerable fear of electoral backlash among Democrats who might otherwise be supportive of or neutral on gay rights.

By this time the United States stood out among industrialized democracies in the intensity and spread of moral antipathy toward homosexuality and the extent to which it was based on religious belief. But the moral codes being defended by such forces were being combatted by the most visible gay and lesbian communities of any country, increasingly becoming a political bloc to be reckoned with. The forces at play in the United States, then, had become more polarized than in Britain, hauling issues of sexual orientation more unavoidably onto the political agenda.

From the eighteenth century onward, homosexual offenses were the subject of moral panics in England, more often and with wider public support than elsewhere in Europe or in North America. (Only in recent decades has the United States surpassed Britain in the extent to which homosexuality is used as a sign of overall moral decay.) The continuity of British political development through periods when other European states and the United States were undergoing revolutionary upheavals helped secure the place of traditional social and political structures and tempered radicalism of all sorts. The early spread of capitalism in Britain, and then of industrialization, produced rapid urbanization and social dislocation throughout the eighteenth and especially the nineteenth centuries. Space was created relatively early for homosexual practice and, ultimately, homosexual identity. At the same time, early economic development propelled into political influence those social classes most likely to develop a culture of restraint.

In the postwar decades, and particularly in the Thatcher period, the foundations for sexual regulation shifted from moral conservatism to a more generalized uneasiness about rapid social change. This allowed for a degree of official toleration of private deviance so long as it was kept within strict bounds and not given public voice—a formula embodied in Section 28. At the time it was unclear whether the events of 1988 would lead to a longer-term chill in the climate for British lesbians and gays, or would represent a last futile attempt to stall reform.

Announcement of sponsors of the parliamentary amendment for an equal age of consent, with Sir Ian McKellan (Stonewall member), Angela Mason (Stonewall executive director), Edwina Currie (Conservative MP), Marjorie Mowlam (Labour MP), and Robert Maclennan (Liberal Democratic MP) (January 1994). Photo: *Gay Times Magazine*, U.K./Bill Short

Demonstration (with singer Jimmy Somerville) protesting the defeat of equality in the age of consent, in front of Parliament (March 1994). Photo: *Gay Times Magazine*, U.K./Bill Short

2

Activist Openings on the Age of Consent

When the Major government ceases to regard homosexuality

as a bar to advancement in the civil service, and begins to

include equal opportunity policies, then something strange is

afoot. . . . One begins to see Section 28 as a Pyrrhic victory—

the last moment of high Thatcherism.

gay activist, June 1992

On the evening of February 22, 1994, a large crowd of gays, lesbians, and their supporters gathered for a vigil outside the Houses of Parliament in the heart of London. They were there to support a legislative proposal aimed at lowering the legal age of consent for homosexual activity from twenty-one to sixteen, the same age as for heterosexual activity. Inside, an unusually crowded House of Commons was seized with debate over the issue for three hours. A vote held just after 10 P.M. narrowly defeated the motion for equality. With disappointment and anger surging in the public galleries inside the House and amidst the crowd outside, MPs then approved a compromise age of eighteen.

The rejection was a defeat for lesbian and gay activists. But what the activist campaign and even the vote tally on that evening revealed was a significant shift in the balance of forces in the years since the passage of Section 28 of the Local Government Bill, curtailing the ''promotion'' of homosexuality (see Chapter 1). The debate over the age of consent illustrated that the issue of lesbian and gay equality had entered the mainstream political agenda in a way that it had never succeeded in doing before. It also showed that gay and lesbian activists themselves had gained access to legislative, partisan, and administrative circles, building on the mainstream legitimacy gained by AIDS activists a few years before.

This paralleled the increased access to the political mainstream being won by gays and lesbians in other countries, including the United States and Canada.

Until the end of the 1980s, the door to statutory change in Britain had largely been kept shut by a combination of the Thatcher government and opposition parliamentary parties reluctant to promote gay and lesbian causes. But the social and cultural visibility of sexual diversity had been growing rapidly in Britain, posing an implicit challenge to the archaic system of legal discrimination. Prior to the 1990s, most calls for a shift from official toleration to equality had been voiced from outside the political mainstream. Progress made by Liberal and Labour Party activists had made only modest dents on parliamentarians of either party, and even less on the legislature as a whole.

The new decade saw an increase in the scale and self-confidence of activism oriented to legislative change, making use of mainstream channels in the media and the political system. From the years of the Homosexual Law Reform Society in the 1960s, there had always been a strand of political activism engaged in mainstream lobbying. The new forms of activism in the 1990s, however, were much less purely "insider" than their predecessors, and were more openly lesbian and gay, better able to establish a presence in the media, and more obviously linked to an assertive constituency.

The age of consent campaign also demonstrated that in some circumstances British activists could overcome the ideological, strategic, and partisan differences that had so deeply fractured lesbian and gay politics in that country. British activists do not operate in a political system that makes enduring alliances across ideology or party easy. Government control over the parliamentary agenda creates few openings for significant advance, and the legislative environment reinforces party division. As a result, there are fewer incentives to create permanent structures focusing on lobbying, and fewer opportunities for such lobbyists to claim victory.

The impediments to legal equality facing the British gay and lesbian movement were still formidable. In the mid-1990s, opposition to equality remained widespread among elected politicians, particularly Conservatives, and electoralist caution continued to pull politicians otherwise in favor of reform back from the front lines of support. The continuing barriers to legal equality, in a system that allows few end runs around the House of Commons and the national government, inevitably created divisions within the activist movement itself. But as elsewhere, openings for political change after the mid-1980s drew more activists than ever into working with and inside mainstream political institutions. The demands of such work, however, and the frustrations created by it, also opened up deep fissures within the movement.

The Sequence of Events

In 1967, homosexual activity was partially decriminalized. The criminal code had penalized all such activity between men, but now allowed consensual sex between two men, in private, if both were twenty-one or over—at that time the legal age of majority. (The age of consent for heterosexual activity was sixteen.) Two years later the voting age was lowered from twenty-one to eighteen, but there was no corresponding reduction in the age at which homosexual activity was decriminalized. Equalizing the age of consent was regularly included in the political demands of lesbian and gay groups from the early 1970s onward, but with no serious chance of effecting legislative change.

The aftermath of the passage of Section 28 led to a higher profile for gays and lesbians challenging legal inequities, and to the formation of two new activist groups. The Stonewall Group was established in May 1989 to lobby governments and take up other forms of mainstream political work. Among its leaders were a few high-profile figures from the arts who had associated themselves with the campaign against Section 28, including Shakespearean actor Ian McKellan and TV star Michael Cashman. It also included long-standing activists associated with earlier lesbian and gay organizing.[1]

One year later the group OutRage was formed to represent quite a different activist orientation. Whereas Stonewall was respectable and reasonable, this new group was confrontational and outrageous. It could trace its roots back to the liberationist politics of the early 1970s, and was influenced by the direct-action tactics of AIDS groups such as ACT UP in the United States, and by the youthful flamboyance of Queer Nation groups in North America and Western Europe.[2] By the end of the year, both OutRage and Stonewall had attained considerable visibility in lesbian and gay networks across Britain, and in the mainstream media. Both groups campaigned for an equal age of consent, though at first with few hopes for change in the short run. In a poll of MPs taken in 1990, 68 percent of Conservatives had favored an age of consent of twenty-one, and only 1.4 percent favored sixteen.[3] Of Labour's MPs, 23 percent favored twenty-one, and only 30 percent favored equality at sixteen.

CHANGES IN PARTY LEADERSHIP. All three parties underwent leadership change in the period between 1988 and 1992. In 1988 the Liberal Democrats sprang from the formal merger of the Liberal Party with most of the Social Democrats who had defected earlier in the decade from the Labour Party. They also chose a new leader, MP Paddy Ashdown, a telegenic ex-marine thought by party activists to be an ally on sexual diversity issues.

Late in 1990 the leadership of the Conservative Party and the government passed from Margaret Thatcher to John Major. Less than a year later, on September 24, 1991, the prime minister seemed to signal a shift in approach to issues of sexual orientation when he invited Stonewall activist Ian McKellen (by now Sir Ian) to Number 10 Downing Street.[4]

Ministers soon began signaling their openness to reviewing sexual offenses laws and their enforcement by police. In November 1991 the Conservative chair of the Home Affairs Select Committee of the House of Commons, Sir John Wheeler, talked of the age of consent of twenty-one as "bizarre," "nonsensical,'' and ''ridiculous,'' indicating that he had come around to favoring sixteen. At about that time the prime minister informed Wheeler that a free vote (to which the normal rules of party discipline are not applied) on the age of consent was possible, although only after the impending 1992 election. At the same time, in March 1992, Major was assuring the censoriously right-wing National Viewers' and Listeners' Association that he had no plans to alter the age of consent.

In the lead-up to the general election there was talk of the ''pink vote,'' with Conservative government ministers reported to be ''wondering seriously and aloud about the possible implications.''[5] Sexual orientation issues did not feature prominently in the campaign, although the press was filled with stories of Conservative MP Alan Amos resigning after being arrested on London's Hampstead Heath for sexual activity with another man.

The Labour Party had led the Conservatives in pre-election polling, but the 1992 vote gave John Major just over half the seats in the House of Commons. With 42 percent of the popular vote, the Conservatives won 336 seats, Labour 271, Liberal Democrats 20, and other parties 24. Labour's defeat led to the resignation of Neil Kinnock as leader, and to his replacement by John Smith. Smith was a cautious leader, in some ways more conservative on moral issues than his predecessor, but widely viewed among gay/lesbian activists as supportive.[6] He included Tony Blair as shadow home secretary, seen to be a centrist on many matters but strong on gay and lesbian issues.

THE CRIMINAL JUSTICE BILL. After the election Conservative ministers were privately expressing the government's willingness to make room for gay-related reform amendments to the Criminal Justice Bill, expected to come up for debate at the end of 1993 or early 1994. The prime minister informed his own party's MPs that he favored lowering the age of consent to eighteen, and that he was considering allowing an amendment to the bill—presumably a free vote.[7]

The Criminal Justice Bill was to be a ''law and order'' bill that would shore up the party's credentials on the right. Such strategy was also in evidence at the party's annual conference in the fall of 1993, where the prime minister talked of going ''back to basics.'' Whether or not such talk was actually intended to defend traditional moral values, it was widely interpreted as such within the party and the press.[8] In November the Queen's Speech at the opening of the new session of Parliament confirmed that the Criminal Justice Bill would go forward. It was to be a grab bag of measures strengthening the power of courts and police, including provisions to limit an accused's right to silence and toughen punishments for some juvenile offenders. Soon after, home affairs ministers confirmed that the government would not obstruct amendments to the bill.

Late in the fall, the Stonewall Group began to draft an amendment to lower the age of consent from twenty-one to sixteen.[9] On December 16 Stonewall learned that a vote could come as early as January, and immediately started to piece together a three-party contingent of backbench MPs to propose the amendment. Conservative Edwina Currie, who had been pressing for reform on the age of consent and other gay-related issues since the spring of 1992, would be the prime mover.[10] The Labour side's most prominent sponsor was Neil Kinnock, the former party leader. The Liberal Democrats were represented by their home affairs spokesperson, Robert Maclennan.

Early signs were not encouraging. Among Conservatives, opposition to any lowering of the age at all might have been as high as two thirds of the caucus, though the stated preference of the prime minister and a few senior ministers for setting the age at eighteen might have reduced such intransigence to one third. Support for sixteen was much lower, estimated by Currie herself to be only thirty MPs, less than 10 percent of all Conservative Members. In the Labour Party, one early January poll suggested that 21 percent opposed any lowering of the age of consent. There would certainly be a Labour majority for sixteen, but there was no clear indication of how large. Stonewall was publicly estimating support for equality across the House of Commons at 250 MPs out of 651, with another 200 undecided.[11]

On January 11, 1994, the Criminal Justice Bill was debated on second reading and approved in principle. Later that evening a Home Office minister confirmed that as long as the Currie amendment for an equal age of consent was accepted on procedural grounds by the House authorities (by now virtually assumed), the government would allow a free vote before the bill as a whole proceeded to detailed examination by parliamentary committee.

A few days later Labour leader John Smith indicated that he would support setting the age at sixteen, joining his home affairs shadow cabinet minister Tony Blair firmly on the side of equality. Increasingly, the opponents in the Labour camp were judged to be few in number and likely not to vote rather than register their disagreement with a position that was, after all, official party policy.

On January 17 more than two thousand supporters of gay and lesbian equality queued up to lobby their members of Parliament—a very large lobby by Westminster standards. By then the activist campaign to mobilize gays and lesbians across Britain was in high gear, using large-scale mailings and full-page ads in the gay press.

Opposition to reform was now becoming more visible. On January 18 a group of Conservative MPs publicized a threat to vote against the Criminal Justice Bill itself if the amendment for sixteen were passed. The group was said to be up to twenty in size (later a dozen or so), and was thought to have contributed to a delay in the timing of the vote to allow Conservative whips an opportunity to estimate the extent of risk. On January 24 the home secretary declared his intention to support lowering the age only to eighteen (it being clear by then that most of the front bench was of the same view). This no doubt provided a lead for many Conservative MPs and a clear signal that an amendment for that age would be proposed (as it was on February 1).[12]

Meanwhile, the Conservatives were reeling from sex-related scandals, the tabloid press having taken some delight in unearthing or publicizing extramarital affairs of Conservative ministers and backbenchers in the wake of the prime minister's talk of going "back to basics." On January 16 yet another Conservative MP was tarred by scandal, this time over fathering an illegitimate child. Some Conservative gay activists and their MP allies were calling this "the worst possible political climate to have this debate and this vote."[13]

A BBC survey of MPs in the second half of January indicated increased support for equality, though not yet enough to win. Extrapolating from the numbers actually responding, the survey predicted a vote of 288 for sixteen, with 31 Conservatives in favor and the same number of Labourites against.[14] But sources in the government whip's office let it be known to Conservative campaigners that their estimates represented only about half of those who favored sixteen.[15] Some supporters of the Currie amendment were now imagining a victory that they had scarcely believed possible two months before.

THE COMMONS DEBATE AND VOTE. Debate on the Currie amendment started in the early evening of February 22, with the chamber much more crowded than for even the most contentious of free votes in the past.[16] (There would be two high-profile amendments debated that evening, the second on hanging.) Eleven speakers took the floor in all: the Northern Ireland MP Ian Paisley defended the status quo; three Conservatives (including the home secretary) argued for eighteen; one Liberal Democrat spoke in favor of seventeen; and seven MPs (four Labour, two Conservative, one Liberal Democrat) supported sixteen. Currie led off, heckled repeatedly and angrily by her Conservative colleagues as she argued for her amendment. She lodged her argument in the laissez-faire tradition of defending the right to privacy against state intrusiveness into "personal" lives; she also talked of British law being out of line with Europe.[17]

Among Labour's speakers, shadow home secretary Tony Blair delivered what many thought was the most effective speech of the evening. It lodged his support for equality in the kind of centrist communitarian framework that would continue to mark his pronouncements when he became Labour party leader and then prime minister: "Yes, there is a powerful mood in this country that the social fabric has been torn, that standards of behaviour have fallen, and that our system of values has become confused and disoriented. Yes, it is the case that any strong society needs good and decent principles to sustain and motivate it. But it should be a society that makes sense of the passage of time, that learns from and evaluates its progress, that has confidence to build its own future, not one that takes refuge in the prejudices of the past because it is afraid to change them."[18]

Openly gay Labour MP Chris Smith (see Chapter 3) forthrightly attacked the concerns raised by opponents that an equal age of consent would clear the way for middle-aged homosexuals to "corrupt" adolescent males. As he pointed out, "Overwhelmingly the problem of abuse is the problem of abuse by older men of younger women."[19] He also attacked the idea that a high age of consent protected vulnerable young men, arguing instead that it prevented them from seeking advice and protection.

Religious belief was only rarely invoked in the debate, though frequent references were made to the role of law in establishing or reinforcing social norms. AIDS was cited on all sides. Conservative opponents of equality claimed that a lower age of consent increased the risk of young men being exposed to HIV through sexual activity. Supporters spoke of the barriers that higher ages of consent imposed for safer sex education, for advice, and for medical assistance.

After a preset limit of three hours' debate, the vote was taken at ten o'clock. Although this was a free vote and party discipline was not being imposed, party whips were making their support or opposition to the Currie amendment visible. On the Labour side, the chief whip and two colleagues were standing prominently by the "no" lobby, signaling that it was safe to oppose the amendment even if the party leader and most of the shadow cabinet were voting in favor of it. (Most of the other MPs in the Labour whip's office were known to support equality.) Chris Smith noticed "some of the Scottish whips who wouldn't naturally be thought of as supporting the issue standing at the entrance into the lobby for the amendment, encouraging people to go in."[20]

Currie's amendment was defeated, 280 to 307. Immediately after, the House approved a second amendment for eighteen, 427 to 162. Despite insistence in some lesbian and gay activist networks on "sixteen or bust," only a handful of MPs favoring equality voted on principle against the compromise of eighteen.[21] Conservatives overwhelmingly opposed equality, 40 percent voting in effect to retain twenty-one as the age of consent. Thirty-seven MPs, 11 percent of the Party's MPs (including two cabinet ministers), voted for equality, and twelve abstained (most of the latter thought to be favoring sixteen). Eighty-four percent of Labour's parliamentarians voted for equality (in contrast to the 30 percent who favored sixteen in 1990). But thirty MPs, including two front benchers, cast votes against, and an additional six abstained.[22] On the second vote, six Labour MPs opposed lowering the age to eighteen on the grounds of opposing any reduction in the age at all, and seven voted no because of a principled rejection of anything less than equality. The Liberal Democrats present in the chamber all voted for equality. One was absent, almost assuredly because she opposed setting the age of sixteen. Most of the representatives of the Celtic nationalist parties from Wales and Scotland also voted for equality. Seven Ulster Unionists, six other MPs from Northern Irish parties, and one Scottish Nationalist voted against any change.

The galleries in the House of Commons had been packed with supporters of equality that evening. They had sat grimly silent as the votes were taken and announced, except for a shout of "Thanks for nothing!" from one veteran activist in response to cheers from the Tory benches. Outside, the thousands who had gathered in vigil greeted the news of defeat of equality with intense emotion, many people weeping, and many surging through police barriers and banging at the door leading to the central lobby of the House of Commons. In a look back at that moment, writer and activist Keith Alcorn captured a sentiment widely shared in that large and diverse crowd: "Last Monday night was a dramatic, spontaneous upsurge of anger by hundreds of activists who had held their breath whilst Stonewall ran a commendably reasonable and persuasive campaign. At 10:35 that breath ran out, and a collective cry of 'Shame' was swiftly transmogrified into anger which an *Independent* reporter described as 'frightening to witness.' . . . On the night we won the most significant law reform since the 1967 Act, under a Government which has made more concessions than all its predecessors, we had the self-confidence to turn round and be seen to say 'Not good enough.' "[23]

PARLIAMENTARY DENOUEMENT. Soon after the House vote on eighteen, the home secretary was reported to be preparing police guidelines suggesting stricter prosecution of homosexual activity for sixteen- and seventeen-year-olds. As Chris Smith sardonically noted, "He didn't tell us that Monday evening."[24]

In April the government approved a number of other amendments to its own Criminal Justice Bill. One brought the age of consent in Northern Ireland into conformity with the amendment for eighteen, since Ulster had initially been excluded from the measure. An amendment introduced by Liberal Democrat spokesperson Robert Maclennan also encoded a long-promised reform decriminalizing homosexuality in the armed forces (though leaving untouched the exclusion of gays and lesbians from the military).

Late that month there were signs of restiveness in the House of Lords on the eve of its debate on the age of consent. The rumors were of a cross-party alliance of peers to restore the age to twenty-one. The issue came up for formal debate on June 20, with the specter of boys being "corrupted" evoked again and again. The debate ended with votes on sixteen (defeated 71 to 245) and on the House of Commons compromise of eighteen (approved 176 to 113).

Increased Activist Visibility

The struggle for an equal age of consent did not succeed in the short run. But it did reveal how sharply the balance of forces had shifted from the late 1980s, and how much access and even influence activists had succeeded in gaining within mainstream political institutions. Even the compromise vote in the House of Commons was beginning to seem anomalous, and wholesale resistance to gay/lesbian law reform on religious or moral grounds more fully marginalized than ever. Among the most important factors shifting the terrain on which political debate took place was an increase in the mainstream presence of gay and lesbian issues, in turn built on the increased visibility of the communities that activists sought to represent.

THE CATALYST OF 1987–88. The passage of Section 28 had been alarming and traumatizing for lesbians, gays, bisexuals, and their allies. But as historian Jeffrey Weeks argues: "There was an unprecedented mobilization of lesbian and gay political energies, supported in the end by important sections of liberal opinion. . . . [F]ar from diminishing the public presence of lesbians and gay men, it greatly contributed to an enhanced sense of identity and community. After many years of fissiparous divisions, lesbians and gay men of various social and political positions found it possible to work together in a common cause."[25] Activist Anya Palmer has a similar view of the period: "Section 28 . . . helped to politicize a new generation of lesbians and gay men, people who like myself who had come out in the early 1980s and were not activists in any sense of the word, who perceived only hazily, if at all, that we were lacking basic civil rights. The marches against Section 28 were much larger than the [Gay and Lesbian] Pride march was at the time, and on a day-to-day level just out in the street it was exciting to see so many people wearing 'Stop the Clause' badges. . . . I had never realized there were so many of us."[26] The Arts Lobby was a particularly distinctive component of the opposition to Section 28, attracting high-profile entertainment figures as openly gay activists, a phenomenon at the time without parallel in either Canada or the United States . This was in part a response to the repressiveness of the British legal and political order.

A number of those who campaigned against the Local Government Bill recognized not only the potential of a new wave of activism, but also the importance of more substantial and skillful engagement with mainstream political processes. As two prominent activists, Lisa Power and Tim Barnett, put it, "Our total refusal to engage with those in power had led us to neglect the impact of legislation and to underestimate the ease with which it could be introduced against us."[27] This was a view that may well have overstated the impact lobbying would have had prior to 1990, but it was an argument in favor of allocating more resources to mainstream processes in the years to come—a view that was gaining increased currency.

A conference held in November 1987 that was aimed at developing an agenda for legislative change also provided an impetus for strategic reflection. It drew over five hundred lesbians and gays from across Britain and from all segments of the political spectrum—from the leftist Labour Campaign for Lesbian and Gay Rights to the centrist Campaign for Homosexual Equality.[28] What proved catalytic for activist redirection was that factionalism prevented any agreement on a program of concrete legislative change. One activist described it as "a pig's ear of a conference—a wasteland of pain and unpleasantness." Peter Tatchell was one of the high-profile figures in attendance. He had been active at the time of the early 1970s Gay Liberation Front, and attracted enormous national attention as the left Labour candidate in the 1983 Bermondsey by-election (see Chapter 1). He was well enough schooled in the fractionalized politics of the left, but was keenly disappointed by the conference. He talked of it as having "betrayed the trust" of the lesbian and gay community.[29]

The Organization for Lesbian and Gay Action (OLGA) was born in the process. But the particular way in which this organization developed, and the circumstances of its formation, persuaded activists with very different ideological and strategic instincts to break from the fractious traditions of the British left. In that sense, OLGA gave birth to the two groups that came to dominate the activist politics of the 1990s—Stonewall and OutRage. One became associated with traditional lobbying, the other with confrontation, but both were in their own ways engaged with mainstream political processes, and both were emphatic in distancing themselves from the legacy that led to the 1987 legislation conference.

A further catalyst for new forms of political intervention came from AIDS activism in Britain and elsewhere. AIDS service organizations such as the London-based Terrence Higgins Trust had gained access to officials and politicians, in part on the basis of the expertise they had developed at an early stage of the epidemic, when government involvement was minimal or wary. The public health crisis posed by the rate of spread created a policy wedge opening up points of access previously unthinkable. More confrontational forms of AIDS activism, exemplified in direct-action groups such as the predominantly American ACT UP, also showed the value of media know-how in gaining publicity for new causes.

THE STONEWALL GROUP. The Stonewall Group was formed in 1989 by the high-profile entertainment figures associated with the Arts Lobby against Section 28, alongside experienced activists such as Lisa Power and Peter Ashman. Reflecting a view widespread in such circles, one activist was particularly frank about how much the group had learned from the Section 28 campaign: "[The] lessons which we drew from it were clearly that you had to talk to the government no matter how much you hated them; that there was no way that you could get a broad-based and politically pure organization in this country; that you had to work on what you could agree to work on, with very limited, specific goals in order to gain any broad base of support; and there was a desperate need for professional lobbying because it was very clear that we were missing those skills—we hadn't the faintest idea how to treat politicians."[30]

From its beginnings the group included members with connections inside the major parliamentary parties and government departments. It consciously chose an organizational format that would insulate it from the kind of factionalism that had mired other groups before it. It was led by a self-selecting board of twenty, without a mass membership but with a rapidly growing mailing list from which it could raise funds and stimulate grassroots action. The board had gender parity; two of its three executive directors from 1989 to 1997 were lesbians.

The group's self-conscious moderation created openings in all of the parliamentary parties. Some gay Conservatives were wary of associating too closely with a group perceived to be dominated by Labour sympathizers but were respectful of the skills of Stonewall's leadership, who in turn welcomed sophisticated advice about lobbying in general, and the development of channels to moderate Conservative officials and MPs. Connections to the Labour Party's parliamentary contingent were also good. One activist's characterization of the contrast with earlier approaches to the party echoes views widespread among Labour MPs and parliamentary aides: "There has never been a group like Stonewall that actually goes and plays sweet reason with them—absolute sweet reason. 'We are not asking for anything more than equality; we are not going to attack you as a person if you don't totally agree with us, but if there's support there, we'll take it.' It's playing at their own game a bit."[31] The trauma over Section 28 had made cross-party contact under the Stonewall rubric easier, despite a political system in which party divisions run deep. After 1988, MPs prepared to stick their necks out on sexual diversity issues began to notice one another and, haltingly, to exchange information and advice about how to advance the political agenda.

Stonewall was preoccupied with law reform, following in the footsteps of groups such as the Campaign for Homosexual Equality (CHE) and the Homosexual Law Reform Association. The organization's growth signaled an increased attention to mainstream lobbying among lesbians and gays of diverse ideological backgrounds, with a broad agenda for equality. The point is illustrated by the fact that Angela Mason, the executive director appointed in October 1992, was once associated with the radical left of the Gay Liberation Front, but by 1994 was acquiring wide respect for her capacity to maneuver in the corridors of Westminster. Almost from its birth the group acquired a very high profile, in part because of the fame of a few of its leading members, in part because of a shift in media treatment of sexual orientation issues and the political and media skills of its staff. This was giving the gay and lesbian movement a sustained and prominent voice that it had never had inside political institutions and major segments of the mainstream media.

OUTRAGE. The challenges posed by Section 28, and the memories of gay/lesbian activist divisions in 1987–88, influenced the second group to emerge at the turn of the decade. OutRage was more clearly within the tradition of radical left organizing around sexual diversity. But it also represented a break from earlier patterns. Those who shaped the group deliberately turned away from a politics centered on large demonstrations—what one activist called "the same boring formula of tramping through the streets followed by speeches at the end."[32] They also sought to avoid the wide-ranging agendas traditionally adopted by left groups in Britain, instead focusing on sexual diversity issues.

OutRage aimed to tap into gay/lesbian anger at discrimination and violence, but also into a trend among young people in particular to be more confidently assertive of sexual difference. It was deliberately focused on establishing a high media profile, taking up a theatrical activism inspired to some extent by the media-wise tactics of direct action-groups in the United States. In fact, OutRage blended objectives that were both radical and reformist with a strategic repertoire that mixed the outrageous with the mainstream. It was committed to confrontation, but avoided much of the fractionalization that had characterized such groups in the past. In addition, law reform, including a call for an equal age of consent, was very much at the center of its concerns, even if its members were more cynical than the Stonewall Group about the political processes through which law reform needed to proceed. In April 1991 activists demonstrating outside the House of Commons dropped their trousers to reveal "EQUALITY NOW!" spelled out on their undershorts. At the same time, they delivered a letter to the home secretary seeking an inquiry into discrimination against gays and lesbians. At the heart of the group, then, was a new style of activism prompting Jeffrey Weeks to talk of "militant reformism" and moving another seasoned observer to describe OutRage as "suffragettes in leather."[33]

ACTIVIST COOPERATION. In the period leading up to the age of consent debate, gay and lesbian activists achieved a degree of cooperation that was highly unusual for Britain. Reaching beyond the mutual suspicion that characterized the relationship between Stonewall and OutRage from the start, some members of each recognized the value of the other. Lisa Power and Tim Barnett, Stonewall supporters from the group's left, commented on activist interventions in the recent past: "While OutRage actions drew attention to the injustices of the legislation, Stonewall lobbyists confronted Conservative parliamentarians and civil servants with the consequences of their actions, and suggested ways to amend it. Both groups successfully exploited their links with the media to obtain sensible coverage."[34] An activist on the group's right agreed in principle: "I think OutRage's attitudes and behavior are outrageous—that's their intention—shocking, wrong, unnecessary, and all the rest. And yet I think there's a need in any movement to have it express itself in different ways. . . . [We] need people who do silly things and say silly things, and we also need people who are prepared to offer the half loaf instead of the whole loaf."[35]

Some OutRage members also welcomed the coexistence of distinct but potentially symbiotic strategic alternatives. One who was critical of some aspects of Stonewall commented in 1992: "Stonewall has more of a lobbying function in relation to Westminster, and I'm happy that they're there. Other people will see them as being toadies, as being assimilationist if you like. I think that's unfair because I think one wants to see legal parity—wants to see anti-discrimination legislation—but that doesn't mean to say that everyone has to do that work. On the contrary, it's generally best to work with people who have professional skills. It seems to me that also leaves our people with the task of much more direct action in terms of policing and so on."[36]

The fact that both groups recognized the importance of law reform on the age of consent indicated a profound shift in the British lesbian/gay movement. OutRage activist and writer Simon Watney, wary of giving law reform too dominant a place in gay and lesbian agendas, nonetheless acknowledged its centrality: "The age of consent matters because it is the symbolic keystone to a whole edifice of reactionary and misleading assumptions and prejudices about homosexuality and, by extension, about sexuality *as a whole*. . . . For at least a quarter of a century, British lesbian and gay political life has been largely retarded by the need to challenge the most blatant anti-gay legal discrimination, focused above all on the age of consent. We have frankly had no choice but to oppose a profoundly unjust and immoral law."[37]

The 1993–94 campaign for an equal age of consent was founded on broad agreement not only over the importance of the issues, but also over the specific objectives to be aimed for and the strategies deployed. Those with divergent views generally acquiesced during the campaign itself, even the most radical recognizing the importance of solidarity.[38] Unity was particularly important on the refusal to discuss compromise. Even activists most inclined to the language of accommodation refused to contemplate the preparation of an amendment supporting eighteen as the age of consent in the event of sixteen failing. Stonewall representatives such as Ian McKellen talked of compromise as an "insult" and a "disaster," perhaps worse than no change at all.[39]

MOBILIZING FOR AN EQUAL AGE OF CONSENT.   Both Stonewall and OutRage contributed to building awareness of the age of consent issue within the political class and the general public.[40] For over three years, OutRage had been bringing this and other law reform issues to the public's attention through well-orchestrated media stunts. In mid-1992 one such event featured signed confessions from sixty gays and lesbians "admitting" to having had sex under the age of consent and challenging police at London's Cannon Road station to arrest them. In addition, on the basis of research on actual prosecutions over the previous year, OutRage was able to point out not only that hundreds of young gay men had been victimized by the discriminatory age of consent, but also that prosecutions and serious penalties were much more likely than in the case of men having consensual sex with girls under sixteen.[41] This information was used widely during the campaign, particularly to counter the claims of some opponents of reform that the law was not rigorously enforced.

Stonewall led the campaign specifically aimed at MPs, one described by Chris Smith as a "textbook model."[42] Others concurred, one Liberal Democratic MP describing the organization as "reasonable, responsible," having done its homework and pitched its argument "exactly right."[43] It was in the Stonewall offices that the amendment for sixteen was drafted and the multi-party team of sponsoring MPs developed. Contact with Home Office officials kept Stonewall members informed about the thinking among ministers responsible for the Criminal Justice Bill.

Perhaps most important, the group developed a database of about thirteen thousand contacts throughout Britain, using it to trigger letters to MPs and visits to constituency "surgeries" (times when constituents can visit MPs in local offices). The database was artfully expanded through the distribution across Britain of fifty thousand copies of a questionnaire on the age of consent, which asked gay and lesbian respondents if they would be willing to write three letters to members of Parliament. The hundreds who agreed received instructions for sending letters to their own MP, the Prime Minister, and the Home Office. The "Case for Change" brochure distributed that autumn also provided ideas for letters and for lobbying MPs in general. Full-page ads were taken out in the gay press, and the letter campaign was amply covered in news stories. Stonewall staff deployed local activists to visit MPs showing signs of wavering. In all this work, the group was aided by local and regional organizations. Outright Scotland assumed a particularly important role.

A large number of gays and lesbians across the country heeded these calls. When Andrew Saxton put a small notice in *The Pink Paper* asking readers to report their MPs' views, he was inundated with letters. At one point the campaign was judged to be so successful that Stonewall urged supporters to stop writing their MPs and to shift to personal visits.[44] For months the Home Office received more mail on this issue than any other. At the peak of the campaign, just three weeks before the vote, a Conservative MP told Stonewall that he had received fifty personal letters in support of equality and only one against.[45] With a weekly total intake of two hundred to four hundred pieces of mail for a typical MP, assisted by only one full-time and one part-time staff person, such a volume of letters on a single issue was impressive. According to one Conservative MP: "Those who were supportive were pleased to have the support. Those who were not sure found themselves thinking very hard about it. One MP came up to me in the House—one older Tory MP—and he said, 'You know, the problem with all this debate is that you're making us think, and we're not very good at that.' "[46]

The willingness of British lesbians and gays to take political action was in part a reflection of Stonewall's skills in building contact lists and providing background materials, and of OutRage's talent for publicizing issues. It also reflected the extent to which those eager for reform had been starved for openings in the central government. The passage of Section 28 in 1988 had jarred many lesbians and gay men out of complacency, moving some to activism, others simply to a sense of injustice that could be tapped at a later date. The persistence into the 1990s of blatant legal discrimination against sexual minorities sustained interest in questions of statutory reform. Even in a political structure that provided few incentives for legislative lobbying, longtime activists and neophytes alike seemed prepared to write and visit MPs, with personal stories of discrimination.

A number of organizations were persuaded to lend public support to an equal age of consent. These included the National Association of Citizens Advice Bureaux; the Council of the British Medical Association (agreeing to support the amendment for sixteen by an overwhelming majority); various other organizations in the fields of health, social services, and youth issues; and several major unions and police officials.[47] Stonewall also engineered a petition, destined for every MP, signed by 150 prominent Britons, including union leaders, bishops, rabbis, and a number of personalities in the arts. One unusual and effective source of support was a group of "agony aunts" (advice columnists), led by Marje Proops of the *Daily Mirror*.[48] Stonewall organized a group of twenty of them to write the *Times* and to deliver a petition to Downing Street—gaining considerable publicity.

MEDIA VISIBILITY. British gay and lesbian activists were skillful in media relations, but they also benefited from increased press willingness to provide evenly balanced or favorable coverage to sexual diversity issues. To some extent, coverage in the media reflected the increased visibility of the gay/lesbian community in cities across Britain, as well as in cultural milieux. It was also a reflection of changed public attitudes toward sexuality. During the Thatcher years, homophobia had been bolstered by the media's shoring up popular resistance to changes in traditional gender, race, or sexual relationships. Until the late 1980s, even the most progressive of British news outlets ignored sexual diversity almost entirely as a political issue, or treated it with patronizing commentary (see Chapter 1).

By 1993, television, radio, and the progressive side of the "respectable" press, represented by the *Independent*, the *Observer*, and the *Guardian*, were devoting much more coverage to such matters than they had in the recent past, though the latter had done so only after repeated protests at their relative inattention. In June 1993, for the first time, the media provided significant coverage of the annual lesbian and gay pride parade and festival. That reflected to some extent the growth of the event, but it stood in stark contrast to the almost complete media silence over the large demonstrations mounted in opposition to Section 28 five years before. More than ever, the press treated representatives of lesbian and gay organizations as legitimate political participants and provided opinion-piece space for those advocating change. Even OutRage's Peter Tatchell acknowledged the difference: "Overall the media coverage on gay issues is now much better than it was ten or even five years ago. It's becoming increasingly routine for lesbian and gay spokespeople to be quoted on issues of relevance. Lesbian and gay issues are getting more regularly reported and on the whole reported in a more objective and dispassionate way."[49]

The tabloids retained their homophobic impulses, though a few reduced the sheer quantity of their diatribes in the years after Section 28, in part as a result of formal complaints.[50] In 1992 even the *Sun* reported rumors about a parliamentary vote on lowering the age of consent without its traditional histrionics. Later on, closer to the 1994 debate, one of its regular columnists confessed to not caring much one way or another about the age of consent, though he tilted toward eighteen.[51] The previously homophobic middle-brow *London Evening Standard* editorialized on the issue by suggesting that "the current differential between ages of consent is a legal inconsistency which criminalizes perfectly honest members of the community—while leaving others free to lead their private lives with impunity."[52] Most of the tabloids retained their essential antipathy to sexual minorities, and the right-wing "quality" papers such as the *Times* and the *Daily Telegraph* generally opposed equality, but they were now more balanced by favorable media attention. The media support that there was for equality, and the relatively low temperature of opposition among the tabloids, helped reassure MPs who were nervous about public opinion. As one activist reported on the reaction of Labour MPs: "I think you could feel it was on the cusp. . . . There were misgivings about whether public opinion had advanced sufficiently to go out now for equality. So various people were beginning to be reassured because they could see we were building support in the media, in the constituencies, amongst other organizations, amongst distinguished figures in society."[53]

In overall terms, enough of the media had expanded their coverage of sexual orientation issues to afford groups such as OutRage and Stonewall (the expanded coverage in part due to the work of those groups) an opportunity to put their case to the general public. At the same time, the increasing number of reporters and commentators supportive of equality provided encouragement to politicians personally favoring that equality but anxious about electoral repercussions. Perhaps most important, the break in tabloid ranks and the increased attention to gay/lesbian causes in the progressive mainstream papers weakened the role of the press in buttressing right-wing moralism.

Openings for Activism within Political Parties

The dominance of the political landscape by party structures and partisan considerations is more complete in Britain than in either the United States or Canada. Electoral loyalty to parties and activist energy devoted to them have declined, but the very continuity of Britain's parties has retained for them a central role in structuring political debate. In the age of consent campaign, activist groups that worked autonomously or across parties took the most prominent roles. But the success of the campaign, which came close to achieving parliamentary victory, depended on important shifts in the party leadership, in the balance of opinion within each of the three major parties, and on the work of activists operating within them.

THE CONSERVATIVE PARTY. The Conservatives' hold on government office gave changes within that party exceptional importance in creating openings for law reform during the early and mid-1990s. No more than a quarter of the party's MPs ever favored significant reform, though that minority did increase after 1988, and became more vocal on the subject in the aftermath of Section 28. A number of Conservative MPs were surprised by the strength of the reaction to that measure. According to a well-connected partisan observer: "What the party noticed was that many of its own members were privately very unhappy about it. The government whip here in the House of Commons felt the full force of a lot of private anger and unhappiness from the more intelligent—the more civilized—of their own party, and they felt it from the constituencies too. They realized they had made a mistake—there's no question at all about that."[54]

To be sure, this realization had more to do with the "massively bad press" the party received than with concerns for the principle at stake.[55] There were a few Conservatives who disagreed with Section 28, but more began to recognize that the party's electoral fortunes, and their own survival as MPs, could be jeopardized by alienating gay and lesbian voters. As one MP put it: "There are enough gays to make a difference in Britain's large cities."[56] Speaking in 1992, activist Peter Tatchell made a similar point: "Among Conservative MPs there's a discernible recognition now that there is a lesbian and gay electorate and that their votes can potentially influence the outcome in marginal seats. . . . John Patton, Home Office minister, speaking to Ian McKellen, admitted that there was a sizable lesbian and gay electorate. Sir John Wheeler, the MP for Westminster North and chair of the Home Affairs Committee of the House of Commons, has made a similar admission. He's sitting on a marginal seat with a majority of about 2,300."[57] As the Conservatives' popular support became more precarious in the early 1990s, fears of alienating this newly talked about constituency increased. The unfounded stereotypes of gay men, and to some extent lesbians, as relatively high income earners also convinced some Conservative officials that there were Conservative votes to be won among them.

Such thinking could be more freely voiced once the Conservative leadership passed from Margaret Thatcher to John Major in late 1990. Major was more of a pragmatist than his mentor on both economic and social issues.[58] His voting record in the 1980s on proposals for decriminalizing adult homosexual activity in Scotland and Northern Ireland had been positive, and early in his parliamentary career he had indicated a preference for lowering the age of consent for homosexual activity (even if only to eighteen). The changed climate was signaled more publicly and dramatically when Major began his September 1991 meeting with Ian McKellan by declaring, "I am interested in the worries of lesbians and gays, particularly on legislative discrimination."[59] There were also modest changes in government policy: homosexuality, for example, would no longer constitute grounds for refusing diplomatic posting or judicial appointment.

In the spring of 1991, an informal group of Conservative MPs committed to law reform began to meet. By 1992 there was talk of about twenty-five MPs being willing to lobby the government on gay issues. These reformers had a formidable representative in Edwina Currie, member of Parliament for Derbyshire South. Currie had been a minister in the Department of Health under Prime Minister Thatcher. She favored both the free market principles of the party's dominant wing and a law and order approach widely popular in the parliamentary and extraparliamentary ranks. In 1987 she voted for Section 28, in part because she was more bound by party discipline than backbenchers, in part because she believed that concerns about the "promotion" of homosexuality to schoolchildren "had some credibility." Nevertheless, Currie was also Jewish and a woman, and thus was aware of some of the ways in which individuals can be marginalized by prejudice and discrimination. She claims, too, that the opposition of gays and lesbians themselves to Section 28 led her to believe that her party "had probably gone too far."[60] Forced to resign her ministerial position in 1989 for unwise words on the subject of salmonella poisoning in eggs, Currie became readier than ever to dissent from her party's majority voice. Since the spring of 1992, she had developed an outspoken profile on gay/lesbian issues, and from 1993 on concentrated on the age of consent. An extremely effective public speaker and writer, she was able to marshal the kinds of arguments that Conservatives would understand. She also had the ear of a few in crucial positions, including the whip's office.

There was, to be sure, a formidable wall of opposition to reform in the party, including the bulk of the Thatcherites who otherwise spoke of keeping the state out of people's lives. The 1990 survey of MPs, after all, had indicated that 68 percent of Conservative parliamentarians favored retaining the existing age of consent of twenty-one. Opponents of equality also included Michael Howard, named home secretary in 1993, and the politician charged with piloting Section 28 through Parliament in 1988. The extraparliamentary party, largely based in constituency organizations, served as an additional brake on social reformism.

But leadership attempts to pander to such sentiment backfired. The prime minister's "back to basics" speech at the 1993 party conference was widely interpreted by the media as a call for a return to traditional morality. This heightened press scrutiny of "lapses" by Conservative MPs and cabinet ministers and evoked cries of hypocrisy even in newspapers normally friendly to the party.[61] Fears about disclosures of homosexuality increased. Whips were rumored to be pressuring bachelor MPs or those suspected of being gay to make a more public show of heterosexuality. Yet they were also rumored to be expressing concern to Conservatives known to be gay about appearing hypocritical by casting an anti-gay vote on the age of consent.[62]

Adding to the discredit of the morally conservative strain within the party was the extremist language used by the Conservative Family Campaign (CFC), the right-wing group most visibly opposed to legal reform. In 1991 its acting chair described homosexual activity as a "sterile, godforsaken, disease-ridden occupation."[63] A number of MPs associated with the group resigned, and many others began viewing it as a fringe element in the party. In the lead-up to the vote on the age of consent, the head of the CFC further marginalized himself, asserting: "I believe I have been called by God to provide leadership for Christians to oppose these moves. . . . Of course this is not the only matter to concern Christians today, but it is *identifiable*, its importance can be gauged by the *effort* Satan's forces are putting in and it is a battle which *Christians can win* in the Name of the Authority of Christ."[64]

The impact on MPs of voices opposing any change at all in the age of consent was no doubt weakened by early indications from the prime minister and most of his cabinet that they would support an age of eighteen. This effectively separated the government from the extraparliamentary forces most adamantly opposed to equality, who insisted on no change at all. Many in the political class who might have been tempted to play on anti-gay prejudice could no longer count on a comfortable ride, and were more inclined to retreat into silence or to acquiesce in a modest reform.

So even with a majority of Conservatives opposed to full equality, the Major era provided some encouragement to reformers in a party that was in any event rife with dissent over other issues. The success of the backbench challenge to Thatcher while she still was prime minister, the depth of the division over European union, and the narrowness of the 1992 Conservative majority in the House of Commons had all weakened the leader's domination over the backbenches. However modest a reformer Prime Minister Major was himself, and however unwilling or unable to force a drastic change in direction on his party, others in the party who were prepared to adopt reformist positions perceived more room for maneuver than ever before.

THE TORY CAMPAIGN FOR HOMOSEXUAL EQUALITY. The expansion of the reform camp among Conservative MPs, and their growing awareness of the potential electoral costs of anti-gay policy, owes much to the emergence of an assertive and visible gay activism within the party. At the party's annual conference in the autumn of 1991, a fringe meeting co-sponsored by Stonewall and the Conservative Group for Homosexual Equality (CGHE), attracted more than one hundred people, unlike the typical meetings of earlier years, characterized as "furtive affairs with everyone sitting rather nervously looking at their shoes."[65] The Tory Campaign for Homosexual Equality (TORCHE) emerged from this new boldness, and was launched officially in February 1992 at a meeting attended by 120 and greeted by a letter of support from the prime minister.

TORCHE's political agenda included the recognition of domestic partnerships, the securing of a right to adopt or foster children by gay or lesbian couples, the extension of immigration rights to same-sex partners, the admission of lesbians and gays to the armed forces, the inclusion of information about homosexuality in schools' sex education, the repeal of Section 28, and an equal age of consent. There was a broad agenda and confidence in the TORCHE program that was largely absent from CGHE materials.[66]

The group was a specifically Conservative formation, giving it at least some legitimacy. Its membership generally adhered to a conception of individual freedom and privacy rights that fit effortlessly with the economic drive of the contemporary party. The group's members were unquestioningly partisan, both loyal to their own party and bitterly critical of others, particularly Labour. Its loyalty to neoliberal Conservative principles, its skill at playing according to the rules, and its rapid growth in membership gave TORCHE a degree of access that would never have been granted to a non-party group.

Those MPs in favor of law reform began to see TORCHE as a valuable resource, providing background information and argumentation that fit with Conservative Party orthodoxy. For those urban MPs motivated in part by a concern to secure electoral support among gay and lesbian voters who would be drawn to the party on economic issues, the group represented a valuable source of legitimacy and assistance. TORCHE members were eager to dislodge as much of the gay vote as possible from whatever left and center-left moorings it may have had. As with other party-based groups, the ambition of TORCHE was not simply to represent certain aspects of a gay agenda to its own party, but to represent its party to the wider lesbian and gay community.

THE LABOUR PARTY. Conservatives played an important role in creating room for a legislative vote, but the extent of anti-gay sentiment in that party meant that the bulk of votes for an equal age of consent would have to come from the Labour Party. In late 1987 the introduction of what came to be Section 28 found the parliamentary party in some disarray over gay/lesbian issues (see Chapter 1). Even after regrouping in the wake of the massive protests against the amendment, Labour's leadership conveyed mixed signals about the firmness of its support for equality. In 1990, for example, only 30 percent of its MPs supported sixteen as the age of consent for homosexual activity.

But the parliamentary party and its leadership did shift toward more pro-gay ground, starting with Section 28 itself. As openly gay MP Chris Smith puts it, the shift arose in part because of the strength of grassroots reaction within the party itself, as well as among gays and lesbians in general: "Labour Party branches up and down the country started passing motions demanding that the Labour Party oppose this clause. When I was talking . . . to the secretary of the parliamentary party, he said he'd never known anything like it—people were ringing up from all over the country."[67] The late 1980s and early 1990s were also a period in which the Labour Party was dislodging itself organizationally and ideologically from its traditional core constituency, the industrial working class. This "modernization" drive was based largely on a centrist appeal that eschewed controversy, but it entailed a shift of values that could inslude equality for lesbians and gays. As Jeffrey Weeks argues: "Value-based politics are likely to be more effective in the postmodern world than class-based politics, as of old Britain. Once one begins to think in terms of values, then you have to define what the values are, and obviously in terms of a party of the left there is a sense of justice, equality, solidarity, and so on. Once you begin to think along those lines, it becomes very difficult to exclude the lesbian and gay community from notions of citizenship."[68]

The increased visibility of sexual minorities in the few years following passage of Section 28 forced most Labour MPs to include issues of sexuality at least in their peripheral vision. Party leader Neil Kinnock was thought to have become more attuned to such issues, moving slowly away from a traditional position shaped by his own background and his leadership of a party not fully united behind an official pro-gay position.[69] Openings in the party's front ranks were apparent in mid-1991, when Labour's deputy leader Roy Hattersley promised a reform of sexual offenses law, and in October when a policy document on family issues seemed to broaden its range of commitments on issues of sexuality.[70] Although the emphasis was on the rights of individuals to be free from discrimination, policy documents extended commitments to parenting and child care rights, and to all areas of law that impeded genuine equality.[71] The 1992 election manifesto was stronger on gay/lesbian issues than the 1987 manifesto, with detailed briefings provided to MPs and relatively strong model answers to barbed questions. The selection of a new party leader in the wake of the 1992 election defeat provided further openings to issues of inclusion. John Smith, who had been shadow cabinet spokesperson on Treasury matters, sent positive signals simply by his selection of ministerial colleagues. Weeks said at the time: ''I think on social issues he's actually more progressive than Neil Kinnock. . . . [Y]ou can see that in the way he constructed his shadow Treasury team. He has two women in it [Margaret Beckett and Marjorie Mowlam], one black man [Paul Boateng], and one openly gay man [Chris Smith]. And I think there's a certain level of understanding in Smith about correcting imbalances.''[72] During the buildup to the final debate on the age of consent, Smith clearly signaled his support for equality. He did not speak in the debate itself—none of the leaders did—but he very deliberately returned from an engagement in Geneva in time to cast his vote for the age of sixteen.

Under Smith's leadership, Tony Blair was placed in the critical Home Affairs slot, and was soon vocally supporting lesbian and gay equality. True, as one media report suggested, ''in terms of the Labour Party's historical baggage—class war, union power, anti-capitalism—Blair travels very light indeed.[73] He was, according to one observer, ''fairly conservative—high Anglican, pro-family, and so on,'' and certainly wary of being thought too far ahead of public opinion.[74] But he was less locked into the rigid idealization of family life that had been so central to the Labour Party's industrial working-class base. He seemed open-minded and prepared to think in broader terms of justice and equality, not on the basis of tolerance for private deviation, but on the grounds of creating a more inclusive citizenship.[75]

LESBIAN/GAY ACTIVISM INSIDE THE LABOUR PARTY. In the extraparliamentary Labour Party, the way toward firmer support for pro-gay positions had been cleared by formal resolutions approved at conferences in the mid-1980s (see Chapter 1). This patient and tedious work had been performed largely by the Labour Campaign for Lesbian and Gay Rights, most effective in the few years leading up to pro-gay party conference votes in 1985 and 1986.

By the early 1990s, the group's role inside Labour was diminished by its decline in membership, its continued positioning of itself on the far left of the party, and the parliamentary party's distancing itself from unpopular left causes from the mid-1980s onward. In any event, even at its height the Labour Campaign had been more interested in influencing the extraparliamentary party than members of Parliament. Like other groups on the left, it tended toward skepticism about the parliamentary party's willingness to support official party policy. In the lead-up to the February 1992 vote on the age of consent, Labour Campaign members were more pessimistic than most other activists working on the issue about the extent of support among the party's MPs.[76]

But by 1992 there were other vehicles for influencing the parliamentary party. A group of of about twenty lesbian and gay staffers engaged themselves actively in the age of consent campaign, pooling information about how MPs were leaning and what arguments might be effective with them. In addition, the Stonewall Group had always included members with close links to Labour Party insiders. The group's high-profile members and moderate style gave it access to precisely those portions of the party executive and parliamentary leadership most removed from the influence of the Labour Campaign.

There was also a sizable core of Labour MPs who were outspoken in favor of equalizing the age of consent. Chris Smith, Tony Blair, and others sent letters to their colleagues urging their support. Neil Kinnock, now the most prominent of Labour's backbenchers, had agreed to be the leading opposition sponsor of the amendment. As in the past, women such as Clair Short, Angela Eagle, and Marjorie Mowlam were prominent supporters of equality.

LIBERAL DEMOCRATS. The Liberal Democrats are generally not major players in Parliament, but outside the legislature, and during elections, they can exert a degree of influence on the debate over issues on which they are relatively united and outspoken. The Liberal Party had a long record of commitment to civil liberties for gays and lesbians, though party resolutions often did not translate into firm leadership support (see Chapter 1). The formal merger of Liberals and Social Democrats in 1988 resulted in the election of Paddy Ashdown as leader, a stronger supporter of lesbian/gay equality than any of his predecessors. (Most of the party's MPs had favored his rival Alan Beith, a veteran MP much less at ease with such issues.) Soon after his election as leader, Ashdown chose Robert Maclennan to handle Home Affairs, which included responsibility over issues such as the age of consent. Maclennan was from the Social Democratic side. A highly reserved, understated Scot from a Calvinist background, he admitted that his preference on the age of consent was for eighteen, for heterosexuals as well as homosexuals. But he had been active in the parliamentary opposition to Section 28, and conceded that on the age of consent he was in a minority and in the end would vote for sixteen.[77]

With hardly a word of dissent, the party's 1989 conference adopted "Partners for Freedom and Justice," referred to in one national gay/lesbian newspaper as "the most radical and comprehensive lesbian and gay rights policy yet seen in mainstream British politics."[78] It committed the party to making "discrimination on the grounds of sexual orientation unlawful in all fields both legal and social," and emphasized the age of consent in particular.[79] The manifesto prepared for the upcoming 1992 election largely repeated the policy commitments laid out in 1989. On the age of consent, it hedged slightly by committing to equality without explicitly mentioning sixteen. But when, in the midst of the 1992 campaign, Ashdown was challenged by a question on the matter by a BBC interviewer who claimed that favoring sixteen as an age of consent was "pretty exotic" and "a bit risky," he responded unequivocally: "It's not exotic; it's fair; it's absolutely essential that people are treated equally."[80] Under Ashdown's leadership the gap between extraparliamentary commitments and parliamentary party support was narrowing. The growing firmness of party conventions, as well as the clear commitment of the party leader, was making it increasingly difficult even for cautious MPs to dissent in public.

Liberal Democratic policy was supported and strengthened by the network of activists who joined together under the name Liberal Democrats for Lesbian and Gay Action (DELGA) at the time of merger in 1988. In 1991 the group launched its own campaign, "16 or Bust," insisting that the party remain uncompromising in its commitment to an equal age of consent. This helped secure support across the party, and focused attention on the importance of this issue in the broader campaign for equality. By the time of the parliamentary maneuvering leading up to the 1994 vote, the intentions of only one or two MPs remained in doubt.

In all three parties, then, important shifts had occurred since the passage of Section 28. In the Labour and Liberal Democratic parties, support for equal treatment of gays and lesbians had spread from official party policy to the belief of an overwhelming majority of parliamentarians. Even in the Conservative Party there was now a vocal minority prepared to argue for individual equality.

Weakness of Extraparliamentary Opposition

The shifts toward greater parliamentary support for equality were accelerated by the lack of organized anti-gay opposition outside the House of Commons. In striking contrast to the Canadian and especially the American cases, the campaign against gay-related law reform was modest and poorly-organized. In earlier years campaigns against abortion and pornography had been mounted by groups that were also anti-gay, based in both the secular and the religious right. But in the debate over the age of consent, no single group or individual emerged to rally opposition.

The speed with which the government moved to schedule debate on the amendments to the Criminal Justice Bill, once they were convinced that allowing an amendment made sense, was certainly one factor that limited opponents' capacity to mobilize. The opposition was also weakened by division. Those most fervent about the issue favored retaining the existing age of twenty-one, or even re-criminalization. But by 1994, a majority of politicians opposed to equality, and a great many members of the general public, were ready to compromise at eighteen as an update of the Wolfenden formula setting the age of consent at the "age of majority."

Few religious groups protested the change. Levels of religious devotion in Britain today are modest in comparison to most countries, particularly the United States; religious fundamentalism is not nearly as widespread as in North America and has little credibility in contemporary politics. Individuals and groups that do use the language of American fundamentalists tend to alienate both public and politicians. During the age of consent debate, those few parliamentarians who echoed such sentiments were more marginalized than ever among their colleagues.

Although the Roman Catholic Church has been a vocal opponent of gay and lesbian rights measures in a number of countries, the British Catholic hierarchy was notable for the moderation of its voice. Cardinal Basil Hume seemed to take special pains to set limits on the political implications of church doctrine condemning homosexual acts. He spoke of the "homosexual community" as a "group that has suffered more than its share of oppression and contempt." In this specific context he counseled caution, but said that Catholics could "reasonably" argue for any of the ages being proposed. He also suggested that the church did not expect that "acts that are morally wrong should, by that fact alone, be made criminal offenses."[81] It is true that constituencies with heavily Catholic populations were assumed antipathetic to reform. One Labour MP is reported to have responded to a query about his inclinations: "I represent a large Catholic constituency—Need I say more?"[82] Still, there was little sign of the sort of clerical mobilization that has marked reform attempts in North America.

The influence of the Church of England was diffused by the fact that its bishops were not of a single opinion about an appropriate age of consent. Most were split between twenty-one and eighteen. The archbishop of York prominently backed the latter, while the bishops of Durham, Edinburgh, and Monmouth favored equality at sixteen, precluding cohesive opposition. The church had also been rent for years over the question of homosexual priests, and seemed loath to take on a political issue that would intensify its internal debates.

As a result of opposition being so weakly organized, MPs received little of the barrage of anti-gay letters and visits that their North American counterparts routinely face. One Labour MP's assistant reported receiving almost no mail opposing change in the age of consent, and virtually no anti-gay letters on other fronts in recent years—this in an office that receives about four hundred letters a week.[83] Conservative MPs also reported receiving very little negative mail to match the substantial numbers in favor of equality.

Changes in Law and Policing

Another lever creating an opening for reform was the threat of embarrassment in European legal institutions to which Britain was tied. The European Parliament (the relatively weak legislative assembly of the European Union) had been moving for over a decade toward official recognition of gay and lesbian equality rights.[84] Progress had also been effected in the twenty-eight–member Council of Europe, with consequences for rulings of the European Court of Human Rights. Increasingly, nationals of member states were taking legal cases to the European Court, including those raising questions of human rights. Adverse judgments against both the British and Irish governments on sexual orientation issues in the 1980s were not binding, but by the early 1990s legal officials in London were becoming concerned about the most obviously discriminatory statutes affecting Britain and its dependencies.[85] (In mid-1993, Ireland equalized the age of consent, at least in part because of pressure from the European Court.)

Before the parliamentary debate on the age issue, the Stonewall Group had found young gay volunteers prepared to challenge the British law at the European Court of Human Rights.[86] The potential for political embarrassment was increased in January 1994, when word was received that the European Commission on Human Rights had ruled that the legal case challenging the British age of consent would be heard by the court.

Although most British politicians (along with activists and the general public) are disinclined to look to Europe for examples, many could not avoid being struck by the fact that Britain had the highest age of consent for homosexual acts in Europe. Of the twenty-eight members of the Council of Europe, only seven retained unequal ages, and none other than Britain with an age higher than eighteen. The fact that legal change on such fronts had been mothballed for so long, widening the gulf with other countries, had led Home Office officials to undertake some background work on a cluster of sexual offenses reforms, "waiting for a minister with the political confidence to pick it up and deal with it."[87] That contributed to a willingness among some officials to meet representatives of gay groups such as Stonewall, providing the sort of civil service access that is rarely attainable for social movement activists, and was never available to gays and lesbians other than those working on AIDS.

The early 1990s were also marked by changes in policing practices. Police training began to incorporate sexual diversity issues, and some police forces took steps to recognize and counter anti-gay violence. There was also an increasing willingness in some cities to turn a blind eye to the sort of "public" sex that would have received only a mild rebuke for heterosexuals but criminal prosecution in the case of homosexuals. There was a recognition within law enforcement and Home Office circles that moral policing had little support in a general population that was increasingly exposed to stories of police corruption, mistaken prosecution, and discrimination. Changed practices, too, reflected to some extent the "Thatcherite razor." As one activist observed: "This regressive parsimony from the Treasury is actually making the police begin to account for their operations. And the sort of moral policing under which homosexuality has thus far lain has actually been edged out. It doesn't offer very clear results; it's not value for money; it's not a clear response to public demand. It's all of those horrible economic liberal arguments which are actually having a positive effect."[88]

Impediments to Equality

As we have seen, the age of consent was not equalized at the end of the parliamentary debate of February 1994. Much shifting in the balance of opinion had occurred in the few years since the passage of Section 28, but there was a large number of opponents within the governing party, and an opposition bloc inside Labour more determined than expected. John Major himself was both less egalitarian and more opportunistic than Conservative reformers asserted at the time. Even one of his gay supporters was prepared to agree: "Major is prepared to make all the nice gentle noises, but the moment when it comes to actually doing something, he doesn't."[89]

The Labour Party's leadership was much more committed to equality, but persisted in treating it as a matter of conscience, and therefore beyond the ambit of the party whip. Labour supporters of equality in or close to the parliamentary party also underestimated the size and tenacity of the dissenting minority. Even in retrospect, one Labour MP talked about lobbying colleagues as unnecessary: "These arguments don't need to be won in the Labour Party. We've got overwhelming policy declarations. We are a party that rates equality above most other things."[90] In September 1993 Chris Smith had predicted that 90 percent of the parliamentary Labour Party would support the age of sixteen, and that most of those opposed to it would abstain. Looking back, he acknowledged the mistake: "I had expected that most of our Labour colleagues that were unhappy about going for equality would abstain rather than vote against, and I was wrong in that judgment . . . [G]iven that it was a basic principle of equality, I thought that they would be reluctant to express such unhappiness."[91]

To some extent, opposition to equality in Parliament reflected public unease. In Britain no less than elsewhere, public attitudes toward gay and lesbian issues are inconsistent and volatile. Surveys show strong majorities in favor of equal treatment but continuing majority disapproval of homosexuality—a pattern evident in other countries. Polling about the age of consent in particular showed the support of three quarters of the population for the principle of equality, but explicit questioning about setting the age at sixteen saw levels of support plummet to between 13 and 16 percent.[92] Such a drop reflects widespread fear about risks to adolescents and children, reflected as well in opposition to gay and lesbian adoption or fostering, though it does not translate into nearly as intense a popular concern for the well-being of heterosexual girls, or into a call for raising the age of consent for heterosexual activity.

Opposition to equality from the right-wing press played on these popular fears, even if there were fewer fanatically anti-gay voices than in the past. The *Times* supported modest change but opposed equality, evoking fears of schoolboy victimization: "Most older homosexual men are not predatory; but some are. Most young teenagers are not vulnerable to such attentions; but some are. Protecting this minority from acts which they may later regret and a sexual path which may leave them isolated and unhappy should remain a priority."[93] Some tabloids offered similar comment, warning of a "predator's charter" leading to "sadness, exploitation and ruined lives," and wondering what chance a sixteen-year-old boy stood against a confident adult pedophile![94]

The Aftermath of Defeat

The period following legislative defeat in 1994 illustrated the seriousness of the challenge facing gay and lesbian lobbyists. Gulfs across activist strategies and partisan affiliations opened up. Pro-gay reformism within the two major parties seemed persistently equivocal.

ACTIVIST CONFLICT. The combination of increased access and difficult progress for gay and leasbian activists fissured the relationship between Stonewall and OutRage after a period of at least grudging mutual regard, despite their determination to avoid the worst of British extraparliamentary fractionalization. Tensions among activists appeared in the crowd outside Parliament on the very night of the vote. The thousands who had gathered that evening were angry at the result, and some attempted to storm the door. Stonewall leaders tried to quiet the crowd, one of its leaders angrily demanding that OutRage activist Peter Tatchell "take responsibility" for controlling it.[95] While most gay and lesbian journalists wrote nonjudgmentally about the anger shown that night, believing it justified under the circumstances, Stonewall representatives joined with virtually all of the mainstream press in condemning the demonstrators. Some Stonewall activists had harbored skepticism or even antipathy to OutRage since its formation. OutRage tactics were seen as media stunts that unnecessarily alienated the public and politicians.[96] Even those who acknowledged a role for direct action often claimed that the lobbying work of Stonewall was more significant and productive.

Many OutRage members reciprocated with impatience or anger at what they saw as assimilationist politics. They viewed Stonewall as a "self-perpetuating oligarchy" prepared to accept halfhearted change.[97] The group's apparent access to inside channels intensified the suspicions of many activists on the outside. One journalistic observer commented: "Maybe people are wondering, 'How did they get those contacts.' There is a sort of inevitable wariness because there hasn't been an organization of this nature before which has actually been able to get into the process. They're seen as having access, and people who would also like to speak to those politicians are saying, 'Why is Stonewall's point of view presented to these people and other points of view not?' ''[98] Here is the classic divide between those favoring the tactics of the parliamentary lobby and those who prefer confrontational direct action, the one adhering to the established rules of the game, the other having no faith in the established political culture.

The gap was further widened by differing interpretations of how much had been gained in the course of the debate, and how much more could be achieved by pursuing the same sorts of strategies that prevailed during the previous months. There was optimistic talk at Stonewall about the prospects of winning a future round in Parliament, and in the meantime of pursuing legal cases and lobbying the home secretary to temper the enforcement of the new age of consent. OutRage activists were disdainful of "exaggerated claims of success" and more than ever inclined to forsake the incremental strategies they had hesitantly supported during the campaign for sixteen.[99]

By the autumn of 1994, the gay press was reporting a "sniping campaign" between the two groups, reflecting profoundly different emphases on the potential for change within existing institutional frameworks. The gap between the groups was widened later in the fall, when Tatchell questioned whether the age of consent should be lower than sixteen.[100] Then OutRage came to embrace "outing"—publicly revealing the names of closeted homosexuals. The group had been divided and indecisive about the issue as recently as 1991, but resentment over the outcome of the age of consent vote had shifted opinion toward more provocative tactics, particularly against gay MPs and other public figures who opposed equality.

The fissures that opened up after the night of the Commons vote were not just between Stonewall lobbyists and OutRage confrontationalists, but between activists separated by partisan loyalties. In any political system, cross-party cooperation is tenuous. In Britain, cooperation is made more difficult by the fact that gay/lesbian groups have tended to position themselves within their own parties in ways that widen their distance from the groups in other parties. Most TORCHE members are free market libertarians, intensely devoted to rolling back state on virtually all fronts.[101] By contrast, the Labour Campaign is dominated by a socialist conception of social justice, one that is highly critical of an emphasis on individual rights at the expense of group or collective rights. Liberal Democratic activists share an individualistic framework with libertarian Conservatives but oppose drastic curtailment of state authority, and in any event believe that the Conservative Party is hopelessly resistant to individual civil rights and freedoms. Even where agreement exists, there are important differences in objectives. TORCHE, for example, focuses largely on the elimination of statutory discrimination, and rejects the sort of proactive anti-discrimination policies favored by many Labour activists. And of course each group seeks to convince gays and lesbians across Britain that they have a natural home in its party. (In late 1996 TORCHE's new leader, David Allen, said that if he lived in the constituency of Exeter, he would vote for Dr. Adrien Rogers, notoriously anti-gay head of the Conservative Family Campaign, running against openly gay Labour candidate Ben Bradshaw.)[102]

Once the campaign had peaked and failed, these differences emerged with considerable force. Activists in all three parties were quick to blame parties other than their own for the defeat. TORCHE was the most vocal, dividing the blame between the Labour Party and activists demonstrating outside Westminster—this from within a party that until 1995 barred even as uncontroversial an organization as the Terrence Higgins Trust, Britain's largest AIDS group, from having a stand at its annual conferences.[103]

POLITICAL BACKTRACKING? Tony Blair became the Labour Party's leader in the summer of 1994. His role in the age of consent debate might have suggested further optimism for law reform, given the prospect of victory in the next general election. But late in the year Blair promised only a free vote, and only when it was feasible. The centrist drive of New Labour became more obvious as the 1997 election loomed closer. The draft manifesto prepared for the election included only a general statement that "attitudes about race, sex and sexuality have altered," that the party "stands firm against prejudice," and that it commits itself "to end unjustifiable discrimination wherever it exists."[104] Soon after Labour's victory in the 1997 election, there were further signs of caution. After one cabinet minister speculated that an equal age of consent would gain overwhelming support in a free vote, the Prime Minister's Office promptly announced that the new government had no plans to reduce the age to sixteen. [105] (See chapter 3 for more on the 1997 election.)

As for the Conservatives, signs of a readiness to countenance reform were more than balanced by retrenchment. In the spring of 1996 the leadership opposed lifting the ban on gays and lesbians in the military, and imposed party discipline to minimize dissent among its own MPs. In June, Prime Minister Major himself cynically played the anti-gay card when he publicly criticized the National Lottery Charities Board for offering funds totalling about £50,000 to gay, lesbian, and bisexual groups, calling the decision "ill-founded and ill-judged."[106] William Hague, who replaced John Major as Conservative leader after the 1997 election defeat, was one of the minority of the party's MPs who voted for sixteen as the age of consent. During his campaign for the leadership, he expressed support for gay marriage, and later sent greetings to London's gay pride marchers. But only a quarter of his colleagues voting for equality in 1994 had survived the election, and among the losers were strong defenders of equality such as Edwina Currie and openly gay Michael Brown. The MPs appointed to handle home affairs were described by one observer as making the ministerial home affairs team under John Major look "dangerously liberal."[107]

On the Liberal Democratic side, there had always been more MPs who were uncomfortable with full gay/lesbian equality than activists in the extraparliamentary party publicly admitted, particularly on the subject of relationship recognition. One was Alan Beith, who had contested the leadership of the party at the point of merger with the support of most of his parliamentary colleagues. As Home Office spokesperson for the Party, Robert Maclennan had become an outspoken advocate of gay and lesbian equality; but after the age of consent debate, a front bench shuffle placed Beith in that position.

There were some positive signs as well. Liberal Democratic leader Paddy Ashdown continued to assert his support for gay and lesbian equality. In March 1996 he unveiled a policy statement on sexual diversity that included an equal age of consent, a complete overhaul of sexual offenses law, antidiscrimination legislation, an end to the armed forces ban, a reform of police training, establishment of hate crime police squads, and a repeal of Section 28. It also included equal rights in fostering and adoption, a subject about which Ashdown had once expressed reservations. The aftermath of the age of consent debate was also marked by overwhelming support for equality in party conferences—a resolution calling for an equal age of consent and recognition for same-sex relationships receiving 97 percent support in 1994.

The 1997 election produced a swing to Labour that significantly shifted the balance of opinion in the House of Commons toward pro-gay positions, especially in light of that party's contingent including more young MPs and women. Support for equality among Labour MPs was strong enough that backbenchers were talking publicly about the importance of legislative action. If a private member's bill were to be given parliamentary time, there is no doubt that the Labour majority would secure its easy passage. The government itself had been cautious enough about making commitments on the age of consent, but dropped its opposition to the legal challenge on the issues being taken to the European Court in late 1997. There were also favorable announcements on immigration rights for same-sex partners, and on the incorporation of the European Convention of Human Rights into British law.

The vote on the age of consent and its aftermath demonstrate the continuing difficulty of taking large steps toward equality in Britain. This is a political order still heavily laden with fears about social change in general and sexual diversity in particular. Its party system is still dominated by two parties, one ready to play on anti-gay sentiment, the other still nervous about the capacity of its opponents in Parliament and the press to tarnish its reputation with anti-gay slurs. The vote for equality was lost largely because the Conservative Party, despite openings created within it for change, was overwhelmingly dominated by politicians who did not, and still do not, understand sexual diversity. It was also lost because the Labour Party's MPs were not as united on this issue as they ought to have been. The House of Commons persists in being an environment in which pro-gay reforms are thought risky, and are almost always relegated even by supporters to the small category of issues of conscience rather than of elemental justice and party policy.

The Britain of the 1990s, however, is not the Britain of the 1980s or earlier. The cultural visibility and political profile gained by gays and lesbians is on more secure foundations. The diversity of activist networks, some operating within parties and some across parties or outside the party system altogether, some of it moderate in tone and some of it confrontational and outrageous, increases the potential for mobilizing large numbers of lesbians and gays who are bridling under a statutory regime that is still censorious and discriminatory. Social movement resources and access to mainstream politics will not guarantee major steps to equality in the immediate future, but they will make gay and lesbian issues harder to avoid, and over the long haul they will make compromises on equality more difficult to maintain.

Chris Smith, MP, in front of Parliament (1995). Photo: *Gay Times Magazine*, U.K./Richard Maude

3

The Parliamentary Ascent
of Chris Smith

"You're better-looking than I thought you were," says one

of the slipper-clad pensioners, flirting with her local Labour

candidate. Chris Smith . . . crouches chivalrously at the old

ladies' feet as he helps to untangle their pension problems

on his pre-election visit. In their admiring eyes he is a cross

between a dashing vicar and a favourite grandson.

Adriana Caudrey, *New Society*, June 1987

In front of a thousand people gathered in Rugby in late 1984 to protest the local council's anti-gay action, the fourth speaker opened by saying, "My name's Chris Smith, I'm the Labour MP for Islington South and Finsbury, and I'm gay." With that, the thirty-three-year-old parliamentarian elected only a year before with a dangerously slim majority became Britain's first openly gay national legislator, and one of the first anywhere in the world. The dramatic announcement was made in a political climate that was not friendly to lesbian and gay issues, dominated as it was by a Thatcherite rhetoric of traditional family ideology, in a country with a long-standing antipathy to public discussion of sexuality of all sorts and homosexuality in particular (see Chapter 1). Over the next few years, Chris Smith gained considerable respect among parliamentary colleagues, particularly in the Labour Party. In the early 1990s he began a steady ascent that culminated in his appointment as heritage secretary following the 1997 general election.

Smith has maintained enormous standing among gays and lesbians across Britain, for whose rights he has been an unswerving advocate. In the British political system, however, a gulf exists between the world of parliamentarians and that of social movement activists. A member of Parliament such as Chris Smith, who so clearly represents a cause simply by virtue of being openly gay, can keep one foot in a social movement. But inevitably his body weight is largely on the other foot, anchored in constituency activity and in the highly partisan work of a parliamentarian. Smith's ascendancy within Labour's front benches and to the cabinet has provided him with a more influential position from which to press for policy commitment, while making it even harder for him to serve as the tribune that his counterparts in Canada and the United States can still be. The tension between such roles is reinforced by the traditionalism of the House of Commons, and the limited flexibility available to individual legislators. At times Chris Smith has played an important role in forthrightly speaking out for gay and lesbian issues in a parliamentary environment that for a long period had few such voices. But as with the broader social movement, there have been only limited opportunities over the span of Smith's career for such a voice to make a difference.

The limits on his role as representative of a larger cause are partly a product of personal style. Smith is an understated person, careful in his discussion of issues, reluctant to criticize others, seemingly incapable of raising his voice. At rallies he has spoken with deep conviction that taps enthusiastic admiration in his audience, without stirring up their anger or defiance. But the role that he plays is essentially shaped by the institutional setting in which he operates. The parliamentary environment discourages specialization, especially in an area thought to be of marginal interest. Smith also operates within a party that has long been wary of sexual orientation issues, not least because of the traditional willingness of other parties and the tabloid press to pander to anti-gay sentiment.

There is substantial disagreement in gay/lesbian political communities about the utility of operating within established political institutions. At the level of activist politics, there has never been agreement on the value of working within the Labour Party or of using the mainstream parliamentary networks within which Smith moves, and to which he is loyal. As much as in any political system, there have always been tensions between activists who use traditional lobbying tactics and those who stand in radical opposition to the frameworks and goals of mainstream politics. The demographic makeup of the House of Commons is enough to convince many activists that it is a world entirely removed from their concerns. They distrust the politics of compromise that so permeates legislative environments; many also resent what they see as the precedence of party loyalty over principle among all parliamentarians.

Chris Smith is nonetheless widely respected among activists, though engaged in what many of them consider an assimilationist and elitist form of politics. That view is widespread even within the Labour Campaign for Lesbian and Gay Rights. Gay and lesbian activists within the other major parties are respectful of Smith only in a distant way, because of the chasms created by party loyalties. For activists who are not engaged in party-affiliated organizing, the influence of partisanship may not be as pronounced, but it still remains a factor. The emergence of a group such as Stonewall has marked a reduction in the distrust of the political mainstream and a new unwillingness to work across party lines. But the high profile of that group, and to some extent of its rival OutRage, shifts onto organizational shoulders whatever expectations might have been urged upon Chris Smith to represent a national gay constituency.

The Diary of an MP

Whatever the difficulties, Chris Smith has devoted enormous energies to the roles of both tribune and parliamentarian. No more powerful illustration can be provided than an account he prepared for the *Guardian* of his diary during the week of February 15, 1994, the week leading up to the parliamentary vote on the age of consent (see Chapter 2), by which time he had become a member of the Labour Party's parliamentary leadership (shadow cabinet).

Tuesday
Start the day with a visit to a young constituent who is doing an A-level project on the age of consent issue. . . . I arrive late at the House of Commons to chair a meeting of the Environment Protection Team. We decide to launch an assault on the Government over Britain's dirty beaches. . . . Spend hours in my office, catching up with a tidal wave of paper, before voting late at night on the Welsh Revenue Support Grant and heading wearily home.

Wednesday
Do an interview with a journalist from the *Evening Standard*, about what it's like being an openly gay MP and what I think is going to happen on the age of consent. I'm optimistic, but by no means complacent. Amazingly, the *Standard* have been remarkably supportive. Questions to the Secretary of State for the Environment: I lay into them on the evils of compulsory water metering. . . . On to Shadow Cabinet, where we talk through the Parliamentary business for the coming week. . . . I arrive late (the story of my life) at my constituency party's general committee meeting.

Thursday
On the train to Norwich. . . . A speech to the Labour Club at the University. . . . Questions come thick and fast: about motorway building, about student grants, about global warming, and of course, about the age of consent.

Friday
Representatives of the Water Companies Association come to see me. . . . Confer assiduously (as I've done all week) with the Stonewall Group, about tactics for Monday night and how the lobbying is going. Stonewall's work on this campaign has been a textbook model. The key has been getting individual gay men and their families and friends to contact their own MP, to put the case in their own way and their own words. And many MPs have listened. Off to my own constituency for my Friday evening surgery. It's supposed to finish at 8:00 P.M.. Finally emerge at 11:00 P.M., traumatised

by the sheer weight of distress so many people have to endure. This is not a nation at ease with itself.

Sunday
Return to London [from a visit with friends]. Tomorrow's debate looms and I have to sit down and think what I'm going to say in the debate. One of the most difficult speeches I've ever made in the House, this one.

Monday
The day of the age of consent debate. I spend much of the morning racing from studio to studio. I'm still telling everyone that we have a good chance of winning equality at 16. Something deep down inside me—chilled by the sad news of [gay filmmaker] Derek Jarman's death—warns me not to be over optimistic. But it's so obviously the right thing to do. The debate begins just after 7:00 P.M.. Edwina Currie, Neil Kinnock, Tony Blair, Tristan Garel-Jones: they're all excellent. I sit nervously hoping that I'll be called. A variety of Tory interventions lapse quite deliberately into homophobia. The Home Secretary makes an unconvincing job of a thin speech that appears to rely wholly on one sentence from the Wolfenden Report published 27 year ago. So when I'm called I decide to take his argument apart. And I say to the House: yes, we as gay men are different. We have a different sexuality. But that does not mean for a moment that we are not every bit as valid and worthy as any other citizen of this land. Surely democracy is about the protection and the nurturing of diversity? The first vote is bungled and has to be taken again, but it becomes achingly clear. We are 27 votes short of achieving equality at 16. Eighteen goes through, yes, but it still enshrines discrimination in law. All the hope, all the expectations, all the lobbying and arguing, all ends in perpetuation of injustice. As I march over to talk to Newsnight I'm disappointed, angry, upset, and just for a moment close to tears.[1]

Candidate and Constituency

Chris Smith has secured extremely high standing among both his constituents in the London district of Islington South, and his local Labour Party association. His partisan opponents have attempted to raise the gay issue, but Smith's own campaigns have succeeded in convincing local voters that he is not a one-issue candidate. He has never been afraid to speak out on gay-related questions, but he has also recognized that his local reputation relies on solid constituency work, overwhelmingly focused on other matters.

Smith has a reserved, courteous manner that endears him to his constituents as well as to parliamentary colleagues. He is culturally and historically literate, able with unpretentious ease to cite his favorite plays, novels, poems, and music.[2] His intellectual depth was evident from his undergraduate years, when he received a rare first in English at Cambridge, and from graduate work leading to a seldom-mentioned Ph.D. Described by one interviewer as a "Fabianesque, Libertarian, Leftist MP," he associated himself through at least the mid-1980s with causes such as nuclear disarmament and nationalizing major financial institutions.[3] In more recent years he has moved toward the center of the Labour Party's "soft" left. Among the political figures he admires, he counts the postwar Labour politicians Nye Bevan and Hugh Gaitskell, and the Americans Robert Kennedy and Martin Luther King, Jr. Following a long tradition in British politics, he marries his socialism with Christian belief.

COMING OUT. At a time when social movement activism was surging on many fronts, Chris Smith chose the route of party politics. He had been a member of the Labour Party since his first year at Cambridge in 1969, when he was eighteen. While there, he was treasurer of the Labour Club, chair of the Cambridge Fabians, and vice chair of the National Young Fabians. He had been born in North London in 1951, to a civil servant father and teacher mother, and he returned to live there, in Islington, working as a housing development officer—a job that intensified his interest in national politics.

He was elected to Islington Council in 1978, and in 1981 became the chair of its housing committee. (In between he contested—hopelessly—the parliamentary seat of Epsom and Ewell in the general election of 1979.) He was part of the lesbian and gay committee on Islington Council, and was a member of the Haringey and Islington branch of the Campaign for Homosexual Equality (CHE), though his activism in these early years was focused on Labour and union politics, not on gay politics per se. Smith spoke out on gay and lesbian issues, and there were certainly people in the area who knew or thought he was gay, but there were many who did not.

In 1981 the sitting MP in Islington South became one of the centrist Labourites who defected to join the Social Democratic Party, making the Labour nomination more easily contestable. The constituency was not far north from the city's center, with established working-class districts coexisting with those being gentrified by relatively young and well educated middle-class residents. Smith won the nomination. The issue of his gayness seemed not to have played a role. In the preparation for the June 1983 election, according to Smith himself: "It wasn't particularly a secret. . . . There were discussions between the agent, party chair and myself, but they revolved around what should happen if someone raised it at a public meeting, rather than should I take the initiative and make a statement. I felt very strongly at that time that I should answer any question openly and honestly, but they were then rather wary about it, naturally."[4] In fact there were whispers in the election campaign, encouraged by Social Democratic campaigners. The SDP in Islington was largely propelled by former Labourites most likely to be antipathetic to the panoply of causes associated with their former party's left wing, including gay rights.

Smith defeated George Cunningham by a razor-thin margin of 363 votes, in a national election won handily by Margaret Thatcher's Conservatives. Cunningham's vote, in fact, substantially exceeded the vote for the Alliance of Liberals and Social Democrats typical of a constituency such as Islington. The reason is hard to pin down: it could have been rumors of Smith homosexuality, or popular discomfort with a local council identified with the "loony left" (see Chapter 1).[5]

In this race, as in almost all races across Britain, a candidate's election depended overwhelmingly on constituent views of the party she or he represented, or of the party leadership. Local election campaigns in Britain are relatively modest in scale. The fact that, unlike in the U.S. system, there is only one race going on in a constituency inevitably gives it prominence, but local campaigning is altogether swamped by the national campaigns. The "personal vote"—that accorded a constituency candidate because of individual qualities, beliefs, or behavior—may be increasing in Britain, but it is still minor in comparison to Canadian and especially American elections.[6]

That does not diminish the highly localized aspect of the MP's role—the considerable time spent on casework generated by the questions and problems of constituents. A typical MP will receive about three hundred letters a week, as well as a substantial number of visits during weekly "surgeries" at constituency offices, all with a total staff complement of about two. Parliamentarians themselves often attach great importance to this "social worker" role, and strong House of Commons norms militate against MPs' taking on casework apart from that which emerges from their own constituencies.

PRESS REACTION. When Chris Smith came out in 1984, there was very little immediate reaction in the press other than a front-page story in the local *Islington Gazette* giving him a reasonable opportunity to discuss it, and favorable comment in the national Sunday paper the *Observer*. The electronic media and most of the progressive or neutral dailies and weeklies were largely silent in the aftermath of his announcement, and there was much less comment from the anti-gay tabloids than Smith and those around him had feared and expected. (The political damage from the Rugby speech seemed so minimal that Smith recalls telling Canadian MP Svend Robinson that coming out politically was smooth sailing.) This was a period when the tabloids were intensifying their attacks on homosexuals, associating gays with disease and epidemic, and relishing every opportunity to associate them with scandal. But Smith's voluntary coming out, with no taint of scandal, had left the media without a sensationalist hook. Trying to decipher the criteria used by Fleet Street journalists to "go after" a gay-related story, one journalist has observed: "There always has to be a separate incident that accompanies the sexual orientation. I think some tabloid story would have to expose Chris as some sort of orgy-goer or child molester. The story that was being run on the *News of the World* prior to the last election was about how [a Labour aide] was living with a married man, which was causing the family of the married man heartache . . . and therefore the story was sort of 'Labour Aide Is Family Wrecker'—it wasn't 'Labour Aide Is Gay.' "[7]

That said, the tabloids were not above giving Smith unfavorable coverage when he associated himself with gay-related causes. A 1985 trip to an American gathering of gay and lesbian officials was widely reported. A small story in the

London Standard (at the time not as disreputable as the bulk of the tabloid press) demonstrated the willingness of his partisan opponents to exploit the issue:

MP "PUT GAY RIGHTS FIRST"

Gay MP Chris Smith, who flew to California for a homosexual rights conference last weekend, has been accused of putting Gay Rights before his constituents. . . . Councillor David Hyams, the leader of Islington's Social Democratic opposition, said: "The people of Islington don't want to read in the newspapers that their MP has jetted off to America to tell Gay Rights activists that England will one day have a gay king or lesbian queen."[8]

In 1986, the *Sun* commented (inaccurately) on an interview statement by Smith in *Gay Times*, criticizing the tabloid exploitation of women in their "page 3" displays: "Chris Smith is Labour MP for Islington South and Finsbury. He is also a self-confessed homosexual. . . . He wants to ban Page Three while at the same time go on allowing homosexuals the right to buy magazines containing sado-masochistic porn. So if Mr. Smith has his way the law would allow nasty-minded perverts to buy material that would sicken normal people while denying the healthy-minded majority their favourite dose of glamour."[9] The *Sun* returned to the attack in 1987, in reaction to a Smith speech at another meeting of openly gay and lesbian politicians in the United States. The language used in the story was vintage tabloid:

SIXTY-FIVE POOFTERS IN THE COMMONS SAYS GAY MP

Parliament is packed with poofters, a leading gay MP claimed yesterday. As many as 65 homosexuals are camping underground on the front and back benches of the House of Commons.[10]

"NOT A SINGLE ISSUE POLITICIAN". This kind of media climate ensured that Smith, by nature calm and low-key in his demeanor, would try to avoid overidentification with a cause that was largely ignored or reviled. He could expect to benefit from incumbency, and from a parliamentary system in which parties and party leaders dominated the electoral landscape. But he was also coming out at a time when gay rights advocacy was thought "loony."

From his first election to Parliament, Chris Smith had shown a willingness to identify himself with gays and lesbians. In the spring of 1984, he had used the pronoun "we" in a talk he gave to a local CHE meeting, and at the autumn annual meeting of the Labour Party, he had been transparent about his homosexuality at a fringe meeting on lesbian and gay rights.[11] After the Rugby speech at the end of that year, he responded willingly to the increased demand for comment from journalists.

It was the attacks on British gays and lesbians being mounted at the time by press and police that had obliged Smith to speak out, especially so because so few politicians were then prepared to defend sexual minority causes. Smith recalls:

It was in the early 1980s that lesbian and gay politics began to hit the national headlines in a big way. . . . The Greater London Council dared to say that it wanted to ensure equal treatment for lesbians and gay men, and was vilified for doing so. . . . From that period onwards, the tabloid press began to treat lesbians and gay men as "fair game," to be hunted, pilloried and railed against in the most wretched and senseless fashion.

And then, of course, came the sorry saga of the Bermondsey by-election [in 1983]. . . . I can vividly remember canvassing for Peter [Tatchell] in that by-election. In a seat that had been rock-solid Labour for decades, it was uphill work. . . . All of us dedicated to a politics of inclusion, a politics that seeks to draw lesbians and gays into the mainstream rights of society, were dealt a savage blow by Bermondsey. . . .

I well remember the time, less than two years after Bermondsey, when we debated the "pretty police" problem in Parliament. Police officers dressed provocatively in tight jeans had been lounging around outside gay pubs and "enticing" men into sexual contact. . . . [We] ended up having a tense debate in Parliament on an amendment to the Police and Criminal Evidence Bill which tried to prohibit any practice of entrapment by the police. It was late at night, but the press gallery was packed. I was absolutely terrified when I spoke. . . . One or two brave souls from the Conservative benches spoke up in favour of an amendment to the law, but the entire presumption of the occasion was that speaking up for lesbians and gay men was somehow rather strange, and certainly politically dangerous.

Shortly afterwards, Customs and Excise officers raided Gay's the Word bookshop in London, impounded a range of books that had been imported, declared them indecent and obscene, and launched a prosecution. . . .

It was against this background that I decided to "come out." A rally was being held in the town of Rugby, against the local council who had declared that they were removing sexual orientation from the list of attributes they would not discriminate against in employment. The decision had been accompanied by stark statements from the leader of the council, about not wanting men coming to work in dresses and earrings, and other similarly nonsensical stuff.[12]

After his Rugby announcement, however, Smith took care to avoid being over-identified with gay/lesbian issues. According to the *Islington Gazette*, Smith was "anxious that constituents should not get the impression that he is going to become a 'single issue politician.' "[13] He repeated the point in a 1985 interview for *New Socialist* and then in a 1986 interview with *Gay Times* "Obviously I stood up and said what I am and no other politician has done so, and because of that I tend I suppose to be asked to take up issues that relate specifically to lesbians and gays. I want to do that, but I've also consciously tried to take up a lot of other issues as well to make clear to my constituents that I'll fight for all of them, no matter who or what their problems are."[14] In the midst of the 1987 election, *New Society* writer Adriana Caudrey reported an interview with the Islington South candidate: "the gay community, if they were hoping for a personal champion, will have been disappointed, because Smith has never made gay rights his preserve. 'I have deliberately gone out of my way to avoid being the gay MP who always skips up and down about that thing.' "[15] She reported him as irritated, in fact, at being questioned on the impact of his sexuality on his public life: "I'd like to see it as politically honest to say I am gay. But so what. Let's get on with the business of being an MP."[16]

SUBSEQUENT ELECTIONS. Smith's campaign for reelection in 1987 almost completely avoided gay and lesbian issues. His literature made no mention of them except for a fleeting and elliptical reference to "sexual and racist attacks" in a brochure section dealing with safety in the streets. The soft-pedaling of these issues may have reflected a recognition on the part of Islington Labour organizers that Smith could be assumed to stand for gay/lesbian equality, but it is hard to escape the suspicion that fears of his being labeled a single-issue candidate resulted in compensatory steps in the other direction. Such fears were undoubtedly intensified by the wariness of the tabloid press that so permeates British political life. The cautiousness of Smith's campaigners was no doubt increased by the fact that the most prominent local paper, the *Islington Gazette*, though not a tabloid in the usual sense of the word, was not above using the gay issue as a smear. Just before the 1987 election, it broke one of the most notorious stories ridiculing the educational programs of London's "loony left," this one about a children's schoolbook, *Jenny Lives with Eric and Martin*, portraying the life of a young girl with a male couple.[17]

The opposition Social Democrats once again tried to make Smith's gayness an issue. Reporting on the 1987 election campaign in Islington South, *Gay Times* referred to a "dirty campaign by members of the local SDP-Liberal Alliance who are reported to have told voters on the doorstep that the Labour Party was going to 'teach children to be lesbians.' Although the local candidate publicly condemned such tactics, there was, according to Smith, "considerable evidence that SDP canvassers deliberately stirred up prejudice, asking electors how they could vote for a gay candidate."[18]

The experience of other openly gay candidates running for local office in the 1980s and early 1990s suggests that all three parties have been capable of pandering to prejudice. In some cases gay Labour councilors have reported vicious campaigning from the Conservative camp, in others from the Liberal Democrats; while Liberal Democratic councillors have found anti-gay sentiment sometimes whipped up by Conservative opponents, sometimes by Labour.[19] The persistence of such patterns suggests that being gay or pro-gay was widely perceived to be a liability well into the 1990s, and despite occasional party disclaimers, playing on such sentiment was still regarded as legitimate and profitable.

Smith's campaigners developed a strategy of responding to voters' questions about the issue by talking about the honesty required to be out: "Wouldn't you rather have an honest politician than somebody who's hiding things like that?"[20] In fact, the issue rarely came up among electors. According to Smith himself: "I think if I had gone on to talk about it endlessly, write about it endlessly, make a meal of it . . . the reaction might have been a bit different. But I made my own decision that the right way to handle it was to say, 'Okay, I've now said this; whenever it is important I will stand up and talk about lesbian and gay rights and I will go and march on Pride Day and I will talk at rallies and go around universities talking to lesbian and gay societies and so on; but the main focus of my political work is about my constituency and about housing and about the environment and about the economy and I'm going to keep on doing that.' Because I deliberately made that decision it probably made it easier to get accepted."[21]

Smith won Islington, though his margin increased only to 805 votes. But since London as a whole had seen an overall swing against Labour, his increased majority could be construed as a favorable result. It was due in part to a return to Labour of votes that had migrated to the SDP in 1983 when that party's local candidate was a sitting MP. But it was also due to Smith's having had an opportunity to demonstrate his qualities as a constituency MP.

The introduction of Section 28 in late 1987, prohibiting local authorities from "promoting homosexuality," launched Smith even more prominently into the limelight as the country's only openly gay MP and an ardent critic of the measure at rallies and in the media.[22] He had gained a profile on such issues at party conferences and in the gay press since coming out. But now he was expected more than ever to make speeches on gay-related issues in the House itself. He made two on the subject of Section 28, the second including this powerful indictment of the principles underlying it: "The proponents of this clause have been saying . . . that there is only one form of relationship, one form of sexuality and one form of lifestyle that is acceptable. That sexuality will be endorsed, approved, applauded and given enhanced legal status, and everything else will become second-class. It is a view which refuses to recognise the difference, the diversity and the very richness of human life and human society. It is intolerant, immature, and undemocratic, and . . . it is profoundly immoral."[23]

In the lead-up to the 1992 elections, however, Smith remained wary of being overidentified with sexual orientation issues. During the campaign itself, his election materials again avoided gay issues, dwelling on economic recovery, health, local taxation, pensions, education, and "family policy," including a call for lower taxation for "ordinary families." The Liberal Democrats (uniting Liberals and most Social Democrats) campaigned on the spending record of the Islington council as a way to attack Labour, finding it difficult to resist the temptation of citing grants to lesbian and gay groups as examples. But the campaign was unsuccessful and generally not well organized.

Smith won his third election with a majority that leaped up to 10,652. Speaking just prior to that election, a local gay activist who identifies himself with the hard left echoed a widespread sentiment: "He has an excellent reputation as a constituency MP. There's a leaflet going around saying 'Everyone's been helped by Chris Smith,' and it's actually true. Taking things up with the local Labour council, tax problems, helping people getting in touch with government departments— that is what carries him through. . . . The people take no account of the fact that he's declared himself to be gay because that's not what comes to mind when his name comes up."[24] Smith is also moderate and soft-spoken, articulate and gentlemanly, and "by his whole appearance demolishes any idea of any sort of popular gay image." The fact that so many local constituents have been helped by Smith also means that many feel they know him, and as one campaigner put it, "would be livid if anybody did anything to hurt their Chris because he's such a nice boy."[25]

If Smith's standing was helped by his reputation as a hardworking and effective MP, it was also helped by the support that his already formidable campaign organization received from gays and lesbians across London. His reelection both in 1987 and to some extent in 1992 was seen as having political importance for sexual minorities across the country, and the local campaign sent out calls for help in London's lesbian/gay newspapers. One activist recalls: "An awful lot of London-based lesbians and gay men worked on his campaign. I actually crossed London to work on his campaign, because he is a person who needed reelection, and he had a very marginal seat."[26] Within the lesbian and gay community he is much loved. Prominent figures such as Michael Cashman (of Stonewall and the popular soap opera *Eastenders*), sporting Chris Smith stickers, visited the constituency, touring Islington's gay bars.

Within his own local Labour Party, Smith recalls strong support in the wake of the Rugby speech: "At the general committee meeting shortly afterwards, a statement was made by the chair of the party congratulating me and offering the party's full support. It was obvious from the mood of the meeting that this had the support of everyone who was there."[27] Before the 1992 campaign, Smith won renomination from his local party by all but two votes out of about four hundred—one of the best results in the country for a Labour MPs.[28]

The 1997 election produced the first Labour victory since 1974, giving the party 44 percent of the popular vote, and with 419 seats, 65 percent of the House of Commons. The Liberal Democrats won 17 percent of the vote, and a significantly increased 46 seats. Chris Smith won his own reelection with ease, increasing his majority to 14,563—63 percent of the total votes cast. The swing to Labour, averaging 10.5 percent, swept aside 177 Conservatives, including Michael Brown, to that point the only other openly gay MP.

Two Labour candidates became the first in Britain's history to successfully contest parliamentary seats as openly gay from the outset. Ben Bradshaw won the Exeter constituency in southwest England, defeating notoriously homophobic Conservative candidate Adrian Rogers by almost 12,000 votes, recording a swing to Labour above the national average. Stephen Twigg scored an upset victory over right-wing Conservative minister Michael Portillo in the London constituency of Enfield Southgate, with a swing of over 17 percent. Their races, along with a few other openly gay candidates for the Labour and Liberal Democratic parties, provoked only modest tabloid response.[29] (The readiness to countenance openly gay standard bearers did not extent to the Conservatives.)

Stature in Parliament and Party

Chris Smith has become highly respected in the House of Commons as a whole as well as within the Parliamentary Labour Party. His hard work as a constituency MP stood him in good stead from the beginning; just as important was his combination of party loyalty, cross-party civility, and intelligence. But like most MPs, Chris Smith has had little room for maneuver in Parliament. That is the result of tight party discipline, and the traditional norms of the British House of Commons. Also, as an opposition MP for much of his career, he had had few opportunities to shape legislative outcomes. These factors limited Smith's capacity to establish an ongoing role for himself as a tribune for a national lesbian/gay constituency.

PARTY DISCIPLINE. The British policy-making process is dominated overwhelmingly by the executive, with power centered in the cabinet and the administrative offices that line the streets of nearby Whitehall. Party discipline in the House derives in part from the power of the government and the dominance of the prime minister within it. The principle of collective responsibility obliges cabinet ministers, as well as other ministers and parliamentary secretaries, to publicly support government decisions or else resign. Loyalty is expected of the rest of the government party's caucus, and is usually granted willingly. Particularly in Britain, most MPs have years of apprenticeship in their party. They know that dissent can hurt the party's success at the next election; they realize that their promotion to the front ranks will depend on their being loyal; and they recognize that their electoral success depends almost entirely on the standing of their party and its leader.

In most circumstances, the extent of party discipline, the domination of each party's caucus by its front bench leaders, and the cabinet's control over the legislative agenda mean that opposition MPs and backbenchers of all parties have very little policy influence. As one writer put it, in the work of government, "the MP is not a player but a spectator, albeit with a front-stall seat."[30] Some commentators have noted an increase in dissent and rebelliousness in recent years. They cite instances in which governments have been defeated in the House, and cabinets or prime ministers have backed down in the face of caucus revolt. But dissent with any chance of exerting influence is also heavily constrained by norms governing timing, place, wording, and so on. Parliament is in some ways strikingly cut off from the rest of the world, with its clubby atmosphere defined by rules and rituals. In any event, most of the dissent in Westminster is voiced in party meetings or hallway conversations away from public view, providing few of the vehicles for public representation of group concerns that can take place in the American system .

MARGINALIZATION OF DIVERSITY. The difficulty of vocally representing a marginalized national constituency in the House of Commons in exacerbated by the weight of parliamentary tradition and the expectation of conformity to un-written rules. The vast majority of MPs treat politics as a career, and electoral patterns have allowed most of them to secure reelection, the typical MP having more than fifteen years' experience in the House. Accession to the front bench of any party normally requires years of parliamentary apprenticeship and dem-onstrated skill in House debate. Among Britain's legislative traditions is the con-ception of Parliament as a deliberative assembly, not a "congress of ambassadors from different and hostile interests."[31] This view is anachronistic in some re-spects, but it does capture the ethos of parliamentary independence from outside pressure.

The British parliamentary culture discourages the kind of legislative speciali-zation that is common in the rest of Europe and to some extent in the United States. This is in part a legacy of the same tradition that resulted in the long-standing practice of recruiting senior civil servants from the ranks of educated generalists. It is also due to the relative weakness of parliamentary committees, and to the importance attached to the MP's focus on his or her constituency.

The parliamentary norms militating against acting on behalf of any group apart from one's geographically defined constituency has made it difficult for an MP such as Chris Smith to represent a second constituency defined by sexual orien-tation. As one Conservative activist put it: "Does he get a mailbag from gay people from all over the country? If he does, I would hope that what he says to them is, 'Don't put any time into writing to me if you're not my constituents; put [your MP] under a lot of pressure to take up cases for you.' Because that's the way it works in this country. There is a convention here: members of Parlia-ment do not take up cases in other people's constituencies. It's sheer practicality. We have constituencies of, what, sixty to seventy thousand. If you just took up cases at random from all over the place, you would soon find yourself in deep trouble. It would just be unmanageable. It's bad manners."[32]

Parliamentary norms are fully evident in this assessment of the standing of racial minority MPs by a Liberal Democratic MP: "I have seen no sign of any discrimination either against or for them. Probably the most successful black MPs in this House are those that try very hard to avoid being cast as black MPs. Far and away the most impressive of the black MPs in this House is Paul Boateng, who is an extremely capable lawyer, barrister, Labour front bench spokesperson. And he makes nothing of the fact that he comes from a nonwhite racial back-ground. He just gets on with being a very good MP."[33] Women, blacks, Asians, as well as lesbians and gays, automatically risk their reputations as "good MPs," partly because of the stigma associated with focusing too much on a "single issue," but also because the issues themselves do not count as "important" in comparison to "hard" issues such as budgeting and foreign affairs.

The definition of what constitutes an important issue is shaped by factors out-side the legislature, traditionally reinforced by the demographics of the House of Commons. The fact that it has been largely a man's world has had relevance for gay rights, since women are more likely than men to support them. In a House of 651 members, only 41 women (6 percent) were elected 1987, a number that rose only to 60 (9 percent) in the 1992 election, making it one of the most male-dominated legislatures (alongside the U.S. Congress) in the industrialized world. Prior to the 1997 election, one MP suggested that in order to understand the House of Commons, one had to think of the culture of an English public (i.e. private) school. Women MPs from all parties have acknowledged Parliament's "rigidly masculine atmosphere," and have widely accepted the comparison to a private boys' school. One Conservative argued that in some respects it is worse: "a mixture of the armed forces—the army—and a field sport, a disciplined hunt."[34] The 1997 election increased the number of women MPs to 119 (18 percent of the House), perhaps enough to shift the parliamentary culture.[35]

The 1980s saw the entry of a new generation of women politicians, informed by feminism and recognizing a special obligation to represent women as well as their local constituencies. The overwhelming majority were in the Labour Party. They began slowly to chip away at a partisan culture shaped by the white, male, industrial working class. Still, even in this group there were fewer cases of women who openly identified themselves with feminist issues than in either the United States or Canada. In part this reflects the extent to which feminism is marginalized in the British political class, and in part is a function of the distaste for "special interests." (Most Conservative women MPs are disdainful of feminism, and those few who have swum against the current have faced a parliamentary party rippling with antediluvian attitudes.)

For institutional and socioeconomic reasons, Parliament is also overwhelmingly white. A House of Commons demographically reflective of the British population would have more than thirty MPs from Asian and Afro-Caribbean backgrounds. In 1997, however, only eight were elected (all for Labour) up from six in 1992. As in other legislatures, British MPs tend to come from the well-educated, professional middle-class, in turn shaping the gender and racial composition of the House.

THE CULTURE OF THE CLOSET. The public face of the House of Commons is, to be sure, overwhelmingly heterosexual. As one parliamentary aide puts it: "I've always thought this place was very homophobic, the pressure on MPs to have a wife—not a husband—a wife, two kids, two dogs, two cars. . . . This is a boys' place: girls clean up, boys rule, you know. A lot of people in here don't even know how to spell lesbian!"[36]

By focusing on the role of an openly gay politician in the House of Commons, one risks ignoring the pervasive stories of closeted members. There is hardly an MP of any party who is not aware of a substantial number of homosexuals, almost all men, currently or formerly in the House. There are politicians throughout the world who are not open about being gay or lesbian, but there seem to be more in Britain, and more of their colleagues know about them. Close observers of parliamentary politics invariably talk of large numbers, some estimates close to fifty.

At a personal level, parliamentarians are often tolerant of one another's weaknesses and "deviations" from the norm. They spend a great deal of time together, especially with the Commons so often sitting until very late at night. As one MP observes: "A lot of non-London MPs virtually live there [at the House] during the week, come down on the train on Monday afternoon, and spend the whole week there, going back to their constituencies on Friday morning. They spend a lot of time chatting with each other. It's a goldfish bowl; they watch each other all the time. And they know each other—often from university, from business clubs, all that sort of thing."[37] MPs become accustomed to hearing of affairs, divorces, domestic trials, homosexuality. The usual condition of acceptance is that the matter stay out of the courts—and the press.

A crucial component of the culture of the closet in the House of Commons are the stories of MPs whose homosexuality has become known in the context of "scandal," almost always resulting in resignation or electoral defeat. The huge numbers of police arrests for homosexual activity in the postwar years included MPs, who usually denied their homosexuality or excused the incident as an isolated "dreadful mistake."[38] Occasionally the matter would be kept quiet, and the MP would discreetly resign or avoid seeking reelection. Just as commonly the tabloid press would print sordid details, and the story would become part of a centuries-long morality tale of men in positions of responsibility corrupting other men, and endangering the respectability of national institutions.

The notion of homosexuality as a "private" matter is widespread in all countries of the West, but nowhere more institutionalized than in Britain, and nowhere within Britain more deeply entrenched than in the House of Commons. The formula arrived at in the 1960s and culminating in the partial decriminalization of 1967, tolerating sexual deviation when kept within strict boundaries and out of public view, remained dominant in parliamentary culture until the early 1990s, and retains powerful currency still. As much as in any legislative chamber, the homosexual as a person, whether out or known to be closeted, can find acceptance without that acceptance or toleration necessarily translating into support for general equality. This pattern is most pronounced in the Conservative Party. There have been a number of MPs widely known to be gay but closeted who have allied themselves with the moralistic right. Prior to the 1997 change of government, in fact, two front benchers widely thought to be homosexual were among those who spoke most ardently about a return to traditional morality. Their standing in their own party was no doubt maintained by their readiness to abide by party norms about keeping themselves out of the press.

While he was a Conservative MP, *Times* columnist Matthew Parris came out in coded terms during a 1982 speech on extending the 1967 Homosexual Law Reform Act to Northern Ireland, although only other MPs and political insiders were privy to his meaning. Parris knew, however, that even this degree of openness precluded his further rise in what was being judged a promising political career, and he resigned his seat in 1986.

More recently, in 1994, Michael Brown became the first Conservative MP to be fully out—in fact nudged out by a tabloid when he was reported to have gone on holiday with a young man of twenty. He had been partially out in that very British sense that "everyone" knew. He was also exceptional among Conservative MPs in having voted on the side of reform on gay-related issues throughout the 1980s and early 1990s, even voting against the whip on Section 28. In this sense he has probably marked himself as a legislator too closely tied to a "special interest," and a somewhat unpredictable team player. Before the 1997 election, it was not at all clear what prospects Brown had of rising above the relative obscurity of the party's back benches. In any event, he was swept aside by the Labour tide in that election.

Early in 1997, Jerry Hayes, one of the Conservative MPs with a relatively strong record on sexual orientation issues, was "outed" when a young former Conservative activist sold the story of their purported homosexual affair to a tabloid.[39] Hayes survived the selection process in his local Conservative Association, but not the swing to Labour in the general election. Before the election, the chair of the Scottish Conservative Party was eying a parliamentary seat, but resigned his ambitions and his chair after publication of a story about an earlier homosexual relationship.

Also in the lead-up to that election, two members of TORCHE won nominations to constituencies, though in unwinnable races. When a journalist sought comment on their sexual orientation, however, the Conservative Central Office dismissed the implication that they were gay as a slanderous accusation. He then met one of the candidates at a gay party, but could elicit no comment. "A few weeks later, in a move scarcely believable just three years short of the millennium, he was married."[40]

The Liberal Democratic parliamentary contingent, and the Liberal caucus before that, seemed always to include at least one closeted gay MP. One of them, former leader Jeremy Thorpe, was embroiled in scandal and forced to resign, perpetuating a cautious approach to the issue of homosexuality among most of the party's MPs until very recently. Even the significant shift in position represented by the election of Paddy Ashdown as party leader in 1988 has not broken sufficiently with the culture of the parliamentary closet to allow for a Liberal Democratic addition to the tiny group of openly gay MPs.

The Labour Party is only beginning to appear significantly more encouraging of openness. Even Chris Smith's notable success in the House has not drawn more colleagues out of the closet, though there have been several known to be gay or lesbian. One, a longtime key party organizer, still refused to talk publicly about his sexual orientation even after being outed, once by a tabloid and once in a book by a former Labour MP. The 1997 election of two openly gay Labour candidates represented a milestone. Later that year, Angela Eagle, a junior environment minister first elected in 1992 and an active supporter of an equal age of consent, came out as lesbian. Some of the rest presumably fear the social conservatism of their constituents and are no doubt inhibited by the traditional climate of the House.

SMITH'S RISE IN PARLIAMENTARY STANDING. Chris Smith started his career as a left-leaning London backbencher. Within a dozen years he was in the shadow cabinet, respected in both the front and the back benches. His influence expanded considerably during that time, but so did the restrictions on what he could say and do. That would be true enough of any front bench politician, doubly so in a cautious Labour Party long in opposition.

When Smith entered Parliament, he faced suspicion among other Labour MPs, not because of any rumors about homosexuality, but because as a London MP he was part of a group associated in many of his colleagues' minds with the "loony left," which they saw as having cost them so many votes in the election just past.[41] This was not a parliamentary environment friendly to sexual diversity issues within his own party caucus, even less among Conservatives. The Liberals, remembering the damage done by their former leader's association with homosexual scandal, were as eager to avoid the subject as MPs in other parties.

No more profound indication can be found of the parliamentary environment than the reactions to Smith's coming out at Rugby. According to his own account, "the overwhelming response from parliamentary colleagues was total silence on the subject: they never mentioned it; they never made reference to it; they never acknowledged the issue existed."[42] The silence was in fact not quite total, for seven or eight did talk to him about it and expressed their support. But from the Labour leadership there was no reaction at all.[43]

Since those awkward moments in late 1984, Smith has acquired unusual cross-party respect as a hardworking MP and an intelligent parliamentarian. One Liberal Democratic member talks of him as "a very, very highly regarded MP—very capable, very nice, very popular."[44] Another describes him as "a very admirable man—highly intelligent, straightforward."[45] One Conservative MP has spoken flatteringly of his grace under pressure; another less effusive, still believed him to be widely respected.[46] Smith has a personality and style that fit the culture of the House of Commons. As a Labour aide puts it, "Chris is always very measured and reasonable and well-behaved."[47] And of course he is a man, and a white man, in an institution still remarkably homogeneous on those fronts. Smith's openness about his homosexuality is challenging for an institution that for so long was marked by the desire to avoid discussing the subject, but he is also a parliamentarian who has made the grade according to the traditional standards of the House of Commons.

By the time of the 1992 election, Chris Smith had become part of Labour's Treasury team, under the leadership of the shadow chancellor, John Smith. Chris Smith's star continued to rise when John Smith replaced Neil Kinnock as party leader after the 1992 election, and then when Tony Blair became leader after John Smith's sudden death in the summer of 1994. By that time Chris Smith had become a full-fledged member of Labour's shadow cabinet, an advance requiring the approval of both the leader and fellow parliamentarians. To be in the pool eligible for designation to a specific portfolio, an MP must first obtain enough votes in an annual election held among Labour parliamentarians to rank in the top eighteen or nineteen contenders (equivalent to the number of shadow cabinet slots). Smith was first elected in 1992, and for two years was given the environmental protection portfolio. Then in November 1994 he was made shadow heritage secretary, the first position to give him major public exposure. After the 1995 shadow cabinet election, he was given responsibility for social security, and then in 1996 for health, both major portfolios. In most of these elections, voting positioned him at about the middle of those who won shadow cabinet position, though with some slippage in 1996.[48]

Within the shadow cabinet team, Chris Smith was an early supporter of Tony Blair's candidacy for leadership, and was thought to be an ally in the drive for "New Labour."[49] It was Blair who had given Smith the high-profile position of shadow social security secretary in 1995, a position that also placed him on the front lines of Labour's centrist modernization. In June of that year, Smith's announcement of Labour's plans for "flexible" welfare benefits was coming under criticism from some on the party's left, which may have explained the modest drop in his support in the 1996 shadow cabinet elections. In fact, Smith is reported to have resisted cuts to social spending proposed by Gordon Brown, the shadow chancellor, and thereby alienated the cabinet minister-in-waiting, whose influence was second only to that of party leader Tony Blair. In the summer of 1996, Smith was demoted slightly to shadow health secretary. He protested mildly at having to master his fourth portfolio in as many years.[50] In the spring of 1997, on the eve of the election, it was rumored that his performance in that position was perceived by the party leadership as "lackluster," and that he might be further demoted in the selection of cabinet ministers after the election.[51] His being on the side of the debate over fiscal "realism" opposed to Gordon Brown no doubt fueled such speculation, but there was no hint that Smith's sexual orientation was a factor.

After the Labour victory of May 1, 1997, Smith was appointed secretary of state at the Department of National Heritage (to be renamed Culture and Communications), a portfolio with responsibility over broadcasting, the media, sports, the arts, historical conservation, and the National Lottery. Smith himself acknowledged the historic moment: "The fact that someone who is openly gay can be appointed to the Cabinet and can go to Buckingham Palace to kiss hands with the Queen as I did, without the slightest tremor of significance really being attached to it by the great majority of the press, shows that we have come a very considerable way to gaining acceptance from the British people."[52]

LEGISLATIVE IMPACT. One Liberal Democratic MP, asked about Chris Smith's influence on the House of Commons, responded by saying that he "may well have altered perceptions of the nature of homosexuality and of what homosexuals are like. It's surprising how many people are not aware of ever having met a homosexual."[53] Smith has also been influential simply as one of the small minority of MPs willing to speak unequivocally in defense of gay and lesbian equality. In 1987–88 he was one of the few in the Commons who spoke in uncompromising opposition to Section 28 from the outset.

Smith's impact on policy is naturally more widespread within the Labour Party than in other parliamentary caucuses. One lobbyist argues that Smith's presence had enormous significance within his own party during the years in opposition. Particularly among the group who have now come to prominence within the Labour Party, he made the gay issue a real issue.[54] But the most influential of his interventions were probably those inside the Parliamentary Labour Party and the shadow cabinet, and in informal discussions in the bars, tea rooms, and lobbies at Westminster. All such discussion were outside public view, with unknown effect.

Smith has been prepared to criticize his party's reticence to embrace equality in the past.[55] By late 1993, in the lead-up to the parliamentary debate over equalizing the age of consent for sexual activity, though, Smith was arguing that past reticence had largely disappeared. He was one of several Labour supporters who underestimated the number and determination of those opposing equality (see Chapter 2). By 1995 he was even more optimistic, pointing to the support for equality from Tony Blair. Smith talked enthusiastically of the speech given by the newly-selected Labour leader before the party conference in October 1994, "The first time ever that the leader of a major party talked about sexuality in his conference speech. In addition to that, he went to Stonewall's Equality Show at the Albert Hall, as a member of the audience, and did a photo call with Stonewall when he was there. So I don't think there's any question of his commitment."[56] Smith says himself that he has encouraged Blair to take clear pro-equality positions, and in some respects that seems to have been effective.[57]

Smith's appointment to the cabinet after the 1997 election placed him for the first time at the heart of governmental decision making. His increased capacity to act in symbolically significant ways was evident inside two months, when he carried to a rapt audience at London's gay pride march a message that the prime minister "wants a Britain free from discrimination."[58] But as a minister in a system so bound by traditions of cabinet solidarity, his capacity to speak out independently on substantive matters was more constrained than ever.

The new Labour government began its term of office sending very mixed signals, for example, on the age of consent (see Chapter 2). In response to a court case arguing that employee benefits should be granted to a same-sex partner on the same basis as a heterosexual partner (a case argued at the European Court of Justice by the prime minster's barrister wife, Cherie Booth), the government's employment minister announced that he thought the plaintiff had no case and that he had no plans to legislate on gay/lesbian employment rights.[59] As recently as mid-1995, Smith was unable to assert that his leader supported recognizing same-sex relationships, despite the party's annual conference having overwhelmingly approved a resolution in favor.[60]

THE MILITARY ISSUE. Debate over the ban on gays and lesbians serving in the British armed forces revealed both the persistent caution in Labour leadership and the difficulty of the role played by Chris Smith as loyal front bencher. The issue moved into the spotlight in the spring of 1995, when Stonewall helped coordinate the launch of a number of court challenges to the existing ban. Suddenly a firm Labour Party commitment to remove the ban became a commitment to establish a working party to discuss dismantling the policy with the military's service chiefs. There may not have been any intention to recoil from the commitment, but it certainly sounded like backtracking to gay and lesbian activists. Interviewed shortly afterwards, Smith saw no retreat: "We believe, as we always have, that the ban is a violation of human rights." In order to avoid "the Clinton problems" (see Chapter 7), Labour was proposing a working party "to discuss with the service chiefs how to set about dismantling the ban. But there's no intention to retreat from commitment."[61]

In May 1996 an amendment to a routine defense bill was introduced to lift the military ban, led by Conservative MP Edwina Currie, co-sponsored by Conservative Michael Brown and Labour MP Gerald Kaufman. (Conservative ministers had already made their opposition clear enough, and the government whips were to block the measure once it got to the full House.) In a parliamentary committee hearing on the subject in March, the Conservative majority would ensure no surprises for the government. But opposition to the amendment also came from Labour members of the committee, chief among them John Reid, the party's defense spokesperson.[62]

Strikingly, Tony Blair indicated that Labour MPs were free to vote as they wished, and he himself was absent for the May 9 vote following debate in the House of Commons—a vote that defeated the amendment 188 to 120. Eight Labour MPs voted against the Currie amendment, including Reid and the other Labour members of the Armed Forces Select Committee. Reid argued that military personnel had the right to not have "offensive" people foisted on them.[63] In a radio interview the next day, Blair reiterated his belief "that homosexual people should not be banned or discharged from the military merely by reason of the fact that they are gay," but added a qualifying note even more troublesome than his past statements, saying that any change would have to be negotiated "in a way that takes account of the concerns of the military."[64] Another observer reflected on such cautionary language in these terms: "There's no doubt the leadership has the pre-election jitters, and 'gay rights' rivals 'higher taxes' for the phrase that dare not speak its name this side of a Labour victory. Once-friendly frontbenchers no longer return calls from the gay press, manifesto commitments seem out of the question, and Blair is desperately trying to avoid a Clintonesque clash with the chiefs of staff on the military issue."[65]

Labour supporters could point out that eleven shadow cabinet members supported the Currie amendment, and that in general four of its five heavyweights had strong records on gay and lesbian rights.[66] Still, the shadow cabinet ministers as a whole continued to be hesitant about those rights, some of them associated with "old Labour," like John Prescott, some with "New Labour," like David Blunkett.

The ministers appointed to defense portfolios in the new Labour government did not provide much room for optimism. The lead cabinet minister talked of the ban being lifted soon after taking office, but then joined with the Prime Minister's Office in backtracking. A policy review would be conducted, but only after court cases had gone to the European Court—cases that the government still intended to oppose. Two of the second-ranked ministers in the defense area firmly opposed lifting the ban, including John Reid. As armed forces minister, with formal responsibility over the issue, Reid was still repeating the opposition to lifting the ban that he had voiced in the 1996 Commons debate. There was persistent reference to the prime minister's caution being reinforced by the lessons of President Bill Clinton's failed initiative on the same front in the United States (see Chapter 7).

Chris Smith was undoubtedly pressing the case for equality within the cabinet, but was quiet on the issue in the first months of the new government. More outspoken and visibly tied to the extraparliamentary lobbyists was Stephen Twigg, one of the two newly elected gay MPs, as a backbencher less hamstrung by norms of strict adherence to the government's line and the prime minister's caution.

Standing among Lesbians, Gays, and Activists

There are many more Labour MPs than Conservatives who believe in the importance of maintaining links to extraparliamentary social movements, although party discipline limits their ability to do so. Tony Blair may be the most egalitarian of recent Labour leaders in his approach to sexual diversity, but he also insists on a degree of discipline in his front bench that places more impediments than ever on those who might wish to speak for a social movement agenda independently of the party position. Chris Smith's rise coincided with his party's rising fortunes leading up to the 1997 election. His public appearances and interviews began to take on a different tone than in the early years after he first came out. By the mid-1980s, he sounded more like a minister in waiting than an outspoken advocate of a cause. According to one observer of his appearance at a late 1994 Stonewall fund-raiser, attended by Tony Blair as well, Chris Smith seemed more cautious than he had the year before, striking a tone that was less "one of us" and more "glad to be here." After the 1997 election, more than ever, his growing responsibilities in other areas limited the amount of time he could spend on issues such as sexual diversity.

OVERALL RESPECT. Even before coming out at Rugby, Smith was warmly regarded by large numbers of lesbians and gay men for his willingness to speak in favor of their rights. After his announcement, the affectionate respect intensified. A gay pub in his own constituency began stocking his favorite whisky, and many gays and lesbians across Britain sent him their congratulations. Throughout the 1980s and into the 1990s, interviewers and reporters for the gay press conveyed genuine admiration.

He has earned respect across a wide political spectrum, with many in and outside the activist movement admiring him even though not always agreeing with his politics. On the left, traditionally riven by factional disputes, some applaud his ability to mediate across political divides. One activist recalled a time when Smith was secretary of a local union branch: "He was absolutely nonsectarian. The way he handled it was really impressive—the extent to which he was able to make everyone feel included. He was very democratic—he wasn't rude or derogatory about any point of view or any position."[67]

A number of extraparliamentary observers admire Smith simply for having spoken out, thereby serving a national gay/lesbian constituency from a political position with real constraints. One activist on the left noted in 1992: "There may be issues he won't want to speak on, because of electoral liabilities possibly. . . . He has to make his strategic decisions. But I've never thought he was a man who hesitated or lacked moral courage or ethical responsibilities to his double electorate—his actual constituency and also the wider constituency of lesbians and gay men. I think he handles that with grace and delicacy, and occasionally with great aggression, very explicitly and forthrightly."[68] Smith's appointment as a cabinet member was treated by countless activists and gay press observers as a historic moment. A *Gay Times* assessment of the significance of Labour's election talked of Smith's potential influence over substantive policy in his own ministerial domain, and over the cabinet as a whole. It also argued that "by any standards this is a highly symbolic political development."[69]

RELATIONSHIP TO LABOUR-BASED GAY/LESBIAN ACTIVISM. If in the British political system a gulf separates parliamentary politics from extraparliamentary activism, that has traditionally been as apparent within the Labour Party itself as anywhere else. In the first few years of Chris Smith's career as an openly gay politician, the Labour Campaign for Lesbian and Gay Rights was at its most active, successfully preparing the ground for gay-positive resolutions at party conferences in 1985 and 1986 (see Chapter 1). But at precisely that time the party's leadership and most of its parliamentarians were distancing themselves from the left, and from causes traditionally associated with the left. The relationship between the Labour Campaign for Lesbian and Gay Rights and the parliamentary party had always been a distant one, apart from contacts with individual MPs on the left most obviously sympathetic to their interest (for example, Tony Benn and Jo Richardson). The group's focus was on the passage of resolutions in the extraparliamentary party, in part because the organizing principles of the party historically suggested that such support was a prerequisite to further progress, in part because of a belief widespread in the group that MPs should be made subservient to the party membership represented at conferences. The group was also dominated by activists on the left who distrusted parliamentary politics itself, and who were prepared to be as uncompromisingly critical of Labour leaders and MPs as activists from other parties—a very different relationship to the party from that which was expected of party insiders.

The LCLGR leadership's distrust of the parliamentary party meant that it would not have thought of an openly gay MP like Chris Smith as a central player in the struggle for liberation, and would have treated him with at least a dose of wariness as potentially representing the forces of compromise. Smith says: "To the majority of people in LCLGR I was a useful speaker at meetings, a respectable face to call upon, and to a certain extent a conduit into the leadership of the party. To a minority I was a dangerous revisionist, not one of the true far-left socialist faith and therefore not to be approved of in any way."[70] At the 1987 annual conference that "minority" voice was an influential one, and an LCLGR fringe meeting barred Smith from speaking to it (although a later meeting of the group's national membership censured the national committee for that decision).[71]

There can be no disputing the contribution of the Labour Campaign in effecting a shift in party policy during the mid-1980s—a shift that has been a crucial prerequisite to change in Labour's election platforms and parliamentary preferences. The work to be done in solidifying support within the parliamentary party, however, was in effect very different from the work the Labour Campaign had engaged in. This meant that Smith's voice was in some respects an isolated one through the 1980s. Inside his own party he was certainly closely associated with the cause of gay and lesbian rights, but he was never obviously at the head of an intraparty movement. To some extent that suited his political style, but it is also a product of the Labour Campaign's character and of its historical relationship to the rest of the party.

THE STONEWALL GROUP. The formation of the Stonewall Group in 1989 introduced new forms of activism, both within and beyond the scope of the Labour Party, to which Smith was more drawn. Smith had close contacts with the group's founders from the beginning, and has regularly talked of its indispensability: "Apart from the occasional very private conversation between myself and Matthew Parris [then Conservative MP, now openly gay journalist] back in the mid-eighties, nothing really happened until the Stonewall Group got going. The advent of the Stonewall Group has been the catalyst for getting parliamentarians from both sides of the chamber together on these issues. . . . And the emergence of a small but nonetheless effective group of Conservative MPs who are prepared to do some work and lobby on these sorts of issues has been extremely important. . . . And it's only really happened because Stonewall sat down and did the basic groundwork of getting to know them, providing them with information, and doing very good briefing material for them."[72]

It is within a group like Stonewall that respect for a parliamentarian like Smith is greatest. Such groups include in their membership individuals who are comfortable moving within political institutions, including parliamentary ones, and for them, gay-positive politicians are invaluable contacts. During the lead-up to the debate on the age of consent, Stonewall's leadership regarded Chris Smith as one of the most important players in their network.

But even in such networks Smith could not be relied on too heavily, in part because of the nonpartisan character of Stonewall. In a political system and legislative arena so shaped by party opposition, Conservative activists would see the role of a Labour MP, however worthy, as marginal so long as their own party was in power, and vice versa. What would matter most would be the exercise of influence inside the governing party. Stonewall's Labour members had to avoid seeming to rely too heavily on Smith to maintain the group's cross-party connections during the years of Conservative rule. Smith's promotion to the front bench and then to the cabinet intensified his association with the Labour Party, and reduced his capacity to speak independently. Stonewall activists were confident of Smith's willingness to put their views to the cabinet, but the relationship would necessarily be more distant.

As Smith himself points out, there are now a number of MPs, from all three major parties, who are prepared to speak forthrightly on gay rights issues. For a time, the Conservative Matthew Brown worked closely with Stonewall in keeping gay equality issues at the forefront, as did a number of non-gay politicians from all parties. This reduced the indispensability of Smith himself for lobbyists, and increased his identification with a specifically Labour Party voice. After the 1997 election, openly gay/lesbian Labour MPs Ben Bradshaw, Stephen Twigg, and Angela Eagle became important voices for equality, Twigg being especially willing to identify himself with the Stonewall group.

The formation of a mainstream lobbying organization like Stonewall reduces the indispensability of an openly gay politician for the press. Both the mainstream and the gay/lesbian media now have a media-conscious activist organization to go to for analysis and comment on gay-related issues, one that will speak with a voice not wholly tied to a single party. As one gay journalist said of Smith in 1995: "He's no longer the obvious expert on everything. We have Stonewall now, with its wide range of potential experts on all sorts of things. You don't need the sort of generalized comment from a gay member of Parliament that you used to."[73]

The admiration for Chris Smith as a person, a parliamentarian, and an advocate for gay rights does cross some of the lines that have traditionally riven British gay and lesbian activism. Chris Smith occupies an enormously significant role illustrating the possibilities of being open about sexual orientation even in a highly traditional institution like the House of Commons. The courage required to come out in such an environment and to speak about gay and lesbian issues deserves and receives enormous credit. But because of characteristics in his personality and the partisan and parliamentary arenas in which he works, he has chosen not to be an "identity" politician in a way that would link him too closely to the gay and lesbian activist movement. To have done so would inevitably have created tensions between his various roles: he has simply chosen to reduce the potential for such tensions.

As a member of a Labour cabinet, Chris Smith will have limited room for maneuver. His parliamentary party and its leader remain more cautious on sexual diversity issues than Smith himself would like to admit, and public debate on matters such as relationship recognition is very new. Britain has nothing like the religious right opposition that slows progress on gay rights in the United States, but the 1996 failure to lift the ban on gays and lesbians in the military indicates that equality can be just as difficult to attain in Britain. It also indicates that whatever shifts in the balance of opinion have occurred within Tony Blair's New Labour Party, sexual diversity is still an issue to be approached with hesitation and a readiness to compromise. As historian Jeffrey Weeks argued in 1992, "The Labour Party does reflect the unresolved issues in the wider society—the traditionalism of the old labour constituency, the moralism of the Roman Catholic constituency, the confusion of liberal opinion."[74] The Labour Party in that sense is a microcosm of the national debate.

That said, the Labour government and its parliamentary backbenches are a far cry from the Thatcherite and Majorite governments preceeding it. They have offered a serious prospect of incorporating the European Convention of Human Rights and other protections into British law, abolishing Section 28, changing immigration rules, and enacting hate crimes legislation—all in the direction of greater inclusiveness and equality. Even in the areas in which Labour's caution was greatest—the age of consent, the armed forces, the recognition of same-sex relationships—the government seemed open to initiatives by its own backbenchers.

In the cabinet there were active proponents of equality, supported by a backbench caucus that included more women than ever, and a significant number of young members considerably more comfortable about sexual diversity than their elders. They were bolstered by a Liberal Democratic caucus also more accepting of such diversity than ever, backed by elaborate and assertive party platforms. With suitable caution at the end, Stonewall's executive director Angela Mason said after the election: "It's the most wonderful opportunity we've had. It is a new dawn. We are in an entirely different climate now, but it's Labour who has won. We haven't won yet."[75]

CANADA

Parliament Hill press scrum on Bill C-33, with EGALE representative John Fisher (May 1996). Photo: Brandon Matheson/*Capital Extra*

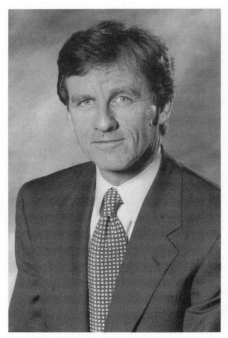

Justice Minister Allan Rock. Photo: Courtesy Allan Rock Constituency Office

Reform Leader Preston Manning, in the House of Commons. Photo: Courtesy of Reform Party Leader's Office

4

The Canadian Human Rights Act and Liberal Party Pragmatism

We are discussing amendments to the human rights act. We

deal here not with abstractions but with people, with hu-

mans. Gays and lesbians are not abstractions. They are very

real, with very real entitlements to dignity and respect. They

are our brothers and our sisters. They are our sons and our

daughters, our neighbours and our friends. They are our col-

leagues.

Justice Minister Allan Rock,

House of Commons, 30 April 1996

For a decade, justice ministers had promised to add the two words "sexual orientation" to the Canadian Human Rights Act in order to prohibit discrimination
against lesbians and gays in areas covered by federal jurisdiction. For just as
long, the fulfillment of such promises was postponed repeatedly. Finally, in the
spring of 1996, Liberal justice minister Allan Rock was given the go-ahead to
introduce Bill C-33 before the House of Commons. Soon it was passed into law,
and the parliamentary opposition to gay rights was left, at least for the moment,
tattered and discredited.

Whatever the limitations of legal and statutory change, Canadian lesbians and
gays have won more progress through political and legal systems than their coun-

terparts in either Britain or the United States, and for that matter in all but a few countries in the world. At the federal level, they have done this with activist resources more limited than those available to national groups in Britain, and on nothing like the scale of American organizing. In a large, politically decentralized, and linguistically divided country, lobbying efforts at the federal level often get eclipsed by activism at the local or provincial level. Political mobilizing around the Human Rights Act was particularly challenging for those activists who had developed lobbying networks. The long years of promises by successive justice ministers made it difficult to generate energy at any one point in the process. Those who followed court decisions also realized that much of what would be secured through a Human Rights Act amendment had already been won through litigation.

But Canadian activists work within a political order, a partisan environment, and a social setting that provide significant opportunities for change. For all the inconvenience it produces, governmental decentralization has allowed for major gains at the local and provincial level in the country's most populous regions. The Charter of Rights has created a legal environment that has offered protections for gays and lesbians, and that in turn has provided inducements for legislative change. Public opinion in Canada creates more room for an equity agenda than in Britain. And what is most striking in the contrast with the United States is the relative weakness of the religious right.

What accounted for victory on the Human Rights Act was a shift in the political environment and circumstances—what some would call the opportunity structure—strengthening the proponents of reform and weakening the forces opposing it. The change was not so much in the balance of forces within parties, as it was in Britain, but in a massive realignment of partisan forces resulting from the 1993 federal election, which created incentives for socially reformist Liberals to press ahead on gay rights. Victory was also facilitated by the extent to which opponents from both parliamentary and extraparliamentary forces discredited themselves. This was particularly important in creating a media climate highly favorable to the passage of Bill C-33, in turn shoring up popular support for the measure.

The Institutional Context

Canadian social movement activists seeking to influence public policy operate in a complex institutional environment. It fragments their energies but also sometimes allows for doors to be opened at one level of government even if they remain closed at another. The decentralized Canadian political system makes a stark contrast with the United Kingdom, from which "British North America" inherited so many institutional characteristics in the nineteenth century. The Canadian federation is rivaled only by Switzerland in the extent of jurisdictional devolution to regional governments, and it continues to move in the direction of even greater decentralization. The ten provinces have almost complete control over education, health policy, housing, and social welfare—in other words, most of the jurisdictional terrain of interest to lesbian and gay activists. (There are two territories in addition to the provinces, which increasingly behave like provinces.) Provincial and territorial human rights and equity legislation also covers more institutions in the public and private realm than does federal legislation, though all such statutes must conform to the constitutionally entrenched Charter of Rights and Freedoms. The power of provincial governments creates opportunities for lesbians and gays to exert influence at one level, which in turn helps to create a lever for change at the federal level.

Decentralization is reinforced by very strong regional attachments, intensified by historical and geographic factors. Linguistic duality also separates the predominantly French-speaking province of Quebec from the other provinces, all but one of which (New Brunswick) are overwhelmingly English speaking. The country's three largest cities, Toronto, Montreal, and Vancouver, are separated by fundamental linguistic and cultural divisions or by geographical distance that is equally vast in psychological terms.

The major exception to the decentralist impulse in Canadian federalism is the justice system. The criminal law, including a number of statutes regulating sexuality, is entirely within Ottawa's jurisdiction. The federal government appoints most judges, in a system that has a single hierarchy of courts rather than the dual system operating in the United States, although the provinces are responsible for the administration of justice. The federal government has also been a more important player in social policy than its jurisdictional terrain would suggest, since it has traditionally used its expansive taxing powers to develop a role in sustaining national standards in health, welfare, and education (though it is now cutting back in that role).[1]

If federalism creates opportunities and alternatives for social movement activists, the parliamentary system in place at the provincial and national levels allows for only occasional access. Within each level of government, authority is concentrated in executive hands, as in Britain. The dependence of governments on legislative majorities leads to firm executive control over the agenda of the popularly elected House of Commons, and the appointed Senate is roughly equivalent to the British House of Lords in having little effective power. All party leaders, particularly on the government side, have access to rewards and punishments to reinforce adherence to the party line, most dramatically illustrated by the prime minister's right to make appointments to the cabinet and many other positions.[2] Throughout most of the twentieth century, the selection of party leaders in Canada has depended on support in large conventions in which MPs play only modest roles. One experienced observer of political leadership in Canada describes the prime ministership as "the most powerful head-of-government position in the democratic world."[3]

As in Britain, backbench legislators (those not in the cabinet or the front ranks of the opposition parties) have the freedom to voice their own views in regular meetings of their party's caucus, but much less power to give them public voice. Almost all abide voluntarily by the norms of "sticking together" in public. They realize full well that they are elected primarily on the basis of their party affiliation and the leader under whose personalized campaign they run.[4] At least as much as in Britain, then, social movement activists seeking a change in public policy confront legislative and administrative sturctures that allow only limited scope for autonomous action. That creates considerable opportunity for change when the political executive is headed by favorably disposed leadership, and very little when it is not.

The party systems are quite different at the two levels of jurisdiction, sometimes with significant disconnection between federal and provincial parties using the same label. Canadian voting patterns are as volatile as those in any industrialized democracy, with turnover of legislative membership of 30 percent in a single election not unusual. Until recently the Canadian political landscape at the federal level was dominated by two centrist parties, the Liberals and the Progressive Conservatives (or Conservatives). In the 1980s the Conservatives shifted toward the neoliberal right, embracing free trade with the United States, deregulation, and (in rhetoric more than practice) cutbacks in social spending. They were less drawn to moral conservatism than either the U.S. Republicans or the British Conservatives. The Liberals have at times represented a center-left reformist alternative, but have always brokered a wide range of regional and ideological interests. On balance, in recent years they have shifted toward the neoliberal positioning of their Conservative predecessors in government, although on questions of gender, race, and sexuality, the Liberals have fewer morally right wing MPs than the Conservatives.

The social democratic New Democratic Party was for decades Canada's "third" party. It has at times occupied power in three of the western provinces, and during the first half of the 1990s in the province of Ontario, but has never risen above minor party status in Ottawa. Of the three established parties at the federal level, it has had the longest-standing and, relatively speaking, the most solid commitment to the rights of lesbians and gays, along with the rights of women, minorities, and aboriginals.

Historical Chronology

The first step toward a more liberalized treatment of sexual diversity was taken in 1969. As justice minister, Pierre Elliott Trudeau had argued famously that the state had no business in the bedrooms of the nation, and introduced a package of reforms that liberalized laws on divorce, birth control, and abortion, and partially decriminalized homosexual activity.[5] The legislation was passed with little controversy.

In 1976 the Canadian Human Rights Act was passed, securing equality rights for federal civil servants and employees of federally regulated companies (such as transportation companies and banks)—all told about 10 percent of the work force. A few MPs had sought to include sexual orientation among the grounds on which discrimination was prohibited, but to no avail. The governing Liberals were opposed, and firmly in control of the legislative agenda. The Canadian Human Rights Commission came into being the following year, and it soon inaugurated an annual ritual of recommending the addition of sexual orientation to the act.

At the end of 1977, Quebec became the first province to add sexual orientation to a provincial human rights code when a sovereigntist government quietly amended the Quebec Charter of Rights (though with an additional amendment explicitly precluding access to benefits by same-sex couples). Like other provincial human rights codes, the jurisdiction of the Quebec Charter includes provincial public institutions, employees in provincially regulated firms, accommodation, and the provision of most services. The addition of sexual orientation had been accompanied by little sustained activist mobilization and provoked virtually no controversy. The fact that it occurred in Quebec, and under a sovereigntist government widely reviled outside the province, gave the move little visibility in the rest of Canada.

CHARTER OF RIGHTS AND FREEDOMS. In 1980 a Special Joint Committee of the Senate and House of Commons took up constitutional proposals of the Liberal government headed by Prime Minister Trudeau. Svend Robinson, one of two New Democrats on the committee, himself gay though not yet openly so, moved an amendment to add sexual orientation to the equality rights provision (Section 15) of the proposed Charter of Rights. Despite the resolution of their own party's 1978 convention, however, the Liberal majority on the committee followed the lead of then–justice minister Jean Chrétien and rejected the amendment.[6] Robinson had been more successful in working behind the scenes with Justice officials and the committee chair to ensure that Section 15 included open-ended wording that could be interpreted to include gays and lesbians.

In 1982 the Charter became part of the Canadian Constitution, giving courts a significantly expanded role in judging the constitutionality of government acts and legislative statutes, including human rights codes. In order to give legislatures and governments time to adapt to this new legal regime, Section 15 of the Charter was to come into effect only in 1985. Its final wording included an enumeration of specific grounds on the basis of which discrimination was prohibited and the vitally important general wording that would provide courts with flexibility, in addition to a subsection explicitly opening the door for affirmative action.

(1) Every individual is equal before and under the law and has the right to the equal protection and equal benefit of the law without discrimination, and in particular, without discrimination based on race, national or ethnic origin, colour, religion, sex, age or mental or physical disability.

(2) Subsection (1) does not preclude any law, program or activity that has as its object the amelioration of conditions of disadvantaged individuals or groups including those that are disadvantaged because of race, national or ethnic origin, colour, religion, sex, age or mental or physical handicap.[7]

CONSERVATIVE EQUIVOCATION. In 1984 the Conservatives came to power and Brian Mulroney became prime minister. Their election victory can be viewed as part of a more widespread rise of "neoconservatism" from the late 1970s, but this was a moderate version of the New Right politics then ascendant in Britain and the United States. Despite a sizable "family caucus," the party leadership was dominated by centrists, and even included a few moderate reformers on issues of gender and sexuality.

The prospect of the crucial Section 15 coming into force in 1985 induced the House of Commons Justice Committee to launch a subcommittee inquiry into equality rights, in part to sample Canadian opinion.[8] The subcommittee operated with uncharacteristic independence, not least because it was not subject to the party discipline that would have been in place if it had been considering legislation. As a result of hearing powerful testimony from gays and lesbians across Canada, and with prodding from Svend Robinson, the subcommittee included in its October 1985 report *Equality for All* a recommendation that federal and provincial human rights codes be amended to include sexual orientation explicitly. The following March, Justice Minister John Crosbie responded by declaring: "The Government believes that one's sexual orientation is irrelevant to whether one can perform a job or use a service or facility. The Department of Justice is of the view that the courts will find that sexual orientation is encompassed by the guarantees in section 15 of the Charter. The Government will take whatever measures are necessary to ensure that sexual orientation is a prohibited ground of discrimination in relation to all areas of federal jurisdiction."[9] Opposition to reform among the government's own MPs stalled moves that would have included sexual orientation in the federal Human Rights Act and lift the ban on homosexuals' serving in the military.

In the meantime, most provincial governments were beginning the process of reviewing existing statutes to eliminate conflicts with the Charter. In 1985 Ontario's legislature began deliberations on an omnibus bill (Bill 7) intended to bring the province's laws into conformity with the Charter. After acquiescing to a New Democratic Party amendment to add sexual orientation to the provincial Human Rights Code, and enduring internal division over the matter prior to its coming to a vote, the Liberal government passed Bill 7 in late 1986. Within the next few years, most of the other Canadian provinces and territories followed suit.[10]

In 1991 the Canadian Human Rights Commission issued another strong statement condemning delay in amending the federal Human Rights Act. In September, in *Haig v. Canada*, an Ontario court added force to the commission's view when it ruled that the act was unconstitutional because it did not include sexual orientation, a view sustained in appeal of that decision and in other cases adjudicated over the following year. The decision was based on a widening judicial consensus that the open-ended wording of the Charter's Section 15 did indeed provide protections for lesbians and gays, constituting a group analogous to others specifically enumerated.

In early December 1992, Conservative justice minister Kim Campbell intro-

Table 4. Canadian federal election results, 1988–97

| | 1988 | | | 1993 | | 1997 | |
	% Vote	Seats[a]		% Vote	Seats	% Vote	Seats
Conservatives	43%	169	157	16%	2	19%	20
Liberals	32	82	80	41	177	38	155
NDP	20	43	44	7	9	11	21
Reform	2	0	1	19	52	19	60
Bloc Québécois	0	0	8	14	54	11	44
Others	3	1	5	3	1	2	1
Total	100	295	295	100	295	100	301

[a]The first column indicates seats at the first sitting of Parliament; the second is the distribution of seats at the dissolution of the House, reflecting defections from the Conservatives to the Bloc Québécois and by-election results. At the Parliament's end, there were also three vacancies, and two members sitting as Independents.

duced long-promised amendments to the Human Rights Act, including one adding sexual orientation, though coupled with a provision stipulating that marital status (including common law relationships) was to be defined in exclusively heterosexual terms. Even this qualification failed to quell backbench dissent, and no attempt to put the measure before the House of Commons was made before the end of the parliamentary session. Conservative government members were soon caught up in a leadership contest, won in June by Campbell. Shortly afterward Parliament was dissolved, and an election was called for October 25, 1993.

A LIBERAL GOVERNMENT AND A LIBERAL JUSTICE MINISTER. The Liberal Party's election campaign focused on a red-covered book of promises that included a commitment to amend the Human Rights Act, though without specifying sexual orientation. It also promised hate crimes legislation, on this explicitly including sexual orientation. Jean Chrétien, the Liberal leader, challenged the media to hold him to those and other "Red Book" promises.

The 1993 election produced the most fundamental shift in parliamentary representation in the postwar history of a country already known for electoral earthquakes. The Liberals won with a significant parliamentary majority. Close to two thirds of the sitting MPs were defeated, all but two of the huge Conservative caucus eliminated. The New Democratic Party was reduced to a contingent below that required for official party status, effectively denying its MPs automatic voice in parliamentary debate and committee membership. Two parties that had been formed just in the previous few years each received over fifty seats. The Bloc Québécois became the official opposition party, its members elected on a platform centered on Quebec sovereignty and moderate social democratic stands on social and economic issues. The Reform Party, heavily concentrated in western Canada though growing in rural Ontario, represented a neoconservative mixture of free enterprise economics and morally conservative social policy. The fact that these two opposition parties were both inexperienced in federal politics and had virtually nothing in common strengthened the hand of the Liberal government.

The new cabinet formed by Prime Minister Chrétien included Allan Rock, a first-time Toronto MP given responsibility for the Justice portfolio. He quickly acquired one of the highest profiles in the cabinet, brandishing a fistful of issues that caught the media spotlight. By May 1994 he was including gay and lesbian rights among them, promising to introduce legislation by the end of the year. He also raised the prospects of reviewing the federally regulated pension and employment-related benefits presently available to heterosexual couples, with a view to broadening the range of relationships considered eligible for them.

Dissent within the Liberal caucus surfaced quickly. In mid-May at least four Liberals warned that they would vote against any gay rights bill. Among them was Tom Wappel, an MP from the eastern suburbs of Toronto already known for his religious right views on issues such as abortion and homosexuality, and a new MP from Nova Scotia, Roseanne Skoke.

Meanwhile, in the late winter of 1994 Ontario's provincial government, controlled at the time by the New Democratic Party, had decided to proceed with Bill 167, sweeping legislation to accord the same benefits and responsibilities to same-sex couples as were granted to heterosexual couples (see Chapter 5). Although the provincial Liberal caucus was largely opposed to the measure, its leader, Lyn McLeod, had committed herself to supporting same-sex benefits a year before. During a March 1994 provincial by-election campaign in a rural constituency northeast of Toronto, the provincial Conservatives associated both the New Democrats and Liberals with support for gay rights. The Liberals had expected to win the constituency, but lost it and blamed their defeat largely on being thought pro-gay.

The debate over and defeat of Ontario's Bill 167 amplified the federal Liberals' disarray. More than ever, a number of Ontario's federal Liberal MPs wanted nothing to do with even the narrowest of legislative initiatives on the subject. The disarray was on public display during a biennial policy convention in mid-May. Delegates did pass a resolution supporting the inclusion of sexual orientation in the Canadian Human Rights Act, but voted almost two-to-one against a resolution calling for legislation recognizing same-sex marriages and common law relationships.

HATE CRIMES LEGISLATION. In September 1994 Rock introduced Bill C-41, hate crimes legislation providing for tougher sentences in the case of crimes "motivated by bias, prejudice or hate based on race, nationality, colour, religion, sex, age, mental or physical disability or sexual orientation of the victim." Only the two words "sexual orientation" provoked serious controversy in this, the first federal legislation ever to include the words in a positive sense.

Liberal dissent was given public voice in the House of Commons on September 20, when Roseanne Skoke decried the inclusion of sexual orientation in federal legislation as "imposing upon and insisting that all Canadians condone what in my opinion is immoral and unnatural."[11] Media attention was focused on those remarks, first by Svend Robinson mounting an attack on them, then by Bloc

Québécois MP Real Ménard publicly declaring his own gayness as part of his response to them. Some Liberals openly condemned Skoke's remarks, but in public Prime Minister Chrétien said only that she was entitled to speak her mind but would have to vote the party line in the Commons.

At the regular meeting of his caucus the next day, the prime minister warned Liberal MPs "firmly" that dissension was divisive and harmful to the party. He talked not only of public disagreement on hate crimes but also of gun control legislation that was on the legislative agenda, also sponsored by Justice Minister Rock. That afternoon a question lobbed from a sympathetic Liberal backbencher, planted in the hour normally dominated by confrontational questions from the opposition, allowed Rock to reiterate the government's determination to proceed with measures to end discrimination against homosexuals, with "thunderous" applause from the Liberal side.

Over the next two months, Rock and the Prime Minister's Office repeated assurances that the government would proceed with both hate crimes legislation and the long-awaited amendments to the Human Rights Act. One such assurance was conveyed in writing to the Ottawa-based lobby group Equality for Gays and Lesbians Everywhere (EGALE). But by now, Liberal dissidents were reported in some newspaper accounts to number between two and three dozen.[12] There was increasing press coverage of the divisions that various "justice" issues had provoked inside the governing party, in a legislative system normally marked by at least the appearance of partisan unity.

Early in 1995 the prime minister was publicly suggesting a more cautious tack on the Human Rights Act amendment, referring to the fact that the government's mandate still had three or four more years to run. In March the Canadian Human Rights Commission Report commented once again on the absence of progress on this front, and once again newspaper editorials criticized the government.[13] At the same time, MPs were receiving a steady stream of petitions on gay rights issues, the overwhelming majority opposing both the hate crimes legislation and the promised amendment to the Human Rights Act.

In mid-June the Liberals faced divisive legislative votes on hate crimes and gun control. In one caucus meeting the prime minister reminded his colleagues that he had to sign their nomination papers for the next election and could prevent their running as Liberals. He was reported to have said that he considered such votes a personal attack on him: "If the leader is hurt, the whole team is hurt. I am a tolerant man, but I'm only going to take so much. When you do this, you do it to me."[14] Both measures passed, but voting on amendments targeting the sexual orientation provision of the hate crimes bill revealed that up to eighteen Liberals were prepared to defy their whip.

REFORM PARTY EXTREMISM. Not surprisingly, the Reform Party's MPs voted solidly against the government bill. More surprisingly, their opposition to gay rights was coming to be viewed by much of the press as an indicator of right-wing extremism. The 1993 election platform had been carefully crafted to avoid inflammatory language on issues of diversity and morality, focusing much of its attention on right-wing economic issues and on populist platforms for new forms of governance. The party's first post-election assembly in October 1994, however, made clear the discriminatory sentiments that motivated the activist core of the party.

There were warning signs during that summer of extremism in the policy preparations for the assembly. Calgary MP Jan Brown resigned from the Reform Caucus Task Force on the Family in August, writing in a then-confidential memo that she was "disappointed at the homophobic approach to the issue of sexual orientation and the narrow and inflexible approach to defining the family"[15] In the report eventually sent on to the convention, the Task Force echoed the language of the American religious right in disparaging claims for protections against discrimination of a group defined only by a "preference" for certain sexual behavior. A survey of 3,800 party members showed that 90 percent opposed inclusion of sexual orientation in the Human Rights Act. The Reform assembly ensured the public airing of these and other views. To cheers from almost all of the few hundred delegates in the room, MP Myron Thompson declared, "I do not hate thieves, I hate thieving; I do not hate murderers, I hate murdering; I do not hate homosexuals, I hate homosexuality," all the while criticizing the media for characterizing the party as hateful.[16] This was a turning point for much of the national press, which was now more alerted to the prejudice underlying the Reform Party's appeal.

Back in Parliament, an April 1995 debate over an ultimately unsuccessful private member's bill on same-sex relationship recognition provided Reform MP Art Hanger a vehicle to talk of the gay rights movement as the most radical and sinister of challenges to morality: "Homosexuality, to anyone who has not been brainwashed by the last decade of effective propagandizing by the gay lobby, is unnatural. It is a repudiation of nature. . . . Homosexuality is nihilistic. It protects nothing, it defends nothing, it continues nothing, and it sustains nothing."[17]

BUILDUP OF PRESSURE ON THE HUMAN RIGHTS ACT. The next public ministerial pronouncement on the Human Rights Act was on February 20, 1996, in the week leading up to the Throne Speech for the new session of Parliament, when Allan Rock acknowledged that it was : "a commitment we're going to be held accountable for."[18] Some Liberal MPs supportive of gay rights had raised the issue in the caucus meeting earlier that week, and one from a Vancouver constituency with substantial gay and lesbian visibility had predicted confidently that the government would proceed. The prime minister, though, told them that he wanted to drop the issue, supposedly to reduce the pressure on rural MPs.

At the end of the month, Conservative senator Noel Kinsella revived a bill amending the Human Rights Act which he had first presented to the upper house in 1992 in response to Kim Campbell's inaction as justice minister. Debate began on the new bill three weeks later, though little noticed in the press, since the work of the upper house in general, and of private members in particular, usually has little if any impact. (The Senate's power is usually minor, and legislation passed by it and sent to the House can be easily defeated.)

What was more widely noticed was a press conference called on March 19 by Max Yalden, the head of the Canadian Human Rights Commission, to release his annual report. Front-page headlines were given to his criticism of the government for failing to add sexual orientation to the act.[19] The very next day, embarrassed by press focus on unkept promises, and fearing further awkwardness if a human rights bill from the Senate were to land on the House of Commons' agenda, the government announced that it would in fact introduce legislation to ban discrimination on the basis of sexual orientation. The justice minister had always intended to combine such a measure with other Human Rights Act amendments, but it was now clear that the Liberals wanted to rid themselves of the gay rights issue and proceed as rapidly as possible.

Late in April the Liberals were embroiled in headline-producing controversy over the government's apparent reneging on a campaign promise to eliminate a much-disliked goods and services tax (GST). The Reform Party led the attack in Parliament, and the furor was widely seen as producing the worst week for the Liberals since their election. Then without warning, on April 26 the government served notice in the House of Commons that its legislation on the Human Rights Act would be introduced the following week.

That weekend the Ontario wing of the federal Liberal Party held a policy convention in Windsor. A motion calling for the inclusion of sexual orientation in the Human Rights Act was passed 236 to 96, its passage by such a convincing majority greeted by "a lot of cheering and clapping."[20] But the split in the Ontario wing was evident in their approval of a motion resolving "that the Liberal Party of Canada support and encourage the traditional, heterosexual institution of marriage through government policies."[21]

BILL C-33 AND REFORM PARTY EXTREMISM. On Monday afternoon, April 29, the justice minister introduced the Human Rights Act legislation. Bill C-33 proposed the addition of sexual orientation to all those provisions of the act except that which envisaged affirmative action. This was a significant exception which implied that discrimination against gays and lesbians would not warrant the kinds of positive measures envisaged for discrimination on other grounds. Bill C-33 also included a preamble intended in part to reassure critics who claimed that it undermined the traditional family. It proclaimed that the government of Canada "recognizes and affirms the importance of family as the foundation of Canadian society and that nothing in this Act alters its fundamental role in society." An information booklet released by the justice minister on the day of the bill's introduction was mostly taken up with denials: the bill would not have a negative impact on the traditional family; it would have no bearing on definitions of "marriage," "family," or spouse"; it would not lead to adoption by same-sex couples; the government planned no changes to other federal legislation.[22]

Headlines the next morning were divided between announcing Bill C-33's introduction and highlighting Liberal dissent over the issue. One Toronto daily topped its front page coverage with "MPS TO DEFY GAY BILL VOTE," and speculated that as many as twenty Liberals were ready to vote against the bill. Then just as debate on second reading was set to begin, a Reform MP from British Columbia provided the Liberals with an opportunity to deflect attention from their own division and indecision. On April 30 Reform Party whip Robert Ringma was quoted in a newspaper interview defending the right of a small business to fire a homosexual who was losing business for him, and to move a black employee whose race was driving away customers "to the back of the shop." Party leader Preston Manning, in British Columbia at the time, responded cautiously about the possibility of misquotes. In that afternoon's question period, the prime minister went after the Reform Party, characterizing Ringma's statements as outrageous and "just about the worst statement we could hear in Canadian society." He returned to the issue several times before the hour was out, taking full political advantage of a chance to embarrass the Reform Party for prejudicial statements not altogether dissimilar to those of dissidents in his own party.[23]

After a caucus meeting the next day, Ringma announced his resignation as party whip and apologized for his remarks. The deputy leader, who had refused to criticize her colleague the day before, now spoke for the party in repudiating his remarks as "completely inconsistent with Reform policy." But within a day, reports began spreading of a radio interview in which Alberta Reform MP David Chatters had said, "When you go into the issue of homosexuals and lesbians, I think it is in the interests of society to discriminate against that group."[24] A few moderate Reformers talked of leaving the party unless extremist elements were expunged, Calgary MP Jan Brown most publicly and forthrightly. Early the next week Manning decreed a six-week suspension of the two MPs who had spoken in favor of discrimination. But his attempt to shed the caucus of its extremist image was tarnished by his expelling Jan Brown at the same time. It was also damaged when, on the same day, another Reform MP spoke with rabid anti-gay prejudice on the floor of the House of Commons, repeating his remarks later for the benefit of reporters.

In the meantime, Bill C-33's passage through Parliament was proceeding at the breakneck speed the government was setting for it. At the Liberals' May 1 caucus meeting, the prime minister had announced that MPs would be freed from party discipline. He did so despite the objections of Justice Minister Rock and many MPs, and in defiance of earlier assurances from his office that the issue would be subjected to the same discipline as other government measures. There was no question that the bill would pass, since the majority of Liberal MPs in support of the amendment would be joined by Bloc Québécois and New Democratic Party members.

Debate resumed on approval in principle of Bill C-33 that afternoon, with a second reading vote—the most important of the votes—called by dinnertime. The vote was 178 to 53 in favor of the bill, with twenty-three Liberals voting against it and as many as ten more who were uncomfortable enough with the bill to stay away rather than vote no.[25] All Bloc Québécois and NDP members who were present supported the bill; all Reform MPs present voted against it.

The House Standing Committee on Human Rights and the Status of Persons with Disabilities began its detailed consideration of C-33 at 6:00 P.M. on Wednesday May 1, within an hour of its approval in principle by the full House.[26] Allan Rock was first to appear before the committee. He repeated the assurances that the bill would not in itself result in the provision of benefits to same-sex couples. He suggested leaving the matter of relationship rights to the courts, though he had earlier defended Bill C-33 on the grounds that legislative action would avoid leaving policy questions for the courts. He also specified that the government had no intention of amending the Income Tax Act, which contained a heterosexist definition of family that constituted an impediment for employers wishing to provide same-sex benefits, particularly in the area of pensions.[27] His caution around the issue of relationships was evident as well in his response to questions about the preamble's affirmation of the family. Rock clearly wanted to avoid a narrow interpretation of "traditional" family, but pointedly avoided mentioning same-sex couples among the nontraditional relationships he cited as examples.[28]

After Rock's testimony, supporters and opponents presented briefs throughout that evening and the next day. A variety of amendments to qualify or weaken the measure were proposed, but all defeated handily. In the meantime, opponents outside the legislature were marshaling their forces. Letters, phone calls, and petitions continued to flow in, mostly mobilized by the religious right.

Bill C-33 returned to the full House on May 7 for clause-by-clause approval. Twenty or so amendments were being proposed for consideration on the floor of the Commons, several introduced by dissident Liberals who thereby secured prominence in the first day's debate. Roseanne Skoke once again condemned homosexuality as unnatural and immoral, directly attacking the justice minister's speech to the Commons.[29] Tom Wappel had circulated a discussion paper arguing that the bill's passage would protect necrophiles and pedophiles. The next day Jean Chrétien sought to rein in his caucus by reminding them of the advantage they had gained the previous week at the expense of the Reform Party, and indicating that a free vote on the principle of C-33 did not mean they could support amendments at will. "You've got one leader and I'm it. Don't throw a stone at your leader. We're not the Reform Party. We're not going to unravel over this."[30]

All of the amendments were in fact defeated, and the remainder of the bill's formal passage through the House was completed by the end of the next day. The final vote on third reading was 153 to 76, with twenty-eight Liberals joining forty-five Reformers, one Conservative, and two independents (both former Liberals) in voting "nay." There were almost assuredly a few Liberals who stayed away rather than oppose the bill publicly, and there were thought to be three Bloc Québécois members who abstained rather than challenge their party's position on the issue.[31]

Allan Rock left the House reportedly looking "less than triumphant" and insisting for what seemed the hundredth time that the passage of the bill would not lead to more same-sex benefits, gay marriages, or gay and lesbian adoptions.[32] Outside the Parliament buildings he was heckled by a small band of protesters, one of them calling him ''Alice Rock,'' others predicting vengeance of biblical proportions.

Visibility and Legitimacy of the Gay/Lesbian Agenda

Among the factors that contributed to the passage of pro-gay legislation at the federal level was the visibility and legitimacy gained by lesbians and gays, and their equality agenda. The story of Bill C-33 indicated that lobbying networks trying to influence the federal government of a decentralized political order, with only modest resources at their disposal, can in particular circumstances shift the balance toward legal change. They can do so in part because they represent an array of communities that have gradually acquired visibility and legitimacy. In the case of C-33 in particular, gay and lesbian activism was accompanied by the media's willingness to hold the government accountable for promises made in the 1993 election.

EQUALITY FOR GAYS AND LESBIANS EVERYWHERE (EGALE). Governmental decentralization as well as the vast distances and linguistic divisions separating Canadian regions had always inhibited the development of national lesbian and gay networks. Prior to the mid-1990s, there were a number of unsuccessful attempts to establish a national organization representing gay/lesbian concerns. Those efforts had usually been linked to the perceived need for a campaign to press for legislative change at the federal level—for example, amending the Canadian Human Rights Act to include sexual orientation. But such initiatives had come to little in the way of ongoing lobbying presence. The establishment of the Canadian AIDS Society at the end of the 1980s, with strong gay representation in the affiliated groups and the national administration, was an exception, maintained largely through substantial federal funding.

Equality for Gays and Lesbians Everywhere (EGALE) was formed in the mid-1980s as a lobby group devoted to pressing for legislative and administrative change exclusively at the federal level.[33] However, in its first decade the group was based almost entirely in Ottawa, fully dependent on volunteers, with only modest connections to groups and networks in other centers. It was almost entirely male and Caucasian, and widely seen both inside Ottawa and beyond as unrepresentative of gay/lesbian diversity. It was also dominated by a low-visibility style of lobbying, with little interest in large-scale grassroots mobilizing, and no capacity for it. It was made up of people who worked for or had connections with the federal government, and was infused with a degree of political caution then characteristic of the capital and still widespread.

EGALE made significant strides in the early 1990s, particularly with the hiring of a paid executive director in 1994. Its resources were paltry by comparison to its mainstream counterparts in London and especially in Washington. It had one small office, one staffer, and one phone line serving a telephone, a fax machine, and a computer. That limited the range of issues the group could work on at one time, restricted the time available to build contacts with individual MPs, and made the development of grassroots connections across the country nearly impossible. The Ottawa location, with its physical separation from large urban concentrations of gays and lesbians, made certain kinds of mass action associated with new social movements unimaginable.

But with all its limitations, EGALE did begin to build a legitimate profile prior to the 1993 election. It prepared a comprehensive election guide and distributed it widely in the gay/lesbian press. John Fisher, the first executive director, brought to the group a thoroughgoing bilingualism, legal training, political sophistication, and extraordinary energy. By the middle of the decade, he and several active members of the board had engaged in cross-country consultations to build both visibility and connections from one end of Canada to the other. Just as important was the increased credibility gained by EGALE and its executive director with the parliamentary press gallery.

Media visibility made it possible for EGALE to extract responses from party representatives to its preelection questionnaire on gay/lesbian issues. Although the Liberals' Red Book did not specify the addition of sexual orientation when it promised amendments to the Human Rights Act, a letter from Jean Chrétien to EGALE did, making it possible for that group, the press, and supportive Liberals to treat the amendment as a campaign commitment. After the election, letters extracted from the Prime Minister's Office promising both the amendment and a disciplined party vote on it were also usefully released to the press as part of a campaign to hold the government to its declared course.[34]

EGALE was particularly effective in playing on the loss of credibility suffered by the Ontario provincial Liberal leader Lyn McLeod when she changed positions on same-sex benefits. Although the 1994 debate over Ontario's Bill 167 was widely seen as damaging to the cause of law reform in the rest of the country, gay activists and the media were quick to point out the dangers of going back on election commitments on the issue. Press coverage of the February 1996 waffling by the prime minister included speculation that he might soon face demonstrators sporting the giant flip-flop sandals that had been used to dog Lyn McLeod in her disastrous election campaign of 1995. EGALE's John Fisher was quoted as pointing out that McLeod had been felled by the integrity issue, and deliberately positioned large flip-flops behind him in press interviews. One activist involved in the campaign spoke of the impact of such tactics: "The Prime Minister's Office would always bristle and fume whenever we made casual reference to the Ontario election or flip-flops. . . . As long as it was a gay issue, they couldn't commit and were not going to do it; once it became an integrity issue focused on the prime minister, his advisers realized that he stood to sustain more damage by not doing it than simply by getting it out of the way."[35]

EGALE was in an especially useful position with a justice minister prepared to treat consultation with gay/lesbian groups seriously. It was able to provide arguments on the logic of a human rights amendment, and information on the extent and impact of discrimination. Fisher's personal access to the justice minister created opportunities for influence over the provisions of the hate crimes and Human Rights Act amendment bills. Adding to EGALE's influence was its readiness to be bluntly critical of the government even while enjoying considerable access to it. When the government was equivocating on the introduction of the Human Rights Act amendment, EGALE did not hesitate to release to the press a written promise on the legislation from the prime minister's office. When Chrétien decided on a free vote, EGALE released to the media a letter from one of the prime minister's senior aides providing earlier assurances of a vote along party lines, and then publicly burned it. Progressives inside the Liberal fold, including no doubt the justice minister himself, resented the resistance to reform within their own party, and seemed not unduly perturbed at EGALE's criticism of the government and prime minister.

LONGER-TERM ACTIVISM. EGALE's role in supporting Liberal progressives and embarrassing the hesitant was built on the earlier work of local activists in pressuring provincial and territorial governments to amend their human rights codes, and in mounting court challenges based on Charter arguments.[36] EGALE did not have the resources to coordinate that work, but activism across the country was moving in compatible directions.[37] A substantial majority of court cases that reached resolution were successful, particularly those dealing with the rights of gays and lesbians as individuals, bolstering activist claims that federal law reform was overdue.

Also critical to success was the two-decade history of activists pressing and educating politicians at the local, provincial, and occasionally the federal level on the need for legislation to combat anti-gay discrimination. The impact of the witnesses and briefs presented to the 1985 Commons subcommittee on equality was a function of social movement activism. That committee began its work with a Conservative majority, and only Svend Robinson firmly on the side of gay/lesbian rights. It ended unanimously supportive of his proposals for gay-related recommendations. During the final debate on the bill Sheila Finestone, the Liberal representative on that committee, told the House:

In 1985, the committee met Canadians of all ages, professions and religions who were gay. For many of us this was our first contact with people who professed this kind of lifestyle. In all honesty and all candour, we were a bit shocked. First, we were shocked by the number of people we met. In every city we went to, in all the towns and villages there were people who had chosen a lifestyle that we had not chosen. . . . We heard details about physical abuse, and psychological oppression from which they have suffered. We heard about the hate propaganda which had been targeted toward them and that they had been demonized in many ways. We heard about the outright discrimination they faced in employment, in housing and in services. . . . That was what the situation in Canada was like just 10 years ago, in a country that boasted of its justice, compassion, tolerance and mutual respect, but did not extend them to people with a different sexual orientation. . . . Last week when the standing committee heard witnesses on this bill I learned that not much had changed.[38]

Parliamentary support for including sexual orientation in federal human rights and hate crimes legislation also benefited from the work on issues of violence and discrimination done by activists in Toronto, Vancouver, Montreal, and Ottawa itself. The May 1994 report by the Quebec Human Rights Commission highlighted the issue of gay-bashing, for example, and in both Toronto and Ottawa, local police forces were becoming more responsive to it. As a result, a large number of reporters and politicians were made aware of violence directed at gays and lesbians, and general patterns of discrimination against them.

Gay and lesbian visibility in the 1990s was built on activist work in the 1980s and 1970s, primarily at the local level, as in other countries. In Toronto, Montreal, and Vancouver, the visibility of activist networks was paralleled by the growth of gay/lesbian residential and commercial communities. Activism on sexual orientation issues in Canada was on a smaller scale and less institutionalized than in the United States. And in comparison to Britain, gay and lesbian themes were taken up less widely and forthrightly in Canadian theater, literature, and television drama. But from the mid-1980s, and more clearly toward the end of that decade, activists and the communities they sought to represent acquired an ongoing visibility in the news media. In urban areas they also developed a degree of political legitimacy that was still a few years away in Britain, and more hotly contested by anti-gay forces in the United States. The educational and political work on AIDS moved activists to develop links with the media, as well as to a wide range of state agencies, and to develop the skills needed to lobby for changes in public policy. For a time, especially during the mid- and late 1980s, the unavoidable focus on AIDS work made political organizing on other fronts more difficult, but it also created skills in media relations and government lobbying that would serve well on those fronts in the 1990s.

Gay rights activists benefited from the support of a wide range of allies. The vocal and impatient support of the Canadian Human Rights Commission over many years was of particular importance in maintaining the profile and legitimacy of the issue. Over a number of years, gay and lesbian rights had been supported by some of the country's largest labor organizations (including the Canadian Labour Congress) and a number of their highest-profile leaders. Bill C-33 in particular was supported by briefs from organizations such as the Canadian Association for Community Living (an organization for people with mental handicaps), the Council of Canadians with Disabilities, the Canadian Jewish Congress, B'Nai Brith Canada, the gay religious groups Dignity and Integrity, the YWCA, the United Church of Canada, and the National Association of Women and the Law.

OPPONENTS. There is no question that gay/lesbian activists, even with such allies, were outgunned by anti-gay opponents, particularly from the religious right, in mobilizing the weaponry of letters and phone calls to politicians. Though not nearly as powerful a set of political players as their American counterparts or with nearly as large a constituency, the various components of the religious right in Canada are still able to motivate large numbers of citizens to register their opinions with elected politicians in a political system in which only a small proportion of the population does so. Like the lesbian/gay movement, the religious right's strength is primarily at the local level, but unlike political groups representing feminist, racial minority, and sexual diversity concerns, its grass roots support is widespread geographically rather than concentrated in large urban centers, and more easily coordinated. Those grassroots can be mobilized from local pulpits as well as by fundamentalist Christian broadcast media emanating from both Canadian and American centers. Its networks can generate passionately written letters from individual voters in a large number of constituencies, in addition to even larger numbers of form letters and petitions.

The religious right swamped pro-gay forces in sending letters and petitions to Parliament Hill. On hate crimes, for example, one MP reported that by the final vote, the total number of signatures on petitions opposing the inclusion of sexual orientation stood at over 83,000, whereas those on petitions favoring the move totaled only 7,250.[39] At one point Roseanne Skoke reported receiving 10,000 letters and phone calls in support of her anti-gay position. In the case of the Human Rights Act amendment, pro-gay petitions totaled 20,000 signatures, but were still vastly outnumbered by the other side. The influence of such voices is evident in the number of parliamentarians in English Canada who are nervous about constituency reactions to pro-gay legislation. It rural areas in particular, where support for such measures is weak, the mobilizing capacity of the right can easily convince legislators that it represents the overwhelming majority of constituents even when it does not.

The religious right, however, is a less powerful political force in Canada than in the United States, in part because the Protestant fundamentalism that acts as its vanguard is perceived as politically extreme by Canadian standards. The terms and arguments used in briefs presented by anti-gay organizations such as REAL Women and the Evangelical Fellowship of Canada avoided religious language, but were obviously imports from U.S. religious right networks. A substantial number of the individual letters mobilized by such groups were less coded than the briefs and petitions presented to the Commons. In House debate some Liberals talked of being shocked by the tone of the letters and phone calls they had received. Liberal Whip Don Boudria was one of them, though on record as opposing same-sex relationship recognition, and representing a conservative constituency in eastern Ontario. "Never, since first arriving in this House a long time ago," he said in debate over Bill C-41, "have I read letters from constituents and others expressing such disturbing grievances."[40]

Fundamentalism attracts fewer adherents in English Canada than in the United

States, and imperceptible numbers in francophone Canada. Almost all French speakers, and a great many Canadians who speak English and other languages, formally belong to the Roman Catholic Church, which can be anti-gay enough in its official posture, though unenergetically and ineffectively so in Quebec. Even in the event of a common position arrived at in, for example, the Canadian Conference of Catholic Bishops, most politicians could not imagine it speaking for Roman Catholic voters in any significant way.

In the case of Bill C-33, the capacity of fundamentalist networks to mobilize letters, petitions, and phone calls was hampered by the government's control of the legislative timetable. Once the Liberals decided to proceed with the matter, they were able to do so with considerable dispatch, and the protests that were mobilized were fewer in number than might otherwise have been sent. There had been a more or less continuous flow of letters opposing gay/lesbian rights since the justice minister first spoke of including sexual orientation in federal legislation, but no one moment until the final debate created the sort of "firestorm" that can paralyze governments.

NEWS MEDIA. The national media played a crucial role in raising the profile of gay rights in a way that forced the government's hand and provided publicity on issues whose proponents had only modest resources. The media also exposed extremism among anti-gay forces, preventing their extraparliamentary and legislative voices from claiming mainstream legitimacy. In Britain a shift in media treatment of sexual diversity had created an opening for a well-organized campaign on the age of consent, though not as widespread across media outlets. In the case of the Canadian Human Rights Act amendment, the Canadian news media seemed more generally agreed on the appropriateness of change, and the attention they gave to the bill helped ensure its ultimate passage. Their focus was in part a product of activist skill in presenting a case in ways designed to attract media attention, but it also reflected an increased readiness to treat gay activists as legitimate players in national politics. One Ottawa-based reporter described a considerable awareness of sexual orientation issues among the CBC reporters in the lead-up to debate over C-33.[41] An activist agreed: "I think most [reporters] are genuinely supportive of the issues themselves. I am amazed at how many media people at interviews mention their gay brother or their gay sister-in-law or whatever. We did a lot to try and cultivate the media, but I have to say that I didn't expect the strength of response that we got."[42]

The shift in media treatment of sexual diversity was evident from the mid-1980s. The coverage of AIDS certainly had its distortions and blind spots, but not on the scale of the British or U.S. media. The mainstream metropolitan media in Canada seemed more open to influence by AIDS activists themselves, and more prepared to discuss the gay-related issues provoked by AIDS in at least a moderately sympathetic light. On the right, Canada also has nothing like Britain's powerful tabloid press or the right-wing religious and secular broadcasting of the United States. Religious right broadcasts in Canada are less ubiquitous and more regulated. In some larger cities, such as Toronto and Calgary, right-wing tabloids regularly oppose pro-gay initiatives, though not with the ferocity, the high circulation, or the national profile of their British counterparts. The *Toronto Sun* even supported the inclusion of sexual orientation in the Human Rights Act.[43]

The shift in press treatment of gay rights issues during the Liberals' tenure of government office also reflected a larger-scale shift in the Canadian media treatment of politicians. Following in the post-Watergate footsteps of their American counterparts, reporters had been developing a more cynical relationship to parties and politicians for some years. According to one analyst: "The prevailing ethic demands that journalists not only be sceptical but aggressive in questioning and exposing the motives of political leaders. Journalists are expected to be tough on all politicians as a way of displaying their neutral credentials and proving their professional mettle."[44] The media have also long been drawn to issues that reveal open conflict within parties, and public dissenters provide special titillation for reporters constantly on the lookout for "leaks" and for breaks in the normally polished party facades. Both the Liberal and Reform parties provided ample temptation in this direction.

A number of prominent reporters and editorial writers had chosen to highlight the Liberal government's delays in fulfilling its promises on the Human Rights Act. The *Globe and Mail* of Toronto was one of the media outlets wanting to "hold the government's feet to the fire" on this issue, and though not quite the "national" newspaper it claims to be, it is influential in business and political circles. Its criticism of the Liberals' equivocation was scathing, and reflective of widespread media reaction. One editorial commented in response to Roseanne Skoke's House speech in September 1994 that the prime minister "had an opportunity—nay, an obligation—to show leadership on a moral question. He showed none."[45] Reacting to talk of delay in February 1996 the same paper editorialized: "If he were a less cautious man, Mr. Chrétien might say to his caucus: 'This is the *Liberal* Party of Canada. Fighting discrimination and protecting the rights of minorities is at the core of what we are about. I am sorry if this decision causes you headaches in your constituencies, but it is the right thing to do, we promised to do it and we are going ahead.' Instead, he mutters about crowded parliamentary schedules and leaves his Justice Minister to twist in the wind."[46] When the prime minister finally decided to proceed with the Human Rights Act amendment, one Vancouver paper complained of "two years of shameful dithering and political weaselry."[47]

The pressure from this and other media voices was very much felt in the Liberal leadership, and according to a Liberal aide finally helped persuade the prime minister to "get it over with."[48] Delay on legislative commitments is hardly news, particularly in a period so shaped by preoccupation with the debt and deficit. Any government's first term usually has a flurry of promises to follow through on, and arguments about a crowded agenda are treated as routine and to some extent plausible. Right-wing mobilization and gay activist attentiveness helped raise this issue's profile, but so did the national press, in a way that became increasingly embarrassing for a party shifting course on so many other fronts. As one Liberal aide put it: "I think it came down to the PM's personal credibility and the fact that he had made a very clear written promise during an election, and certainly his advisors are very much aware of what happened to Lyn McLeod."[49]

Alongside the press attention to Liberal delay and internal dissent was a dramatically increased media scrutiny of the Reform Party since its dramatic showing in the 1993 election. With notable exceptions, reporters covering that election had been complacent in largely accepting the party's presentation of itself, failing (with notable exceptions) to explore the raw prejudice that underlay the smoother language of campaign rhetoric. Its success at the polls, and the Liberals' legislative proposals, created incentives for looking more closely.

Favorable Balance of Partisan Forces

Whatever their increase in visibility, sexual orientation issues still occupy the margins of the federal political agenda, and their activist proponents work only at the fringes of political influence. Such issues requiring legislative action are very much buffeted by party forces, and decisions about them are heavily shaped by questions of partisan advantage. Here as elsewhere, parties may well be dimmer stars in the overall political firmament than they once were, losing grassroots engagement, to some extent in favor of social movements. But inside Ottawa, and especially on Parliament Hill, parties remain powerful shapers of political debate.

In some respects the 1993 general election changed little, substituting for the center-right Conservative government of Brian Mulroney a Liberal Party under Jean Chrétien which had campaigned on a center-left platform but was soon governing toward the right. But the Liberals included a higher proportion of social progressives than the Conservatives, and a much smaller number of morally conservative MPs. Just as important, the election transformed the face of the parliamentary opposition, in the end creating a partisan advantage for the Liberals in appearing to be progressive on equality rights

THE LIBERAL PARTY IN GOVERNMENT. The Liberal election victory of 1993 brought to power a cabinet and caucus with substantially more proponents of gay and lesbian equality than its Conservative predecessors. To be sure, on this issue and all others the Liberal Party has always been a broad church. Its leader Jean Chrétien was thought a centrist on most social and economic policy matters, with no record of supporting gay-positive initiatives. The Liberal caucus as a whole also had a weak record while in opposition. Certainly there were individuals strongly supportive gay rights, but most were unwilling to take vocal stands or press for legislative change.

Historically the Liberals have had a sizable reformist wing. Interest in rights issues on that side of the party was strengthened during Trudeau's leadership, helping to ensure passage of resolutions favoring gay rights at policy conventions since 1978 (though little in the way of legislative initiatives). One survey of MPs conducted in the mid-1980s asked what beliefs were shared by members of their party: Conservatives talked of family and free enterprise, NDPers highlighted social justice, and Liberals referred to tolerance and diversity.[50]

Since about that time, but most dramatically after the 1993 election, most of what social policy reformism there was in the parliamentary party has been side-lined by the deficit preoccupations of the Chrétien government, leading to major cuts in federal social spending. But that shift may well have strengthened the voices of progressives on issues that do not directly affect such spending, for movement on at least some elements of an equity agenda would allow the party as a whole to portray itself as holding firm to "liberal" principles of social justice.

Justice Minister Allan Rock was the most strategically placed of the reformist Liberals. He was articulate, forthright, and photogenic, appealing to the media and more than prepared to take on issues that leaped to the headlines. According to a Liberal aide, Prime Minister Chrétien tended to let ministers run their own show, provided only that everyone was "singing from the same hymn book." In addition, Rock was "very, very much admired by the prime minister" and by his close advisers, and so had more influence and leeway than most of his cabinet colleagues.[51]

Rock was committed to extending equality rights to gays and lesbians, and saw the issue as important, even in a policy envelope with a substantial number of difficult, high-profile issues. To an unusual degree in cabinet government, he made his commitment visible even at times when the prime minister's interest in pursuing gay rights was flagging, thus helping to keep the issue in the news and fueling the media fire to push the Liberals on an election commitment. He was also willing to consult with gay and lesbian activists, something that no justice minister before him had done seriously.

Within the prime minister's inner circle there were strong supporters of sexual minority rights, including Chaviva Hosek, policy adviser and onetime head of the National Action Committee on the Status of Women. Other supportive advisers, such as senior aide Eddie Goldenberg, repeated pledges of action on the Human Rights Act at crucial stages after the election, providing additional ammunition to those who detected hesitation in the prime minister himself.[52] "Talking points" sent to MPs by the Prime Minister's Office on October 7, 1994, reflected their efforts: "As longstanding party policy and a matter of fundamental human rights, this bill will *not* be subject to a free vote. . . . This amendment is *long overdue*." Among the advocates of change were a few prominent women MPs. Deputy Prime Minister Sheila Copps had been an outspoken supporter of lesbian and gay rights since her earliest years in the Ontario legislature. She had been among the small minority that had pressed for the inclusion of sexual orientation in the Ontario Human Rights Code at the beginning of the 1980s. When she became a federal MP, she was a frequent critic of the Mulroney government, and one of the few Liberals who spoke out about the unfulfilled promise on the Human Rights Act.

To some extent the "liberalism" of progressive MPs was strengthened by the extremism of the most vocal Liberal opponents of gay/lesbian rights. Roseanne Skoke marginalized herself in the caucus from the beginning of debate on gay-related issues. Tom Wappel's fundamentalist arguments struck most of the caucus as incomprehensible and as misrepresenting the issues at stake. A number of dissidents were newly elected MPs from areas that traditionally voted Conservative, and were therefore easily characterized as inexperienced, and as not "real" Liberals. Their challenge to party discipline angered most of the Liberal caucus, especially when rebels persisted just as the Liberals were scoring points against extremist statements from Reform Party MPs. Open conflict also forced the prime minister to respond more forcefully than he normally would. According to one close observers: "The prime minister felt that perhaps things were getting out of hand—that he was facing the possibility of some kind of caucus revolt. I think what concerns the prime minister more than the actual substance of the issues is maintaining a tight ship in caucus."[53]

Partisan considerations played a role in convincing hesitant Liberals, including the prime minister, of the merits of proceeding even with an issue that was dividing their caucus. In late April 1996 the controversy over the Liberals' apparent failure to deliver on their election promise to eliminate an unpopular tax on goods and services (GST) became the most damaging challenge to their credibility and popularity since the 1993 election. Introducing the Human Rights Act amendment held out the promise of appearing true to an election promise, distracting public and media attention from the GST. It also provided a vehicle through which Reform MPs might say embarrassing things. As one Liberal observed on the morning the legislation was introduced, the party was "hoping that Reform is going to make a lot of noise about this and sound like the kooks that they are."[54] As the *Globe and Mail* later observed: "Mr. Chrétien and his advisers shrewdly saw that raising the issue would expose deep faults within the Reform Party, releasing all kinds of demons. They cued the music, and the dance of the dinosaurs began."[55] Progressives and some others inside the Liberal camp were also aware of the imminent arrival on the Commons' agenda of the Senate bill amending the Human Rights Act, sponsored by Conservative senator Noel Kinsella. If an amendment were to become law, they were eager that Liberals be able to take credit.

Once the government was persuaded to proceed, the leadership was able to retain control of the legislative timetable and thereby contain dissent within the ranks. They determined when debate on Bill C-33 would begin, providing very little advance notice, and they imposed strict limits on debating time for each stage of the bill's passage through the House. The prime minister had conceded a free vote to Liberal opponents of the measure, but was still able to limit opportunities for his own caucus members to amend the legislation and to impose time limits on debate with almost no dissent. He also realized that support for the bill from the official opposition party ensured a wide margin of victory.

THE REFORM PARTY'S DISARRAY. No factor could have played a more surprising role in advancing gay/lesbian rights than the Reform Party's opposition to them. In Canada as in other countries, the willingness of a political party to hoist the anti-gay flag can still scuttle pro-gay legislative proposals, in part by acting as a conduit for hostile sentiment, in part by holding out the threat of using a volatile issue at the next election. In the case of the Human Rights Act amendment, though, Reform opposition encouraged equivocating Liberals to proceed with a measure that was dividing their own caucus.

Like other protest parties before it, Reform has been torn between the instincts of party and social movement. The rise of the party provided a channel for right-wing voices as clear as any they had achieved before at the national level. As one close observer has remarked, the activist core of Reform "are the people who are really upset by the visibility of gays and lesbians, by immigration, by abortion, all these sorts of cultural issues that, until [party leader] Preston Manning came along, no political party gave legitimacy to."[56] This is a populist movement in which most adherents share an antipathy to normal politics and the media, and a determination to adhere to the principles that gave birth to their movement. The beliefs and policy preferences of voters and activists are not to be shaped, combined, distilled, or moderated in party forums or on the floor of the House of Commons.

There are others in the party, less numerous among activists but an important force in the party's inner circles, who are preoccupied with deficits and big government. Their attitudes toward moral and rights issues are roughly in tune with those of the rest of Reformers but often more moderate, tempered by a fear that focusing on such policies will prevent the party from expanding beyond its core supporters.

Preston Manning has his feet in both camps of his party. His own evangelical religious foundations have never left room for doubt about his commitment to the morally conservative beliefs of many of his adherents. He has strong objections to abortion and to homosexual activity, having once publicly stated that "homosexuality is destructive to the individual, and in the long run, society."[57] Nevertheless, he saw the dangers of appearing too extreme, and during one trip to Washington, D.C., recoiled at what some Republicans were saying and doing.

The 1993 election had been fought on the basis of a strategy that avoided blatantly inflammatory language. But Reform was a new party, and those who held strong views on moral issues, as well as on immigration, Quebec, and crime, were providing the activist engine for the Reform movement. Manning's parliamentary caucus included a number of MPs whose views were reflective of that activist core, who came from milieux in which the open expression of anti-gay prejudice is thought entirely appropriate and saw no reason to speak differently on Parliament Hill. Worth remembering, too, is the fact that even Reform MPs who considered themselves moderates were still voting against gay-positive initiatives, using rationales transparently influenced by the American right.

The Reform assembly of October 1994 provided inescapable evidence of the strength of homophobic sentiments inside the party, and the convention's location in Ottawa ensured ample coverage by the parliamentary press gallery. Conservative commentator Dalton Camp gave voice to the widespread revulsion: "The speechifying gives off acrid whiffs of xenophobia, homophobia, and paranoia—like an exhaust—in which it seems clear both orator and audience have been seized by some private terror: immigrants, lesbians, people out of work or from out of town, and criminals."[58]

The Reform assembly, and the voting record of Reform MPs on the government's hate crimes legislation, widened suspicions among reporters and electors that the party was dominated by anti-gay sentiments, distinguishing it from the Liberal caucus, where only a minority shared such views. At the time of Bill C-33's introduction to the House of Commons, MP Bob Ringma's "back of the store" comments became the final straw. Even the *Globe and Mail*, which had expressed some sympathy for Reform in the last election, was scathing:

> Oh, what an awful price we pay for Bob Ringma and the Reform Party of Canada. We elect them to Parliament and endow them with authority, respect and stature. We offer them a forum for their beliefs and a vessel for their ambitions. In return, we ask diligence, responsibility and judgement. Happily, most parliamentarians understand their influence and their impact. . . . For most politicians, it is instinctive. But not for Bob Ringma and his troglodytes. Driven by a sophomoric defiance, misplaced individualism or artless earnestness, they say whatever comes to mind, thinking it innocuous. When the country recoils, they shoot the messenger and blame political correctness. Eventually, having counted the political cost (rather than the moral damage), they offer half-hearted, forced apologies.[59]

The party's own moderates were highly critical of anti-gay outbursts, adding internal divisiveness to Manning's woes. Moving desperately to control the damage, he then made things worse by suspending moderate Jan Brown along with those who had made discriminatory remarks.

Reform's anti-gay sentiments were kept in the public eye during a national assembly held early in June 1995, in the wake of its disastrous performance over the Human Rights Act. Arriving delegates encountered highly organized sessions and a leader constantly exhorting his party to avoid the sounds of extremism. But such warnings were only partly effective. The delegates approved a motion affirming the equality of every individual, but only after the phrase "without discrimination" was removed. They further emptied the gesture of significance by calling for the elimination of group specification in all human rights legislation. They reaffirmed (by a 93 percent vote) that the only acceptable definition of family involved those related by blood, marriage, or adoption. Another motion calling for tighter regulatory control over people with HIV was supported by 84 percent. One delegate objected that the party would look anti-homosexual if the motion were to pass. Another voiced a sentiment bubbling just below the surface throughout the convention when he responded, ''I did not join the Reform Party to bow down at the altar of political correctness.''[60] The strength of that sentiment was evident in the standing ovation that greeted Ringma when he first arrived at the convention.

SUPPORT FOR GAY/LESBIAN RIGHTS FROM OTHER OPPOSITION PARTIES. The Bloc Québécois's support of gay rights facilitated the introduction and passage of the Human Rights Act amendment, helped marginalize opposition to it, and allowed the government to avoid protracted debate. Its votes also ensured passage, and therefore opened up the option of a free vote, in turn easing the Liberals' internal management of the issue. Social democrats are prominent in Quebec's sovereigntist movement, and most are intent on portraying the movement as an inclusive one. Relatively liberal attitudes toward sexual diversity are part of what they see as distinguishing Quebec from the anglophone regions of Canada. Pro-gay sentiments within the Bloc itself have been strengthened by the growing outspokenness of the now openly gay Montreal MP Real Ménard. A majority of the caucus, including its most prominent leaders, supported not just individual rights for lesbians and gays but the legal recognition of their relationships. In a fall 1994 caucus meeting, then-leader Lucien Bouchard had given his personal support to a private member's bill on relationship recognition that Ménard was proposing to introduce, and the votes in favor of it the following September included that of Bouchard's successor.

There were Bloc MPs opposed to or uneasy about gay and lesbian rights, most of them former Conservatives, joined by a few MPs from small towns or rural regions of the province.[61] When Bill C-33 came to a vote, at least three Blocistes were known to have been opposed, and one MP intervened publicly in House debate in a way that seemed to give credence to right-wing concerns about the prospect of same-sex benefits and relationship recognition.[62] Nevertheless, the leadership and most of the caucus supported a party vote, effectively imposing discipline even on a measure declared a free vote by the government. Those who opposed the measure absented themselves.

The New Democratic Party also played an important role in the Canadian Human Rights Act amendment—a role going back more than a decade. Over the years before the 1993 election, Svend Robinson had been crucial in keeping gay equality issues before federal parliamentarians, this in a legislative arena that rarely accords opportunities for individual MPs and minor parties to have much impact on public policy. After coming out in 1988, Robinson served as a constant reminder of a gay presence, and as a regular proponent of legislative change (see Chapter 6). During almost all of this time, Robinson has been able to rely on the support of the NDP, until 1993 one of the officially recognized opposition parties in Parliament. There were certainly individuals within the caucus who were less than completely comfortable with gay issues, and a number of MPs did not like

Robinson's political style, but public dissent on the sexual orientation issues that he has raised in the House of Commons has been virtually non-existent.[63]

Other Factors Supporting the Amendment

Among the additional factors that played a role in reinforcing arguments for the Human Rights Act amendment, three merit further discussion. The first is the legal environment, which exerted much stronger pressure for reform on Canadian politicians than their British or American counterparts experienced. The second is the decentralization of political power in Canada, which allowed gay/lesbian activists to make gains at the provincial level despite resistance at the federal, and which also allowed federal authorities to narrow the ambit of their law reform. The third is public opinion, which was ambiguous enough to provide no strong lead either way, but which provided some encouragement to progressives.

LEGAL FRAMEWORK. The constitutional and jurisprudential environment in which gay and lesbian activists and the federal justice minister were operating was the key element of the institutional setting generating pressure for statutory reform. Soon after the Charter of Rights came into play, legal opinion was coalescing around the view that sexual orientation was covered under the open-ended wording of its equality provision (Section 15). The 1985 recommendations of the parliamentary subcommittee report *Equality for All* reinforced this trend, as did the views of human rights commissioners across the country. (Senator Noel Kinsella, who had twice proposed adding sexual orientation to the federal Human Rights Act, had served as chair of the New Brunswick Human Rights Commission.) The persistent call for statutory change by successive chairs of the Canadian Human Rights Commission served as a reminder of this consensus and a vehicle for media spotlighting of government inaction.

Judgments rendered by Canadian courts in the early 1990s regularly interpreted the equality provisions of the Charter of Rights as implicitly prohibiting anti-gay discrimination. This offered the justice minister a crucial argument that an amendment to the Human Rights Act was inevitable. A flurry of decisions by courts and tribunals in 1992 added weight to this view. There were decisions (or court-induced government concessions) eliminating de facto differentials in the age of consent for sexual activity, removing the ban on gays and lesbians serving in the military, and mandating employers (including the Ontario government) to provide same-sex benefits. One Ontario judgment (*Haig v. Canada*) effectively "read" sexual orientation into the federal Human Rights Act on the grounds that it would have to include those words in order to conform to the Charter.[64]

In May 1995 the Canadian Supreme Court announced a judgment in the case of *Egan and Nesbit v. Canada* that was somewhat ambiguous, as well as incoherent. The court denied federal pension benefits to a gay male couple, but it ruled unanimously that the Charter protected lesbians and gays against discrimination. That ruling provided support for Rock's argument that amending the Human Rights Act was inevitable, and it bolstered his claim that prohibiting discrimination would not in itself lead to the provision of benefits to same-sex couples.

GAINS AT THE PROVINCIAL LEVEL. Federal decentralization played an important role in easing the passage of the bill adding sexual orientation to the Canadian Human Rights Act. Proponents of the bill could point to the passage of similar measures by most of the provinces and territories, introduced by governments of varying political stripes, which appeared to suffer no losses in the elections following even the most fiercely contested legislative battles.

The jurisdictional limits on federal power in Canada also allowed the justice minister to sideline a number of the arguments against Bill C-33. The primacy of provincial jurisdiction in a number of the areas judged by mainstream parties to be most controversial made it easier for federal authorities to portray the legislation as entailing only minor change. The justice minister regularly reminded opponents that adoption and other family law matters lay within provincial jurisdiction.

PUBLIC OPINION. The willingness of politicians to make commitments on gay/lesbian issues, and of the media to accord significance to such commitments, reflected a shift in public attitudes that was certainly more favorable than in Britain, and perhaps also the United States. (According to one sophisticated survey, Canadians in the late 1980s were more likely than Americans to support guaranteed equal rights for homosexuals in jobs and housing—63 versus 53 percent).[65]

As in other countries, popular beliefs about homosexuality in Canada include a volatile mixture of contradictory impulses, highly susceptible to influence from organized groups, the mass media, and state institutions: support for the principle of equality for lesbians and gays coexists alongside disapproval of homosexuality. Proponents of the Human Rights Act amendment were able to cite 81 percent opposition to anti-gay discrimination and a ten-year record of polls showing over 70 percent in favor of prohibiting it. Opponents, however, were able to cite polls showing not only 60 percent moral disapproval of homosexuality, but also opposition by about the same proportion to legal recognition of same-sex relationships and to the rights of gays and lesbians to adopt.[66] But the extent of disapproval and opposition has declined, and on the question of adoption is significantly lower than in Britain. According to one 1996 poll taken at the time of debate over Bill C-33, 42 percent of Canadians were reported to be in favor of giving gay and lesbian couples the right to adopt, with 52 percent opposed.[67] The same poll revealed that 49 percent supported legal recognition of same-sex marriages, with 47 percent opposed. (See Chapter 5 for additional data on relational rights.) One 1995 survey showed that 48 percent of Canadians believed that homosexuality is ''not at all wrong,'' a significant increase from a 1980 poll indicating that 31 percent agreed that "sexual relations between two people of the same sex is sometimes all right."[68]

The intense debate over same-sex benefits in Ontario during the first half of 1994, along with a proliferation of court judgments extending elements of recognition to same-sex relationships, established a closer link in the popular mind between the questions of individual and relationship rights. That linkage was regularly evoked by opponents of the Canadian Human Rights Act amendment, knowing that such linkage increased public unease. It was probably that association with relational issues that resulted in a lower-than-expected level of public support for Bill C-33 at the point of its introduction (an Angus Reid poll showing 60 percent support, 36 percent opposition).[69] But there was still majority approval.

Supporters of gay and lesbian equality at the federal level benefit from the particularly strong level of popular support in Quebec. One poll taken in 1993, for example, showed that 85 percent of Quebeckers agreed that "it would be fine if one my children turned out to be gay," compared to about 49 percent in other provinces.[70] Quebec nationalists exaggerate the differences in order to sustain their arguments about the distinctiveness of Quebec society, but such arguments help to reinforce the difference and spread the view among ordinary Quebeckers that hostility to sexual minorities is a peculiarity of puritanical English Canada. The relative liberality of Quebeckers undermines already shaky claims that Canada's large Roman Catholic population is an impediment to political progress on gay and lesbian issues. It also augments the number of population centers, beyond the major cities, in which at least moderately liberal attitudes dominate. This contributes to the capacity of rights advocates and the media to characterize virulent opposition as a geographically isolated and non-mainstream phenomenon.

The Limits on Lesbian/Gay Equality

However important the passage of Bill C-33 for gays and lesbians, it represented a modest step, unlikely to be followed soon by others. Liberal politicians gave incessant assurances about how narrow the ambit of the legislation was, and the prime minister's behavior suggested that he would not soon allow another major gay-related issue to enter his government's legislative agenda.

CHRÉTIEN'S LIBERAL "PRAGMATISM". The Liberal caucus had always been divided over gay rights, and Prime Minister Chrétien's handling of the issue encouraged dissenters until very late in the debate. Liberal ambivalence about gay-positive measures was evident in an early 1993 EGALE survey of MPs. Only five of the eighty Liberals (including the leader's office) bothered responding. All of them supported the addition of sexual orientation to the Human Rights Act, but only one of them answered yes to even half of EGALE's questions. None agreed to the same-sex extension of benefits for federal employees; only one agreed to allowing same-sex partners of Canadian citizens entry to the country as landed immigrants.

A large number of caucus members and some members of the cabinet shared the opposition to relational rights expressed in the Liberals' policy convention of 1994. One Liberal insider anticipated the negative reaction: "There is a relatively passive non-discrimination view in the party, and my assumption is that for our party, like with all parties, there is discomfort with the rest, and confusion. We had an extremely wide-ranging policy conference in 1992. A lot of issues were discussed. We remained very progressive on all kinds of issues. . . . The [relational rights] issue didn't even get put forward. There wasn't even a resolution out of the three hundred resolutions that came from every single riding in the country that even touched the issue."[71]

Most Liberals in and out of Parliament had no desire for their party to be too closely identified with gay rights or similar issues. Asked about the influence of groups such as EGALE, one pro-gay Liberal insider answered: "It's increasingly common in the Liberal Party to dismiss groups like that as special interests or narrow interests. Liberals see that as a reason why the NDP has done so badly or why the Democrats in the U.S. have done so badly in relation to the president. They were seen as prisoners of narrow interest groups. I think EGALE has made a lot of strides in a couple of years . . . but I don't think they are very influential."[72]

Open dissent in the Liberal Party was encouraged by the large number of new MPs elected from areas that had previously sent Conservative representatives to Ottawa and that were providing the Reform Party with substantial support. A number of both newly elected and established MPs were facing the prospect of serious challenge from Reform candidates at the next election, a challenge based in part on what would be characterized as an urban-driven agenda on issues such as gun control and gay rights.

But Liberal hesitation on sexual orientation issues was not simply a product of electoralist fear. One study of Canadian attitudes to social issues undertaken in the late 1980s contradicted widespread claims that political elites were more tolerant and egalitarian than other citizens. Asked about guaranteeing equal rights for homosexuals, Liberal parliamentarians at both federal and provincial levels were only slightly more supportive (61 percent) than Conservatives (56 percent), and slightly less so than the average Canadian (63 percent).[73]

Prime Minister Chrétien's handling of dissent on gay-related issues demonstrated the weakness of his own commitment to equality. Serving as justice minister at the time of the initial drafting of the Charter of Rights, Chrétien had dismissively opposed the inclusion of sexual orientation, and his record since has implied no transformation of his view. According to one Liberal activist, commenting in late 1994, "He doesn't talk about it: he's never said 'gay' in public."[74] According to another: "His understanding of the issues is not always that good. On gun control there was a special caucus committee which [worked out a compromise]. . . . And he thought this was really great, and at one point in caucus apparently said something like, 'Well, maybe we can do something like this on the sexual orientation stuff.' And, you know, it's totally different. The amendment on the Canadian Human Rights Act is two words. There's not a great deal of room for compromise on that. So he clearly hadn't really thought that one through.''[75] In the fall of 1996, asked about same-sex marriage, the prime minister responded, ''I'm not very comfortable with that.''[76]

Chrétien's initial weakness in responding to the early anti-gay outbursts of Roseanne Skoke did little to discourage internal opposition. Soon afterwards, in the privacy of caucus, the anger he showed seemed focused on the strategic harm of public division rather than on the principles being voiced by dissenters. Although he applauded the expulsion of Bob Ringma from the Reform caucus, he never sent nearly as strong a message to his own caucus members.

By the time the government introduced Bill C-33, Chrétien was angrier than ever at dissidents, but he still managed the issue as if it were tainted goods. His decision to allow a free vote implied that gay/lesbian rights did not have the same standing as those for women, racial minorities, aboriginals, or the disabled. There are other issues regularly submitted to free votes, but they invoke issues of life and death—capital punishment, abortion, euthanasia. Placing gay rights amidst such company reinforces their characterization as controversial even when supported by strong popular majorities. The long history of delays in presenting an amendment to the Commons, despite pressure from the courts, sends the same message. So too did the Liberal government's constant reminders of the limited scope of its legislation.

The 1994 debate over and defeat of the Ontario government's bill on same-sex relationship recognition intensified Liberal caution over such issues. Until that time, Justice Minister Rock had often talked of eliminating discrimination against a range of relationships beyond the heterosexual family. There was to be a discussion paper prepared by his ministry on the subject, eagerly anticipated by gay and lesbian activists. But when controversy erupted over the Ontario bill, he put himself at some distance from it by calling any attempt to redefine ''family'' or ''spouse'' as ''unduly provocative.''[77] In response to a question in the House of Commons on the subject in late May 1995, he reiterated his support for extending benefits to people in a range of relationships beyond the traditional family, but talked of it only as a personal view, indicating that there was no plan to introduce legislation.[78]

Though clearly driven more by principle than pragmatism, Rock was increasingly defensive in discussing the government's intention to amend the Human Rights Act. The October 1994 memo to MPs outlining the issues before them provides clear illustration: ''This amendment will not result in the extension of benefits to same sex partners. The question of benefits is a separate matter and is already the subject of litigation under the Charter. This simple amendment does not in any way deal with the matters covered in Bill 167 proposed by the Ontario government this past year. . . . The proposed amendment will simply guarantee individual rights—it has no bearing on definitions of family or spouse. As such, it does not promote any particular lifestyle. It in no way contradicts the importance of strong, healthy families in our society.'' Note in particular the memo's insistence that an amendment to the Human Rights Act would not promote a ''lifestyle''—language taken directly from the right.

When Bill C-33 was introduced and debated, Rock and other Liberals obsessively repeated assurances that it would not in itself lead to same-sex benefits, adoption rights, or other components of the Bill 167 package. A private member's bill on same-sex relationship recognition, introduced by Bloc Québécois MP Real Ménard in 1995, elicited little support from the Liberal benches. There was no chance of its surviving, and many MPs were absent during the vote. Still, only eighteen Liberals voted for it, and among the many voting against it were three ministers and the party whip.[79]

The Narrowing of Legislation and the Pressure to Compromise

Bill C-33 passed with repeated government assurances of what it would not do, setting limits on the extent to which the government was prepared to go toward full equality, and potentially sending signals to the courts on the future adjudication of gay-related litigation. Speeches by the justice minister and most other Liberal proponents of the measure included repeated denials about the measure's reach, particularly in the realm of relationship recognition. The bill came with a preamble affirming the importance of the family and denying any wish to alter the family's role in society. Courts seeking direction on interpreting this legislation could glean many signals about an exclusive and heterosexual reading of ''family'' from ferreting through parliamentary debates for signs of legislative intent.[80] Although predictions by the justice minister about what the courts would do on the matter of benefits and recognition were studiously neutral, he reminded MPs of the Supreme Court judgment in *Egan and Nesbit v. Canada*, which denied a specific benefit claim, as a way of assuring critics that Bill C-33 would not automatically lead to successful claims.

Fears about the impact of such qualifications during parliamentary debate were intensified in the aftermath of the bill's passage. The Justice Ministry fought relational rights cases brought by gays and lesbians to courts and human rights tribunals. In one case a foreign affairs officer relocated to Indonesia was denied moving expenses for his partner. The government opposed him in argument before the Canadian Human Rights Tribunal and then appealed a judgment in favor of the plaintiff.

Bill C-33 was also limited in that it did not add sexual orientation to the section of the Human Rights Act that envisaged affirmative action (Section 16). There is no doubt that positive steps to counter anti-gay discrimination would have to be different from those used to respond to discrimination on other grounds, but the complete exclusion from Section 16 seemed a preemptive concession to those opponents who talked of all gay equality measures in terms of ''special rights.''

This reinforced a distinction made between sexual minorities on the one hand and all those other groups thought worthy in Canadian law of positive measures to counter discriminatory patterns.

To some extent, gay and lesbian rights activists were caught in a dilemma when lobbying on this and other legislation. During this mid-1990s, Canadian groups working on these issues gained enormous visibility and access, in part with the help of supportive urban media. EGALE was particularly fortunate in the access it enjoyed to a justice minister with principled commitments to gay and lesbian equality. But such access inevitably confronted activists with expectations that they would acquiesce to the compromises judged essential to legislative success.

The group's representatives, for example, ended up supporting the "family" preamble to Bill C-33, though it fell short of their ideal.[81] EGALE had also pressed the justice minister to include sexual orientation in Section 16. Rock had informally promised to address that concern in further amendments to be submitted to Parliament later.[82] Despite their recognition that sneaking such an additional change in amidst other changes would not likely go unnoticed by Liberal rebels, EGALE activists agreed to support the bill as it was. The hate crimes legislation that had been passed earlier in the Liberal government's term was also a more limited measure than activist predictions of victory would have suggested. It was restricted mostly to sentencing issues, thereby dealing only with the outcome of those few cases that managed to make it through a full trial. As one activist experienced in the issue remarked: "They have taken one tenth of what a hate crimes package should look like, but they're getting away with the credit for introducing hate crimes legislation. All they're doing is telling judges to respond to hate crimes. Well, what about police, what about the Crown [prosecutors]? None of that stuff is covered."[83]

The promise to add sexual orientation to the Canadian Human Rights Act was notable for the tortuousness of its journey over more than a decade. The final weeks of that voyage were also notable for the concessions made to opponents in the wording of the bill, and by the constant assurances from its legislative proponents of its limited effect. The Liberals had faced dissent on other issues, but nothing so disruptive as this. The opposition to gay rights within their own caucus, intensified by the debate over same-sex benefits in Ontario, forced even the strongest proponents of legislation into a defensive posture. That defensiveness took the form of adopting the right-wing language of "special interests" and "special rights," not in a way that challenged its credibility, but only to deny its applicability to the specific legislation at hand.

The Liberals won reelection in June 1997, though with a diminished majority. (Most Liberal opponents of Bills C-41 and C-33 won reelection, though Roseanne Skoke failed to secure nomination as a Liberal candidate.) The Reform Party won the same percentage of the popular vote, but in parliamentary seats it edged out the Bloc Québécois to become the official opposition party. Despite the heated debate over the previous three years, sexual orientation issues were virtually invisible in the campaign. Reform candidates avoided them as part of a general effort to avoid seeming extreme. The Liberals did not flag them in touting their legislative record, nor did they make further promises. The new cabinet sworn in after the election saw Allan Rock shifted from the Justice portfolio to Health. A pro-gay minister in such a position had some administrative leeway in AIDS-related matters, though constrained by the government's continuing preoccupation with deficit cutting. On other fronts there seemed less likelihood of advancement toward equality, at least in the short run.

During the early 1990s, to some extent, lesbian, gay, and bisexual activists have become legitimate players within the political mainstream, with access to legislators, officials, and even ministers. AIDS activists helped pave the way for such access, though other forces at work from the late 1980s also opened doors. But as in Britain, such access is not enough to tip the balance in favor of gay rights policy outcomes without other factors at play. Gay and lesbian lobbyists have little capacity to generate the kind of grassroots mobilization increasingly needed by a group still thought to represent a "special interest." Parliamentarians in most parties may be skeptical about the waves of letters and phone calls mobilized by the religious right, and less influenced by it than their American counterparts. But any group that cannot muster significant pressure from its natural constituency cannot help but be measured against its opponents. EGALE made up in part for this weakness by using considerable lobbying skill and taking advantage of the media's focus on the unfulfilled promises of the Liberal government. Even with that support, and with an "opportunity structure" more favorable to law reform than ever, the changes legislated in 1994 and 1996 were hemmed in to such an extent that limits could be imposed on future progress in courts and tribunals.

Gay/lesbian activists and their supporters had reason to hail the addition of sexual orientation to the Canadian Human Rights Act as an important victory. Legislation such as this at the provincial level has demonstrated that such legal change can be empowering. In 1986 the addition of sexual orientation to Ontario's Human Rights Code engaged a substantial number of activists who believed that it was a largely symbolic gesture with no obvious impact on daily life, not least because of the ineffectiveness of the administrative apparatus appended to the act.[84] In fact, the passage of the law led to a dramatic rise in the sense of lesbian and gay entitlement and to a resulting increase in grassroots challenges to discriminatory institutional practice.

The passage of statutes that incorporate lesbian and gay concerns also creates legitimacy both for the issues they address and for the activists behind them. The framework within which the issues are taken up may narrow and distort the agendas first established by social movement groups, in the case of sexual orientation assimilating demands to a continuing heterosexual framework. But the recent history of litigation over same-sex relationship rights in Canada has provided ample evidence of the degree to which those frameworks can be unsettled.

If for now the progress that has been made is on behalf of those gays and lesbians who portray themselves as normal, responsible, fitting into safe categories, that does not mean that change will benefit only them. The movement of boundaries since the mid-1980s could scarcely have been predicted at that time; the impact of ongoing political and legal changes can hardly be predicted any more easily.

Premier Bob Rae and Attorney General Marion Boyd in the Ontario legislature, during debate on Bill 167 (June 1994). Photo: *Toronto Star*/D. Loek

Demonstration in the Ontario legislature building on defeat of Bill 167 (June 1994). Photo: *Toronto Star*/D. Loek

5

The Fight for Relationship Recognition in Ontario

Maybe it was when the police put on their latex gloves.

Maybe it was then, when OPP officers and security guards

began to push demonstrating gays and lesbians down the

stairs at Queen's Park, that the dimensions of yesterday's

same-sex vote hit home. For the defeat of the NDP govern-

ment's same-sex bill did not occur merely on the plane of

abstract principle. It was also about a living, breathing group

of people—a group already considered disease-infested out-

siders who, the authorities figure, literally must be handled

with rubber gloves. "Shame," the demonstrators shouted.

They were right.

Thomas Walkom, *Toronto Star*, 10 June 1994

When Ontario's New Democratic Party government introduced Bill 167 in the spring of 1994, it received national media attention. This was the second time in eight years that gay and lesbian equality rights had moved into the legislative spotlight in the province. In 1986 a Liberal government had been pressured by the NDP into passing Bill 7, adding sexual orientation to Ontario's Human Rights Code, making it the second of Canada's twelve provinces and territories to do

141

so. In this round, the agenda had shifted from the extension of individual protections to the recognition of gay and lesbian relationships. The bill proposed amendments to scores of provincial statutes to eliminate discrimination against same-sex couples, and came close to meeting the demands for comprehensive change that had come from gay activist networks since the formation of the government in 1990. This time as before, Ontario's large population and economic importance in the Canadian federation lent the story national prominence. And because governmental decentralization gives provinces important jurisdiction over human rights, health, family law, housing, welfare, and education, the potential advances for gays and lesbians were of major significance. Toronto, the country's largest city, also contained its most visible lesbian/gay communities.

The passage of Bill 7 had depended on an unusual constellation of political factors, almost all of them beyond the control of the pro-gay lobby. By 1994 that lobbying presence had been strengthened immeasurably, and was now able to push onto the political agenda an issue that otherwise would have been far removed from it. Prior to 1989, relational rights had been raised in a couple of pioneering court cases but in few other arenas. Even political parties that had formal policy commitments to gay and lesbian rights had rarely been asked to consider the question of benefits. Then, only eight years after Bill 7 passed into law, a proposal for change as sweeping as anything ever discussed in Canada, and as comprehensive than any legislation elsewhere on the globe, came close to victory, though in the end was defeated.

The rise and fall of Bill 167 shows how far the human rights agenda for gays and lesbians has expanded in the short time since 1986. It also illustrates a growing sophistication in political mobilization and an expansion in access to the apparatus of government. But even if some factors were more favorable to success than ever, others militated against passage of the sweeping package of same-sex benefits that the campaign insisted on. The readiness of the Progressive Conservative Party to play on anti-gay sentiment intensified fears among government members, already nervous about extraparliamentary mobilization by the Christian right. The wide compass of the legislation created more openings for bigots to play on volatile public opinion and on the appearance of anti-gay consensus outside the province's major cities. The willingness of legislators from all three parties to put partisan advantage ahead of human rights, and the strategic ineptitude of some key players, helped seal the fate of the bill long before it came to a vote.

The Chronology of a Campaign

In 1985 the Liberal Party took the reins of government in Ontario after over forty years of Progressive Conservative Party rule. Since the Liberals held only a minority of seats in the provincial legislature, they depended on the support of the New Democratic Party for survival. Later that year the government introduced Bill 7, an omnibus bill designed to bring provincial law into conformity with the Canadian Charter of Rights and Freedoms (see Chapter 4). An NDP amendment added a provision that would explicitly include sexual orientation in the Ontario Human Rights Code. After lobbying on both sides, and despite the religious right mobilizing impressive numbers of letters, petitions, and phone calls opposing gay rights, Bill 7 passed. At the end of 1986, then, Ontario became the second province (after Quebec) to formally prohibit discrimination against gays and lesbians.

By the end of the decade, a scattering of institutions had been successfully pressured to offer same-sex benefits, and a number of community activists had launched human rights complaints against their employers for failure to provide such benefits. On a midsummer weekend in 1989, the Coalition for Lesbian and Gay Rights in Ontario (CLGRO) convened a debate over the issue of relationship recognition. For the previous fifteen years the group had acted as a link among gay and lesbian groups in cities across the province, and had led the fight for legislating equality rights. The conference ended with a statement of principle that sought a middle ground between those who supported a high-priority campaign for "spousal" benefits and those who opposed what they saw as a privileging of couples and an assimilation to heterosexual norms.[1] A CLGRO working group of six lawyers spent the next two years identifying scores of statutes in need of amendment in order to eliminate discriminatory treatment of same-sex couples, for the first time giving activists a sense of the full range of changes entailed by calls for relationship recognition.

NDP DELAY. In the midst of these preparations, the New Democratic Party had been caught almost completely off guard by winning the 1990 provincial election. In the early 1980s its commitment to gay rights had been irregular and highly suspect, but the party's crucial role in the passage of Bill 7 bespoke a stiffened resolve, reflected in firm extraparliamentary party support for pro-gay positions. Optimism among activists ran high that the new government, led by Premier Bob Rae, would introduce sweeping change on several fronts.

There were encouraging signs almost immediately. On December 20, 1990, cabinet minister Frances Lankin announced on behalf of the government an extension of employee benefits to same-sex couples within the Ontario public service, and held out the prospect of more sweeping legislation that would affect the private sector as well.[2] The government also appointed a few prominent lesbians and gay men to boards and commissions. The following March, the NDP's provincial council unanimously adopted a policy on same-sex benefits that largely reflected the gay and lesbian activist agenda. By this time, the cabinet had agreed that the attorney general would conduct a major review of the issue, working up a range of options.

In the spring of 1992, CLGRO increased its lobbying presence, widely distributing the "Happy Families" brief that encapsulated its legal research and for the first time publicly identified seventy-nine statutes in need of amendment. A September 1992 decision by an Ontario Human Rights Commission tribunal, in a case brought by Crown prosecutor Michael Leshner, attracted additional media attention. The judgment acknowledged the legal right to same-sex benefits and obliged governmental and quasi-governmental institutions to act on the matter. Doubts among activists about the government's resolve on the issue were increased, however, by an announcement in early 1993 that the attorney-general would interpret the judgment narrowly.

Behind the scenes at Queen's Park, (site of the provincial legislature), a working group from the offices of relevant ministers was established at the premier's direction to work out a package of reforms. At least one meeting was held with gay and lesbian NDP activists to sound them out on the possibility of a compromise policy, and to urge them to work persuading recalcitrant NDP caucus members. Once the activists made clear their unwillingness to provide prior clearance for government compromise, they were not contacted again by the working group or informed of its progress.

The working group prepared an options paper for the inner cabinet, suggesting a bill that dealt with employment benefits but not with the wider package redefining spousal and adoption rights. It was never discussed. Movement was delayed first by the national constitutional referendum of that fall and then by the pressure of other events that drew the premier's attention away from an issue that was thought to be controversial enough to need his direct intervention.

BY-ELECTION IN ST. GEORGE–ST. DAVID. By early 1993, continuing inaction led to greater cynicism among activists, including NDPers who had by this time constituted the Lesbian, Gay, and Bisexual Committee within the party, reviving the work once undertaken by an earlier Gay Caucus formed in 1974. Their first opportunity to display their discontent was in the lead-up to an April 1 by-election in St. George–St. David, a constituency that included Toronto's gay ghetto. In protest at governmental inaction on benefits, the NDP riding association refused to nominate a candidate or to fund the candidate eventually designated by the party leadership.

Candidates from all three parties then vied with one another in supporting the principle of same-sex benefits and claiming their leaders' support for the idea. Nancy Jackman, the Conservative candidate, declared, "My leader, Mike Harris, is encouraging me to work to redefine the term 'spouse' in all legislation."[3] Liberal leader Lyn McLeod went much further in support of candidate Tim Murphy, challenging Premier Rae to end discrimination against lesbians and gays, and announcing her intention to act on the matter in the event she replaced him as premier. She reiterated her support for same-sex benefits in a letter to CLGRO signifying her sympathy with the group's "Happy Families" brief.[4]

Though unnoticed outside the Liberal caucus at Queen's Park, McLeod's commitment had provoked a number of her colleagues, especially those from rural areas. One Liberal recalled, "When McLeod made her commitment during the by-election campaign, she did so without full consultation with her caucus and got hell at caucus meeting the next week for having climbed out on a limb like that."[5] When the victorious Tim Murphy raised the subject of a private member's bill in early May in order to address the by-election commitment on same-sex benefits, his caucus colleagues were reluctant. In the words of the same observater, "They were prepared to go as far as allowing Murphy to introduce the bill, figuring like the rest of us that . . . it wouldn't go anywhere."[6] But they wanted to ensure that it would be a limited measure.

The result was Bill 45, introduced in June, a modest proposal that aimed to amend only the Ontario Human Rights Code.[7] Most of the Liberal caucus had agreed to a strategy of staying away from the vote on Bill 45 to avoid embarrassing their leader, who had to support a bill she herself had delimited. But their assumption that the measure would die like most private member's bills was shattered by NDP support of the measure. Before the summer recess, Bill 45 passed first and second reading.

NEW DIRECTION FROM A NEW ATTORNEY GENERAL. A cabinet shuffle in early February 1993 had replaced an attorney general not very interested in moving on gay rights with one who passionately supported them.[8] From her first days in the job, Marion Boyd made clear her intention to introduce a comprehensive package that echoed the demands being made by gay activists. By late spring and early summer, Boyd was acknowledging that there was opposition to same-sex relationship recognition within the NDP caucus, but was still signaling her intention to amend all statutes that defined "spouse" in heterosexual terms. She also seemed to have at least some backing from the premier, who had reiterated his commitment on the matter at an NDP provincial council meeting earlier in the spring.[9]

Tim Murphy's introduction of Bill 45 increased the pressure on the government to act, and appeared to provide a strategic solution to the difficulties Boyd was facing among her fellow provincial leglislators (MPPs). The government and caucus agreed to use public hearings on Murphy's bill as a Trojan horse for more sweeping legislation. This would allow the NDP to avoid assuming sole responsibility for what was seen as a controversial measure, and would get around what was known by then to be formidable caucus opposition to treating the issue as a priority.[10] Public hearings on the bill would allow a period of education for the public and for caucus members, creating an opportunity either for expansive amendments or for the introduction of a wide-ranging bill sponsored by the government itself.

The passage of Bill 45 through its first legislative hurdle, however, energized the Christian right. Petitions and letters began flooding Queen's Park during the autumn session, protesting Murphy's bill as well as another private member's bill on hate crimes that included sexual orientation.[11]

The same-sex benefits issue failed to emerge as a priority from an NDP caucus retreat in September. This ensured that the Trojan horse strategy would remain.

And yet, in an early November meeting with the New Democratic MP who chaired the legislature's Justice Committee, activists expressed their concerns about the strategy, especially on learning that the pressure of other legislation would delay hearings on Bill 45 until the New Year, too close to the next election. Within a few weeks the strategy was falling apart. In mid-November, Tim Murphy informed the Committee chair that he did not favor the strategy of piggybacking on Bill 45 in order to develop broader legislation. In December the NDP's legislative managers failed to get agreement from either of the opposition parties to hold hearings on Bill 45 over the ensuing weeks.

By mid-February 1994, although most activists were becoming more pessimistic than ever about legislative progress, promises of action were still being made by Marion Boyd. A priority-setting exercise that had begun in the fall was moving towards its climax with a February cabinet retreat, and gay/lesbian activists stepped up their pressure. Fifty CLGRO members and supporters staged a sit-in outside the premier's office, and a demonstration in front of Boyd's office was planned for March. In the meantime, an NDP caucus retreat planned to begin on February 27 in the town of Orillia provided one last opportunity for Boyd to get clearance to go ahead with legislation before the election. By a one-vote majority, the caucus agreed to proceed with legislation, though without agreeing on its scope.[12] Two days later the attorney general announced to the press that measures to extend same-sex benefits would in fact proceed.

THE BY-ELECTION IN VICTORIA-HALIBURTON. The timing of the Orillia retreat so shaped by the forthcoming election was ironic for it took place during a by-election in nearby Victoria-Haliburton, a constituency in a rural area northeast of Toronto which the Liberals were expecting to win. Most of the Conservative caucus, including the chair of the election team, were eager for the local candidate, Chris Hodgson, to use the gay issue aggressively. Questions were already being posed at candidates' debates, by audience members widely thought to be Conservative "plants." Then on March 9, the Conservatives launched the final stage of their campaign with a newspaper ad in the *Lindsay Daily Post* playing the anti-gay card forthrightly, even if not as strongly as caucus members would have wished.

SOME PEOPLE HAVE THEIR PRIORITIES WRONG

The NDP and the Liberals have their priorities all mixed up. The NDP Government's new priority is to introduce a law that would provide gay and lesbian couples with the same family benefits as married couples. The Liberals not only support this idea—their leader, Lyn McLeod, has been pushing it personally for months. Chris Hodgson feels that government should be focused on job creation, not on new spending schemes that will increase the cost of doing business in Ontario and drive jobs away. If you think that jobs should be the first priority for Victoria-Haliburton, support Chris Hodgson on March 17.

When the Conservatives won the by-election, overcoming a preelection Liberal lead, the Toronto-based media attributed victory to the Conservative deployment of the same-sex benefits issue. That interpretation was shared by a number of politicians from all three parties, but most widely by Liberals in the local constituency and the caucus at Queen's Park. The by-election also gave additional courage to opponents of same-sex benefits inside the NDP caucus, and it reinforced caution among cabinet members disinclined to treat the issue as a priority.

Attorney General Boyd was still determined, though, and at the party's provincial council meeting in March she indicated to gay and lesbian activists that the government would be pressing for the maximum package. She also talked of a free vote, for the first time signaling a possibility that activists had never planned for. All of this was in some ways speculative, though, for the caucus still had to vote on how extensive a package would go forward.

THE INTRODUCTION AND DEFEAT OF BILL 167. During April there were signs of skittish delay, until finally at an April 26 meeting government MPPs were presented with three options ranging from a minimum to a maximum package.[13] The caucus remained deeply divided, with about half still opposing the general principle of proceeding with legislation at all, and a number of opponents giving increasingly public vent to their views. A few days after the late April caucus meeting, Premier Rae indicated that he respected fellow New Democratic MPPs who intended to vote against same-sex benefits: "I think you've got to recognize on an issue of this kind, you're going to have very strong views and that's only natural."[14] For the first time he publicly aired his willingness to use a free vote.

The issue was now closely followed by the media and described as a "powder keg." Finally, on May 10, the caucus approved the maximum package by "the slimmest of margins." Boyd was obviously delighted as she announced the decision to the press, describing the impending legislation as the "jewel in her crown." There would in fact be a free vote—a critical trade-off in getting caucus go-ahead for the package. She certainly knew it would be a difficult fight, and was concerned that activists were not mobilizing enough support.[15] Nevertheless, she was predicting that there would be enough votes to carry the measure.

Gay and lesbian activists were delighted at the decision to proceed with what seemed close to the full package they had been so insistently demanding. Recalled one: "We were shocked. It was as if we had been pushing at this door for ages, and suddenly the door opened. We had such conflicting stories flying about it; when it finally happened, when it came out the way it did, we thought, 'Oh my God, we did the right thing.' They'd been saying all along that it was impossible; we'd been pushing them and pushing them, and now all of a sudden here it is."[16] Mobilizing in favor of the bill accelerated almost immediately. A new group was formed to coordinate lobbying, consisting largely of activists from the Coalition for Lesbian and Gay Rights in Ontario and the NDP's Lesbian, Gay, and Bisexual

Committee, though with a few Liberal gay activists tied to it directly or through intermediaries. The Campaign for Equal Families hired four full-time employees to staff their office in the heart of Toronto's gay ghetto, and very soon it attracted hundreds of volunteers. Within a few weeks, they were able to trigger visible support for Bill 167 from a number of groups and mobilize over twenty thousand supportive letters.

The Conservative leader, Mike Harris, immediately declared his opposition to the NDP's same-sex proposal, describing the changes as "very offensive" to a lot of people in Ontario. As for the Liberal leader, "Ms. McLeod looked like a deer caught in headlights as she was pressed repeatedly for her position after Ms. Boyd's announcement on Tuesday, saying she would not comment until seeing the bill itself."[17] Some of her colleagues, including two who had voted for Bill 45, were not waiting, and declared their intent to vote against the measure.

News media polls of MPPs indicated almost immediately that the chances of victory were slight. Despite their delight at the introduction of a wide-ranging package, gay activists had been saying for months that legislation would lose in a free vote. Within a week of Boyd's announcement, there was talk of opponents' garnering enough support to defeat the measure on first reading, even before a debate on principle. (First reading votes are almost always automatic, signaling the formal presentation of the full text of a bill.) Inside the NDP, opposition was being mobilized more visibly than ever by George Mammolitti, who said he wanted to see the bill "destroyed," as well as other backbenchers and, according to some, one member of cabinet.[18]

Bill 167 was introduced on May 19, and survived first reading by five votes. Ten of the NDP members voted against it, including two cabinet ministers. The Conservatives mounted an all-out assault, Mike Harris flying in from an Ottawa engagement expressly to record his opposition. The overwhelming majority of the Liberal caucus also voted against the measure. The Liberal leader, in her own constituency on other business, issued a statement indicating her intention to vote no on the bill's second reading, citing as grounds the bill's redefinition of "spouse" and its extension of adoption rights to same-sex couples.

There had been lobbying against gay rights since the introduction of Bill 45 in mid-1993, much of it organized by Protestant fundamentalists. Shortly after Bill 167's first reading, the Roman Catholic archbishop of Toronto urged parishioners across the archdiocese to write to their provincial representatives protesting the proposed legislation as "a matter of considerable urgency."[19] Shortly after, the Ontario Conference of Catholic Bishops joined the archbishop in opposition to Bill 167.

By the time debate on second reading began on June 1, only a handful of MPPs were signaling indecision, and hope was fading that opponents in either the NDP or the Liberal camp would stay away for the final vote. At the last minute the government tried to salvage its bill by floating ideas about amendments on the most contentious issues. But almost immediately McLeod was reported as leaving no room for a deal on a watered-down version of the bill, going further than ever in contradicting her earlier claims by stating that as premier she would not introduce legislation of her own. Gay Liberals in the extraparliamentary party had formed Liberals for Equality Rights just a few weeks before, publicly criticizing Liberal opposition to the legislation at first reading. Now they were reiterating their criticism in language that pulled no punches: ''People are stunned that the Leader and her caucus are opposing what is a very basic human-rights issue, particularly given Mrs. McLeod's previous statements in support of gay and lesbian rights.''[20] Behind the scenes, NDPers were stepping up their attempts to discuss strategy with Liberals, but McLeod was refusing any contact, either formal or informal.

Talk of amendment was yielding no sign of changed positions, even within the NDP. There was no longer any point in delaying. The vote on second reading was held on June 9. Bill 167 was defeated by eight votes to cries of ''shame, shame'' from supporters who had filled the public galleries. (NDP members voted fifty-nine to twelve in favor; Liberals thirty-two to three against, and Conservatives unanimously against.) Hundreds then vented their anger inside the legislative building, greeted by security and police officers whose latex gloves added insult to injury. Later the same day thousands more demonstrated outside the building.

Openings to the Mainstream Agenda

Even though Bill 167 was defeated in the end, a number of factors created leverage for gay and lesbian activists pressing for same-sex benefits. The legal environment was particularly favorable, and in some important respects public opinion was positively disposed. Holding the reins of government was a political party that was committed officially to gay rights and that included a number of influential ministers, MPPs, and political aides whose support was firm and comprehensive. And while the Liberal Party ended up almost united in its opposition, gay and pro-gay extraparliamentary Liberals had acquired unprecedented visibility and shown their readiness to go public with their anger.

LEGAL ENVIRONMENT. Adding considerable force to the influence of the campaign for relationship recognition was the developing consensus in legal circles that the Charter of Rights and Freedoms prohibited discrimination on the basis of sexual orientation (see Chapter 4). The courts were less unanimous on the question whether a prohibition against discrimination translated into a requirement that same-sex relationships be recognized, but a number of important cases were leading in that direction prior to the introduction of Bill 167. The most important of them—the 1992 Leshner decision—was doubly so because it was a case against the Ontario government itself and because it successfully challenged the hurdle to full benefits represented by federally regulated pensions.

The addition in 1986 of sexual orientation to the provincial Human Rights Code had helped create a legal and administrative environment conducive to further change. The passage of the measure gave an element of legitimacy to gay/lesbian communities previously denied routine access to the political system. Bill 7 also combined with early Charter victories in court to embolden lesbians and gay men both within and outside activist networks to challenge discrimination in government statutes and private-sector practices. Because benefits programs were among the most obvious instances of formal and statutory discrimination ostensibly prohibited by the code, they became the focus of intensified grievance and litigation.

The legal gains already made by the early 1990s, and the prospect of a spate of court cases mounting successful challenges to existing statutes, convinced a number of elected politicians and strategically placed officials that preemptive legislation was required on same-sex benefits. For some years, for example, lawyers and policy advisers in the provincial attorney general's department had favored amending provincial statutes to eliminate discrimination against same-sex benefits.

Another aspect of the legal environment that facilitated campaigning for same-sex relational rights was the progress that had been made in Canada in recognizing common law relationships among heterosexuals, far in advance of the United States and Britain. That stripped defenders of the status quo of the argument that only marriage justified rights and obligations, and allowed pro-gay activists to avoid invoking the heavily laden symbolism of marriage, which would only have intensified opposition, reduced public support, and divided gays and lesbians from one another.[21]

The case for same-sex benefits was also made easier by the Canadian medicare system: the universal availability of basic health services made the extension of benefit programs to same-sex couples much less expensive than in the United States. As a result, many private corporations and public institutions were prepared to offer such benefits at the time of debate over Bill 167. The Income Tax Act created impediments for pension benefits (through its capacity to allow deductions for pension contributions and income), but there was no obvious statutory or fiscal barrier to other benefits.

PUBLIC OPINION AND THE MASS MEDIA. In general, the campaign for relationship recognition benefited from a climate of public opinion that had shifted in favorable ways since the passage of Bill 7, even though anti-gay sentiments remained widespread and publicly voiced. Support of the principle of equality for lesbians and gays had already exceeded 70 percent in public opinion polls taken since the mid-1980s. For Torontonians especially, gay visibility had become more of a commonplace. Even outside the metropolis, there was significant growth in the number of people who knew of friends or relatives who were openly lesbian and gay. Media visibility prompted heterosexuals to accommodate to sexual diversity, if only silently. The issue of same-sex couple rights was a newer and more difficult one, but polling from 1992 on indicated public support of between 52 and 55 percent for pension and employee benefits (see Table 5).[22]

If the urban media were favorably disposed to the addition of sexual orientation to the Human Rights Code in 1986, they were even more positively inclined on the spousal benefits issue in the 1990s. With important exceptions, the Toronto-based media in particular had developed a style of coverage that implied acceptance of gay and lesbian communities within the city and the country as a whole, evidenced in most press treatment of Toronto's huge gay and lesbian pride celebrations. One particularly striking example of favorable coverage of the benefits issue was the harsh media response to Lyn McLeod's "flip-flop" when Bill 167 was introduced.

ALLIES. A number of groups came forward in support of Bill 167, some of them mobilized by the campaign, others not. Two major press conferences were organized by the campaign itself, one with well-known entertainment figures and another with high-profile religious figures. Spontaneous support came from a petition signed by four hundred clergy across Ontario, and from endorsations by the Ontario Association of Professional Social Workers and the Children's Aid Societies of Ontario.

More significant, however, was the support that the campaign received from a few labor unions actively pressing for change—significant because of the links between the NDP and organized labour.[23] There were public declarations from the convention of the Canadian Labour Congress, the Ontario Federation of Labour, and the Ontario Division of the Canadian Union of Public Employees. Others, such as the Ontario Public Service Employees Union and the Canadian Automobile Workers, had also been pressing for same-sex benefits at the bargaining table. Some union leaders engaged actively in lobbying on the issue at Queen's Park—enough that some of the recalcitrants in the NDP caucus were "extremely perturbed."[24]

The tacit support for benefits from some business quarters was just as significant, and perhaps even more so in light of the government's preoccupation with building or maintaining investor confidence. Although there were predictable complaints from some small-business quarters about the supposed increase in benefit package costs, the press commentary on business reaction suggested either indifference or support. The lead story in the business section of the May 21 *Toronto Star* was "Same-Sex Plan Just Ho-hum to Bosses." A number of other stories pointed to the growing number of institutions in the private and public sectors that had already extended benefits to same-sex couples, and reinforced activist claims that the financial costs were small.[25]

Table 5. Attitudes to same-sex relationship recognition in Ontario, 1992–95

	Agree with rights of gay and lesbian couples:	
	to pension and employee benefits	to adopt children
1992 (December)	52%	30%
1994 (April)	55	37
1994 (July)	53	29
1995 (April)	56	34
1995 survey: Categories of respondents		
Sex		
Male	52%	31%
Female	59	38
Age		
18–24	70	51
55+	41	21
Community size		
> 100,000	61	39
< 10,000	45	30
Party affiliation		
NDP	59	41
Liberal	59	34
Conservative	44	29

Source: Environics Research Group, *Focus Ontario*, no. 4, (1992): p. 33; no. 1 (1992): p. 42; no. 2, (1994): p. 36; no. 1 (1995): p. 24, and information supplied directly by Environics.

Notes: Question asked was: ''Do you strongly agree, somewhat agree, somewhat disagree, or strongly disagree that the Ontario government should ensure gay and lesbian couples have the same rights as heterosexual couples in such areas as . . . (a) pensions and survivor and employee benefits? (b) the right to adopt children?''

There are strong party differences in strength of agreement and disagreement. On adoption, for example, 23 percent of NDP supporters, 14 percent of Liberals, and 11 percent of Conservatives strongly agree; and 43 percent of NDPers, 51 percent of Liberals, and 56 percent of Conservatives strongly disagree.

THE NEW DEMOCRATS' ELECTION VICTORY. In the configuration of political party forces during the period leading up to Bill 167, the single factor deemed most likely to work in favor of the campaign for same-sex benefits was the NDP's victory in the 1990 provincial election. In 1976 the provincial NDP had become the first party in Canada to propose formally the addition of sexual orientation to anti-discrimination legislation. More recent conventions had approved resolutions on same-sex benefits with very little opposition. Official policies could be ignored by the parliamentary party, but the importance attached by the NDP to its membership corps and to internal democratic processes made convention resolutions somewhat harder to ignore than in other Canadian parties.

When the NDP assumed the reins of government in 1990, almost all of the influential members of the government seemed at the very least open to gay initiatives, and several were assertively supportive of them. According to one insider, the Policy and Planning Board—essentially the inner cabinet—was ''full of people eager to move on this issue,''—people who were also aware that the courts would likely continue producing favorable rulings.[26] There were certainly periods in the early 1980s when the parliamentary party's commitment was insecure, and there were still some MPPs in the 1990s who opposed the recognition of sexual diversity; but the balance of forces in the NDP government was highly favorable to pro-gay initiatives.

Marion Boyd was one of those most committed to gay and lesbian rights, and to a broad interpretation of what such commitment required in legislation. She had strong feminist principles, with a background of administrative work at a day care center in metropolitan Toronto and a battered women's clinic in the southwestern Ontario city of London (the location of her electoral constituency). She was respected by many within the parliamentary and extraparliamentary NDP, particularly on the left, and widely admired among social movement activists. One insider close to the leadership remarked while the NDP was still in office: ''She's articulate, principled, and tough as nails. Even people who disagree with what she's doing and why she's doing something end up respecting her for the honest way she goes about it.''[27] Gay and lesbian activists, as well as party insiders, also recognized the indispensability of having a strong advocate within the cabinet. As one activist noted, ''Without that, we would not have been even moving on the issue.''[28]

An additional ingredient strengthening the support for same-sex benefits within the NDP was the growth of gay and lesbian activism in the party since the late 1970s, and especially in the 1990s. There were also a number of openly gay and lesbian aides appointed to legislative and ministerial offices who were supportive of the campaign. Some played a role in educating their own bosses on the issues; most provided the campaign for same-sex benefits with information about decisions taken in caucus and cabinet, and in some cases with advice about strategy. This contributed to a sense of connection and alliance between the activist movement on the outside and policy-makers on the inside which had been almost totally absent in the campaign for Bill 7.

Impediments to Success

If circumstances were more propitious than they had ever been for making progress on gay rights in Ontario, there were a number of factors that stood in the way of recognition for same-sex relationships. The sheer scale and complexity of the required changes slowed the process of preparing alternatives for legislation, and some of the issues that were raised posed more radical challenges to established ways of thinking about sexuality and family than the more individualistic changes to human rights codes that had been at stake in Bill 7. The political agenda was under more pressure than in 1986 on other fronts, and in the hands of political masters without experience in governing. And the partisan forces arrayed against the legislation were formidable.

THE COMPLEXITY OF RECOGNIZING SAME-SEX RELATIONSHIPS. More than any other gay/lesbian rights measure seriously discussed by any government in Canada, the question of same-sex benefits brazenly confronted heterosexual norms that were deeply embedded in statute. With a few exceptions in British Columbia in the early 1990s, lesbian and gay relationships had not been given any statutory recognition in Canada, and what was being proposed in Ontario was of unprecedented scale. Because of the complexity of the measures being contemplated, and the opposition bound to be mobilized against them, a same-sex benefits bill would have posed a challenge for any government. But the challenge was particularly difficult for this one, at this time. This, the first NDP government in Ontario history, confronted the high expectations of a wide range of social activists. In the equity area alone, there were other major issues on the agenda, including amendments to gender-related equal pay legislation and a new employment equity initiative.

The changes being demanded by activists and largely embodied in Bill 167 were so wide-ranging that they raised difficult questions even among those who firmly supported gay/lesbian rights. There are activists, writers, and academics who themselves have challenged the idea of same-sex benefits as too derivative of heterosexual marriage, therefore perpetuating traditional norms of family that are oppressive of women and sexual minorities. That, in combination with long-standing critiques of the construct of "the family," led to opposition or silence among some feminists in and out of government.[29] Even during the weeks immediately preceding the introduction of Bill 167, there were debates inside the government about whether family law issues should be rolled into a broader package of "family equity" reforms that would go beyond same-sex equality to include issues such as division of pension benefits on marital breakdown. Some policy makers feared that by opening up such areas, the government would subject itself to intense pressure from other activist networks, in the words of one journalist, "creating a massive political headache."[30]

The broad sweep of the proposed legislation also brought to the surface public anxieties about sexual diversity. Human rights measures that speak largely to the rights of individuals easily dovetail with the popular view of homosexual orientation as a private matter. But because of the extent to which heterosexual norms have insinuated themselves into law, legislation dealing with relationships forces to the surface a great many issues that arouse particular discomfort, especially in the realm of family law. Demands for such changes evoke in the public mind images of what homosexuals do rather than simply what they are. For many people, this legislation went beyond simple toleration of individual difference to treating same-sex relationships as practically and morally equivalent to "traditional" family relationships (see Table 5).

The fact that employee benefits were an important component of the legislative package also contributed to opposition in some quarters, particularly in rural Ontario. One Conservative MP from a rural constituency commented that most workers in areas like his do not have benefits at all, and would say, "We're talking about people who have full-time, good-paying jobs who want ice cream after-wards, and I'm really having trouble getting the meal on the table.''[31] Strength-ening this view is the increasingly widespread stereotype of lesbians and especially gay men as a privileged minority, blessed with ample political access and material well-being. This imagery is partly a product of right-wing propa-ganda, reinforced by income surveying based largely on the unrepresentative pop-ulation of gays and lesbians who are in a position to be open about their sexual orientation. The recession and growing economic insecurity also increased pop-ular sympathy with arguments that sexual orientation issues were a low priority, fueling perceptions that the government was spending time on things other than ''bread-and-butter'' issues. Such views were particularly strong in rural and small-town areas, where such issues are thought to be the peculiar preoccupations of big cities, especially Toronto.

The belief that only economic issues are important resonated powerfully within the NDP government itself. The recession had hit the province very hard, and the government's attempt at expansionary policy in its first budget met ferocious business and press attack. From that point on the economy came first, social issues such as child care and education reform second, with other social issues far down the priority list.

Even the most favorably disposed media organizations helped feed fears about Bill 167. The press repeatedly referred to same-sex benefits as ''controversial,'' obsessively pointing to the adoption issue as especially inflammatory, despite the fact that individual gay men and lesbians already had the right to adopt children. Even when early poll results suggested that almost 40 percent of the public sup-ported the right of same-sex couples to adopt, commentators and reporters con-tinued to treat this as if this were an extreme demand. One reporter who followed the issue closely agreed that the media understated public support for the measure, instead focusing on stories about ''MPPs getting flooded with petitions from right-wing fundamentalist small-town Ontario,'' too easily concluding that 'this is a real loser of an issue.' ''[32] After an onslaught of this kind of coverage, not sur-prisingly, public support for adoption rights fell.[33] Polling by Environics showed that support for adoption rights stood at 37 percent in April 1994, then dropped to 29 percent by July (see Table 5).

CHRISTIAN RIGHT MOBILIZATION. As in all parts of North America, the chief source of opposition was the Christian right. This had been true in 1986 as well, but the character of the opposition had changed in important ways. In the earlier round, the anti-gay campaign had been waged by a highly visible coalition of Roman Catholics and fundamentalist Protestants, with the latter taking the lead. The principal representatives of that coalition sometimes used temperate language, but not always, and most of the messages sent to Queen's Park in support of their position were rife with hateful stereotypes. The transparent bigotry of the coalition had actually contributed to the passage of Bill 7.[34]

Since that time, groups such as the Evangelical Fellowship of Canada, representing more than two dozen right-wing denominations and one thousand churches, had learned important lessons. Following the lead of their American counterparts, the opponents of same-sex benefits softened their tone and lowered the public profiles of their political organizations, while increasing their capacity to stimulate local activism from the center. This time around, elaborate guides were produced to assist members in putting arguments forward, advising them to avoid spiritual references and extreme language. Though partially funded and frequently directed by provincial and national organizations, the new-look homophobic campaigns portrayed themselves as the voice of concerned individual citizens.[35]

The Roman Catholic hierarchy joined the battle immediately after the first reading of Bill 167, also changing its tone from the earlier round. Implicitly denying his own role in 1986, Toronto's archbishop declared that he had never opposed protectiing the rights of *individual* homosexuals. The Roman Catholic hierarchy had more weight in provincial politics than at the federal level in the confrontation over the Canadian Human Rights Act (see Chapter 4). The church in Ontario was dominated by a conservative archbishop adamantly opposed to the extension of gay rights, at the head of a Roman Catholic constituency that included many with equally conservative views on sexuality. The Ontario hierarchy was also practiced at political intervention, for example, in defense of Catholic schooling.

Part of the impact of this more subdued campaign, focusing on the preservation of families, was that it provided a number of politicians and journalists with a language that did not seem as far outside the mainstream as the opposition to Bill 7 some years before. And of course the legislation at hand, as distinct from federal human rights legislation, explicitly took up "family values" and the recognition of relationships with which most Ontarians felt at least a degree of discomfort. As one journalist observed: "About a third of the way through the debate, the leaders of the right awoke to say, 'You do not need to feel ashamed— it's not that you're homophobic, it's that you believe in the traditional family.' That helped to galvanize the right."[36]

More than in 1986, the campaign against same-sex benefits convinced a number of politicians and some reporters that public sentiment was more opposed than it was, especially because so many people with pro-gay sympathies were reluctant to speak out. Rural and suburban MPPs from all three parties reported receiving dozens or even hundreds of letters opposed to Bills 45 and 167 for every one in favor. Support for the legislation was lower in such areas than in large cities. Nonetheless, the disparity in letters and phone calls was many times greater than in actual public preferences (see Table 5). That vocal opposition in part reflected the capacities of right-wing Christians to mobilize their grassroots, but was also a function of the reluctance of small-town and rural dwellers to be "controversial" by diverging openly from what they perceived to be the majority view.

The particular sequence of events in the Ontario debate over same-sex benefits gave politicians a preview of the scale of opposition. The introduction of the relatively moderate Bill 45 provoked a flood of letters and phone calls, with no significant campaign being organized on the other side (not least because the bill was thought unacceptably weak by gay activists, and in any event unlikely to pass). By the time Bill 167 was introduced, some MPPs were reporting letters running a hundred to one against, and face-to-face encounters in home ridings were even more one-sided. One rural MPP received four thousand letters opposing the bill. The barrage was enough to intimidate some of the NDP members who had voted yes on the bill's first reading. As one observer puts it: "They went back to their constituencies and got the crap kicked out of them and said, 'Omigod, I can't vote for this.' "[37]

Although a number of politicians recognized that the letter-writing campaign was the work of a well-organized and unrepresentative minority, many still took it seriously. One Liberal gay activist recalled: "We had people telling us, 'In my constituency office it's fifty to one against the bill.' These are supposedly intelligent individuals who you'd think could understand that there was an organized lobby effort from the church groups. You'd think they would be able to understand that gays and lesbians getting the message would be nervous about calling them. Didn't occur to them!"[38] Even reporters who ought to have known that far-right mobilization did not necessarily reveal the truth about public opinion were swayed. According to one of them: "There was not a lot of counterpoint. They weren't hearing a lot of people saying, 'Well, there is support.' Reporters tend to make very superficial judgments about things, so the superficial judgment that they made a year ago and right up until the last couple of months is that there was no support for this and that it was going to be vehemently opposed by a strong religious core of voters and that you have to be crazy to take it on politically."[39]

LIBERAL PARTY OPPOSITION. The popular opposition mobilized against same-sex benefits was also inflated by the resonance it had within all three political parties, and in particular by the willingness of the Conservatives to play on that opposition. The Liberals were now a very different party from that which had governed before the election. It had lost most of its reformist members while retaining a large number of the rural and small-city members who had kicked up a storm of internal opposition to Bill 7. It had shifted to the right in part as a reflection of its caucus and leader, but also in response to the rising popularity of the Reform Party in Ontario. The provincial party had a higher proportion of MPs from rural, small-town, and small-city areas than its federal counterpart, and for most of the postwar decades it was to the right of the federal Liberal Party on social issues.

The mail and phone reaction to Bill 45 intensified the concern about the party's being identified with this issue and amplified the perception that the Conservatives were whipping up the opposition. Increasingly, caucus members came back from ridings with stories of opposition to same-sex benefits, reporting a flood of calls and letters running 95 percent against the bill. The Victoria-Haliburton by-election defeat, according to one Liberal MPP, "caused great panic in our caucus," intensifying resistance to any support of gay rights."[40] Even Liberal MPs with relatively reformist credentials began arguing that support for gay rights would eliminate the Liberals' lead in public opinion and hand the election to the Conservatives. None but a handful of supporters were prepared to stand firm against this onslaught, particularly when Lyn McLeod announced her opposition to Bill 167.

There was virtually no one in the caucus or the front bench who could act as a tribune on human rights in general and gay rights in particular. On equity matters, though not at first on gay issues, former attorney general Ian Scott had been that figure in the previous government, but no one of his strong beliefs or stature had replaced him. Tim Murphy's inheritance of Scott's seat in an area that included many gay and lesbian voters might have given him that kind of profile on human rights issues, but he was not perceived by his colleagues or by Liberal gay activists as having a highly principled commitment to such issues.

The personal position of the party leader was difficult to decipher, and close observers vary in their estimation of her social policy position from "feminist" to "traditional." But most believed, like this Liberal activist, that McLeod was personally uneasy with some of the changes proposed in Bill 167: "Like a lot of people, she sees that families today are not what they were twenty or thirty years ago, but is very reluctant to enshrine the changes. She was very, very clear that the adoption provisions bothered her a lot, and denied vehemently that that was related to concerns about gay men being pedophiles, but was related to her feeling that that changed the nature of what we really recognize as being a family."[41] By the time the legislation was introduced, whatever doubts she had about the expansive definition of "benefits" now on the table were reinforced by electoralist fears. One gay Liberal described a meeting with McLeod after her first reading announcement of opposition to the bill:

I went in expecting her to give me some indication of sympathy [in committing herself to benefits]. But it was like running into a brick wall. We explained to her why it was important that this legislation should pass; we explained what it meant in terms of human rights in Ontario, personally. And she looked through her eyebrows, as she does when she wants to make a point and look serious, and said, "I cannot guarantee that I would move on this issue through legislative means." So we started talking to her about the symbolism of the issue [which] was just as important as the actual developments—it was time that our leader said it's okay to be gay. She didn't get it. She said she had problems with the adoption issue. We confronted her with that and said, "Lyn, you're calling us pedophiles—you're sending out messages that it's okay to go to Church Street and beat up my friends."

"That's not the message I want to send!"

"But that is the message you're sending."

We realized very quickly that there was no way she was going to move on this.[42]

CONSERVATIVE PARTY OPPOSITION. The Conservative Party's opposition to gay rights was just as severe an impediment as the Liberals', though never in doubt from the outset. The Conservative caucus had been reduced to a third-place rump by the 1987 election, in ways that shifted it to the right. According to one insider: "You begin to look at who survives the tide. Those who survive . . . represent ridings that are more classically conservative [than] any sort of profile you would give the electors and therefore likely to be more 'conservative' Conservatives than progressive Conservatives."[43]

The selection of Mike Harris as party leader after that election reinforced this shift. The "Common Sense Revolution"—the label given to the Conservatives' new policy directions—promised massive cuts in government spending, deregulation, and privatization. To some extent, the emphasis on neoliberalism simply marginalized other issues in the policy mix rather than imposing a morally conservative viewpoint on them. Some Conservatives were speaking honestly when they asserted that same-sex benefits were not a priority, only economic issues were. But the party was not without prominent members prepared to play other cards in the neoconservative deck. And while official Conservative policy documents have said little about a return to traditional family values, there could be no doubt that this "other shoe" of modern-day neoconservatism was part of the package. (One small illustration of the Conservatives' position on gay rights is the absence of sexual orientation from the party constitution's nondiscrimination provision, and the refusal of the party's leadership to amend it when challenged on the subject.)

The invocation of these kinds of issues was of course partially designed to stem the Reform Party tide in Ontario and reduce the incentives to establish a provincial wing of that party. This was one of the factors thought to have contributed to the strategy adopted in the Victoria-Haliburton by-election, located as it was in a region in which Reform had done well in the federal election. A rural area was a perfect setting in which to characterize the Conservative Party as distinct from other parties driven by agendas foreign to most Ontarians. According to one NDP observer of the by-election: the Conservative message was, " 'We gotta send a guy down there who represents us, who knows us, who's one of us, who plays hockey, has a family.' And there are a number of ways you can communicate that message: [Bill] 167 was only one of them. They used it because it was a good issue which said, 'This is a big city–type issue and this is the kind of stuff we get from big government—from Liberals and NDPers—and we're different.' "[44]

Most Conservative MPPs took advantage of anti-gay sentiment from mid-1993 onward by reading petitions into the legislative record, routinely signaling their sympathy with the petitioners. In debate they used the familiar right-wing language of "special interest groups," juxtaposing them to the rights and best interests of children, presumably under threat by the legislation, although they did avoid the worst of the inflammatory language that they had used in opposing Bill 7 in 1986. A substantial portion of their backbenchers, and some of their leaders, no doubt shared the sentiments of Reform MPs in Ottawa, so evident in debate over federal legislation from 1994 to 1996, but they restrained themselves. And when Mike Harris flew in from an Ottawa engagement just to cast his vote on the first reading of Bill 167, he sent a very strong message to any potential dissenter from what had become the party line.

DIVISION WITHIN THE NDP CAUCUS. Both principled and opportunistic opposition to same-sex benefits would not have had nearly the impact it did without its resonance inside the governing party. About half of the caucus opposed treating same-sex benefits as a priority, and for some time had expressed concerns, as one journalist noted in mid-1994, "that implementing same-sex rights could put them in a vulnerable position with very traditional, very conservative rural voters. Remember that the NDP was elected with only 38 percent of the popular vote, as compared to the Liberals at only 35 percent. . . . [F]rom the moment they took office, there was a sort of strange fragility about them, so they were becoming cautious and thinking about being reelected."[45] Dissent was especially pronounced among the substantial numbers of NDPers elected for the first time, without years of experience of debate over gay rights issues inside the party. Like a number of federal Liberals in 1993, some NDP candidates had been selected without any expectation of victory, and presumably without the scrutiny usually given to potential winners as to their fit with party policy.

The caucus had of course been seriously divided over a number of issues in the past. But as one caucus member put it: "This one involved people's minds and bodies in a way that was much more visible—more painful to all of us. Everybody felt pressure to deal with this issue and *not* to deal with it. Even the Social Contract [overriding collective agreements to cut back public sector salaries], as much as there was debate and a whole history on that issue that is much longer, it wasn't as passionate as this one."[46] The idea of a free vote was launched in part as a tradeoff for waverers in the caucus, but it was also a recognition of the fierceness and intransigence of some of the rebels, and the risk that defections from the caucus could be fatal to the government. An NDPer close to the premier described Rae's thinking: "His view on this issue is that there are some people who are genuinely uncomfortable with the equivalence of marriage . . . and that there really wasn't any way that he could persuade them to be comfortable with it. He and Marion [Boyd] agreed that it just wasn't something . . . that should be forced. It's not the kind of issue that you can whip people into line over."[47]

Caucus division of this sort would always have been an impediment to legislative action, but it posed special difficulties in light of earlier crises within the caucus and a resulting shift in decision-making patterns within the NDP. By the end of 1993, the practice had become institutionalized of taking issues to caucus for approval after they had gone through cabinet committees but before they went to the Planning and Priorities Committee for the final legislative go-ahead. As one NDP insider put it: "Morale had been so badly battered over the three years.

You know, the backbencher in a government knows less than in opposition, and it's a pretty lonely life going back [to the constituency] every week-end explaining why some new stupidity is in the paper and why you're not doing anything—and you can't even tell them very much because you don't even know very much. The Social Contract had sort of focused all of that, and the government woke up and said, 'Gee, we can't get ourselves elected with these people unless they're in the picture.' ''[48] Adding to the new influence of backbenchers was the low public esteem in which the government was held, and the growing likelihood of defeat in the next election. This reduced the persuasive power of the premier and compounded the loss of political capital among backbenchers incurred in earlier battles over government policy that had deviated from party policy. This was in contrast to the federal Liberals, who were still doing well in polls, and who in any event had never given backbench MPs much leverage over the parliamentary agenda.

THE ABSENCE OF AN NDP CHAMPION. The delay of legislative action on same-sex benefits was a factor in generating electoralist panic about any identification with ''contentious'' issues, making the NDP caucus more difficult to hold together. The delay can be partly explained by the obvious division within the caucus and the press of other business, especially that most directly associated with economic recovery. But it can also be partly explained by the absence of a strategically located person to champion the issue in the crucial early years of the government's mandate.

A number of ministers who were favorably disposed to gay rights in principle were still new to the idea of relationship recognition. A few were on board from the beginning, but none was in a position to exercise leadership. A number of activists believed that the kind of educational and political work needed to advance the issue could have been effected more quickly if there had been an openly gay advocate within the cabinet prepared to take it on. In their view there was a candidate for that role who might have made a difference. The minister in question, however, never did act as much of an advocate on the issue in cabinet or caucus. Even if he had, he would have been dismissed by opponents as having too personal an interest in the debate. He had also alienated a number of caucus members and cabinet colleagues on other fronts, and did not have the kind of influence needed to carry the day on a controversial issue.

In the absence of other champions, movement on this issue in the early years depended completely on the commitment of the minister formally responsible for the matter, Attorney General Howard Hampton. He seemed unopposed to legislation in principle, but he did not want to be a leader on an issue that he believed to be controversial, perhaps owing to a fear of Reform Party sympathies in his own riding. His caution was evident in the aftermath of the 1992 *Leshner* decision of the Ontario Human Rights Commission, when he announced that his ministry was adopting a narrow interpretation that the decision applied only to provincial government employees. Some observers believed that Hampton wanted to let the courts decide the issue, permitting gains without allowing the NDP to get pummeled.[49]

The attorney general's weakness on the issue could have been compensated for by a stronger commitment from the premier's office, but that was not forthcoming. There was no serious doubt that Rae was supportive of gay rights in principle. He had been forthright in his support for Bill 7 in 1986, and apparently had not been bothered by taking a certain amount of heat for that. But according to one insider, he saw the issue of same-same sex benefits as more divisive: "He had decided at some point that it was going to be very complicated; it was going to arouse all the wrong emotions; that it was going to chew up a huge amount of time and push everyone off track and just divert attention. . . . His private view was that this should happen, that it ought to have happened years ago, but that in terms of the life of this government, it was not something that he was interested in doing."[50]

The premier's reluctance was shaped by his view that the right track was the economic one, a view shared by a majority of the cabinet and reflected in priority-setting exercises until 1994. Other issues did of course intervene, and contributed to the fact that same-sex benefits were never even discussed in cabinet. At about the time that most of the preparatory work on the issue had been completed, there was intense debate within and outside the party over public auto insurance, reducing the government's willingness to open up a new policy front that was bound to be controversial. Then, in the autumn of 1992, much of the premier's attention was taken up with the constitutional negotiations that for a time seemed to consume the whole country.

Opinions vary as to Rae's view of same-sex relationship recognition during the period of his government. One NDP insider very active in pressing the party's leadership to move sooner on the benefits issue believed that Rae never fully understood gay-related questions, attributing that limitation both to his background and to the failure of people around him to work with him on the issues.[51] An NDPer close to the premier disagreed: "Rae evolved, in that he used to see [gay rights] much more as a matter of privacy, and I think in the last while he's come to feel that it's got less to do with privacy and more to do with affirming one's identity, and as a human right—the right to be who you are. . . . If you look back to his speeches, the speech he gave in '86 [on Bill 7] was very much a speech about people's right to privacy, and the speech he gave in '95 [on Bill 167] was more about how we affirm who we are, and I think that's been an evolution."[52] But according to another NDP insider, Rae also saw the issue as a matter of individual conscience, a view that allowed him to opt for a free vote: "Rae said a number of things . . . about how this should be nonpartisan and how this was about rights. On difficult issues that you could characterize as issues of conscience, whatever that is, the NDP's preferred position was to have a policy and then basically leave it to people's conscience."[53]

For some time apparently the premier was of the view that a modest package, excluding a number of the family law issues (especially adoption), would have been able to pass in the legislature. But he was inclined to leave the matter to the minister in charge, and when Boyd became that minister, he and other cabinet ministers knew that she would accept nothing less than the full package. Rae and other ministers favoring a lesser package also recognized that they would be strongly criticized by gays and lesbians if they compromised. And as one government member asked, why proceed with such a measure if it was of no interest to gays and lesbians themselves?[54]

For a variety of reasons, then, the premier took neither a public nor a private lead on the issue. Even when the question was raised in caucus, after Boyd's accession to attorney general, Rae remained hesitant. The temperate tone he adopted until the end emboldened opponents to make their views public, and probably allowed them to solidify as a group. One MPP suggests that it also convinced a large number of his own colleagues that Rae did not want to engage the issue at all.[55]

Absolutely clear in retrospect, and arguably clear in prospect, was that Rae ought to have pressed the issue onto the government's agenda earlier than he did. He and his office should have been able to gauge the determination of well-placed proponents of legislative change, and recognize the increased dangers of waiting until the next election was in sight. Rae himself was said to have wished that he had moved much earlier and faster.

POLITICAL INEPTITUDE. Even hampered as they were by the opposition within all three parties, including their own, the legislative strategists of the NDP were blinkered at crucial stages in the development of the issue. Their most obvious error was in calculating the likely level of support from the Liberals in a free vote. As one NDP insider put it: "We were a bit naive as to how the politics would play out, particularly in the Liberal Party. . . . What I thought at the time [of Bill 45] was that the Liberals were being cute and staying away . . . [insisting] that's it's the government's responsibility to put forward the bill. I thought that's what that was all about—not about not supporting the initiative."[56]

It may have been difficult to extract useful information from Liberals, who were often guarded about an issue they wanted to run away from, but it would not have taken much effort or perceptiveness to recognize from the moment when Bill 45 was introduced that Liberal support for sweeping reform was slight and slipping. In journalist Thomas Walkom's retrospective view, the NDP strategy was particularly "kamikaze" in light of the Victoria-Haliburton by-election: "A good month before the government introduced Bill 167, McLeod's office made it clear to anyone who would listen . . . that the Liberal leader would not support a wide-ranging measure that included adoption."[57] For Marion Boyd and her government allies to have continued to believe that a maximal package was winnable in the late winter and early spring of 1994 borders on the incomprehensible.

Strategic errors made by NDP proponents of same-sex benefits extended to their marshaling of support within their own caucus. Boyd brought to the office of the attorney general a feminist-activist commitment to social justice. But while she had earned considerable respect among many of her colleagues, she was also thought by some not to have done enough of the one-on-one political work needed to convince reluctant individuals within the cabinet who might have been useful in caucus debates. According to one close observer, Boyd's attitude was that "it had to be the full package or no package; and she was not prepared to bend, or negotiate, or discuss."[58]

The controversy inside and outside the caucus called for a single highly placed political office or individual to coordinate players and handle the media. As one frustrated aide put it, Boyd's office "always kept a certain distance from the nitty-gritty networking thing."[59] According to another insider, the attorney general's office in any event lacked the political experience required to push this legislation through its final weeks.[60] Until the very end, the absence of "handling" by the minister's office was not made up by the premier's office, though intervention from that quarter would normally be more prominent on difficult issues. A number of aides at Queen's Park and activists outside the legislative system have commented on the absence of even *apparent* activity from Rae's inner circle. As someone intensely involved in the issue commented, "The premier's office had absolutely nobody managing this issue."[61]

Impeding the process further was the NDP's inexperience in government. The signs were evident from the start, with extraordinary delays in the making of political appointments—in part a function of a highly centralized premier's office without any capacity for making either short-term or longer-term strategic plans. The government planning capacities were further hampered by strained relations with the civil service, exacerbated by the NDP's early unwillingness to trust even those in the public service who were allies on policy. The cabinet was plagued by ministerial fumbles from the beginning, adding to the tendency to govern from crisis to crisis. As business and the press ganged up on them after their first budget, the siege mentality persisted, as did a defensive fixation on the next election.

The NDP was ill equipped for working honestly and constructively with the social movement activists pressing in upon them. Pro-gay NDP ministers (along with some who were not so pro-gay) offered activists constant assurances that legislation on same-sex benefits was impending, despite the fact that the ducks were far from being lined up within their own caucus. Those assurances reduced the incentives for activists to mobilize support among legislators inside the NDP and the Liberal Party.[62] The NDP's unfamiliarity with the politics of governing led to an erratic oscillation between declarations of principle more appropriate to a party in opposition and hastily assembled compromises to deal with the constraints of office. Their long years on the opposite side of the legislature, and the considerable experience of many of their members in social advocacy, had not equipped the NDP leadership for handling complex or controversial issues within their own caucus or with the media and thence the public.[63]

INSTITUTIONAL RIGIDITY. The extent of opposition among MPPs to same-sex benefits increased the importance of mobilizing support outside the legislature and of forging cooperative strategic links across party lines within the legislature. The parliamentary system in place at Queen's Park, however, militates against both. In a political setting such as the Ontario provincial legislature, as in all parliamentary systems, there are few opportunities for social movement activists to intervene. Political mobilizing is particularly difficult in the early developmental stages of a policy issue—precisely the time when politicians are locking themselves into positions (see Chapter 7 for similar commentary on the issue of lesbians and gays in the U.S. military). The institutional disincentives for developing elaborate lobbying organizations prevents the longer-term buildup of resources, including specialized skills, that are indispensable currency in policy circles. This reduces opportunities for moving beyond advocacy to active participation in policy-making "communities," a crucial threshold for the development of political influence.

The centralization of power in the hands of the government of the day also creates few incentives among activists to develop ongoing ties with or relationships to political parties, a weakness that in the end probably hurt the campaign for same-sex benefits. As activism around sexual orientation has grown within the New Democratic Party, there has been an increased overlap with groups such as CLGRO, but with only a small group of people acting as links, and virtually no long-term representation in other parties. The Campaign for Equal Families was able to forge some links to the Liberals and to a number of activists with experience in the inner workings of government, though too late to have much impact.

Another institutional impediment to the advancement of gay and lesbian rights is the intensity of partisanship in parliamentary systems such as Ontario's. Party discipline can of course facilitate the passage of legislation that has clear government backing. But because parties so often retreat from gay/lesbian issues by claiming that they transcend party loyalties, governments usually depend on other parties to secure the passage of pro-gay bills. From mid-1993 onward, supporters of same-sex benefits inside the government chose strategies that required a degree of cross-party interaction at which few legislators in Ontario were adept and to which few were disposed. The depth of animosity between almost all of the protagonists interrupted information flow and narrowed the room for strategic maneuvering in the final stages of the legislative process. Tim Murphy's introduction of Bill 45 created an opportunity to effect progress without identifying only the NDP with the issue. NDP supporters tried to use the bill as a Trojan horse for wider changes, not recognizing the signals which suggested that the Liberals were disinclined to play along. Liberals accurately detected and resented an NDP attempt to avoid full responsibility, and were in any event seeking to maximize their own distance from the issue.

Cross-party ties had become even more difficult to achieve than usual, given the bitterness that had marked the relationship between Liberals and NDPers since the late 1980s. On this issue, as with most others, operatives in all three parties were inclined to Machiavellian perceptions of other parties. However illogical, the belief was widespread in opposition circles that the NDP was introducing Bill 167 solely to embarrass the Liberals. The NDP, for its part, was suspicious of the Liberals' motives. One member of the government recalled: "There was kind of a difficult relationship with the Liberals, because we frankly didn't trust them and they didn't trust us. . . . So there was this kind of game playing going on, and [it was] very difficult to get an actual meeting where you say, 'Here's what we're planning to do,' fearing that as soon as we did that, the Liberals would leak it and then we'd have more difficulty with our own people and more difficulty in the Liberal caucus.''[64] One gay Liberal thoroughly exasperated with his party's MPPs for not recognizing the human rights essence of the legislation accused them of framing the "problem" as the fault of the NDP: "[Liberals] were saying, 'I'm so angry with the NDP mismanaging this whole issue.' . . . [I]t became 'a bad piece of NDP legislation'. . . . [I]t was like watching a cult. They talked themselves into believing that [the bill] was indicative of NDP mismanagement and therefore had to be defeated—completely disconnected to the merits of the contents of the bill.''[65]

Gay/Lesbian Activist Resources

The combination of forces and circumstances that led to the introduction of Bill 167 required a level of activist mobilization that was virtually impossible to achieve at the stage in the political process when it would have been most usefully applied. In retrospect, it seems clear that the Toronto-based activist networks that had primary ownership of the same-sex benefits issue might have done more, but little in their experience prepared them for what in the end was needed. Perhaps no social movement representing a group traditionally on the margins of institutionalized politics could have managed to counteract the forces that were arrayed against gays and lesbians in this particular round.

POLITICAL AND MEDIA VISIBILITY. Much more strikingly than with Bill 7, extraparliamentary activists were able to call on the full range of resources and contacts that had been accumulated in a variety of gay and lesbian activist networks over the previous two decades. Lesbian/gay political networks in Toronto had long been the most developed in Canada's major cities. Political organizations did not emerge as early as in Vancouver, and gay liberationist political activism did not mushroom as dramatically as in major American and British cities. But the late 1970s and early 1980s were periods of considerable growth in organizational density and visibility.[66]

From the beginning, activism in Toronto (as well as in Ottawa) incorporated a range of strategies that created room for the development of sophisticated tactics suitable for mainstream politics. Even while early mobilization was marked by distrust of state institutions akin to that shared by other "new social movements," police raids on gay institutions in the late 1970s and early 1980s created a generation of activists with expertise in the media and legal system, experience in legislative briefing, and the skills required to mount demonstrations and raise funds.

AIDS hit this newly politicized community very hard during the 1980s, generating a number of political networks, some based on ties forged in earlier activism. The demand for governmental action, and for fundamental changes in health care delivery, increasingly brought gay and lesbian activists into close relationship with the mainstream media and direct negotiations with state officials.[67] The success of AIDS groups in generating favorable public attention and influential pressure on policy makers was to a major degree a function of the diverse strategies they adopted.

Until 1986, gay community mobilization in Ontario had only sporadically concentrated energy on attaining formal legal rights, even if the activist agenda had always included calls for such rights. As a result, the Coalition for Gay Rights in Ontario (later the Coalition for Lesbian and Gay Rights in Ontario) had only a modest profile within the community. But it had built up considerable expertise in human rights legislation. Particularly in the 1981 campaign for an amendment to the Human Rights Code, it also identified and expanded the network of allies in organized labor, religion, and other equity-seeking networks. The campaign for Bill 7, in which CGRO was a partner alongside the Right to Privacy Committee (organized in response to police raids on gay bathhouses), moved human rights legislation to the top of the gay and lesbian agenda, and pressed more allies than ever into vocally endorsing gay rights.

The visibility of political activism focused specifically on same-sex benefits had increased in the early 1990s. Gay and lesbian employee groups were forming in a number of private sector firms, public institutions, and unions, calling on employers to end discrimination and challenge marginalization. Spousal or family benefit programs became a routine target for these groups, representing the most obviously discriminatory practices.

One measure of community support for the spousal benefits campaign was the sheer number of volunteers who came forward when the Campaign for Equal Families was launched. Four paid staffers and over one hundred volunteers were working out of the offices at the peak of the campaign, and there were knots of activists in more than twenty-five communities around Ontario. Although the campaign was too centered on Toronto (as I discuss later), it galvanized gay/lesbian communities outside the metropolis in unprecedented ways, confronting politicians and citizens in some smaller cities with their first pro-gay demonstrations.[68]

The resources available to proponents of same-sex benefits were applied with considerable skill. One activist with substantial experience in government lobbying was impressed by the work of the Campaign: "They had their act together.

. . . [T]hey got lists of names and petitions rolling and jammed every fax machine at Queen's Park. . . . Every time they tried to do something in the way of media coverage, they got media coverage—and it was a nice mix of controlled press conferences and larger demonstrations, rallies, and things that involved lots of people and showed them there was a base of support. There's no question that [they] won the media battle.''[69]

The Campaign ensured a steady flow of news. Press conferences were organized with religious and entertainment figures; the press was provided with ''human interest'' stories, and the everyday mechanics of maintaining contact with reporters were attended to. For the Toronto-based media in particular, coverage was made easier by a campaign that was extremely well organized and responsive to reporters' needs. One journalist remarked: ''Representatives of the gay and lesbian community have just been unbelievably vigorous and professional and persistent. . . . Tom Warner [of CLGRO] is an example. . . . [H]e will fax you, he will answer any question, he will put you in touch. It might sound sort of small, but the truth is that a highly responsive lobby really does get action. I think that is one of the reasons that this has really gotten into the media as much as it has.''[70] Media reports, in turn, drew on Campaign activists for comment, making them more visible participants in the political process than their predecessors had been in 1986. This was in part a product of effective media strategy, but it was also a legacy of the profile acquired by CLGRO at Queen's Park and elsewhere, particularly since the inclusion of sexual orientation in the Ontario Human Rights Code.

Another factor contributing to favorable media coverage was the air of calm reasonableness that had characterized the campaign over Bill 7 and had long been the style of CLGRO leaders. A reporter commented: ''I remember they did a sit-in—a very polite but in-your-face sit-in at the attorney general's office. . . . [T]hey protested with a kind of dignity that kept the focus on civil and human rights. . . . They somehow managed to shame people. They got quoted all the time; they were outspoken. They had protests; but they picked their spots.''[71]

CONSENSUS ON POLICY AND STRATEGY. The efforts of activists working on same-sex benefits were strengthened by widespread agreement on the issue among lesbians and gays themselves, nurtured by careful treatment of the issue from 1989 on. The extraordinary burden of health costs borne by those living with AIDS or HIV gave the gay community a special interest in the benefits issue, as well as the broader range of issues encompassed by relational rights. The growing number of gay men and especially of lesbians with children also increased community interest in adoption rights and family law in general.

What was particularly distinctive about the campaign for same-sex benefits was the integration of gay men's and lesbians' policy priorities that it effected—a mark of campaigns for equality in Britain and the United States as well. Political organizing prior to the late 1980s had been dominated overwhelmingly by gay men. Women had joined in the early campaigning for human rights and in early

AIDS activism, though in a minority position. But in the fight for relationship recognition, leading roles were played by lesbian activists from the beginning. Karen Andrews launched the first court case challenging heterosexist restrictions in the benefits package of the Toronto public library system, and feminist union activists had long been active in pressing unions to take up such issues. Over time, this interest came to be reflected in the composition of the activist core of the Coalition for Lesbian and Gay Rights in Ontario and of the Campaign for Equal Families which it spawned.

Not that there was community-wide consensus on the importance of the benefits issue. When CLGRO convened its 1989 conference to debate whether the pursuit of such benefits ought to be a priority, they faced a considerable range of opinions. But activists sought compromise language, talking of the right of individuals and couples to the benefits accorded heterosexuals. Calls for more radical changes in family law and benefits legislation were accommodated to some extent by acknowledging the need to take a wider look at such laws while asserting the shorter-term need to end discrimination. Unity was strengthened by skirting the issue of marriage, made easier by the legal recognition accorded common law heterosexual relationships.[72]

To a considerable degree, agreement was widespread not only on treating same-sex benefits as an important issue but also on interpreting the goals broadly and thus seeking a sweeping package. As had been true of political mobilizing around sexuality issues in the past, activists came to this issue from widely divergent ideological backgrounds. The insistence on a comprehensive package reduced the potential for open splits and helped retain the support of most of those with doubts about the benefits strategy as a whole.

The role and perspective of gay Liberals in the campaign for same-sex benefits illustrates the extent to which consensus was built around the idea of sweeping change. In general, Liberal activists were prone to an incrementalist view of legislative progress and a cautious approach to the formulation of political demands. But the campaign that was organized to press the issue forward, and the government's ultimate willingness to introduce the comprehensive package that it did, moved the goal posts even for some of the moderates. One Liberal activist remarked: "[Bill] 167 has mobilized us by showing us what is possible. Back then it never occurred to me to ask for more than workplace benefits. But now I see that 40 percent of Ontarians say that it is a possibility, that it came close to second reading. I'm sorry, I'm not going to settle for anything less than that. So I think that 167 changed the whole tone of the debate."[73]

Another source of activist strength in this and earlier struggles was the relatively low temperature of disagreement over strategies as well as substantive priorities. On the tactical front, in these activist circles as well as in gay and lesbian organization in Ontario generally, there had long been a relatively uncontentious mixture of direct action and mainstream approaches. The scale of attacks against gay institutions in the past had secured a degree of legitimacy for mass protests and angry denunciations, but the development of workable legal defenses and effective media strategies had always been thought natural accompaniments. There was to be sure a degree of caution about mass demonstrations, but little of the categorical rejection of direct action typical of some activist organizations preoccupied with legislative lobbying in other countries.

POLITICAL WEAKNESSES. Gay and lesbian communities in Canada still commanded nothing like the positioning and resources required to exercise sustained influence, let alone power. Like all other social movements advancing the concerns of the politically or economically marginalized, gays and lesbians do not have the power to invest capital or to create jobs which has so much currency in the post-Keynesian state. They do not, therefore, have the virtually automatic access to policy makers that the corporate sector has always enjoyed, now more than ever.

Neither do most social movements have the resources to create the ongoing institutions that are needed for continuous lobbying and policy development. As I argued earlier, parliamentary systems such as Canada's federal and provincial governments create fewer openings than the U.S. congressional system for applying pressure, and therefore fewer incentives to maintain a continuous lobbying presence, let alone the specialized staff that would be most effective in maintaining influential contacts inside policy networks. (AIDS organizations are to some extent exceptions, in part because they formulated responses to the disease before government policy makers were prepared to, thereby developing skills and services that turned out to be indispensable, and in part because they have been able to secure government funding in the process of organization building.)

Some of the inherent difficulties in working on the fringes are illustrated by the Coalition for Lesbian and Gay Rights in Ontario. Although a large potential constituency lay at its doorstep in downtown Toronto, it had never developed a repertoire of techniques for activating that constituency or for raising money from it. For a number of years after the mid-1980s, that may have resulted from a realistic assessment that community concerns were more focused on AIDS than human rights. The post–Bill 7 connections forged with provincial and municipal human rights policy networks also increased demands on already overstretched activists, without necessarily providing the kind of publicity that could mobilize a constituency.

Another of the challenges that gay/lesbian activists never fully overcame was the need to demonstrate that the support for legislation on same-sex benefits extended beyond downtown Toronto. As one active participant in the campaign has commented: ''From the outset, it was clear that among NDP caucus members relationship recognition was perceived as a downtown Toronto issue. . . . CLGRO's lobbying effort only reinforced that impression by continually bringing MPPs face-to-face with downtown Toronto queer lobbyists instead of their own constituents. CLGRO activists were told as early as 1991 that their top priority should be showing MPPs from outside of Toronto that there was support across the province for relationship recognition. However, such a strategy never became a priority.''[74] Even if there was activist mobilization on an unprecedented scale outside Toronto, particularly in a few of the medium-sized cities that had well-established gay/lesbian networks, it was not large-scale enough, widespread enough, or early enough to have much impact. Even if, in theory, CLGRO's membership in cities across the province gives it a large grassroots potential, in fact it has always been coordinated by a small steering group concentrated in Toronto, with one paid staff position at most.

The proponents of same-sex benefits were weakened by exaggerated optimism following the 1990 election. "When the NDP got elected," one activist recalled, "we were all in the clouds; we thought, 'They will take care of us.' Every movement backed off: the environmental movement backed off, the gay and lesbian movement backed off, the labor movement backed off. All of us said, 'We elected an NDP government with a specific platform, and they promised us.' ''[75] The continuing reassurances from the NDP government from 1991 on helped convince activists that their approach made sense, especially in a parliamentary system with disciplined legislative voting. As Tom Warner of CLGRO has admitted, "In the early days, people didn't think it was necessary to do lobbying because the NDP was on side and it was just a matter of time."[76] Openly gay Ottawa region councillor Alex Munter argues that activists were regularly sent messages to the same effect:

> Indeed Frances Lankin's December 1990 statement . . . was seen as a sign of the government's commitment. At the March 1991 NDP provincial convention, Lankin—one of the government's most influential ministers—led the fight to have the convention adopt a resolution calling for relationship recognition. Throughout 1992, at closed-door meetings between lesbian, gay and bisexual New Democrats and officials from the Premier's Office and Ministries of the Attorney-General and Citizenship, government representatives continued to give the impression that change was imminent. . . . At every 1993 meeting of the NDP Provincial Council . . . Marion Boyd and the Premier always said the measure was months away. As a result, each time the issue was about to go to a cabinet committee or caucus meeting CLGRO's focus was on making sure the measure successfully cleared that hurdle, which was usually described as the last step needed before legislation was introduced.[77]

Even after some activists realized that more should be done, there was a constant sense of urgency that kept energies focused on the short run. Under these circumstances, a significant shift in mobilizing strategies and diversifying lobbying targets might well have been impossible.

Some errors in judgment may also have been made about when a high-profile campaign was most crucial. CLGRO was not plannng to launch a major campaign until after the government introduced an omnibus bill. An organizational strategy that aimed at peaking only with the introduction of legislation actually delayed beyond the point at which it could have had its most significant impact. It is difficult, of course, to mobilize a constituency in the absence of a concrete legislative proposal—and the media publicity accompanying it.

In addition, the preoccupation of almost all activists working on this issue were focused on the NDP. One leading advocate admitted: "To be honest, once the NDP got elected, we put all of our energy into lobbying NDPers. . . . [F]oolish as this was, and naive as this was, we really did not entertain the idea of a free vote until the [end of April]. . . . It wasn't until then that we realized, 'Omigod, what a whole new universe: we have not been lobbying Liberals. We've been sending out briefs and that kind of thing, but we haven't been working on them.' "[78] Lobbying, in other words, assumed a party vote that would render backbench opposition from any party irrelevant. The error here lay not simply in failing to anticipate the possibility of a free vote, but in believing that a party vote did not require working more closely with Liberals and backbench NDPers. Work was needed to reduce identification of the legislation with a single party and to contest the strategic arguments within the opposition that pro-gay stances were necessarily vote losers. This, of course, would have required resources that were unavailable to proponents of same-sex benefits until very late in the process.

THE DIFFICULTIES OF PLAYING PRAGMATIC POLITICS. Both the CLRGO and the Campaign for Equal Families were criticized by a number of political insiders for not playing according to the rules of pragmatic politics. At the very end, for example, when the government was floating trial balloons about amending the package in the face of certain defeat, one government insider was struck at how inflexible activists still were: "They were unable to bring themselves to a decision. . . . they felt very strongly at that point in time that they would lose every credibility from various elements of the gay community, and as leaders would be seen as having sold out. . . . I believe that if you can make major progress, it's important to do it in steps. So I tried to convince them, but I was unsuccessful. Their reading of their constituency was that people were even harder-lined about getting a whole package than they were."[79]

CLGRO and the Campaign had been constantly confronted with the question of compromise. In fact, a full year before the introduction of Bill 167, they had concluded that the full package would never be supported by a majority of the NDP caucus, and therefore assumed that they would have to settle for something less. Some had considered what degrees of anger or outrage should accompany various possible compromises. But they resisted endorsing any particular package. They did so in part because they were always getting mixed messages, as one CLGRO activist recounts: "One person would tell you, 'No, no, we're solidly behind everything you put into your brief,' and others would say, 'No, I don't really think there's enough support for that—it's going to be something less.' It was really hard for us to figure out exactly what it was that they were going to do. The other frustrating thing about it was that the government didn't involve CLGRO or any other group outside of the NDP family in any formal or organized way. They would talk at party functions or private settings with party members who would then come back to us. It was only at the point that they made the decision to introduce the bill that they even started talking to us."[80]

There was also a strong view among activists, including the lawyers who had been responsible for CLGRO's brief on the issue, that a compromise bill made no sense if one of its principal objectives was to address the growing wave of litigation on relationship issues. If a legislative package did not resolve most of the litigation that gay and lesbian couples were launching, what was the point?

Even more critical was deciding which issues would be jettisoned in the event of a compromise. Activists knew that to compromise on family law would reinforce the prejudice that gays and lesbians are unfit to raise children. It would also jeopardize the sometimes fragile cross-gender alliance that had been built over the benefits issue. According to one lesbian activist: "We were vulnerable inside the community because the critique was that employment benefits is a white male issue. What about the rest of the community who has a whole series of concerns, including the lesbian community? When you started thinking about that, you started realizing that compromise, while a legitimate question to ask about, could ultimately end up splitting the community."[81]

Some activists central to the campaign recognized that compromise might be inevitable, but that it was the responsibility of politicians to make the appropriate judgments. It was after all the job of politicians to gauge support for proposals in the general public, the legislature, and the party caucus, and as a result to know what was winnable at the moment. Central to that job was weighing the principled costs of formulating a succesful legislative package. As one CLGRO activist put it, if the politicians had presented a compromise and said, " 'This will be a first step of a long process in gaining equal rights,' we would have been critical, but we would have also understood. . . . It's fine and well for politicians to ask everyone what they want, and what's acceptable to them, but we're not in the House."[82]

The firmness of resolve and the resistance to compromise typified NDP activists as well as nonpartisans. To some extent this was a source of strength in the campaign, but it also exposed the NDPers to accusations of disloyalty to their own party. One of the charges leveled by government insiders at gay NDP activists was that by criticizing the government, they undermined the party that was strongest in its support of their cause. The NDP felt, as one insider has commented, "We're getting the shit kicked out of us by people who should know better and who are treating us worse than they're treating people who are their enemies."[83]

Gay and lesbian NDPers had gained valuable entry into policy networks that would otherwise have been denied them, but what was expected in return was a degree of loyalty that most were unprepared to offer. The perception inside the NDP that some activists were not playing according to the rules was most intense in the wake of the St. George–St. David by-election. NDP activists' refusal to nominate a candidate and provide funds for the campaign provoked anger among some elements in the party hierarchy, including a few who were unequivocally supportive of gay rights.

For some members of the NDP inner circle, this kind of protest may have been perfectly understandable, but it spoke to an inability to understand the difficulties of governing. The point, of course, has broader application than the NDP and Ontario. A legislative environment almost always demands uncompromising partisan loyalty, apart from those groups with so much clout that they can claim to stand above party politics. But most of the social movements that emerged from the 1960s on were not built by activists with that kind of attachment to the party system; they were built, in fact, by generations of activists with substantial reason to be distrustful of party politics. In Canada in particular, gay activist circles had never attracted the sort of party loyalists who were being held up as models by NDP insiders. The long-standing record of parties bluntly opposing gay rights or running away from even moderate commitments to them had discredited people whose loyalty to party was uncompromising, however rational it may have been to favor one party over another. There was also, of course, no evidence that partisan loyalty within the NDP or any other party had produced better results than disloyalty.

The Aftermath of Defeat

It was Liberal leader Lyn McLeod whose image was most tarnished by the defeat of Bill 167. Some Liberal insiders publicly quit their jobs in frustration, including two staffers in McLeod's office. The issue of relationship recognition remained prominent throughout the autumn, as both Premier Rae and McLeod were challenged on their views. A provincial election was called for early June 1995. Although economic issues were the focus of attention, the question of same-sex benefits was raised repeatedly, and demonstrators wearing flip-flop sandals made repeated appearances at the Liberal leader's campaign stops. McLeod's change of heart on Bill 167 was cited regularly in the press as evidence of her indecisiveness and unreliability, and her response to a question on the issue during a televised all-candidates debate was widely seen as damaging.

The election had once been considered the Liberals' to lose. But on June 8, the Conservatives won handily with 45 percent of the vote, the Liberals trailing with 31 percent and the NDP with 21 percent. Among the NDP candidates who lost were all twelve who had voted against same-sex benefits. Marion Boyd and other active proponents of the legislation survived the Tory tide, and there was no evidence that support of gay rights lost votes in areas where the issue was raised.[84] The new government moved aggressively to undo some of the NDP's highest profile legislation, for example, on labor rights and employment equity, and to reduce the size and scope of the public sector. They did not explicitly invoke sexual orientation issues, but the attorney general did begin intervening in the courts to oppose challenges brought to existing statutes by gay and lesbian couples.[85]

Elsewhere in Canada the defeat of Bill 167 was treated as a major news story, and widely interpreted as a cautionary note for politicians prepared to take steps in the direction of law reform. As we saw in Chapter 4, the defeat of the legislation had major reprecussions in Ottawa, Justice Minister Allan Rock insisting that his approach to relationship issues was quite different from the Ontario government's. Premier Jacques Parizeau talked of the Quebec population as not yet being ready for major change.

Court challenges to existing law continued to be fought, some with help from the Foundation for Equal Families, a litigation spinoff from the Campaign group which had led the fight for legislation.[86] In 1995, the Ontario Court of Appeal agreed with four lesbian couples challenging the legal restriction on same-sex couples' adopting children. The Manitoba Court of Appeal ruled the same year that the provincial government had to extent benefits to same-sex couples in its employ. In 1996, shortly after the House of Commons added sexual orientation to the Canadian Human Rights Act, a federal human rights tribunal ordered the federal government and federally regulated companies to offer health benefits to same-sex couples. It also ordered the government to survey all existing statutes, regulations, and directives with a view to eliminating provisions that discriminated against same-sex couples.[87] Soon after, an Ontario human rights tribunal came to a similar conclusion in relation to municipal employees. In late 1996 the Ontario Court of Appeal ruled that same-sex couples had to be treated the same as heterosexual couples under family law.[88] One major setback on relationship recognition was the Supreme Court of Canada's 1995 decision in *Egan and Nesbit v. Canada*, which confirmed that the Charter of Rights offered protection against discrimination on the basis of sexual orientation, but decided by a narrow majority that some forms of discrimination against same-sex couples was justifiable.

Outside of courts and legislatures, the list of institutions recognizing same-sex relationships was growing rapidly. Some even worked around federal income tax restrictions so as to include pension benefits in their packages; in some instances they were required to do so by courts or tribunals, in others they were pressured to do so by lesbian and gay employees or by unions.[89] By late 1996 most banks, universities, telephone companies, and several city administrations had recognized same-sex relationships for benefit purposes. News headlines were more likely to single out companies refusing than those accepting such moves.

Some of the nervousness over the issue of relationship recognition in legislative arenas seemed to be subsiding. Public opinion polling indicated a rise in approval among Ontarians and other Canadians for legal recognition of same-sex relationships (see Table 5). The Parti Québécois government passed legislation in mid-1996 eliminating explicit prohibitions in the Quebec rights charter on extending benefits to same-sex couples. In the same year British Columbia's New Democratic government proclaimed changes to its Adoption Act allowing same-sex couples to adopt children. In mid-1997 that government moved further by proposing legislation that would recognize same-sex couples as equivalent to common law heterosexual couples with regard to child custody, child support, and access. The term "spouse," in other words, was to be redefined in the province's Family Relation Act (with the provincial government promising to examine other provincial laws to ensure that they complied with the expanded definition). By late July, the legislation was passed with only a modest flurry, despite last-minute efforts by religious leaders to mobilize opposition.[90]

The organizing and maneuvering for same-sex benefits confronted activists with challenges they had not anticipated. A political party most of them thought would deliver on pro-gay promises was more divided than they anticipated. Here, as in other Canadian jurisdictions and other countries, the normal rules of politics did not apply. The campaigners for relationship recognition were also faced with the powerful pressure to compromise that invariably permeates legislative politics—pressure applied by some of their strongest allies.

But in the wake of defeat, the kinds of fissures that opened up between activists in Britain after the age of consent vote were notable for their absence. There were a few voices of disagreement over strategy and future prospects by gay Liberals and Conservatives, but nothing on the scale or intensity of the partisan sniping that occurred between gay/lesbian activists in the three party camps in Britain. In any event, as in the rest of Canada, only a very small portion of sexual minority activism was directed at party politics, and most of the organized communities in the large cities retained a degree of skepticism about the likelihood of any party delivering on gay-related issues. Perhaps most important, gays and lesbians were emboldened by the campaign. In the weeks and months after Bill 167's defeat, individuals and groups confronted party leaders about their record on the Bill, angrily challenging those who had voted against it.

The defeat of Bill 167 certainly constituted a setback for the activist movement and a reminder than even parties formally committed to equality face rough rides in following through. But this defeat was of a different order than the defeat on an equal age of consent in Britain or on overturning the ban on lesbians and gays in the U.S. military (see Chapter 7). By 1994 in Ontario, the goal posts had been moved significantly from the days of demands for individual rights which had been at the center of the debate over adding sexual orientation to the provincial and federal human rights codes. The scale of the step being proposed at least temporarily legitimized a right-wing opposition that was being discredited at the federal level in Canada, as in Britain. The scope of the legislation also contributed to the slowness of response, even from a sympathetic government.

The election of a Conservative government in 1995 ensured that no further legislative advances could be expected in Ontario in the short term. Legal interventions by that government would also attempt to stem the tide of court judgments in favor of same-sex relationship recognition. But activists in all kinds of institutions were continuing to challenge employers through union grievance, litigation, and political mobilizing. Legislative moves in British Columbia demonstrated that "family" could be defined more inclusively in the face of religious right opposition. Regardless of the political timidity of some within the legislative arena and the heterosexist frameworks of others, the pressure for change was undiminished.

Svend Robinson at Toronto's lesbian and gay pride march (July 1995).
Photo: David Rayside

6

The Activist Roles of
Svend Robinson

> For Svend, any minority—he doesn't care—he's out there
>
> flying the flag. If he feels you're being mistreated, you've
>
> got him right there and he's working on your behalf.

NDP activist

In February 1988 Svend Robinson generated cross-country headlines by becoming Canada's first openly gay MP. He had already achieved public recognition rare for individual members of Parliament. After 1988 his reputation grew, not only as an outspoken advocate on sexual orientation issues but as Canada's "protester-in-chief" on other fronts as well. He was twice charged as a result of anti-logging protests on the West Coast, once investigated by the Royal Canadian Mounted Police for attending at an illegal doctor-assisted suicide, and asked by the Chinese government to end a visit to that country after he challenged its human rights record.

Robinson balances the sometimes conflicting roles that an openly gay legislator plays in a different way from most others, such as Britain's Chris Smith. The character and political positioning of his party have allowed him to remain a social movement activist. So have his political skills and his talent for making news.

Robinson is an unusually independent MP in a parliamentary system that creates little leeway for autonomous action, and in a party system that rewards loyalty more than dissent. He has used that independence to place sexual orientation issues and other equally contentious questions on the national legislative agenda. He has also energized lesbian and gay political activism when pressure on federal government institutions seemed likely to have an impact.

And yet there are tensions inherent in managing the roles of activist and legislator at the same time. Most social activists in Canada are wary of forming close ties with any single party, and impatient with the arcane norms and procedures associated with intraparty decision making and parliamentary debate. They generally attach more importance to the interests of their group or community than to advancing any single party's agenda. A parliamentary party, by contrast, is suspicious of what is seen as the social activist's single-mindedness and resistance to compromise. Such tensions have been evident for some time in Robinson's relationship with parliamentary colleagues in his own party, and became more obvious when he decided to run for the leadership of his party in 1995.

Robinson may be a maverick in some ways, but he has a strong partisan attachment to the New Democratic Party in an electoral system that leaves little room above the local level for the election of candidates unaffiliated to parties, and in which ridings are won or lost almost entirely because of swings in support for parties and their leaders. More than his counterparts in the U.S. Congress, Robinson operates as a party representative in his constituency election as well as in his parliamentary activity.

The NDP was formed in 1962 to replace and reconstitute the Cooperative Commonwealth Federation (CCF). The two parties were consistently on the social democratic left through the postwar period, and in elections regularly placed third behind the Liberals and Progressive Conservatives. The NDP's largest pockets of support were in western Canada, the only region in which it had ever held provincial government office until the surprise 1990 victory in Ontario. The party's support was weak in the Atlantic region, and almost nonexistent in Quebec. A number of the country's largest unions and federations have been formally linked to the party, although the NDP was never able to win the bulk of the working-class constituency it sought. The party's periods of relatively electoral success were always dependent on a range of constituencies, and its organizational culture was never as thoroughly dominated by industrial working-class norms as some of the leftist parties in Europe. A substantial number of its members have had links to other social movements. In fact, many have seen the NDP as part social movement, part political party, and in some ways have been quicker than their European counterparts (especially the British) to take up issues of gender, race, and sexual orientation.

NDP parliamentarians at the federal and provincial level have been significantly more supportive of gay/lesbian equality than legislators in almost all other parties, rivalled only by Quebec's social democratic sovereigntist Parti Québécois. As we saw in Chapter 5, there have been internal divisions and a failure of nerve in some of the provincial parties, but even in Ontario the level of support for gay equality in the provincial NDP caucus was very high in 1994, and in the other party caucuses very low. One late 1980s survey indicated that support for guaranteeing equal rights in jobs and housing was half again as high among NDP legislators than among Conservatives and Liberals (see Table 6).

In Canada, parties have never had the reach into civil society that their counterparts in Europe have. They are also not as permeable and localized as their American counterparts, and so are less attractive to social movement activists at the grassroots level, where links are often easiest to forge, not least because social

Table 6. Attitudes of partisan elites on sexual orientation issues, 1987

	Partisan elites				General population
	NDP	Liberal	Conserv.	PQ	
Guarantee equal rights in jobs and housing	91%	61%	56%	84%	63%
Custody rights for lesbian mothers	96	88	73	96	72
Equal rights for homosexual teachers	92	72	48	92	51

Source: Paul Sniderman et al., *The Clash of Rights: Liberty, Equality, and Legitimacy in Pluralist Democracy* (New Haven: Yale University Press), pp. 105–7.

Note: Questions asked were:

"For the most part, local ordinances that guarantee equal rights to homosexuals in such matters as jobs and housing (1) damage Canadian moral standards, or (2) uphold the Canadian idea of human rights for all." Percentages in first row refer to those choosing (2).

"Would you approve or disapprove of a law allowing lesbian mothers the right to be granted custody of the children in a divorce, if the court finds her otherwise capable of taking care of the children?"

"Do you approve or disapprove of allowing homosexuals to teach school in [the respondent's province]?"

movements tend to be highly localized phenomena. Canadian parties, including the New Democratic Party, do have constituency associations as their primary base, but these are generally inactive between elections. The ongoing networks that count are focused on provincial and national legislative arenas, and these are relatively inaccessible for most social movement groups and uninteresting for many movement activists. The NDP's third-rank placement at the federal level from the 1960s to the 1980s reduced the attractiveness of hitching social movement hopes to its star.

Svend Robinson identified himself with that wing of the NDP most eager to forge links with the new social movements of the 1960s and beyond, while retaining close ties to organized labor. In an era when a great many politicians on the left, particularly in North America, avoid the labels traditionally associated with the left, he describes himself repeatedly and unequivocally as a democratic socialist. His speeches also include recurrent reference to issues affecting women, people of color, and those with disabilities, as well as to the mistreatment of aboriginals and of Native rights in Canada.

The Burnaby Constituency

Svend Robinson's capacity to survive as an "out" politician, and to act as a different kind of MP even within his own caucus, is built to some extent on the solidity of support in his parliamentary constituency in greater Vancouver, as well as in the support for his positions in the extraparliamentary NDP in the area. He has built this support through his local roots, his work for individual constituents in Burnaby, and his defense of union causes. His coming out as gay may well have reinforced the strength of his local electoral base by securing his reputation as honest and principled. His high profile has allowed him to develop more of a "personal" vote than most Canadian MPs enjoy, and significantly more than is possible in the British system, where individual campaigns are even more dominated by parties and party leaders.

Robinson, like most of his counterparts in other national legislatures, was first elected by constituents who generally did not know that he was gay, in a district without an unusually large gay population. Experience in Canada and elsewhere suggests that winning first election as openly gay or lesbian is extremely difficult, and has so far not been accomplished at all on the federal level. Robinson's success in retaining electoral support in his constituency is an important indicator of the potential for gays and lesbians to enter into mainstream politics, but it is not the same test that would be provided by a candidate starting out as openly gay.

BUILDING LOCAL SUPPORT. Robinson was born in 1952 of parents clearly on the left, his mother a nurse with a passionate social conscience, his father an academic. They left the United States in part because of the war in Vietnam. As Robinson has said, "They didn't want to contribute taxes to an immoral war."[1] In 1965, Robinson's father got a teaching position at Simon Fraser University, a new institution known for the progressivism of much of its faculty, located in what was then a largely working-class district, just east of Vancouver. Burnaby is now a mixed area, having strong working-class roots in addition to a sizable middle-class spillover from Vancouver, with strong social democratic traditions. The Robinson family of five moved into a residential area of Burnaby called Capital Hill, once referred to as "Red Hill" for its feisty and generally progressive politics. But it is also an area characterized by traditional values on issues of family and sexuality. (Robinson himself, when pressed to come out publicly in 1981, claimed that his constituency was very conservative on such issues and was not ready.)[2]

A provincial election was held in 1966, and the fourteen-year-old accompanied his mother in campaigning for NDP candidate Eileen Dailly, joining the party at the same time. One local NDP activist recalls his being around the committee rooms a lot, "working and handing out literature and goodness knows what else at a fairly young age."[3] As with most elected politicians in Canada and almost all in Britain, Robinson's early political apprenticeship occurred inside a party more than in non-party social movement activism. He continued his intense interest in politics through his university years, enroling in law school at the University of British Columbia in part because of that interest. In 1973 he was a delegate to the party's federal convention and became a member of the party's provincial council. In 1974 he was elected president of the province's Young New Democrats, and for the next two years served on the provincial executive.

Robinson asserted his independence from the NDP hierarchy in his first foray into electoral politics. In the spring of 1977 he began to work for the NDP nomination in the Burnaby riding, a seat that had been safe for the NDP and the

CCF before it. Close to the October nomination meeting, Simon Fraser University president Pauline Jewett announced that she would enter the race. This was to be a lustrous candidacy, much favored by the party's leadership, but Robinson was not about to back down.

By then he had already gained the support of many party veterans. As one recalls, "That was the surprising part: he won over the older members in the party, and I think he did it out of his enthusiasm and high energy level and working hard."[4] His local roots certainly helped, as did the contrast between his years of NDP experience and the more recent conversion of Jewett from the Liberals. He also gained support in some local NDP circles by firmly identifying himself with the party's left. His campaign literature hammered at cutbacks in federal payments such as medicare, the second-class status of women in Canada, and the sellout of Canada's resources to multinational corporations. One flyer read: "Now more than ever Canada needs a democratic socialist government committed to redressing the economic and social injustices that threaten the very fibre of our nation."

He made no mention of gay issues in this literature, and few party members knew that he was gay. He had married a high school sweetheart in 1972, and although within a few years the need to "make sense of these feelings I have" led to divorce, there were few open signs of sexual difference.[5] Robinson had little if any involvement in the surge of gay liberationist activism that began in the spring of 1969, or in the small circle of social networks and commercial institutions that were surfacing in Vancouver.

In early October 1977 Robinson won the Burnaby nomination, and over the next two years he walked the length and breadth of the constituency knocking on doors. In 1979 he contested his first election and won, though by a narrow 1,400 votes. Aged twenty-seven and looking no more than twenty, he had become a member of Parliament.

Another election followed a year later, precipitated by the fall of a Conservative government with only a minority of MPs in the House of Commons. By this time there were rumors about Robinson's sexual orientation—enough that his Conservative rival was referrring to him as "a faggot" in door-to-door campaigning.[6] But he won again, increasing his majority. Before long he was gaining a reputation as outspoken on a number of issues, including gay and lesbian rights. In 1981 the *Vancouver Sun* claimed that scarcely a week went by without his name appearing in the news.[7]

By the 1984 election, his third, Robinson's homosexuality was widely known though not publicly declared. He was vocal in support of gay causes, and by then was attending events such as Vancouver's gay and lesbian pride march. During the election campaign itself, as one local NDPer recalls, "there was a lot of innuendo, a lot of snickering" from opponents.[8]

Robinson built constituency support in part by paying close attention to local needs. There is no one associated with the local NDP who does not speak of his indefatigable devotion to constituency work. His local office is located on the main commercial street of the riding, and a large storefront picture window enures that passers-by can see him at his desk for long hours on weekends and during parliamentary recesses. He makes the 1,800-mile flight from Ottawa to the constituency at least once every two weeks when the House is in session. He checks in with the Burnaby staff every day, and demands close and rapid attention to requests from constituents. Party activists are biased of course, but their praise echoes sentiments widespread among the voters. According to one: "He would have done whatever it would have taken to defend or support somebody in a difficult situation. . . . The stories people would bring in, they would just sort of go right to his heart, and he would try and find a way to help people out."[9] Another said: "He's probably the best member of Parliament I've ever seen—does a hell of a job. He comes [home] Saturdays, when he's been in Ottawa all week working like hell, and then Saturdays he goes banging on doors, talking to people."[10]

Robinson has always been careful to nurture his relationship with local party activists. One Burnaby party veteran speaks for many others in describing their MP's relationship to the local association: "He just inspires loyalty in people. And he would have such a grasp of the issues he was working on. . . . So even though people might want to be angry, he would always manage to bring peace to the troops. He was a consensus builder, by and large, and worked really hard with his riding—brought people around, brought them back into the fold. If he heard that someone was upset about something, he'd be right in there."[11]

COMING OUT AND ITS ELECTORAL AFTERMATH. In early 1988 another election was looming. Robinson knew that Conservatives in his riding would be attempting a more intensive anti-gay smear campaign than they had ever mounted against him. He was also more discontented than ever with the implicit dishonesty of not being out, and was under increased, though still gentle, pressure from lesbians and gays across Canada to come out. The experience of a few legislators in other countries—Chris Smith in Britain, Gerry Studds and Barney Frank in the United States—suggested that constituents would not likely be alienated.

In January 1988 he informed his riding executive and caucus colleagues in Ottawa of his intention to go public. Rumors circulated in Ottawa and Vancouver that he would be making an "announcement," the build-up made that much more dramatic by vandalism of his constituency office. On the evening of February 29, the news was formally released in the course of television interviews on both the English and French networks of the Canadian Broadcasting Corporation. Headlines appeared across the country, and the comments of columnists and politicians kept the issue in the news for well over a week. Negative comments came from two provincial premiers, British Columbia's Bill Vander Zalm and Saskatchewan's Grant Devine, both worrying about the message being sent to young people.[12]

In the election campaign of November 1988, the Conservatives tried to use the issue of homosexuality against Robinson from the beginning. At the party's nomination meeting, John Bitonti was introduced as the standard-bearer in these terms: "You're running against a publicly declared homosexual . . . is that really what you want as a role model for your children?"[13] During the campaign itself, the language of "family" was regularly evoked as a code to remind constituents of the difference between Bitonti and Robinson. Midway through the campaign, Conservative Prime Minister Mulroney snidely joked, "Can you imagine—Svend as minister of defence?" The Liberals were not as blatant, but their campaign too emphasized "the family," and suggested that Robinson's gayness would cost him votes. Fundamentalist Christians joined in the attack. A four-page flyer titled "Life Gazette" attacked Robinson in a front-page story headlined "SODOMITE INVASION PLANNED FOR 1990," featuring plans for the 1990 Gay Games. Concerned Citizens for the Family distributed a leaflet alerting constituents to the dangers posed by "the new deviant amorality of a highly vocal minority."[14]

In general, constituents were unmoved by these attempts to marshal anti-gay sentiment; few expressed outright homophobia of the "nudge-nudge-wink-wink 'I wouldn't vote for *him!*' "variety.[15] Robinson himself recalls very little anti-gay sentiment in encounters with voters. By then, they were seeing him in the media regularly, making news in other countries as well as in Ottawa. And of course he was still highly visible at his desk in his constituency office window.

Many supportive constituents adopted the view that being gay was about what one does in one's private life, and that it should not impinge on someone's political capacity. They may have remained uncomfortable about homosexuality, but were willing to separate that part of Robinson's life from the person they knew. A union supporter characterized the reactions of his fellow workers: "Most of our guys think it's none of their goddamn business: we don't give a shit what else he does; that's nobody's business."[16] One journalistic profile explained the support of unionized workers partly in terms of Robinson's stand on labor issues: "The only times the guys on the waterfront get a little spooked is when they spot Svend Robinson perched on the back of an open convertible with another man in yet another gay parade. But they avert their eyes and vote for him anyway. After all, when the federal government tries to pass back-to-work legislation during a strike, Robinson is the first person on his feet to protest in the House of Commons. When a union calls for safety equipment for its workers routinely injured on the job, Robinson prevails upon a federal minister by threatening to take a camera crew on site."[17]

The sheer range of issues on which he had been outspoken helped ensure that his gayness was placed in a larger context. An NDP activist commented: "Now and again a gay issue will come up and he represents it, but he's also representing women's issues, visible minorities, or whatever, so that he's consistently taking the minority position, defining, protecting, or enhancing. . . . So when he's taking that position, people don't think he's doing that out of his own interest, but because he's consistent and he's out there."[18] Many of his electors, as well as social movement activists in the Vancouver area, see Robinson's commitment as principled. According to this NDP member: "I've seen him do three or four events in an evening with groups that aren't really going to help you get elected anywhere. For instance, I saw Svend speak at a Palestinian hospital. . . . There weren't any media there, so he wasn't going to get anything outside of that. He's willing to take risks on behalf of his beliefs."[19] "In an age of political milque-toasts," an editorial in the *Vancouver Sun* once put it, "Robinson dares to say what he thinks and stands ready to take his lumps if all society disagrees."[20] Many voters admire that, particularly in an age of political cynicism. Robinson believes, as do a number of other openly gay and lesbian politicians, that even voters uncomfortable about homosexuality might have been drawn to his candidacy by his coming out: "At a time when there is enormous cynicism about politicians and political leadership, I think there is a certain value placed on honesty. I have had constituents say to me, 'Look, if you can be honest about this very fundamental, very personal matter, I expect you'd be honest with me about other things.' To that extent it is a benefit."[21]

Robinson's 1988 campaign did not underplay sexual orientation issues; the candidate himself made regular reference to them as well as to the smears directed at him. Of course he talked about the many other issues with which he had firmly identified himself, but as he says himself: "I have no doubt that for the vast majority of my constituents, the first lens through which I am viewed is as a gay man. They look at me and they know that about me. And if a woman in the shopping center in Burnaby had to explain to her visiting sister who this member of Parliament was, she would almost inevitably say that is openly gay. But then she would go on to say that he is a really hard worker, and he has represented this community for many years, and he is very high profile in this country—that sort of thing."[22]

THE 1993 ELECTION. Svend Robinson was returned to the House of Commons in 1988 with a margin of 7,700 votes over his closest rival, an increase from the 1984 margin of 6,200 votes. The message that victory conveyed about his constituency's readiness to accept Robinson's gayness was reinforced in the next election, perhaps even more forcefully in light of the NDP's losses elsewhere.

In 1993 the NDP was slumping in the polls, and the Liberals were far in the lead nationally. The right-wing Reform Party appeared to be gaining in western Canada in particular, pulling some supporters from the NDP though most from the Conservatives. The NDP had nineteen sitting MPs in British Columbia (forty-four across Canada), and there was widespread talk of losing most of them.

In the lead-up to the election, the Reform Party candidate in Burnaby-Kingsway made clear his opposition to "special interest groups"—a coded reference to Robinson's support for gays and lesbians. He also called for a reduction in taxes, in part to ensure that wives who wanted to stay home with children could do so. While not singling out sexual minorities, he left no doubt in constituents' minds that he upheld a set of "family values" utterly at odds with beliefs associated with Robinson.

Early in the campaign, the Liberals distributed Chinese-language literature that described Robinson as "a bad influence on your children." Candidate Kwangyul Peck apologized profusely, claiming an oversight, but Robinson knew that the smear had been intentional, and kept the matter before constituency audiences and the press. The NDP campaign office was soon deluged with requests for Robinson signs, many from disgruntled Liberals. Some were Chinese Canadians, insulted by the racist assumption that they would be more susceptible to an anti-gay campaign than other constituents. According to Robinson's campaign manager: "There was a real turning point with Mr. Peck's letter to the Chinese-Canadian community. We knew right then that his support dropped and people were coming to us, and we had a lot of momentum out of that. There were Liberals calling in, saying, 'We took down our sign, we want one of yours,' and the phone rang for days after that."[23]

There were also surprising examples of groups embracing sexual diversity. A longshoremen's union newsletter published just before the election included a message from the president criticizing the Reform Party. One of the risks posed by Reform gains, the message indicated, was to lesbian and gay rights. During the last candidates' debate, held at the Capital Hill Community Centre on October 20, two gay-related questions were posed after opening speeches in which the issue was not mentioned. Both were framed in antagonistic ways, and both were greeted by loud and widespread boos from the audience. When Robinson answered a question unequivocally supporting the right of gay couples to the same status as heterosexual couples, he was greeted with warm applause. By this time it was clearer than ever that anti-gay attacks were backfiring.

Robinson won the election. Although his majority slipped to 4,200, he was one of only two NDPers in the province, and nine nationwide, who survived the election. In this campaign, as in the previous one, Robinson benefited not only from incumbency but also from his extremely high profile as an MP—and this in a parliamentary system that rarely puts individual legislators in the spotlight unless they are cabinet ministers or party leaders. Any opposition critic trying to characterize him as a one-issue politician would confront a record indicating the contrary, and a record widely known to the local electorate.

For less well known candidates, the lack of a legislative track record may well provide anti-gay prejudice more play. In the 1993 election, openly lesbian Betty Baxter was running for the first time as the NDP candidate in Vancouver Centre, a constituency with a substantial concentration of gays and lesbians. In contrast to Robinson, who reported little evidence of homophobia in his own door-to-door campaigning, Baxter recounted a mixed experience: "I had people open the door, and a look of absolute terror would go across their face. They would close the door behind them and step slightly into the hall and say [in a whisper], "You're the lesbian candidate?" And I would go, "Yes I am." I didn't know whether I was about to get punched or what was going on, but usually these were reasonably civil meetings. . . . The negatives were sometimes a bit more bold. About six months before the campaign, there were people who would phone me at two and three in the morning, and say in rather obscene terms that no lesbian should ever be able to run for political office."[24]

Robinson's reelection after coming out was partly eased by his visibly fitting in to what might be perceived as the Canadian mainstream. He is gay, to be sure, and on the left, but he is also youthful, good-looking, well educated, white, and male. Whether constituents would acknowledge this or not, his cultural background enables them to see him as the hometown boy that he is, and his being a man made it easier for him to enter the electoral fray at a time when women politicians were still something of an oddity.

In this election, as in the previous one, Robinson's being openly gay boosted support among local gays and lesbians, even more so than in Chris Smith's campaign in London. As one envious colleague once observed, Robinson has access to a very large volunteer base, something that is difficult for most politicians to maintain, especially without the cachet of government office. Gays and lesbians also seem readier to volunteer energy and money to a political candidacy such as Robinson's, in contrast to campaigns of activists associated with other social movements. The 1988 campaign had a worker corps of more than a thousand volunteers, many of them lesbian and gay, and the 1993 campaign had close to that: by comparison, the Liberal and Reform campaigns had one hundred to two hundred each. The campaign was also able to raise donations from gays and lesbians across the country, using lists of names built up by Robinson's efforts to alert activists to federal developments.[25] Robinson's role in spotlighting sexual orientation issues had given his race a national significance, especially in English Canada.

THE 1997 ELECTION. The election called for early June 1997 posed a serious challenge for Robinson. His constituency was re-shaped as "Burnaby-Douglas," losing an area with relatively high NDP support and gaining one with low support. The NDP was also not predicted to fare well nationally. At the same time, the Liberal Party had decided to target the constituency, and secured the nomination of Mobine Jaffer, a national vice president of the party and a well-known immigration lawyer. Her candidacy was supported by constituency visits from the prime minister and the justice minister. Robinson's campaign was strengthened, as it had been in the past, by large numbers of lesbian and gay volunteers. He was also able to raise considerable money, the fundraising appeals intensified by the anticipation of a tight race.

The local campaign, like the national, made few references to sexual orientation issues. The Reform candidate was intent on characterizing Robinson as "extremist," but focused on the issues of logging and asssisted suicide rather than gay rights. The Liberal candidate indicated that she shared many of Robinson's views, though Deputy Minister Shelia Copps had made a point of Jaffer's "commitment to family values" at the nomination meeting in January.[26] Robinson himself believed that sexual orientation played no significant role in the campaign.[27]

Robinson won the election, increasing his percentage of the vote from 34 to 43, and his numerical margin from 4,200 to 7,200 votes. As in 1993, the Reform and Liberal candidates each ended up winning just over a quarter of the votes cast. (In the same election, ten other candidates had run successfully as openly gay or lesbian, all of them with the NDP, only one having had much of a chance of winning a sizable vote—Bill Siksay in Vancouver Centre.) The NDP nationally did better than expected, winning twenty-one seats and consequently returning to official party status in the House of Commons. Robinson thus returned to the House of Commons as a member of a party caucus with the resources and visibility attendant on official status restored.

The Legislative Role

As assertively as any openly gay or lesbian politician in any country, Svend Robinson has used his legislative platform to highlight gay and lesbian issues, to protest government inaction, and to stimulate activism. He has been able to do so because of the extent of support for gay rights inside the NDP's parliamentary caucus, and because of his skills as a legislator and a publicist. In addition he is a loner, willing to buck parliamentary traditions and partisan norms. That has cost him support among parliamentary colleagues who value party loyalty more than he does, but it gains him access to reporters hungry for the unpredictable.

Unlike Chris Smith in Britain, Robinson was a maverick from the beginning, and that affected his standing in a legislative chamber laden with norms of team play. His independence, intelligence, and hard work earned him considerable respect in Burnaby, among social movement constituencies, and among a number of MPs in other parties, but not always among his NDP colleagues.

THE PARLIAMENTARY CONTEXT. The Canadian parliamentary structure generally marginalizes dissenters. The conduct of elections at the constituency level may seem to entail a contest between local personalities, particularly in a period when traditional partisanship is distrusted, but in fact party and leader matter as much as ever. In the House of Commons, party discipline is high, even in comparison to other parliamentary systems, and a world away from the U.S. congressional system, which provides so much leeway for policy entrepreneurship. The individual backbencher will only rarely be given debating time that is visible in the media, and will almost always speak from a script largely shaped by party leaders.

The NDP has a more uninterrupted history of internal conflict over policy than the other parties, not because its members are more ideologically diverse than those of the Liberal and Conservative parties, but because party membership and policy debate have greater significance for the New Democrats, as they have for most social democratic or working-class parties.[28] The fact that the federal NDP has never come close to achieving government office has also reduced the power of leaders to dangle cabinet appointment as a means of luring dissident MPs into conformity. Audrey McLaughlin, the party's leader from 1989 to 1995, loosened the reins on MPs more than her predecessors. But the decline in party strength during her term no doubt buttressed the view among party pragmatists that her choice was ill advised. NDPers recognized, too, that reelection is largely a function of party factors, and that public opinion will look more favorably on a unified team than a fragmented one. Parliamentary politics is dominated by respect for the process of resolving political dispute through debate and compromise. The extraordinary effort and the political apprenticeship required to win elections is generally accompanied by commitment to the art of the possible.[29] The pressures to conform come not just from the partisan discipline that is so central to Canadian parliamentary politics, but also from the rituals associated with the legislative arena as a whole. Accounts of the experience of women in such arenas have revealed the assimilative power of parliamentary norms and their potential for excluding those who do not fit in. Such norms do not have the weight in Canadian parliamentary practice that they do in Britain, but in some respects the standing of the individual MP in Canada is even more hemmed in by the primacy of party. This is not a context in which a born activist and dissident easily fits.

HOUSE DEMOGRAPHICS AND THE MARGINALITY OF DIVERSITY. The fact that parliamentarians have a higher level of education than the average Canadian may encourage greater toleration of diversity, but other factors appear to work in the opposite direction. The higher-than-average age of politicians would suggest more traditional attitudes toward sex and sexuality. The demands on and expectations of elected politicians may, as one Parliament Hill insider argues, accentuate traditional norms among men especially: "There are any number of elected politicians—male—whose wives stay home and take care of the kids. . . . Now the reason for that is partly because when the man is doing this kind of a job, someone has got to be home. I think the profile of political families is more old-fashioned than the profile of regular folks out there. Part of that is scrutiny. It is like the family for the United Church minister. They are subjected to a certain kind of scrutiny, and basically people expect them to live the fantasy of how we wish to live. . . . Even if they are politically progressive on a lot of issues, their display of self, or how they behave, is more socially conservative than perhaps they would be in a different job."[30] Such norms are more powerful in Britain than in Canada, but the parliamentary culture in Canada is still one in which those who claim to rethink family roles and sexuality are construed to be on the fringe.

Gay and lesbian parliamentarians, like those from other marginalized groups, are likely to experience more pressure to fit in, and to have more difficulty satisfying other MPs that they do truly fit in. As one openly gay politician in Canada has put it, "You've got to be twice as good, you've got to work twice as hard, you've got to be careful."[31] Carving out and retaining a distinctive role can be difficult under such pressures, and gaining policy influence is even more challenging, especially within a parliamentary environment in which room for innovation is minimized.

The challenges facing gays and lesbians within legislative environments parallel those facing women, members of racial minorities, and other marginalized groups. Women MPs, who make up only one fifth of the House membership, still describe the House of Commons as a boys' club, though less ubiquitously so with an increase in their number and a reduced tendency for MPs to stay in Ottawa for long stretches and socialize together.[32] Women who have entered legislative politics with an affinity for feminist principles have routinely experienced the tensions between the conventional politics of parties, elections, and legislatures and the more autonomous idealism of social movement activism.[33] They often cite the difficulty of retaining a distinctive role, either in the policy agenda with which some women enter the legislative arena or in the procedural style they would prefer to use. One Liberal MP identifying herself as a feminist commented: "While your colleagues are supportive, there are two things that you have to know about. One is sharing power is never easy; no matter how nice and kind and supportive they are, every politician is looking for her or his own turf. The second is . . . you can't relax for an instant or you'll be back asking questions about tea parties. I don't like the term 'women's issues,' but there is a perception out there that these are soft issues—these are the issues that women can deal with."[34] In a period when governments are preoccupied with deficits and cutting social spending, policy objectives entailing public expenditure are marginalized on new grounds rather than on the basis of traditional attitudes toward women and gender. This means that a legislative arena such as Parliament Hill may be more genuinely welcoming toward women than before, but as resistant as ever to new policy initiatives that cost money.

Male dominance has an obvious impact on attitudes toward homosexuality, reinforcing anxiety about sexual diversity and a reluctance to discuss it. As one Parliament Hill Liberal comments: "Clearly for men masculinity is not a given; it has to be constantly proved. This means that they are uncomfortable with homosexuality, whereas most of the women I know, including those who are quite old-fashioned in all kinds of ways, are not nervous about this. There are men who are extremely concerned about aboriginal rights, people who are comfortable talking about women's issues to some degree, but I think on this issue still might be uncomfortable because suddenly it is about them in some way. You want to say to them, 'This is not about you.' They don't believe you."[35]

The demographics of Parliament also marginalize visible minorities. The 1993 and 1997 elections yielded parliaments with fewer than 5 percent of MPs from aboriginal or racial minority backgrounds. (Estimates in 1996 suggested that minorities make up 12 to 13 percent of Canada's population, and 30 to 35 percent of the population in metropolitan Toronto and Vancouver.) Those MPs have varied across party affiliation, ideology, cultural background, and interest in race or culture as an issue. To some extent this is reflective of the social, cultural, and linguistic diversity within minority groups. Those who enter legislative politics at the federal or provincial levels are often those who are most assimilated to European-Canadian cultural and political norms, in part because their electability in highly diverse constituencies may well depend on it. In fact, most MPs from racial minority backgrounds in recent Canadian history have not been unusually progressive on social policy issues, nor particularly outspoken even on issues of race. The marginality of race issues in the Canadian legislative agenda is reinforced by Canadians' belief that there is no serious problem of racial discrimination in their country, certainly in comparison to other countries, especially the United States (though many would acknowledge mistreatment of aboriginal peoples).

The demographics of legislative politics in Canada make it much more likely that homosexuality will present a white male face rather than a female or non-Caucasian face. That reinforces a tendency in the general public to associate homosexuality with white men, itself a product of many factors, including media portrayals of sexual minorities, the makeup of most gay/lesbian institutions, and the greater difficulty that women and people of color have in coming out publicly. The traditional white male dominance of gay political groups, though challenged with some success during the 1990s, has provided men with more elaborate networks for both campaigning and fund-raising. Women can compensate to some extent with connections to feminist networks, but the geographic dispersal of both feminist activists and the constituencies they seek to represent creates less of an electoral advantage.

Canada is typical of other countries in the extent to which successful openly gay candidacies are undertaken by white men. That is true of the two federal MPs, two provincial legislators, and the gay city councilors who have been elected in Vancouver, Edmonton, Ottawa, Kanata, Montreal, and Toronto. Lesbians have contested school board and local elections in Vancouver and the greater Toronto area, but largely unsuccessfully.

Once in the legislature, an openly gay man risks being thought of by his colleagues as a single-issue politician. A white lesbian, a black gay man, or a lesbian of color, would be even more commonly thought consumed by issues of identity politics. In a legislative environment in which economic issues are privileged, the compounding of marginal status makes being heard on non-equity issues very difficult. As with women, though, the principal difficulties facing lesbians as well as both gays and lesbians of color are those that they face in the world outside the legislature, and these make the very aspiration to political office unlikely.

ROBINSON AS ADVOCATE OF GAY/LESBIAN RIGHTS. The Canadian Parliament has not been an environment friendly to rational discussion of sexual diversity throughout most of Svend Robinson's tenure in it, even if it is not as unwelcoming as the British House. It is a legislature in which almost all successful bills are sponsored and passed only in a form approved by the governing party, and it has a composition that has often militated against the serious treatment of any form of diversity. Still, Robinson has had unusual success in raising sexual orientation issues, creating vehicles for lesbian and gay spokespeople to acquire legislative visibility, shining media spotlights on government-sponsored discrimination—and occasionally changing law.

In 1980 and 1981, parliamentary debates over the development of a constitutionally entrenched Charter of Rights contributed significantly to Robinson's interest in and profile on the rights of sexual minorities (see Chapter 4). He began pursuing the government on issues such as the armed forces' ban on lesbians and gays and the government's failure to amend the Canadian Human Rights Act to include sexual orientation. He tried to have discrimination on the basis of sexual orientation explicitly prohibited in the new Charter, as one of two NDPers on a committee dealing with the Constitution. Robinson himself counts that early work as among his most important: "I was instrumental in getting the gay and lesbian community before that committee. . . . I moved an amendment to include sexual orientation in the Charter of Rights, Section 15, which was defeated twenty-three to two. And when we lost the specific amendment, I worked a lot behind the scenes to get them to open up Section 15—to leave it open-ended. The original Section 15 just said there'd be no discrimination on grounds (a), (b), (c), (d), (e). . . . So when we lost the sexual orientation–specific inclusion, I worked with officials and other people . . . behind the scenes."[36]

In 1985 the Justice Committee of the House of Commons launched a subcommittee inquiry into equality rights just as Section 15 of the Charter of Rights was coming into force. Robinson convinced Justice Minister John Crosbie that discrimination on the basis of sexual orientation should be included in the committee's mandate, in part on the strength of the open-ended wording of Section 15 which Robinson himself had originally pressed for. He then spearheaded a mobilization of activist groups to present briefs on sexual orientation during the committee's planned cross-country hearings—the first large-scale mobilization of activist resources in the direction of federal policy making. The briefs and personal testimonies had a powerful influence on committee members, who in October recommended that federal and provincial human rights codes be amended to include sexual orientation. As Robinson himself recalls: "The hearings kicked off in Burnaby, at my suggestion, and one of the first witnesses was a group of lesbian mothers, and they brought pictures of their children—family pictures. The pictures were passed around the committee table, and it was just the most remarkable experience. [W]hat I was trying to do with the committee, was to drive home the human dimension of what we're talking about—and that's what made the difference, as it so often does."[37]

Following a commitment by Crosbie in 1986 to amend the Canadian Human Rights Act accordingly, and to address discrimination that persisted at the federal level, Robinson was virtually alone among MPs in dogged pursuit of a Conservative government retreating from that promise. Robinson also played a role in the launching of a court case that in 1992 forced the Canadian armed services to drop their ban on homosexuals. After having publicly pestered defense ministers since his early days in the House, he helped persuade a young former officer named Michelle Douglas to pursue her cause, and arranged for free legal representation by one of the country's best-known lawyers.[38]

Robinson was also visible in his advocacy on other gay-related issues in the House of Commons. He attacked the targeting of gay and lesbian bookstores by customs agents. He worked both in public and behind the scenes in effecting the recognition of gay and lesbian relationships in immigration decisions. He was active in the effort to equalize the age of consent for sexual activity, and to eliminate the criminal code section on "gross indecency" which had been used by police and the courts to regulate homosexual activity.

In the period following the 1993 election, even though his parliamentary voice was weakened by the NDP's losing official party status, Robinson played a role in drawing media attention to homophobic pronouncements by MPs. Early on in the new Parliament, he knew about the anti-gay views of Liberal MP Roseanne Skoke. When she rose to speak against her own government's hate crimes legislation, Robinson dashed over to the House to confront her, and then called a press conference to spotlight her anti-gay remarks. Robinson also knew about the extreme views of the Reform Party's Bob Ringma. When a Vancouver reporter called in the spring of 1996 seeking comment about the government's bill to add sexual orientation to the Canadian Human Rights Act, Robinson suggested that he contact Ringma for comment. The resulting quotes triggered a highly embarrassing sequence of events for Reform and its leader, Preston Manning.

Knowing that the Liberals were retreating from commitments made by Justice Minister Allan Rock on widening the range of relationships eligible for federally regulated benefits, Robinson filed a complaint with the Human Rights Commission on behalf of same-sex couples working on Parliament Hill. On this occasion, too, he garnered national press attention and focused it on the issue of gay and lesbian equality.

Robinson's impact has extended beyond sexual orientation issues, though these are the issues with which he is most often identified. More than is the case with Chris Smith or any of the openly gay members of Congress, Robinson's sexuality is never far from view. When asked if legislative colleagues might have adjusted to his homosexuality by ignoring it, Robinson responded: "I don't think there are many people who bracket my gayness. I try to make sure that people are aware of that, and if they forget, I remind them of it—that's an important part of who I am and . . . why I'm doing this—so that they don't forget, so that . . . when they deal with me, it's not invisible. My gayness is just as visible as Jesse Jackson's blackness or Audrey McLaughlin's womanhood.[39]

PARLIAMENTARY LEVERAGE. Robinson gained leverage, even from the benches of a third party, in part on the basis of hard work, intelligence, legal skills, and knowledge of parliamentary procedure. Politicians of various partisan stripes describe him as the most intelligent MP in the House of Commons. According to a Liberal aide, MPs say: " 'He is a mean son of a bitch, but by God I respect him.' They know he is fiercely intelligent; they know he is everywhere. He will, in a given day, go from a press conference on one issue to two committees on two other issues, speak in the House on overflights [low-altitude military test flights], and still be in his office at nine o'clock that night. The energy and the capacity for work and excellence is well known and respected."[40] In a 1994 interview, one Bloc Québécois MP reported on attitudes toward Robinson in the House overall and within his own party, including those of its then-leader,

Lucien Bouchard: "Mr. Bouchard respects him a lot; so do Bloc colleagues. Before Svend Robinson said he was gay, what the veterans here say is that he had the reputation of being the best MP in Parliament. In the Bloc's second caucus meeting [after the 1993 election] . . . Mr. Bouchard said that Svend Robinson had been the best member of Parliament in the House for a long time—a very good MP for his constituents and a very good MP in the Chamber. He is very, very, very respected."[41] The respect owed to Robinson from Bloc MPs is enhanced by the extent of his understanding of Quebec nationalism and his fluency in French. The openly gay Bloc MP Real Ménard appears to have treated the more experienced Robinson as a confidant and source of advice, thereby bolstering his reputation among most of Ménard's colleagues.

Robinson's coming out did not affect his standing at all adversely. The fact of his being gay was of course already widely known among MPs and reporters, and they were unsurprised by one more illustration of his outspokenness. One parliamentary aide argues that the House has an ethos that would work against judgmentalism against fellow MPs—an ethos similar to that in the British House, and to some extent the U.S. Congress: "In some ways Parliament is incredibly representative of all of our human foibles—not in class, race, and sex terms, but other things. And look at parliamentary delegations—these people eat together, drink together, sleep together. They have traveled around the world together. So they know who is gay and who is not, who is an [alcoholic] and who is not . . . they know all of these things about each other. The fact that Svend chose to come out—'Well, that's Svend.' It doesn't surprise them at all. It doesn't particularly scare them either. Svend is one of them."[42]

Respect among his colleagues for Robinson's decision to come out was probably amplified by the homophobic jibes regularly directed at him before that. He and others recall his being harassed by right-wing MPs. As one Liberal says, "He'd stand up [in the House] and then five or six guys on the other side would start giving it to him."[43] Among the more notable occasions was in October 1985, when a Conservative MP shouted across the aisle of the House, "Why aren't you at Rock Hudson's funeral?" Another backbencher, this one from Quebec, once referred to New Democrats as the "PD Party," playing on the French insult for pederast. In early January 1987, after Robinson suggested to the prime minister that he was hiding behind the skirts of the RCMP, Mulroney shot back, "From my skirt to yours."[44]

The Canadian media have not needed to be pulled in Robinson's direction. They chase him. They saw him as newsworthy even before he came out, and after that their interest in him intensified. Major profiles appeared in mainstream magazines as well as in the alternative press. In 1994 *Maclean's Magazine* devoted a four-page cover story to him, without any prominent news hook apart from the gay-related legislation being considered by the Liberal government. As Robinson's staffer Bill Siksay said: "Svend does things that are newsworthy and worthy of attention, that people are interested in, and then he gets the coverage.

He rarely does a press release, whereas other [MPs] are constantly sending them around trying to get somebody to bite on a story. I've seen other MPs phone the media and try to bribe a story to them. I've never seen Svend do that."[45]

Robinson's capacity to speak out aggressively on gay and lesbian rights has benefited from support in his own party. In contrast to Britain's Labour Party and the U.S. Democratic Party, the federal NDP has had little vocal opposition to such rights since the 1980s. As a partisan Robinson himself is hardly neutral, but he makes a plausible point about the extent of his party's backing: "I have received nothing but support at every instance in which I have raised this issue, whether it is in the House or on the election platform. I'm talking about the federal party. In terms of our national platform—as, for example, whether or not equality for gays and lesbians will be part of our platform—absolutely. We have already agreed that we will have a specific platform document for gays and lesbians, setting out our priorities."[46] The support of Audrey McLaughlin, leader from 1989 to 1995, was particularly important. Robinson says: "Audrey has been a solid and consistent supporter. I remember when I went to ask a question about two women in the Yukon who were seeking recognition of their relationship— not the slightest hesitation at all. It's just been a given, and anyone that has not agreed has certainly never voiced that disagreement in caucus."[47] One of Robinson's former colleagues agreed that inside the federal NDP caucus, gay-positive positions are enough of "a given" not to require debate.[48]

Robinson acknowledges that support for pro-gay positions in provincial New Democratic parties is sometimes less solid. He notes one important difference: "By and large, to be elected as a federal New Democrat to Parliament, you have to have a fairly good grounding in history, in the movement. You don't get a nomination in a winnable seat at the last minute. You have to have commitment, some history with the party."[49] On occasion he has had to provide a nudge, reminding some of the party's spokespeople of gay-related issues within their portfolios. He acknowledges, too, that on some occasions the caucus has needed more than just a little goading. In describing his attempts in the late 1980s to obtain an equal age of consent for homosexual activity, he reports taking "tremendous flak" from his colleagues, particularly as a campaign on the issue organized by the religious right began to surface.[50]

There are party insiders who would argue that there is more hesitation around sexual orientation issues than Robinson would acknowledge. As one such insider in Ottawa put it in 1992: "In my opinion the level of understanding is fairly limited. Sometimes it seems to me that it is very convenient—I'm not sure if this is just for NDP members, but very convenient for the public to say Trudeau's line about privacy: 'The state has no business in the bedrooms of the nation.' For many people it is a convenient means whereby they can avoid dealing with the issue or exploring it further or taking a particular stand on it—saying, 'Of course I'm in favor of it . . . it is a very private matter.' "[51] But in fact little of that discomfort is made public, for most MPs bow before the party's official stand on these issues. And because Robinson is present, and persistent, he is able to push his caucus colleagues to the limits of their zone of comfort, and sometimes beyond. Potential dissenters also realize that they cannot keep the issue of sexual diversity bottled up.

Support from most NDP colleagues seemed heartfelt when Robinson told his colleagues in February 1988 that he planned on coming out. Party leader Ed Broadbent was reported to be supportive, and Robinson's announcement to a caucus meeting was met with applause and hugs from colleagues. Some of the respect with which the decision was greeted came from a recognition of the political risk he was taking, particularly in coming out in the year of a general election.

Robinson realizes that one of the sources of his impact on the standing of gay/lesbian issues in the legislative arena is simply his being there: "For many of my colleagues, they have been forced to deal with a real person and not an abstract concept, in the heart of the institution, in the heart of Parliament itself. And let's face it, not just for parliamentarians, but for Canadians generally, a lot of them really don't think they know anyone who is gay or lesbian. . . . But more importantly, I guess my colleagues know that, and any time this issue comes up, they know that they are going to have to deal with me as a gay man."[52]

One Liberal agreed on the significance of having an openly gay MP within a party's caucus, and lamented the absence of one within her own caucus in 1993, just as it was facing hotly debated legal reforms:

It is going to be a difficult fight, and one of the difficulties is that there are no announced gay members of our caucus. There are gay members of my caucus, but not prepared to come out. I think it is a very personal decision, but until we have a real advocate within the caucus, it is going to be more difficult, because it is a lack of real knowledge, and just lack of association in a sense, that creates fear and bigotry. You lack the punch. When I stand up and speak about women's issues, I know whereof I speak, in spite of the fact that I am a privileged, educated woman. I'm still a woman, and I suffer the discrimination of being a woman, and therefore there is a certain resonance that is there. The same thing for someone who is going to advocate on behalf of gays. When Svend stands up, the same resonance is there with him, and that is what you need.[53]

One Liberal MP who thought that "people shouldn't talk about their sexuality" nonetheless acknowledged that he had learned something from Robinson's coming out: "I never understood gay pride until watching Svend do what he did, and the result of it. What gay pride means is that you are allowed to be just as proud of being gay as other people are of what they are. In that sense I think he performed quite a service for public consciousness, and that maybe justifies making a private issue public. [His being out] made it impossible for the kinds of slurs that were being made against his gayness to go unanswered."[54]

As an opposition MP, Robinson has had only a few opportunities to make a concrete difference in legislation. His work in 1980–81 and then again in 1985 helped bring sexual orientation to the fore in debates over the Charter of Rights, at a time when little lesbian and gay activist energy was focused on the issue at the federal level. From that time until 1993, Robinson was a member of the Commons Justice Committee and respected among other veterans. On a number of occasions he was able to get changes made to bills by his willingness to work across party lines, and by his impressive grasp of the legal and political issues at stake. He was also a constant thorn in the side of justice ministers forever promising to add sexual orientation to the Canadian Human Rights Act. In that sense he played a long-term role in the lobbying process culminating in the 1996 addition of those two words to that act.

CRITICISM. Robinson does of course have detractors among MPs in other parties as well as his own. He is a partisan NDPer in a highly partisan environment, though the animus directed at the NDP by other parties before the 1993 election was not as great as that directed by Liberals and Conservatives at each other. Some opposition MPs see him as "badgering" in style, unwilling to give quarter when he disagrees, though most recognize that as a normal part of legislative politics.

More striking is the resentment occasionally evident among NDP parliamentarians past and present. Recurrent references to him as a "one-man band," a "media hound," and most of all "not a team player" surface regularly in quotes from MPs in published profiles. As early as the spring of 1983, a story on Robinson included the remark: "It's . . . no secret that Robinson has a well-deserved reputation for being abrasive, arrogant and too quick to speak for the party without first consulting his caucus."[55] Such sentiments arise partly from Robinson's record of breaking with caucus ranks in parliamentary votes. In October 1980, his first year in the House, he dissented from his party to vote against a Liberal government motion cutting off debate on the constitutional reform package, in part because of weaknesses in the equality provisions of the proposed Charter of Rights. In 1982 he did so again to vote against the constitutional package itself, in protest against the inclusion of an opt-out clause in the Charter.[56] Robinson had also been leading the movement against incorporating property rights into the new Constitution, breaking from a majority of his own caucus. More recently he supported the Liberal government's 1995 gun control legislation, opposing the position taken by the rest of the NDP caucus.

More significant in the development of resentment among colleagues are Robinson's statements and actions outside the House. In 1983 he articulated a version of NDP policy on the decriminalization of prostitution which sufficiently annoyed leader Ed Broadbent that he demoted Robinson for a time from his position as justice critic. In 1985 he enraged many in the federal and provincial party by joining a group of Haida Natives in blocking a road to prevent logging in the Queen Charlotte Islands off the coast of British Columbia. This was, according to some NDPers, potentially damaging to sensitive negotiations on the issue, and in any event infringed on the turf of the NDP's replacement justice critic and MP for the area.

In 1993 he joined a protest against logging on Clayoquot Sound, and once again was perceived as stepping on the turf of an NDP colleague. He was also seen as criticizing a "compromise" struck by provincial government, at the time in NDP hands. At the NDP's 1994 provincial convention, environmentalists and logging unions managed to cobble together a compromise on the issue, but Robinson was not satisfied and proposed an amendment. It was defeated, but many observers saw the move as an attempt to put his individual mark on an issue regardless of the consequences.

Supporters argue that Robinson is often outspoken in favor of official party policy. They will add that he has a sense of popular sentiment on issues, and of the importance of timing, which moves him to act more decisively than some of his legislative colleagues. A longtime Vancouver activist remarks: "He doesn't have great support in the party. People resent him. [They will say,] "Well, we have to discuss this in caucus; we have to go to the environmental community; then we have to check with trade unions.' The process will kill an issue. And Svend just says, 'No, I believe in so-and-so, and I'm going up with the Natives.' He doesn't ask the local weenie MP up there if it's okay. The local MP is hiding. . . . Part of the problem is that he's going to show them up, challenge them, make them look lazy."[57] A parliamentary aide discussing his legislative skills says: "In terms of public opinion, in terms of media savvy and so on, he is just smarter than [his colleagues] are, and I think in the end it bugged the hell out of them. Svend would be freelancing on deals around committee stuff and constitution stuff. If Svend saw an opportunity he would seize it even if it infringed on someone else's area."[58]

It is precisely the characteristics that some of Robinson's colleagues find irksome that have allowed him to help raise gay and lesbian issues inside Parliament, and in Canada as a whole. His outspokenness and independence, his eye for the dramatic, attract the media, and that attention in turn is indispensable for influence. These same traits and skills have built him a standing in the gay and lesbian movement that is unmatched by most legislators representing marginalized groups in Canada, and by most gay and lesbian politicians elsewhere.

The Sexual Minority Constituency

Svend Robinson is unusual among national legislators in the extent to which he has developed links to activist networks across the country. In effect, he has built a second constituency outside of Burnaby, made up of gays, lesbians, bisexuals, and the transgendered. He inhabits a legislative arena similar to that in which Britain's Chris Smith works, but one with fewer strict norms about representation—norms that in any event he would be more inclined than Smith to ignore. Robinson insists on the importance of gays' and lesbians' pressing their own MPs on sexual orientation issues, but he has been more than ready to stimulate that activism, to act as a clearinghouse for it, and to respond to the individual requests of gays and lesbians seeking help with discrimination.

As a young man, Robinson was not rooted in a gay/lesbian community or in its activist offshoots in nearly the same way that he was rooted in the NDP. By the time he might have been comfortable developing links to local community organizing, he was already a member of Parliament. For a while, some observers detected in him a slight unease around the sexual outrageousness and confrontationalism that has been a feature of radical gay politics from its earliest years.[59]

But, as with many other issues, Robinson was quick to learn, and was soon unstinting in his support. Not long after he entered the House, his willingness to speak out on gay and lesbian rights was garnering him a cross-Canada constituency of admirers. His contributions to the 1981–82 parliamentary debates on the proposed Charter of Rights were widely covered in the gay press, and his aggressive questioning of government ministers and officials was widely admired. In the spring of 1983 a full-page profile in *The Body Politic*, at the time Canada's most influential gay magazine, paid Robinson this tribute: "The consistency and tenacity of his attacks on government policy affecting lesbians and gay men have been unique among federal politicians and, as a result of his work, gay issues have come up more often in the current session of Parliament than in all sessions since 1867 combined."[60]

His commitment was not restricted to issues before the House of Commons, and because of that too he gained standing. In a late February 1981 talk at the University of British Columbia, just days after a massive police raid on Toronto gay bathhouses and years before he was fully out as gay himself, he condemned "bully-boy" police tactics, advocated the elimination of the criminal code section dealing with gross indecency and bawdy houses, and called for an equal age of consent. Soon after, he spoke at a rally organized by the Coalition for Gay Rights in Ontario, over the loud protests of an Ontario NDP leadership furiously backtracking on gay rights commitments in the lead-up to a provincial election.

Once he came out, Robinson became even more closely identified with the movement. In June 1988 he led Toronto's gay and lesbian pride march, and was met with a hero's welcome from the thousands who lined the streets. At the 1990 Gay Games in Vancouver, the huge crowd at the opening ceremonies welcomed him in similar fashion. One activist commented about his standing in the gay community: "Regardless of their political stripe, if they're gay and lesbian, [people give him] a tremendous amount of respect. In terms of how he's approached gay and lesbian issues, he's been able to appeal to the broadest group of people. . . . He remains in touch with his constituents; he remains active in the gay community; he's visible all the time; he doesn't take [their support] for granted."[61] Others describe him as a hero or "an icon."[62]

His outspokenness on women's issues has gained him standing among lesbians as well as gay men—and as a different kind of politician. (His first private member's bill as a new MP was a pro-choice amendment to the criminal code provisions on abortion.) A Vancouver activist recalled being "at a function where there were a lot of politicians, and he was so clear-minded and present and politically approachable . . . people's attitudes toward him really went beyond the fact that he was gay or NDP. He had a kind of stature, a presence."[63]

Robinson's standing among young people, especially young activists, is increased by his bluntness of tone, directness of approach, and genuine belief in extraparliamentary street activism, which are unusual among politicians, gay or straight. His willingness to engage in civil disobedience on issues such as forest preservation, even to go to jail if necessary, marks him unmistakably as a different kind of politician. Despite his personal unease with some of the tactics employed by groups such as Act Up and Queer Nation, he is disinclined to criticize: "They're a very important part of this community. Invading church services—I wouldn't personally participate in that. But if your partner is on his deathbed with AIDS and the head of a church tells you that you are responsible for your own death and your own suffering and your own torment, and that your relationship is profoundly immoral—you know you're being treated as a subhuman and someone you love is being treated as a subhuman, and you're going to rage against that. So I'm not going to condemn those people, certainly not. We need more rage in the face of this epidemic, not less."[64]

Robinson's linkage to community networks is sustained mostly by the visibility of his position, but he increases it by making himself available to the lesbian/gay media, as do his counterparts elsewhere. He has granted extensive interviews to radio and newspaper outlets in Vancouver and other major Canadian cities. His unusual facility in French has allowed for the creation of a profile even in Montreal, rare for an English Canadian politician outside the government, and unheard of for an NDPer.

Starting in early 1991 Robinson also launched "Ottawa Update," a newsletter mailed irregularly to gays and lesbians across Canada. It provides information about federal government action (or inaction) on sexual orientation issues, reports on what Robinson has been doing on that front, urgings to write to federal or provincial politicians on issues of the day, and model letters or petitions. Some mailings have essentially constituted lobbying kits, especially in the years before an effective lobbying organization existed in Ottawa.

His links to lesbian and gay networks across the country, and particularly in British Columbia, owe much to Robinson's staff in Ottawa and the Burnaby constituency office. Gays and lesbians have always been prominent among his staff members, and the central figures in both offices have developed rich connections themselves to activist groups—most notably David Pepper (in the Ottawa office from 1985 to 1993) and Bill Siksay (in the Burnaby office before himself running for Parliament in 1997).

An important feature of Robinson's connections to activist networks is that they are direct, not mediated or rivaled by a lesbian and gay caucus in his own party (Chris Smith's role in the British Labour Party being an obvious contrast). There are such caucuses in the NDP, but they are most visible in the provincial parties in Ontario and British Columbia, not at the federal level. Activists do come together for federal conventions but maintain almost nothing in the way of ongoing organization. To some extent the federal party's reasonably good record on developing pro-gay policy reduces the kind of adversarial climate that stimulates internal activism. Robinson's visible role also contributes to the perception that the work needed to keep the party on track is being done.

The low profile of NDP gay/lesbian activism makes it easier for Robinson to achieve standing in the larger community that is not seen as completely framed by partisanship. The federal party's absence of government experience also helps the NDP in general, and Robinson in particular, to retain an unsullied image compared to others who have experienced the travails and pressures of office. The NDP has some parallels to Britain's Liberal Democrats in that regard, although its clearer positioning on the social democratic left has given it somewhat stronger standing in progressive social movements. Partisan attachment is less widespread in Canadian movements than in either Britain or the United States, and therefore has less impact on Robinson's standing in the broader gay/lesbian community and activist movement.

Nevertheless, there are moments when Robinson's partisanship has been at times surprising and nettlesome to gay/lesbian audiences. In March 1981, for example, at a rally called in the wake of Toronto's bathhouse raids, and in the midst of provincial NDP retreat over gay rights, he endorsed the party's candidate in the central Toronto riding of St. George–St. David, provoking boos from the audience. (The only other time that close observers can recall Robinson being booed by a gay audience was during a forum in which he defended a 1992 constitutional accord agreed upon by federal and provincial governments and officially supported by all three parties then represented in the House of Commons.[65]) Vancouver activists are more likely to be aware of his NDP partisanship, which is more evident closer to his home turf than in other areas of Canada.

Some activists also have mixed feelings about Robinson's approach to "process," which runs in parallel with the views of some of his parliamentary caucus colleagues. He is confident in his own political instincts and strategic savvy, sometimes impatient, and occasionally insistent on getting his way. As one Vancouver activist has suggested, "He can be a very powerful person at times: I've heard it said many times that if he doesn't get his way, then you're in trouble."[66] In some respects though, Robinson's confidence and decisiveness, and the directions in which his political instincts take him, earn him respect among lesbians and gays in the street, while at the same time they rankle activists and party heavyweights. Rightly or wrongly, most lesbians, gays, and bisexuals are preoccupied with the substance of what a public figure says, and with the very fact that a public figure speaks honestly and forthrightly about sexual orientation at all, using "we" and "us" rather than "they" and "them."

Robinson's Candidacy for the NDP Leadership

Svend Robinson ran for the leadership of the NDP in 1995, and came close to winning. The race required winning support from thousands of the party's rank and file across the country, and from hundreds of delegates at a convention scheduled for November of that year. His backing within the extraparliamentary NDP was strongest among those who maintained a vision of the party's future as linked to the rainbow coalition of social movements with which he had become so closely identified. None was more obviously identified with his candidacy than the gay and lesbian movement.

But for Robinson to develop the standing in the extraparliamentary party required to win the leadership constituted quite a different challenge than the performance of his legislative role or the winning of lesbian and gay respect. As he himself acknowledged, it called for some skills and instincts that were different from those that had helped him to that point. In his run for the leadership, Robinson benefited greatly from the energies of young social movement activists. But his link to their causes, and to sexual orientation issues in particular, also amplified fears of electoral reaction even in a party so apparently committed to sexual diversity.

SOCIAL ACTIVISM VERSUS PARTY-CENTERED PRAGMATISM. Neither Robinson nor his supporters shied away from acknowledging his distinctiveness. At the campaign launch in late April 1995, the candidate himself responded to press queries about his activist profile by saying, "The NDP and the public want a radical, clear, democratic socialist voice."[67] The style of the campaign was captured in a number of community meetings like this one described by a Robinson organizer. "Svend often started by doing a meeting in the area, where they would invite progressive people who had left the party, a cross-section of people who were in the party, people from social movements. They had one in St. John's, Newfoundland, where a large bunch of them were from Youths for Social Justice, a bunch of labor folks, and folks from social movements in St. John's, people from the gay and lesbian community. They looked around the room at one point and they realized that they had all heard of each other but never sat around the same room together to talk about stuff."[68]

The leadership race was soon joined by two other candidates thought to have a chance of winning. Lorne Nystrom was a federal MP from Saskatchewan, the province with the largest party membership. Preoccupied with fiscal issues and sounding like a candidate awaiting government office, he represented a "pragmatic" alternative to Robinson. Nova Scotia provincial legislator Alexa McDonough also joined the race, persuaded to run by some of the NDP's best-known leaders, including a number of the Ontario "establishment" associated with the now-defeated Bob Rae government.

By the end of the summer, Robinson seemed to be in the lead, increasing media attention and provoking concern in some party circles. Robinson's campaign had been the first to organize fully, and his supporters were, as one campaigner described them, "true believers," giving the overall campaign an energy level that the others lacked. It also gave a fund-raising base, making the $250,000 ceiling entirely achievable even for a candidate perceived to be outside the party mainstream.

His campaign team had worked hard on getting delegates selected from riding associations, and favorable results were also showing up in the regional primaries that were incorporated into the leadership selection process.[69] He had won the very small Quebec primary as the only candidate fluent in French and the only one with any noticeable recognition value in the province. He then won the British Columbia primary with 51 percent of the vote.

Robinson picked up labor support through the summer, crucial in challenging perceptions of him as unelectable among ordinary Canadians and unsupported by unionized workers, widely stereotyped as anti-gay. He was particularly successful in those unions that had carved out progressive profiles on social policy issues, for example, in the public sector and among auto workers.[70] He had been received warmly at Canadian Auto Workers' meetings in Windsor and Port Elgin, confronting the issue of his gayness head-on. In early September he won the support of 83 percent of the union's primary voters (the CAW was entitled to eighty-five delegates at the convention). He was less successful among steelworkers, the bulk of whose delegates went to McDonough, and the United Food and Commercial Workers, whose delegates supported Nystrom. And of course the very powerful British Columbia–based woodworkers union was going to be supporting almost anyone but Robinson, since his protests against West Coast logging of primordial forest were seen as an attack on their jobs.

On the morning of October 12, the first day of the convention, Robinson received surprising support from the editorial page of the establishment *Globe and Mail*. Lamenting what it saw as the poor quality of the candidate field in general, and dismissing the other two contenders' "amiable mediocrity," it went on: "Then there is Mr. Robinson. In 16 years in Parliament, he has sometimes shown bad judgement, but he has also had courage in declaring his sexuality and breaking with his party on issues of personal conscience. He has worked hard as justice critic and demonstrated sophistication, independence from conventional wisdom and a flair for publicity. He is unlikely to win widespread acceptance for the NDP, but this is about survival, not power."[71]

Lorne Nystrom entered the convention strengthened by his recent win of the Prairie provinces' regional primary, particularly influential because of the large number of party members in that part of the country. That built his overall tally to 47 percent of NDP members voting in the regional primaries, as compared to Robinson's 32 percent. He had also emerged somewhat ahead of his rivals in the labor union primaries. In addition, Nystrom had endorsements from more than half of the party's sitting MPs (Robinson, significantly, was supported by no sitting MPs).

Alexa McDonough had trailed badly in all of the primaries except in the Atlantic region, winning a total of only 18 percent of the regional votes and only 29 percent of the labor vote. But by convention time there was increasing talk of her as a compromise candidate who would avoid the polarizing effect of a victory by either the left-wing Robinson or the centrist Nystrom. In the opening night debate between candidates, she raised the "team player" critique that the Nystrom forces had so often invoked against Robinson. More significant, though, was her claim to represent the best chance of reuniting the party.

SOCIAL MOVEMENT ACTIVISM MEETS CONVENTION POLITICS. Once the convention got under way in the shadow of Parliament Hill in Ottawa, there was talk of strategic voting among some of Nystrom's supporters to prevent a Robinson victory. All of the campaigns knew that Robinson was leading in delegate count, with Nystrom second. The Robinson campaign was still the most visible of the three, and infused with the youthful energy that had brought it to first place among committed delegates. A number of Robinson's campaigners, obviously at their first convention, were striking in their contrast to the seasoned partisans making up the bulk of delegates. They could be rubbing shoulders with presidents of provincial federations or other veteran heavyweights and not know it. In the words of one organizer, the Robinson campaign had got to where it was through "raw unharnessed energy."[72] The McDonough campaign's power brokers posed a stark contrast. There were members of the Lewis family, prominent for two generations in the party; several former ministers in Ontario's NDP government; the ex-premier of Ontario; the party leader from Manitoba.

The candidates' speeches on Friday evening may have narrowed the difference in delegate totals for the second- and third-ranked candidates, and in some way reinforced the contrast between the candidates positions and styles. Robinson's probably was the best speech, but as one observer remarked, "It didn't extend what the other camps wanted extended, which was a suggestion that he was going to moderate his rhetoric on things like 'corporate thugs.' "[73] Nystrom performed least effectively, and risked dropping from the second spot.

McDonough's key supporters, feeling that they were within one hundred delegates of second place, increased pressure on pockets of Nystrom delegates to shift on the first ballot, arguing that McDonough had a better chance of beating Robinson. Some supporters were targeting Quebec delegates, others the West Coast woodworkers and the United Food and Commercial Workers. By this time some strategists in Nystrom's camp were coming to terms with his weakening position and the very strong likelihood that Robinson would defeat their candidate on a final ballot. Without Nystrom's knowledge, they were considering sacrificing him to prevent an ultimate Robinson victory. This could be effected either by delegates' shifting to McDonough in the first ballot, or simply not showing up for the vote. By Saturday morning Robinson was still acknowledged to have a first-ballot lead, and while Nystrom was widely recognized to be retaining second place, McDonough was not very far behind.

Balloting began at around 2:30 P.M.. What no one noticed until much later was that about one hundred delegates failed to vote in this first round. Half an hour after the balloting was finished, the counting was done. The crowd quickly quieted as the results were announced in English and French: Nystrom, 514; McDonough, 566; Robinson, 655. Here is Robinson's own account of the moments that followed:

The fact that Alexa was second was certainly a surprise. My strength in the first ballot—655—was a bit lower than I had thought. A lot lower. I thought we'd be at around 700 on the first ballot. But Alexa being second by 566, and Lorne third at 514— the minute I heard those numbers I knew it was all over. . . . I was surrounded by the cameras when the first ballot result was announced. Boy, talk about feeling like I was kicked in the gut. I had to maintain a brave front. I had to kind of get up and wave and you know, "on to victory" kind of thing, right? Things weren't supposed to happen that way. Alexa wasn't supposed to be second.

So I'm thinking, well now, the only possible hope is if some key supporters of Lorne come to me, right? I knew that was virtually unthinkable, but I thought, well, I've gotta wait. . . . So I waited at the table for a couple of minutes, and they weren't exactly flocking. And then . . . I talked to one of my key handlers and just said, "Look, I'm not feeling comfortable just sitting here; I'm gonna go for a little walk." So I walked down the center of the convention right into Lorne's section—just thinking, "I'm just going to see what kind of support there is." It was the longest walk of my life, the loneliest walk of my life. It wasn't there, and in the meantime people were just tripping over themselves—you know, the UFCW leaders and all sorts of other key Saskatchewan people—tripping over themselves to go to Alexa. And of course I walked by Alexa's area as I made that walk.

So I got back to the table and I knew then: "Look, it was just absolutely not there." And at that point one of our key campaign people came to see me, suggested a huddle. So a few campaign people—about half a dozen of us—looked at the options very quickly. We didn't have a lot of time, and by the time I'd done this walk and everything else there was very little time left before they called for the second ballot. So this tremendous pressure—"Look, we gotta make a decision." And we looked at the results, and I just said without any hesitation whatsoever, "I'm going to go to Alexa." And that was it.

So I walked back onto the convention floor through the side door, past my own table. I didn't even have time to consult with my own riding executive on this or anybody else. And just the worst moment of the whole convention occurred just as I passed the table of my own delegation. Half a dozen delegates from Manitoba came up to me, including the three aboriginal MLAs [members of the Legislative Assembly]. These were people who had been committed to Lorne, and they had been under tremendous pressure from Gary Doerr, who had nominated Alexa, and everybody else, to move to Alexa. Well, they'd gotten together, and despite threats in terms of funding, they were going to support me. And so here they came over and shook my hand as I was coming back: "Svend, we just want you to know we're with you." And I just had to look at [them] and I said, "I'm sorry." You know, after having gone through this agony and resisting this incredibly intense pressure, I said, "No, it's all over." So that was just—

oh, it was painful. I had tears in my eyes, and just felt sick. And of course they were angry, and they were stunned, and didn't understand. So I just continued my walk.''[74]

In the midst of this, delegates held up and bobbed the signs of their favored candidate. As reporter Glenn Wheeler commented: ''The Svend team of workers—many of them urban and gay, wearing the rainbow colours—set off on a masochistic mission handing out flyers to Nystrom supporters in plaid shirts and peaked caps. Each looked down on the other, and they were barely on speaking terms. 'Come to Svend—Let's Build Together,' the yellow pieces of paper said. But many of the Nystrom crowd—most of them from Saskatchewan . . . just threw them on the floor or wouldn't take them at all. 'No goddamned way,' one guy responded to the overture''[75]

As Robinson was walking toward Alexa McDonough, an announcement came across to confused delegates that he wanted to speak. He had just told McDonough in person that he was there to support her, interrupting her in startled mid-sentence as she awaited second ballot. Nystrom and his key organizers had been told just seconds before, and their blank stupefaction revealed their incomprehension of a radical break from the unspoken convention rule book. Then, to a stunned convention floor, just a few minutes before 4:00 P.M., Robinson moved that the vote be made unanimous, followed by seconding from an apparently still startled Lorne Nystrom.

As the McDonough delegates went predictably wild, a number of Robinson's showed their anger. A few threw their signs to the ground or against the wall, their candidate's concession not yet comprehensible, the arithmetic not yet having sunk in. Young delegates and observers especially were baffled, some honestly believing that there was a chance of winning on a second ballot, many others yearning for more consultation even in the face of the merciless balloting deadline, wishing for a process that smelled less of party maneuvering. They had seen Robinson as a completely different kind of politician, one who did not compromise or concede defeat. As one observer remarked of the young supporters in particular: ''They often don't have the years of experience and friendship, and it's a bit of a crusade for them, the true believers. Also, they see the other delegates more as sometimes the enemy, while we've been through umpteen conventions together. So I think for the young people this is a very, very hard decision.''[76] Even for some of the more experienced delegates, the Robinson move was too strong a break from the usual convention practice of fighting to the finish. The campaign veterans knew that what he had done made sense, but they were obviously shaken by the suddenness of the defeat. One seasoned campaign worker, reflecting on those moments as Robinson crossed the convention floor, described a sense of complete shock.[77]

A while later, in a wide hallway, Robinson's supporters gathered together with the media and curious onlookers. Their candidate appeared. The cameras rolled as he waded through the crowd to a podium. Like many other unsuccessful candidates in other times and settings, and against all emotional odds, he seemed unflinchingly composed. But instantly, before he could speak, a couple of his own supporters yelled, "You betrayed us!" and "Why did you set us up?" The rest of the crowd became hushed, not least because they knew that the cameras and microphones were on, but the dissenters persisted.

Robinson tried to speak to the whole assembly, arguing that his move was the right one and that McDonough was a worthy choice. But in the end he was speaking to a social movement audience in a partisan voice—an audience in which many had believed he was categorically different from the other candidates, and whose allegiances were not transferable. He delivered a speech steeped in the tradition of concession speeches rallying support to the new leader. Robinson describes the moment:

> It was like an out-of-body experience, because I couldn't speak from the heart to those people. That was the worst of it. . . . It was a terrible, terrible experience, because here were my bedrock supporters, the people that had just sweated to get me elected; that had worked long hours; that had put so much into this campaign; that had joined the party and in some cases had rejoined the party after years of alienation and disgust but had taken this move and were now just bewildered and in some cases angered and feeling betrayal. . . . I had to do this thing about "Let's rally 'round Alexa," and you know, that was important to do—important to say. But fundamentally I wasn't speaking from my heart to them; I was speaking to the media. . . . The message that had to come out publicly was this message of solidarity and unity. . . . So that was terribly frustrating.[78]

It was a moment that embodied the tension between political party and social movement, never far below the surface of NDP politics. The concession was not "old politics", for that would have required fighting to the last ballot; but it was a "new politics" that was still firmly lodged within a party framework. As another organizer put it: "I feel bad for these young people for whom Svend is kind of their leader. I think some of them don't recognize Svend's commitment to the party. These movement people were brought into this party and brought in a lot of their expectations of how they do business, not recognizing that they were coming into an institution that was steeped in all sorts of [tradition]".[79]

Robinson ended with an announcement of a party that evening, closing with an Emma Goldman quotation that several in the crowd knew well enough to join in repeating: "If I can't dance, I don't want to be part of your revolution!" Then out into the rainy evening they went, many gathering again later to party into the night.

THE GAY FACTOR. Was Robinson's homosexuality a factor in his defeat? He himself seems ambivalent, but tends to the view that other factors were more significant:

Yes it had a role. Did it play a significant and decisive role? No, I don't think it did. But there's no question that that was one of the arguments that was used on that intense Friday night by people to stop me. That was the strategy to push Lorne's people to Alexa: "We've got to stop Svend." Well, why do we have to stop Svend? Well, if you're from a small community in northern Ontario or from rural Saskatchewan or North Bay, Ontario—it's true those arguments were used, and to some effect. There's no question about that. . . . But at the same time, just as homophobia was there working against me, there was sexism working against Alexa. There were certainly delegates from Lorne's camp who were saying, "Look, we've done the woman thing, we can't elect another woman." I don't think it was a decisive factor, but it certainly was there.[80]

Other issues were almost certainly more important than the gay issue in denying Robinson the leadership. The race turned on the sort of left-right split that has often divided the party, and Robinson's campaign was clear about its uncompromisingly leftward thrust. The accusations of being an unpredictable loner would have had more weight with caucus members and other party leaders than with the rank and file, but they would have had some impact on moderates, particularly in British Columbia. In fact, the gay issue played an indirect role by reinforcing the beliefs of many party members that Robinson would take their party down a road they did not want to travel, and one that would make it less electable. His gayness highlighted his interest in moving the NDP further than it had ever been in the direction of a rainbow coalition of causes. For some delegates, many of them not at all homophobic, electability was a serious question, and it raised doubts about Robinson's appeal in areas such as northern Ontario and rural Saskatchewan. Many of the rural delegates from the Prairies needed no reminding that an openly gay leader would be a hard sell back home. One ex-legislator from the area spoke of the possibility of running for Parliament, but said that it would not be worth his time if Robinson were the party leader. He liked him personally, but he was too far left and too "alternative" for his constituents.[81] Some delegates also worried that Canadians in general would perceive him as more interested in issues of diversity than in economic issues, at a time when unemployment and social program cuts were uppermost in their minds.

Anti-gay sentiment, therefore, did play a role. One campaign worker on the floor of the convention said later: "I've canvassed for gay candidates, and I'm gay, and I know when it's there. It's that sixth sense. When I was doing that table-to-table stuff [after the first ballot]—'Thanks but no thanks,' and what they're really saying is, 'No fags here.' I got it from a few people."[82] The reaction to Robinson's sexuality was probably strongest in the Prairies, particularly in rural areas, where debates over sexual difference have made fewest inroads. It was also strong among delegates from the West, who were most wedded to a pragmatic concern with winning election or obtaining government office, and therefore preoccupied by "electability."

One journalist covering the convention believed that the issue hung in the air more heavily than most NDPers were prepared to admit:

No one at the NDP leadership convention this week at the Ottawa Congress Centre would ever say he or she is bothered by Robinson's sexuality. But almost everyone there seems to know people back home who would refuse to vote for a gay candidate. The message is that New Democrats are open-minded but the population at large is not. . . .

McDonough's campaigners were out in force Thursday, as the convention opened, twisting delegates' arms by saying Robinson could never get MPs elected in two of the NDP's traditional power bases—northern Ontario and the rural Prairies. . . . Nystrom supporters have long complained that Robinson is captive to, and bankrolled by, "special interest groups." Naturally, the first "special interest group" that comes to mind is an army of rich homosexuals storming Parliament Hill. . . .

The NDP's level of comfort with Robinson's homosexuality was clearly displayed Wednesday evening at a roast held to honour Nancy Riche, the party's retiring president. Someone told a joke about McLaughlin being lonely for male company and having a special panic button in her apartment to summon handsome, Mountie bodyguards. Later in the evening, when Robinson addressed the 400 people, he put a gay slant on the joke, by saying Riche tried to induce him to run as leader by mentioning that special button capable of summoning handsome Mounties.

Robinson's joke bombed. . . . A joke about McLaughlin thinking naughty thoughts about a Mountie was funny. A joke about Robinson thinking naughty thoughts about a Mountie was, to the assembly, embarrassing.[83]

The gay issue may not have been decisive in Robinson's defeat, but it probably weighed more heavily than most New Democrats, including Robinson himself, believe. That is so in part because it worked in combination with other factors to intensify party members' perceptions of him as being on the fringe of the party rather than at its center, and as an electoral liability rather than a asset. Without that additional signifier, he probably would have wooed more delegates with his principled stands on a wide range of other issues, and his obvious skill in garnering publicity.

Svend Robinson balances the role of legislator and activist with considerable skill and energy. The same can be said of Britain's Chris Smith and U.S. Congressmen Barney Frank, but Robinson is quicker than the others to break with legislative and partisan norms. He is an effective parliamentarian, to be sure, having made the most of his position as an opposition MP. He has been one of the few members of the House of Commons to speak assertively about gay/lesbian equality. He has served as a constant reminder of issues unaddressed, promises not kept. His knowledge of law and legislative process has given his interventions legitimacy, on occasion enough to influence public policy.

Robinson's maverick side has alienated parliamentary colleagues, especially within his own caucus, and certainly became an issue in his run for the party leadership. But that did not weaken the support from the caucus on the sexual orientation causes for which he has fought. The very fact that the NDP was in opposition, in minor party position, increased the latitude for a politician to act from an uncompromising position as something of a loner.

The status he has maintained in the gay/lesbian movement, and among gays and lesbians normally inactive in politics, is partly a function of his being a maverick, but also because of his position within a social democratic party that has gained widespread respect even among Canadians who do not vote for it. At the federal level, it has been seen by many as a party of social conscience, able to take principled stands. Many gays and lesbians vote for other parties but still acknowledge that the NDP is more strongly supportive of their rights. The very fact that the federal party has been perpetually in opposition means that its legislative accomplishments cannot be used as benchmarks against which to measure official policies and campaign promises.

The respect given to Robinson within the movement also derives from the relatively low levels of strategic and partisan fractionation within the movement. The very fact that the federal party most likely to be supportive of progressive social movement causes is also a minor party makes unequivocal allegiance to it uncommon. In any event, party activism and social movement activism in Canada have always been relatively separate. Within the gay/lesbian movement, and a number of others, wariness of partisan engagement has not been as intense as it was during the early 1970s in other countries. But neither has it declined. That allows a figure such as Robinson, who has so obviously served as a tribune for the gay and lesbian movement, a standing outside the party he represents.

But there are inevitable tensions inherent in appealing to constituencies as distinct as a political party, a legislative arena, an activist movement, and Burnaby. Those tensions become visible only occasionally, but they surfaced in dramatic fashion in the final stages of Robinson's run for the NDP leadership. The shouts of betrayal spoke to the disappointment of a social movement campaign team confronting the hard realities of partisan politics. Some of the young campaigners in particular were surprised by the extent to which Robinson was, after all, a team player and a party loyalist. He always had been, not least because in a legislative setting MPs almost always have to be. But many had seen him as someone who could escape all of its bounds.

In the aftermath of that leadership campaign, Svend Robinson is still widely admired for his contribution to gay and lesbian visibility, and respected both for his legislative work and the energy he devotes to mobilizing activist attention to federal politics. He recognizes, too, that he acts as a role model for gays and lesbians and their friends, associates, and families: "There have been countless times that I have been either written to or spoken to on the phone, or spoken to personally by people who have told me about how my coming out and continued advocacy really affected them. It made a difference to them in their own personal lives, whether it be young gay men, lesbians, bisexuals, parents. Families have talked to me about their sons and daughters, about how it has helped them come to terms with that. So that is the most fundamental thing I think it did."[84]

UNITED STATES

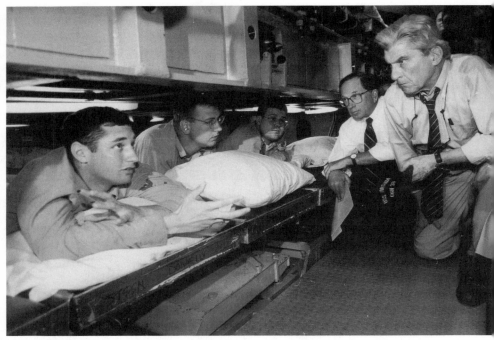

Senators Sam Nunn and John Warner during Armed Services Committee tour of nuclear submarine (May 1993). Photo: AP/Wide World Photos/Steve Helber Slug

Announcement of policy on gays and lesbians in the U.S. military, by President Clinton, with Les Aspin (Defense Secretary) and General Colin Powell (Chair of the Joint Chiefs of Staff) (July 1993). Photo: Archive Photos/Reuters/Ira Schwarz

7

The Military Ban and the Perils
of Congressional Politics

When soldiers began talking about showers and foxholes,

whatever mainstream legitimacy we had assumed, whatever

straight acceptance we thought we had earned, vanished

without a trace.

Urvashi Vaid, activist and writer, 1996

In late 1992 and the opening weeks of 1993, as Bill Clinton's inauguration approached, only a few of the exuberant gay and lesbian activists in Washington took seriously the early sniper fire from the Pentagon, Capitol Hill, and the religious right. The new president had made lifting the ban on gays in the military a signal of his commitment to gay and lesbian rights, and the transition frenzy after the November election lent even more credence to hopes that the issue would be dealt with immediately. Particularly in the area of military policy, which so clearly lay within the prerogative of the executive, doubters seemed out of touch with the energetic policy networks that were forging the new optimism.

By midsummer 1993, like the memories of glittering inaugural balls, hopes that gays and lesbians would become fully a part of the new governing coalition had faded. The proposal to lift the ban was mortally wounded by March and dead by July, with further indignities inflicted on its corpse by congressional and military opponents in the weeks to follow. In what turned out to be the president's first major political battle, the initiative was seized by opponents in the Senate, supported by virtual insurrection in the military's highest command and emboldened by a Christian right focusing on gay issues more than ever before.

The failure to repeal the ban revealed the daunting challenges facing lesbian/gay organizations doing battle in Washington. These groups are the largest and in some ways the most sophisticated gay lobbying organizations in the world. But they had insufficient resources to wage a pitched battle at the national level, and no experience in dealing with an ostensibly supportive administration. Once the issue of gays and lesbians in the military was visibly placed on the national policy agenda, the initiative was seized by opponents on Capitol Hill and in the Pentagon, relegating social movement activists to the sidelines.

Legislative clout has always been greater in the United States than in any other liberal democracy of Western Europe or North America, and has increased with the decline of presidential authority since the 1970s. The military, its influence diminished with the decline of cold war tensions, still demonstrated a willingness to defy executive wishes which had few parallels in other democratic countries. The strength and political influence of extreme anti-gay forces is also great. Right-wing and religiously based networks play important roles inside and outside the party systems elsewhere, but the strength of the religious right in the United States, its growing political sophistication, and its fixation on gay rights issues have no equal.

In addition, heterosexual norms remain deeply embedded in American law. As in most other countries, the legal framework governing "family" relationships assumes heterosexuality. But the United States also contains jurisdictions that are among the few left in the industrialized world that criminalize homosexual activity between adults. The result is a web of legal marginalization in which weaker strands are supported by other, stronger ones. Despite a greater emphasis on individual rights than in just about any other Western country, progress on sexual minority rights is not concomitantly easier.

The Congressional Context

The founders of the American republic were nervous about majorities. Designing a deliberately complex system, they conceived of a division of powers not only to prevent executive tyranny, but also to slow the pace of change and prevent popular "excess." In contrast to the British system, the fragmentation of authority across different levels of government and within each of them creates the potential for innovation in one site as it precludes advance in others. But for all the access the system allows, effecting significant change is a different matter.[1]

Federalism creates a degree of state-level autonomy that simply does not exist in Britain. State governments have little of the jurisdictional breadth of Canadian provinces, or the same ability to levy taxes, but they do have more fully autonomous legal systems, including distinct criminal law systems, areas that are important for groups seeking equity. Municipal governments also have greater autonomy in the United States, creating both opportunities and barriers, depending on the local political climate.

None of this fragmentation diminshes Washington's importance. The federal government is a much more substantial player in domestic politics than is its

Canadian counterpart, and the nation's superpower status provides the national capital with an almost unparalleled aura of power and drama. But the enormous authority centered in Washington is also highly fragmented within it. The constitutional separation of powers may well contribute to the ceremonial mystique surrounding the presidency, but also weakens it in relation to the other branches. Even within the executive branch, the proliferation of administrative agencies creates room for policy entrepreneurship within them that is rare in other political systems. On the one hand, this porous system opens up opportunities for access at the national level, while on the other it imposes barriers for groups seeking large-scale change.

Congress has enormous independence and power, with unusual equality between its two chambers. Even in spheres of executive authority, such as foreign and military affairs, the Constitution explicitly allows room for legislative policy making—an option that is increasingly used by congressional entrepreneurs. In such a setting, determined legislators can block executive initiative even if they cannot always advance their own agendas.

Even during the middle of the twentieth century, when presidential ascendancy was strongest, Congress was more independently powerful than any other liberal democratic legislature. The most "imperial" of presidencies could wield nothing like the legislative power of a parliamentary cabinet, and the reassertion of congressional authority from the 1970s on further sharpened the contrast with other democracies. The first Reagan term stopped and may even have partially reversed the trend, but the growing assertiveness of congressional Democrats in the late 1980s restored it.

The separation of powers and the relative lack of party discipline plant the seeds for the fragmentation of authority within the legislature itself. Partisan cohesion did increase in the mid-1980s, and remained higher in the 1990s than in the decades before. But even within the more polarized congressional environment, centrifugal forces are very powerful, and of a categorically different order from those in other systems. The rebelliousness of British Conservatives over European issues during John Major's prime ministership, and of a few Canadian Liberals over issues such as gay rights, are remarkable for their exceptionalism.

Elections are still party affairs, and every four years the presidential race towers over all others. Even then, individual congressional campaigns are more independent of the national contest than in other systems. The sheer number of elections being conducted at the same time—for the presidency, the House and Senate, state and local offices, and in most areas for a number of ballot initiatives—imposes obligations on candidates for legislative office to rise above the fray with individualized campaigns. The demand for resources, especially money, and the electoral finance rules of state and federal governments weaken candidates' dependence on their parties, and increase their need to use local and regional political networks. The central parties' (and leaders') leverage over constituency-level nominations in Canada and Britain has no parallel at the national level in the United States.[2]

The proliferation of subcommittees in both the House and Senate and the partial devolution of power to them create many opportunities for policy entrepreneurship among politicians with eyes ever fixed on the next election. Independence is tempered in the House, where the large size and the volume of business require more rules and therefore concentrate more leverage in the hands of party leaders. The Senate was once regulated by strong norms of collegiality and deference, but that is less true now. The relative absence of rules accords its members considerable leeway for establishing independent policy profiles. To some extent, this has allowed some liberal senators to champion progressive causes, drawing attention to the upper house as a source of potential innovation. And yet the composition of the Senate, and the power its most senior members retain over committees, gives it a more conservative cast than the House.

Party unity, especially among Democrats, is highly contingent on circumstances and on the particular issues at stake. Congressional party leaders simply do not have the disciplinary powers they might once have had, and cannot easily oblige recalcitrant members to vote in ways that conflict with personal beliefs or home district pressure, especially in the Senate. They have particular difficulty in whipping votes in favor of "controversial" positions, with legislators more concerned than ever about what issues might be used against them in the next election.[3] The growing anti-incumbency mood in the United States electorate, the intensification of negative campaigning, and the dramatically augmented capacities of lobby groups to mobilize grassroots efforts either across the country or within particularly targeted districts, all increase the individual legislator's aversion to risk. This results not simply in taking up issues in ways that accord with perceived constituency opinion, but in avoiding issues that may provoke organized local interests or induce powerful opponents to contest the next election.

Elected politicians everywhere, to be sure, are seldom noteworthy for their courage on gay-related issues. In Canada and Britain such matters are often among the rare questions that are left to free votes, leaving legislators more exposed (see Chapters 2, 4, and 5). Nevertheless, politicians in such systems are less vulnerable to individual attack and negative campaigning. In such systems, too, the electoral fate and career ascendance of a member of the legislature can be shaped substantially by currying favor with party leaders (even highly unpopular ones) in a way that has virtually no parallel in the contemporary American system. Party leaders therefore have more unspoken leverage over legislative compatriots, even in free votes.

The United States system multiplies the sites from which both progressive and regressive initiatives can emerge. Even though many favorable openings are thereby provided, the work required to ensure success is monumental and the outcomes unpredictable. Initiatives to block or undermine progress are given just as many opportunities, and often emerge without warning. Proponents of progressive change thus confront a task more daunting than that faced by activists in virtually any other political system.

The Presidential Commitment

From the 1960s on, the discharge of lesbians and gays from the military had been included in activist chronicles of injustices perpetrated by the state.[4] In the 1970s some members of the armed forces fought their discharges in court, occasionally with success. In 1975 Sergeant Leonard Matlovich achieved a national profile in both the mainstream and gay press when he declared his homosexuality and condemned the ban. The number of legal challenges increased over the following decade, and in 1988 produced the first ruling by an appeals court that the ban was unconstitutional.

The military issue, though, was not a priority in most activist agendas. For most of the 1980s, the spreading AIDS epidemic and the surge of anti-gay measures at state and local levels preoccupied the movement. But the sheer number of discharges, averaging 1,800 per year in the first half of the 1980s and 1,000 per year from 1988 to 1991, maintained the issue's visibility. It was also a matter that affected women as well as men; in fact, women were more likely than men to be discharged because of homosexuality.[5]

At the end of the 1980s, cracks began appearing in Washington policy networks. In 1989 two reports commissioned by the Pentagon (and made public by an openly gay member of Congress, Gerry Studds) admitted that homosexuals were at least as qualified for service as heterosexuals. In 1991 another Pentagon study, also publicized by Studds, questioned the traditional security risk rationale for the ban. By this time more activist attention was being focused on the issue. In 1988 the National Gay and Lesbian Task Force established the Military Freedom Project to organize against the ban in the wake of an anti-lesbian witch hunt at the Parris Island base. The project was operated almost entirely by lesbians, for the first few years with a relatively low profile. By 1991, two national gay/lesbian groups were attaching more importance to the matter—the Task Force and the Human Rights Campaign Fund (HRCF)—though not on the same level as AIDS, anti-gay violence, and broader anti-discrimination measures.

The race for the United States presidency moved the issue closer to the forefront. In September 1991, Arkansas governor and presidential aspirant Bill Clinton started seeking out gay support to bolster his candidacy. He lacked the track record of his rival, former Massachusetts senator Paul Tsongas, and needed to establish his commitment. On October 14, in Los Angeles, Clinton met a small group of West Coast lesbians and gays linked to a political fund-raising group, Access Now for Gay and Lesbian Equality (ANGLE). Tsongas had already met the group, brandishing a campaign booklet containing pledges on the military as well as AIDS and civil rights legislation. Clinton announced that an executive order lifting the ban would be one of his administration's first acts, adding that there was no room for compromise on the subject.[6] The commitment was repeated more publicly at the end of that month, when the candidate was asked about the issue at Harvard University. Clinton made other promises, too: to issue an executive order barring discrimination on the basis of sexual orientation in federal agencies, to support a gay civil rights bill, to intensify federal programs to combat AIDS, and to appoint openly lesbian and gay people to the administration. But the military issue became the most talked about of Clinton's gay-related commitments.

The promise provoked little response from the campaign of President George Bush and his vice president, Dan Quayle. In late August the Republican national convention was riddled with anti-gay vitriol, and in the ensuing election campaign the party sought to distance itself from the perception of right-wing extremism. Republicans had been ready to profile the military ban issue, but polls on the impact of the convention persuaded them otherwise.[7] This reinforced the belief in the Clinton's campaign and among lesbian/gay activists that the ban's removal would be straightforward.

After the early November election, Clinton's victory fueled high hopes for early action as the mainstream press focused increasing attention on the military issue. At his first news conference, held in Little Rock on November 12, Clinton confirmed his intention. Repeating the pledge a few days later in Washington, he cited the estimated $500 million that the military had spent to oust some seventeen thousand lesbians and gays over the previous decade.[8] The presence of a few openly gay members of the president-elect's transition team, and that team's work on options for a civil rights bill, maintained high expectations.

Even as late as the day of the inauguration, January 20, the signals were virtually unequivocal. Encountering Congressman Studds in the Capitol building after his swearing in, Clinton offered assurances that he would deliver on his campaign promise to end the military ban.[9] Although word was getting out that his approach would be first to instruct the defense secretary to stop enforcing the ban, and to draft an executive order only within the next six months, there were no intimations of retreat.

Senatorial Leverage

The initiative stayed only momentarily in the hands of the victorious president. Even before the January inauguration, congressional opponents moved into position and soon appeared able to engineer a checkmate—even before lesbian and gay activists could mount a significant counteroffensive. Democrat Sam Nunn, chair of the Senate Armed Services Committee and central player opposing a lifting of the ban, was emboldened by the Republicans' willingness to engage in aggressive anti-gay politics, by the readiness of the religious right and veterans' groups to mobilize grass-roots opposition, and by the active collusion of anti-gay elements in the military hierarchy.

Congress has formal authority to establish rules for the military and to authorize expenditures. The Uniform Code of Military Justice is an embodiment of congressional prerogative, and it contains a sodomy provision prohibiting anal and oral sex. The need for congressional approval to change the UCMJ meant that even a forthright executive order lifting the ban would leave intact a comprehensive prohibition on gay and lesbian sexual contact.

Although the House of Representatives has always had the power to exercise leverage over military issues because of its powerful appropriations role, the Senate has also established influence over the broader range of issues related to foreign affairs and defense. There, opponents could benefit from the looser party discipline and laxer procedural rules.[10] They could also benefit from the considerable media exposure given to senators, not nearly as available to the more numerous members of the House.

EXECUTIVE VULNERABILITY. Clinton's authority was more challengeable than most presidents' because of the particular circumstances of his election. It was easy enough for other politicians and observers to conclude that Clinton's victory had been a negative vote—a rejection of President Bush. Also, the entry of a substantial third-party candidacy had robbed the victor of the symbolic power of winning more than half of the vote, a source of legitimacy more important in a system with a separate executive election than in parliamentary systems in which minority voter support is more common. As one insider suggested, "Remember this guy's a 43 percent president."[11]

The early days after the 1992 election seemed to increase the room for maneuver among dissenting Democrats. Clinton had a reputation in Arkansas as a politician eager to please, and initial meetings with members of Congress reflected a relatively passive style. Subsequent voting patterns revealed what some insiders had sensed from the beginning: that Democratic senators and representatives would have no particular difficulty voting against the president.

Senator Nunn and other opponents of lifting the ban had an added advantage in the new president's campaign message of focusing attention on economic issues. Once it became clear that there would be more difficulties over the ban than Clinton had anticipated, the White House was strongly motivated to distance itself from the issue.[12] To have engaged in the kind of presidential arm-twisting that might have made a difference would have left the White House even more vulnerable than it already was to charges of being sidetracked.

The new president's perceived weakness on military issues further strengthened Nunn's hand. During the election Clinton's opponents, and much of the press corps, had emphasized his mild opposition to the American conduct of the Vietnam War and his avoidance of the draft. Once in office, his appointment of Les Aspin, known for an interventionist style of policy and an interest in budget cuts, as secretary of defense did little to shore up his standing with the military hierarchy itself.

PLAYING THE ANTI-GAY CARD. The hands of Democratic opponents were greatly strengthened by Republican antipathy to virtually all gay-related causes.

The Republicans' commitment to maintaining the existing ban intact made Nunn look like a moderate on the issue, thereby building his strength among Democratic colleagues.[13] It was no surprise that Nunn could count on Republicans as allies. What was a surprise to the White House and to others working to sustain Clinton's promise was the ferocity of the Republican onslaught. The gay-bashing of the party's August convention, after all, had seemed to do more harm than good, and the Bush campaign had avoided the military ban issue altogether.

Republicans such as Robert Dole and Newt Gingrich, in the leadership of the Senate and the House, were not known to be personally uncomfortable around gays and lesbians. But what one conservative gay activist said about Gingrich could easily be said of both: "I've never found Gingrich to be an ideological homophobe. I think Gingrich is a political homophobe, and I think if he sees it to be in his political benefit to gay-bash he will, and if he sees it not to be in his political benefit to gay-bash he won't."[14] As a gay former Republican said: "Gays and lesbians really don't matter: we're out of the rhetoric. If we begin to matter, they'll not be with us but against us—they will turn against us in a second."[15]

There had been warning signs as early as November 15. On the same day that Nunn, on national television, voiced his opposition to lifting the ban, Dole was expressing similar views on another of the Sunday morning news shows, flagging his party's readiness to pounce on the issue. Late in January, once the Clinton strategy on the military issue was clear, Senate Republican leaders and Armed Services Committee members met to plan their own tactics. There was already talk of encoding the ban by tacking it onto the popular Family Leave Bill or an appropriations bill needed to pay for the military's Somali operations. They were focusing their strategy on the Senate, where amendments are procedurally easier to introduce, and where the support of the Democrat Nunn could be counted on. There may have been as many as twenty-five or thirty moderate Republicans in the House who did not want the opposition to lifting the ban to go too far, perhaps ten or so with strong views. But in the words of one Republican aide, "They certainly didn't want their names in the paper."[16]

SAM NUNN'S HAND. Senator Sam Nunn, not thought by congressional observers to be a man of particular political courage, was able to challenge his own party's president because he held three crucial aces: the deference on military issues among his own Democratic colleagues, the strong alliance of Republicans, and the active collusion of the Joint Chiefs of Staff. By the end of January he would add a fourth ace: the capacity of right-wing forces to mobilize grassroots opposition. In a political system with substantial fragmentation of authority, this hand gave Nunn enough power to transfer the center of the debate away from the executive branch to Capitol Hill and effectively marginalize lesbian/gay activists.

The chair of the Armed Service Committee was in a particularly strategic position, in part because of the power still held by committee chairs in the Senate. Challenge from outside the membership of a committee was particularly difficult

Table 7. Congressional voting on the military ban and all gay/lesbian-related issues, 1993

	#s		% members voting gay-positive on ban[a]		% members voting gay-positive on more than half of gay/lesbian questions		% members voting gay-positive on 100% of gay/lesbian questions		Average pro-gay scorecard vote	
	Dem	Rep	Dem	Rep	Dem	Rep	Dem	Rep	Dem	Rep
Senate										
South	14	12	7%	0%	86%	0%	7%	0%	62%	22%
Midwest	15	9	60	0	93	22	33	0	89	37
West	11	15	73	0	100	20	45	0	88	37
Northwest	16	8	75	38	94	50	63	0	90	60
Total non-South	42	32	69	9	95	31	43	0	87	43
Total	56	44	54	7	95	23	34	0	81	37
House										
South[b]	85	53	31%	0%	40%	0%	15%	0%	45%	2%
Midwest	61	43	61	7	57	5	16	0	60	11
West	55	38	91	5	96	3	42	0	86	9
Northeast	59	42	73	14	78	12	34	0	75	27
Total non-South[c]	179	123	74	9	77	7	31	0	73	16
Total[c]	264	176	60	6	65	5	26	0	64	12

Source: Human Rights Campaign Fund, "Votes of the 103rd Congress, 1st Session."

Notes: Senate votes comprise Feb. 4 procedural vote to block entrenching existing military ban; Feb. 18 vote to codify prohibition on immigration of HIV + individuals; Feb. 18 vote on National Institutes of Health Reauthorization that included AIDS initiatives; May 24 confirmation of nomination of Roberta Achtenberg as assistant secretary for Fair Housing; July 27 vote to allow D.C. to implement domestic partnership registration; Sept. 7 confirmation of nomination of Joycelyn Elders as Surgeon General; Sept. 9 vote on Barbara Boxer amendment to prevent codification of "don't ask, don't tell"; Nov. 4 vote on Dianne Feinstein amendment to increase penalties for hate crimes; Nov. 16 vote on bill penalizing physical obstruction to abortion clinics.

House votes comprise Feb. 4 procedural vote to block entrenching existing military ban; March 11 vote on Sam Johnson amendment to defund a phone HIV counseling program; March 11 procedural motion agreeing with Senate amendment on immigration of HIV + individuals; June 30 vote on Henry Hyde amendment to prohibit federal funds being spent on abortion; June 30 vote on Ernset Istook amendment prohibiting D.C. spending money on domestic partnership registration; Sept. 28 vote on Martin Meehan amendment to prevent codification of "don't ask, don't tell"; Sept. 28 vote on Duncan Hunter amendment requiring military to ask recruits about homosexuality.

[a]Refers to votes on Boxer amendment in Senate and Meehan amendment in House.

[b]16% of the 67 white southern Democrats and 88% of the blacks from the region voted yes on the Meehan amendment. In the Congressional Black Caucus overall, 87% voted yes. David A. Bositis, *The Congressional Black Caucus in the 103rd Congress* (Washington, D.C.: Joint Center for Political and Economic Studies, 1994).

[c]Totals include four House members not included in regions, from American Samoa, Guam, Puerto Rico, and Virgin Islands.

to mount. In the Senate as a whole, and within his committee, Nunn could also count on majority support for his views. He could rely, first, on most southern Democrats. Even if the North-South split had been tempered in recent years, it was still as likely to surface on either gay-related or defense-related issues as any (see Table 7). Among the rest, Nunn's lead on a number of issues was strengthened by his image as moderate—not fanatically right wing or strongly tied to conservative Christian forces. Although this hardly counts as progressive, Nunn had the most liberal voting record on gay-related issues of any of the southern Democratic senators prior to the ban issue.[17] Some have even suggested that his opposition made it easier for others to oppose the lifting of the ban without fear of being branded extreme.

There were of course reliable supporters of pro-gay positions in the Senate, including the four female Democrats. But few were sufficiently vocal or strategically enough positioned at the outset to challenge Nunn's leading position. Even if Democrats on the Armed Services Committee were in the end about evenly divided on the ban, only Senator Ted Kennedy acquired any significant visibility in registering opposition to Nunn's drive. Without a substantial chance of winning the day in votes, few Senators on or off the committee were willing to carve out a high profile on such a "controversial" issue. In any event, the senators who served on this particular committee were disproportionately supportive of the military, making lopsided majorities in favor of relatively conservative positions easier to obtain.

Nunn had more than enough motivation to take advantage of the maneuvering room provided by law and political circumstances. He had a close, symbiotic relationship with the military. These links provided Nunn with valuable political leverage in Washington, ensuring him his share of spending benefits specific to his district, and creating for him a valuable national constituency of enlisted service members and veterans. Appearing strong on defense issues and conservative on social issues also provided a degree of protection against electoral challenge from right-wing forces in his home state of Georgia.[18]

Nunn's personal beliefs also played a role. His voting record signaled his opposition to pro-gay positions on a number of fronts. In letters to constituents at the time of the debate over gays in the military, Nunn indicated his opposition even to general civil rights protections, and later in the year he opposed a domestic partnership measure adopted by the District of Columbia. On two occasions he had been unwilling to support gay Washington staffers when they faced difficulties gaining the security clearance or military cooperation they needed in order to work in his office. His language also indicated a view of homosexuality that had strong parallels with the beliefs of the religious right. In a late May 1993 appearance on *Meet the Press*, he rejected any move by government that would give approval to homosexual behavior. Asked if he considered heterosexuality "morally superior," Nunn responded, "I'm not only saying that, I'm saying the family structure in America has deteriorated, and that's one of our big problems."[19]

"Cooling Off"

Sam Nunn had always seemed ready to confront Clinton directly and publicly about lifting the ban. Six months before the election, he had bluntly warned

Clinton in person that "the military isn't ready for it."[20] Then, only days after the election, appearing November 15 on *Face the Nation*, Nunn expressed his support for the existing ban and called on the president-elect to refer the issue to Congress.

By early January 1993, the White House and the office of the defense secretary had begun to consider a "cooling off" period, an idea that crystallized in a January 18 memo from Les Aspin to Clinton, leaked to the press soon after its delivery. During a six-month period, discharges or reassignments based on sexual orientation would cease, and in the meantime a draft executive order would be prepared by Aspin. That same memo indicated the weak position that Clinton was in on Capitol Hill, citing Senate majority leader George Mitchell's estimate of at most thirty secure votes out of one hundred.[21] It also flagged the difficulty of circumventing the strategies likely to be used by opponents, for example, tagging a codified ban onto a bill that the administration badly wanted (such as the Family Leave Bill).

During the week of January 25, a firestorm of letters and phone calls swept over Congress and the White House, mobilized by the religious right and veterans' organizations. Only late that week did calls in favor of lifting the ban begin to register, though never even approaching the volume against. Midway through the week Nunn voiced strong opposition to the Clinton commitment on the Senate floor, firing a volley across the bow of the administration ship which, even at this stage, surprised many Democrats. If there had been any doubt up to this point that he would seize the initiative on the issue, there could no longer be a shred of it.

By this time Nunn had become a central player in negotiations between the White House and the Pentagon over how to proceed. There no longer seemed to any disagreement about the value of a six-month delay, but considerable debate raged over the regime that would apply in the interim. The "cooling off" announcement of January 29 signaled an important victory for Nunn and the Joint Chiefs, for it allowed commanders to continue processing discharge cases, though relegating those destined for "separation" to the limbo of "standby reserve" pending the final determination of the policy issue.

National lesbian and gay groups were caught off guard by these developments. The Human Rights Campaign Fund and the National Gay and Lesbian Task Force began activating their networks, but among sympathetic Capitol Hill staff there was widespread talk of the ineffectiveness of the earlier response. In February the Campaign for Military Service (CMS) was formed, at first as an ad hoc coalition, to mobilize around the issue, with New York–based Tom Stoddard of the Lambda Legal Defense and Education Fund as coordinator. CMS had much to do in short order, not least prepare for congressional hearings.

SENATE HEARINGS. Now with the administration shell-shocked by the opposition to lifting the ban, and gay/lesbian activists unprepared, the field was clear for Senator Nunn to work his mischief. He quickly set out to schedule hearings and manage them in such a way as to maximize their advantage, not only in the kinds of information that would be offered up to the media, but also in the selection of witnesses. Proponents of lifting the ban were being constantly surprised by last-minute announcements of new witnesses, and so their resources were drawn even more disproportionately to the Senate hearing process. Nunn was also successfully framing the public debate in narrow military terms, with "unit cohesion" as the central issue.

By the end of the first day of committee hearings, on March 29, it was clear that most members had formed their opinions, with enough Democrats opposed to lifting the ban to secure Nunn an overwhelming majority. Even at this early stage, Nunn was raising of the possibility of permanently adopting the six-month interim policy he had played so prominent a role in crafting, allowing gays and lesbians to serve as long as they did not identify themselves as such. On the second day of hearings, military witnesses who began their testimony opposing the lifting of the ban seemed to fall into line behind the Nunn proposal. In some quarters "don't ask, don't tell" was being promoted as a compromise, though in fact it differed only fractionally from the status quo.

President Clinton's own pronouncements subtly prepared the way (perhaps unconsciously so) for compromise. He offered assurances that he had meant only to end discrimination based on "status," and that he favored maintaining a strict code of conduct, and that he had no intention of proposing any changes in the military's existing codes.[22] Before long, Nunn was able to cite such statements as suggesting agreement between his views and the president's.[23]

On April 25, hundreds of thousands of lesbians, gay men, bisexuals, and transgendered people gathered in the capital for one of the largest marches Washington had ever seen. Gays in the military was a featured issue, addressed by several of the headline speakers. But few of the march's participants saw the occasion as an opportunity to engage in mainstream lobbying techniques. In any event, the proceedings in Congress carried on as if nothing had happened.

The Senate Armed Services Committee held its second round of hearings at the end of April, retaining its initiative on the issue and monopolizing the public spotlight. Once again, witnesses were chosen to undercut attempts to lift the ban entirely, among them the Desert Storm deputy commander, Lieutenant General Calvin Waller, an African American called to refute the analogy between anti-gay and anti-black discrimination. Senator Edward Kennedy tried to challenge the way in which the hearings had been stacked, but in a recorded vote he was the only member to oppose the chair. Once again, there were clear signs of an emergent "compromise," one that would forbid routine questioning about homosexuality during recruitment but would characterize even an acknowledgment of being gay as inappropriate "conduct" leading to dismissal.

Then on May 10, the committee embarked on the first of its "field" hearings, staging a photo opportunity tour of a submarine to provide a close-up view of the most tightly packed environment in the military, complete with sailors in their bunks asked to react on camera to the prospect of openly gay shipmates. The media provided precisely the coverage that was intended by the event's stage managers. The ground was now shifting even more rapidly than it had been since late January. Even senators on record as favoring an end to the ban were now suggesting only allowing gay service members to "discreetly acknowledge their sexual orientation," while prohibiting overt or disruptive activity.[24]

HOUSE ALLIES. The original Clinton proposal was always expected to find more support in the House than in the Senate, in part because the lower chamber's rules allow the majority leadership more control over debate and amendments, and in part because there were more outspoken supporters. Openly gay Representative Gerry Studds had addressed the issue years before. In 1991 Representative Barbara Boxer (later elected to the Senate) responded to the increased visibility of lesbian and gay military personnel prepared to challenge the existing policy by proposing a nonbinding resolution urging President Bush to lift the ban.

In May 1992 House Armed Services Committee member Patricia Schroeder moved more aggressively toward forcing the executive's hand, introducing the Military Freedom Bill. Within a few weeks sixty House members had signed on as co-sponsors, with Schroeder herself sensing, perhaps naively, a "reservoir of good feelings on this issue" among her colleagues.[25] Hearings were being presented in positive terms as a means by which the issue could be aired.

The large wave of newly elected House members following the 1992 election promised even more support for pro-gay initiatives, not least because of a sharp increase in women (from 29 to 48) and blacks (from 26 to 39). Committee re-assignments in the new Congress placed into the chair of the Armed Services Committee a strong supporter of Clinton's promise to lift the ban. Ron Dellums was an African American highly respected by his Democratic colleagues, and himself a former marine. Dellums had wanted to launch his own committee hearings in March, in part to counteract the bias he knew would shape the Senate hearings. He was persuaded to delay by activists who were themselves not advanced enough in their own campaign to be prepared for a second set of hearings, and by supporters in the White House and Congress who feared that such hearings would provide House Republicans an opportunity to force an early vote.[26]

Even if Dellums's view had prevailed, he would have had difficulty attracting as much limelight as Nunn on the Senate side. In addition, Dellums would never have been able to benefit from the kind of assistance that Nunn received from the military hierarchy itself—assistance that was crucial in developing and maintaining a high media profile—especially since Dellums had long been a critic of the military. Dellums was also hampered from the beginning by clear indications that he did not have the support of anything close to a majority of his committee. One of his many Democratic opponents on the issue was Ike Skelton, strategically located in the chair of the Subcommittee on Personnel.

Two days of full committee hearings were finally begun on May 4, with personnel subcommittee hearings to be held on questions of implementation at a later date. By then there seemed no way to deflect attention from the Nunn hearings, so artfully constructed to grab headlines. The media paid only scant attention to the House hearings, and whatever positive effect they might have had was swamped a few days later by the media shots of concerned senators and sailors in a cramped submarine.

By this time, too, Dellums, Schroeder, Studds, and their allies faced a groundswell of resentment among House colleagues about having to deal with the issue at all. Even before the inauguration of Senator Nunn's hearings, most members of the House (and probably the Senate) were driven mostly by a desire to have the issue go away. Democratic members of Congress, besieged from both sides since the end of January, constantly asked to comment on the issue by constituents and their local press, were entreating Dellums to put an end to the hearings. This was a view for which there was sympathy in the Democratic leadership, which saw the issue of gays in the military as throwing off the whole legislative agenda.

THE BARNEY FRANK COMPROMISE. At the time when the military ban was being debated, Barney Frank was the only openly gay member of Congress other than his Massachusetts colleague Gerry Studds (see Chapter 8). Frank had not devoted the attention to the ban that Studds and his aides had, but had developed a high profile on other gay-related issues, in both Congress and the gay media, and was widely thought to be one of the House's most effective legislators.

In mid-May, at first in a general and speculative way, then more pointedly, Frank began to talk of compromise on lifting the military ban.[27] He developed a "don't ask, don't tell, don't listen, don't investigate" proposal that would let gays and lesbians be open about their sexual orientation while off duty and off base, but not while on duty. The compromise proposal was motivated primarily by Frank's conclusion that there were simply not enough votes in Congress to sustain the president's commitment on lifting the ban, and that support for a highly unfavorable Nunn policy of "don't ask, don't tell" was solidifying fast both in Congress and elsewhere.

The idea of compromise provoked all but universal criticism from activist groups. Many called the proposal a sellout for encoding the closet and offering solace to cowardly Democrats. Some activists and Capitol Hill insiders, including Studds, were more disturbed by what they argued was precipitous timing and lack of consultation.[28] Not surprisingly, the White House reacted with delight at the help they had been given, and Clinton himself phoned Frank the evening of the May 18 to express his gratitude. The administration had long abandoned the hope of lifting the ban entirely, but had hesitated in clearly stating a compromise. As one Democratic insider put it: "The White House was concerned with the political fallout of a unified national gay and lesbian community in all of its manifestations—electoral, political, grassroots—denouncing, hating, condemning the White House. Barney Frank pulled the middle out of that unified front and made it seem like the reasonable, sensible, politically astute gays (i.e., himself and all others who thought like him) could understand the compromise based on political reality.''[29]

For the administration, the organized community became irrelevant, with the only significant spectrum of opinion remaining being that between Barney Frank on the left and Sam Nunn on the right. On May 27, President Clinton said he was very close to a compromise that would address ''legitimate concern [that] our country does not appear to be endorsing a gay lifestyle.''[30] Nunn seized on that, and on the president's frequent references to imposing strict rules on ''conduct,'' to assert that Clinton was now closer to his own views than to Frank's, at the same time flatly rejecting the possibility of service personnel publicly acknowledging their homosexuality.[31]

In a rearguard action given very little publicity, key gay/lesbian activist groups had narrowed their core demands to three: no discharges based on status, the protection of ''private speech,'' and the equitable application of sodomy provisions to allow private consensual sexual conduct off base. They continued to believe in the possibility of attaining those objectives, and in some respects they were reinforced in that belief by White House representatives who still described the issue as being in flux, and still repeated the president's objective that ''status alone should not disqualify people from serving.''[32] Hope seemed to be alive in mid-June, when even the conservative *Washington Times* reported a survey showing that 143 House members favored lifting the ban, with 81 more still undecided.[33] The same survey showed an unfavorable shift in the Senate from a poll earlier in the year, but still with 32 opposing the ban and 28 undecided. Gay activist polling suggested the possibility of a progressive shift if accompanied by clear presidential leadership.[34]

But the numbers were soft. By late June, a letter circulated by pro-gay members of the House calling on the president to lift the ban garnered only sixty-nine signers, some of them reluctant.[35] More than ever, Democrats in Congress resented being forced to solve what they perceived to be the president's problem, and were appalled that the story had returned once again to the front pages. It seemed increasingly that the particular form of the compromise mattered less than that it get a contentious and difficult issue off the agenda.

ENCODING THE NUNN BAN. By June 22, there was no longer any serious question about Nunn's victory. Les Aspin was reported as supporting an alternative closely resembling the senator's version of ''don't ask, don't tell''—one asserting that sexual orientation (meaning, of course, only homosexual orientation) was a personal and private matter, and that homosexual conduct was inconsistent with high standards of combat effectiveness. At the same time, incredibly,

White House officials were indicating that the option favored by the defense secretary was "not necessarily incompatible" with Clinton's pledge to lift the ban on gays in the military.[36]

In July Nunn made clear his intention to proceed with codification, using as a vehicle what was seen as an almost veto-proof Defense Authorization Bill. In a July 16 Senate Speech speech, Nunn argued that it was essential for Congress to legislate policies on homosexuality in the armed forces. Among the principles that he indicated would have to be encoded was one that had been under much debate in recent weeks: that "the presence in military units of persons who, by their acts or statements, demonstrate a propensity to engage in homosexual acts, would cause an unacceptable risk to the high standards of morale, good order and discipline, and unit cohesion that are essential to effective combat capability."[37]

On July 19 Clinton announced a policy that largely matched the Nunn view, eliciting open expressions of disappointment from allies on Capitol Hill, including Barney Frank. They had been lobbying hard against the most restrictive proposals coming out of the Pentagon, in part on the grounds of defending the president's commitments. They were now faced with a policy declaration that yielded to the military's preferences, but was hailed by Clinton as an honorable compromise and a substantial advance over the previous policy. In the days leading up to the presidential announcement, even Frank had declared, "The victims of prejudice would rather lose with the president on their side than win a small gain with him being perceived as having moved away."[38] Proponents of lifting the ban were now on the other side of the fence from Clinton.

On July 23 the Senate Armed Services Committee voted seventeen to five in favor of the Nunn amendment. It included a statement that homosexual conduct is incompatible with military service; it expressly permitted questioning recruits about sexual orientation; it provided no examples of off-base conduct that might be permitted; and it omitted the Clinton policy's stated objective of enforcing sodomy laws equally for heterosexuals and homosexuals—all of this using language carefully crafted to immunize the new policy as much as possible from judicial challenge.[39] In all those senses it was more restrictive than Clinton's already restrictive version announced only days before, enough to please even some of Congress's most conservative members.[40] An utterly fatigued White House immediately signaled its approval, having already acquiesced in principle.

At about this time, Ike Skelton and his House Armed Services Committee allies were persuaded to follow the Nunn lead by incorporating the Senate committee wording into the House version of the defense bill. So strongly had the pendulum swung against Clinton that some of the committee members who had worked alongside Skelton in opposing any lifting of the ban thought that Nunn might have "gone soft" on the issue as a result of conferring with the president. On

July 27, Ron Dellums proposed an amendment lifting the ban altogether but lost twelve to forty-three.

On September 9 the Senate as a whole voted sixty-three to thirty-three to codify the Nunn policy on gays in the military, after rejecting a pro-gay amendment proposed by Senator Barbara Boxer. (Activists in the campaign to lift the ban had asked their congressional allies to propose such an amendment in order to register the extent of support even in the face of pressure from the White House and congressional leadership to drop the issue.) Thirty-three senators had voted for the Boxer amendment, all but three of them Democrats. These accounted for 69 percent of non-southern Democrats, but only 7 percent of southerners (see Table 7).

On September 28 the House adopted the Nunn language by a vote of 301 to 134.[41] There had been votes on two amendments, one to reinstate the pre-Clinton ban, another to delete references to the ban in the bill in order to allow presidential discretion—the latter a pro-gay amendment formally proposed by Representative Martin Meehan over objections from Democrats sufficiently fed up with the issue to want to avoid a recorded vote. The regional differences so evident in the upper house were also present, though tempered by the recent increase of black representation from the South. Only 16 percent of white southern Democrats supported the Meehan amendment, while 74 percent of the non-southern Democrats did (see Table 7).[42] On November 17 the budget bill to which the amendment was attached was finally sent to the president for signature, without ceremony.

Buttresses to Congressional Opposition

The advantage Sam Nunn and his allies enjoyed over the new president was secured in large measure by the balance of political forces on Capitol Hill and the leverage accorded legislative opponents by the United States political system. But it was also buttressed by forces beyond Capitol Hill.

LEGAL FRAMEWORK. The formal criminalization of consensual same-sex activity in more than twenty states has long been a brake on progress on other fronts. The sodomy provisions of the military justice code in particular were a barrier to full legal equality in the armed forces, and delimited even Clinton's early proposals for lifting the ban. From the beginning of the debate, in fact, the president's inability to change those provisions justified a particularly discriminatory differentiation between status and conduct—one that reinforced widespread double standards about closeting sexuality. Apart from the legal barriers it provided to enacting protections against discrimination, this statutory web contributed to the perception of lesbian and gay sexuality as quasi-criminal.

Constitutional guarantees of equality were not strong counterweights. There had been successful litigation on behalf of lesbians and gays seeking equal rights protections under the Fourteenth Amendment, but appellate courts had rarely moved to scrutinize anti-gay discrimination with the same care as discrimination on racial or gender grounds. Higher courts were also reluctant to challenge military discretion or executive prerogative in such areas even if a number of the legal challenges to the pre-Clinton ban had been successful in their early rounds.[43]

The Canadian case is a clear contrast. Consensual same-sex activity among adults was decriminalized by the federal government (which has exclusive jurisdiction over criminal law) in 1969. The Charter of Rights and Freedoms, enacted in 1982, contained equality provisions that were more flexible and comprehensive than those in the American Bill of Rights (see Chapter 4). The Canadian military had long opposed admitting gays and lesbians, using arguments identical to those used by the United States military. Their resistance had appeared to be weakening in the early 1990s, however, and finally collapsed in October 1992 on the brink of a court case that they realized they were going to lose on constitutional grounds.

The ban on gays in the British armed forces has been less challengeable than the Canadian ban on legal or constitutional grounds, and in Britain as in other countries there is a strong tradition of laws that presume and therefore enforce heterosexuality. But the fact that most European countries have no such ban has strengthened challenges to it, and increases the possibility of successfully appealing to the European Court of Human Rights (see Chapter 3). In the written decision for a 1995 case upholding the ban, Lord Justice Brown of the High Court was moved to comment that "the tide of history is against the Defence Ministry. Prejudices are breaking down; old barriers are being removed. It seems to me improbable, whatever this court may say, that the existing policy can survive much longer.[44]

MILITARY OPPOSITION. The opposition of the United States military to lifting the ban was a decisive impediment to change. There had been precedents for military protests of civilian policy in the past, but none in a half century against a president whose legitimacy on military issues was as vulnerable as Clinton's. As a result, the opposition was more overt and more organized than any within memory, enough that even some in the Pentagon wondered if it constituted insubordination. The military's power to oppose Clinton rested on its size, its prominence in American economic and political life, and the popular support for the military that usually accompanies status as an imperial power, amplified by the war successfully waged against Iraq. The public support for the military is in contrast to popular distrust of political authority—a distrust that has longer standing and currently a more cynical edge than in most other liberal democratic systems.[45] With only modest exceptions, the strength and popularity of the military immunized it from criticism for the baser motives that underlay the resistance to Clinton's commitment.

The military's arguments about cohesion and effectiveness were treated as legitimate even though they constituted an admission of its willingness to acquiesce in the bigotry of enlisted personnel, and its inability to effect compliance with unwelcome orders. By evoking images of cramped sleeping quarters and shared showers, the military played on deep-seated anxieties about sexual exposure and equally embedded prejudices about homosexual predation, particularly widespread among men. The intimacy of same-sex contact in the military, as in the world of professional sports, made the assertion of official heterosexuality that much more essential for maintaining a sense of masculinized security, and that much easier to argue in ways that resonated with the general public.[46]

The opposition of General Colin Powell was especially damaging to Clinton. Powell was an immensely popular chair of the Joint Chiefs of Staff, with considerable political savvy gained as Ronald Reagan's assistant for national security affairs. He was described in one account as "the most charismatic and well connected military leader since Douglas MacArthur."[47] His own African-American background gave him particular influence in deflecting claims about discrimination and in countering arguments about parallels to racial exclusion. Powell was personally and vehemently opposed to lifting the ban. His unwillingness to criticize his more rabid colleagues suggested a degree of sympathy with the deep-seated bigotry on which their opposition was founded, an impression reinforced by some of the language he used to defend the ban.[48]

By January there were reports of senior officers copying and circulating *The Gay Agenda*, a fanatically homophobic video prepared by the Christian right. One Pentagon official reported that "the Marines are passing it out like popcorn."[49] The marine commandant was one of those said to be most actively distributing it, even to some members of Congress. Organized phone-ins were reported on some military bases, and dissenters from the gathering storm of orthodoxy were discouraged from voicing their views. It was now clear that military leaders were orchestrating a virtual campaign against the president, using command structures ideally suited to political mobilization. Outside the Pentagon, they were backed by the Coalition to Maintain Military Readiness, a grouping of several organizations of veterans and active-duty National Guard and reserve personnel. Inside the Pentagon, working groups established to examine the issue were stacked with opponents.

Secretary of Defense Les Aspin was no match for the unified service chiefs. In any event, Aspin was not personally convinced of the wisdom of fully lifting the ban, and was disinclined to expend political capital at the Pentagon by pressing the chiefs on the issue. Aspin had acquired a relatively pro-gay reputation as a member of Congress, and his failure to provide more support and leadership caught some activists off guard.[50] By June, the Joint Chiefs were virtually dictating terms to him. And according to some observers, Pentagon officials were leaking proposals emerging from negotiations over details in order to help secure their position against possible White House erosion. On June 25, Aspin formally presented to the Joint Chiefs a proposal that differed only microscopically from the one they favored, and once again leaks signaled their unwillingness to be moved.

THE RELIGIOUS RIGHT. Only in Catholic Europe have religious groups had a capacity for political mobilization that even approaches that of the United States Christian right. But in Europe, Roman Catholic political groups have long had to confront well-organized anticlerical forces. In any event, they have been weakened by declining levels of religious observance and by a growing willingness even among believers to ignore the political and religious directives of the church hierarchy.

The U.S. Protestant right is of course more rooted in local churches and local preachers with considerable influence over their following (buttressed on some issues by the conservative leaders of the Roman Catholic hierarchy and by right-wing leaders of other religious faiths). The messages of the Protestant right are powerfully reinforced by religious media, fund-raising capacities, and central political organizations without parallel in other countries. While fundamentalist mobilizing can also make a difference in Canada, the numbers of adherents are much smaller, and their language less extreme (see Chapter 4). In the United States, close to 40 percent of the population claims to adhere to a literalist or fundamentalist belief in the Bible, and even if all of these are not supportive of the religious right's political leadership, the potential constituency for anti-gay campaigning is huge and mobilizable. The American religious right, then, is a set of politicized forces with few parallels in other countries, working in a political system virtually unique in its susceptibility to the kinds of resources they are able to deploy.

The Christian right had taken advantage during the Reagan and Bush years of opportunities opened up within the Republic Party for the exercise of conservative political influence. Focusing on homosexuality created a common enemy about which few would dissent. As Peter Applebome reported in the *New York Times* in February 1993, "When the issue was fused to conservative views on the military and the objections of the nation's military leadership, it attained extraordinary emotional power, both for committed conservatives and for Americans in the political mainstream."[51] For an expanding conservative coalition, the prominence given the gay ban in the weeks after the election was "a bonanza for building organizations and raising money."[52]

The church-based facilities and national media resources available to the religious right enabled it to generate the firestorm of protest against lifting the ban in the last week of January. Leaders such as Pat Robertson, Jerry Falwell, and Beverly LaHaye had been railing against the president's commitment since the election, so their constituencies were thoroughly primed. For most of the second week of the new administration, the congressional switchboard was handling more than five times its typical daily total of eighty thousand calls, in some offices producing tallies that ran a hundred to one against Clinton's plan. As one journalist has remarked, "Unlike other powerful interests, [the gospel lobby] does not lavish campaign funds on candidates for Congress nor does it entertain them. The strength of fundamentalist leaders lies in their flocks. Corporations pay public relations firms millions of dollars to contrive the kind of grass-roots response that Falwell or Pat Robertson can galvanize in a televised sermon."[53]

Even if most people on Capitol Hill recognized the degree of orchestration behind the waves of telephone calls and letters, the scale was a reminder of the potential electoral influence of the groups behind the campaign. In the midst of the storm, Gerry Studds was reported to have admitted, "I'm not aware of any group that has the capacity to instantaneously turn on that volume of calls and correspondence. It certainly can be intimidating, which is what it's designed to be." Democratic Congressman Jim Slattery observed, "From the standpoint of delivering votes, they're more influential than the bankers, more influential than the real estate industry and as powerful as any single labor union in America."[54]

Because of the religious right's capacity to mobilize a grassroots movement with strong views on issues such as this, the pressure had an effect. The messages sent to the White House and Capitol Hill were strong and heartfelt, standing out from the lobbying usually mobilized by political action groups. Journalists commented that lawmakers were surprised by the display of "genuine, authentic, public outrage."[55] One congressional aide described the campaign in similar terms: "I think it was one of the most effective grassroots campaigns that have ever been run. I would say that what made it so effective was that it appeared not to be organized by an interest group or by a lobbying organization, because letters came and they were handwritten by people in their words. They weren't scripted, computer-driven letters or postcards."[56]

The decline of party organization and party loyalty in the electorate increases politicians' exposure to the mobilizing of groups such as those in the religious right. The cynicism about politicians that has always been part of the American political culture, and that has increased so markedly in the last generation, further increases the vulnerability to negative campaigning and intensifies fears of taking on causes thought to be unpopular.

THE SOFTNESS OF PUBLIC SUPPORT. Gay-related issues are firmly lodged within that category of issues which provoke close attention to public opinion, and mobilized opinion. In this respect, opponents of Clinton's plan to lift the ban had considerable advantages. Although survey evidence has indicated that a large and slowly growing majority of Americans favor equal rights for gays and lesbians, a clear majority has also consistently "disapproved" of homosexuality. In late summer 1992 a *New York Times*/CBS News poll showed 80 percent in favor of equal rights to job opportunities, but only 38 percent agreeing that homosexuality is an acceptable alternative lifestyle.[57] In mid-1993, another poll showed that 70 percent opposed allowing gays to adopt.[58]

One 1988 electoral survey found that Americans felt more negative toward gays and lesbians than toward any other social group they were asked about, placing them on average at 28.5 on a 100-degree "feeling thermometer."[59] Similar surveys in 1992 and 1994 found the assessment of gays and lesbians less "chilly" but still highly unfavorable, at 37.8 and 35.7 degrees; 28 percent of 1994 respondents scored gays and lesbians at zero.[60] The persistence of prejudice, combined with a widespread reluctance to talk about sexuality in general and sexual difference in particular, creates the potential for considerable volatility in public sentiment. The relatively recent arrival of gay-rights issues onto public agendas exaggerates that volatility and creates an opportunity for protagonists to shape public perceptions.

Opinion surveys on the issue of gays in the military provide striking evidence of that same volatility. Polls taken between 1977 and 1991 showed an increase in support for allowing gays to serve, from 51 percent to 69 percent, this at a time when the ban on their serving was total.[61] But by the time of the January 1993 firestorm, one similarly worded poll found that support had fallen to 47 percent, and three others showed a slide down to the low 40s.[62] Amplifying public disquiet was a growing impatience with Clinton for spending time on this issue rather than on the economy.[63]

A number of Capitol Hill insiders have called public opinion a major problem for politicians sorting out the issue of the ban, and a source of much of the opposition within Congress itself. The strength of feeling among opponents of lifting the ban, and the reluctance of proponents in many areas of the country to speak out, intensified the risk-averse reactions of politicians. According to one Capitol Hill Democrat: "I think the reaction was mainly rooted in a sense of where the public was— in a sense of what the political fallout would be—rather than any free-standing preference on the part of the members. People are well aware of the presence of articulate and well-organized opposition groups—the religious right, in this case the Republican Party or Republican fellow travelers of various sorts, very willing to use this to embarrass the new president. But it's not just that; it's also a sense that there's a certain resonance in the public about these anti-homosexual views and that they could become very damaging politically."[64]

The same judgment would once have been made about abortion, but politicians tend to see opinion on the subject of homosexuality as both more negative and more volatile. On abortion they had fully worked-out positions, and in most cases had been forced to declare them publicly. An aide to a southern Democrat argued that on the issue of gay rights,

it's not just the fringe elements that you're worried about; it's also the resonance in the broader population. A number of these issues have undergone a transition, and this one may as well, but it hasn't yet. . . . For Democrats, our job is to talk about education and the environment and economic opportunity—these bread-and-butter issues—and don't let them get us out on this cultural turf where we're going to get whipsawed. [On gun control and abortion] people want to know what side you're one. And so you figure you're going to alienate some people, but you're going to have to take a stand or else you're going to please no one. And there has also been some shift in public opinion that makes it more profitable to say, "I'm for gun control" or "I'm for choice." But we haven't reached that point yet with gay rights.[65]

These factors weigh much more heavily in the United States than in other political systems. Voter turnouts are lower than in any other liberal democracy in the industrialized world, for reasons that include the sheer number and complexity of decisions appearing on the ballot, the initiative required to register to vote, and the extent of cynicism about the political process. In that kind of climate, the capacity of social movements and political organizations to mobilize letters and phone calls on particular issues comes to stand for the potential to mobilize voters at election time. In other words, even if "mobilized opinion" is widely recognized as distinct from "public opinion," the former becomes an electorally important representation of the latter. Barney Frank has talked at length about this:

> People's ability to organize mail is a pretty good marker for their ability to organize votes. The fact that one group is able to get thousands of people in your district to write you letters and make phone calls, and another group is not, is not irrelevant when it comes to who's going to mobilize people to vote in the primaries and the general election. . . . If you know these are people who are totally out of sympathy with the overwhelming majority of the public, that lessens their impact. But if you know that the public is divided, [what legislators attend to] is the public opinion that registers itself. I guess it's not public opinion, it's voter opinion. . . . That's why the gun control issue became such a difficult one. I do not believe that anyone was defeated in 1994 because he or she didn't support gun control; but a number of people were defeated in 1994 because they did. And the reason is that the great majority of people who support gun control rarely make that their motivating factor, and the small minority that hate gun control often make it the motivating factor.[66]

Frank argues that among elected politicians, supporters are still reluctant to stand up for sexual minority rights; but at the same time a growing number of opponents are uneasy about focusing on the issue. That may have been evident in the annoyance of legislators at being forced into roll call votes in the final stages of the military debate. As Frank argues: "It was where abortion was ten, twelve years ago. When I got [to Congress] you got 100 people pro-choice and 100 people who wanted to ban abortions, and 235 people who thought you're crazy for saying anything. It's about not having to alienate people on either side. For all politicians, conflict avoidance is very important. Some have very little policy core. . . . [T]hey will generally say, 'Gee, I've got enough problems in my life, I don't need high-visibility issues that are seriously problematic.' And what's happening now is that many, many of them see gay and lesbian rights as an issue that will bring them grief.''[67] Fear of controversy may serve to reduce setbacks by intensifying the desire to avoid sexual orientation issues altogether. Of course, that same aversion also reduces the chances of legislative advance.

THE MAKEUP OF CONGRESS. Moderate and progressive members of Congress tend to argue that defeats of pro-gay initiatives such as lifting the military ban are primarily a result of outside forces impinging on Capitol Hill, most notably public antipathy. Gerry Studds was quoted as saying that a secret ballot among members of Congress would consistently produce pro-gay majorities.[68] Barney Frank argues that the military debate itself demonstrated a progressive shift in reasoning among his colleagues: they opposed the removal of the ban as a special case, in part because of prevailing prejudice among heterosexuals in the military, but had no objection to equality rights in general.

There can be no doubt that the attitudes of many Capitol Hill legislators have shifted toward more progressive positions on sexual diversity. But in some respects there is less movement than there appears to be. The moderation in language used to oppose pro-gay measures is not in itself a reliable indicator of changed perspectives, and may well speak only to a desire to avoid seeming hateful. A lobbyist for one right-wing Christian group admitted in 1992 that ''privately members of Congress and staff use the f-word—faggot—but they won't say it publicly.''[69] The avoidance of extremist labeling is widespread in Britain and Canada, and has been noticeable even in those right-wing parliamentary circles in which anti-gay voting patterns have not altered (see Chapters 2 and 4).

In 1992, according to one Washington-based activist, firm supporters of gay/lesbian rights numbered only about one hundred in the House and ten to fifteen in the Senate. The number of national politicians prepared to stand up and speak forcefully in pro-gay terms is smaller. In 1992 one Democratic congressional aide illustrated the challenge facing pro-gay advocates such as Gerry Studds, who has since left Congress. He cited Studds's belief that most members of Congress ''understand what the right thing is,'' but continued: ''Gerry has talked about flying back from somewhere with a member of Congress who—and this is a critical part of the story—who is a co-sponsor of the lesbian and gay human rights bill, who says, 'You know, I'm on the bill, but I really don't understand why we would need this.' And Gerry says, 'Well, for example, you could be fired because you're gay.' And he will say 'No, that's not true!' 'Or someone could kick you out of your housing and they wouldn't be subject to any lawsuit— they could deny you housing and tell you [it's] because you're gay.' 'No, that's not true!' And this is a co-sponsor!''[70]

Many legislators use public opinion as a shield for their own prejudice or ignorance. In confronting sexual orientation issues, a number of genuinely gay-positive politicians in Canada, Britain, and the United States have taken pains to explore the range of opinions in their constituencies, often uncovering strands of decency not evident in polling or in letters. Politicians, in other words, will read the conflicting public opinion messages that routinely emerge on a particular issue through the lens of their own information and opinion.

The members of the Congressional Black Caucus generally represent districts with African-American majorities, which for a variety of reasons are not unusually disposed to pro-gay positions. And yet the caucus was highly favorable to lifting the military ban. The most likely reason for their support was their own experience and knowledge of sociopolitical marginality. A similar argument can be made about women. In the 103rd Congress (1993–95), the voting records of women in the House of Representatives (twelve Republicans and thirty-five Democrats) showed that their support of pro-gay positions on the military was up to twice that of men, the gender contrast much sharper than in the general public.[71]

Jean Schroedel has conducted a survey of elected officials at the state and local level which demonstrates the tenacity of anti-gay sentiments. Of those who were not openly gay or lesbian, fully 45 percent believed that homosexual relationships between consulting adults are "always wrong" or "almost always wrong."[72] That was lower than the figure that such a question would elicit from the general public (closer to 55–75 percent), but still high enough to ensure substantial opposition to pro-gay initiatives. Only 45 percent of non-gay respondents favored laws to protect the civil rights of lesbians and gays, and 47 percent favored lifting the military ban. An extrapolation to the federal legislature, taking into account even more unfavorable gender, race, and age profiles, would not be likely to produce more positive results.

The retention of the military ban in Congress, then, was not simply a product of "exogenous" factors, however important such factors were. It was also a product of the paucity of core support for pro-gay positions, the substantial number of congressional representatives personally opposed, and the sizable number in the middle, relatively indifferent to and embarrassed by such issues, and more than prepared to take their cues from mobilized opinion.

WHITE HOUSE WEAKNESS. There were questions long before the election about Clinton's commitment and clarity of vision on sexual orientation issues. His record in Arkansas provided little encouragement to lesbians and gays, and local activists remained surprised by the support he acquired over the course of 1992. At the Democrats' July convention, Clinton had to be reminded to include explicit mention of gays and lesbians in his acceptance speech.[73]

At the time of the Republican Convention, Clinton was asked once again for his views on the military ban. He confirmed his promise, but with qualifications flagging the complexity of the issue. He talked of the need to "guarantee a certain level of privacy, a certain level of security against sexual overtures, a certain level of cohesion. . . . There would have to be something besides the simple statement of status. But I think everybody understands that any kind of inappropriate behavior would be grounds for dismissal."[74] Though not much noticed at the time, these remarks seemed to open up the potential for a double standard of conduct. This impression was reinforced when Clinton subsequently implied that he would not change the sodomy provisions in the military code effectively criminalizing most homosexual activity.

At a March 23 press conference, Clinton refused to rule out restrictions on duties or deployment of lesbian/gay service personnel—in other words, segregation.[75] Then on May 27 he made his comment about not appearing to endorse a "gay lifestyle," invoking, whether accidentally or willfully, the phraseology of the religious right. He further distanced himself from the cause he had once espoused so passionately with his July announcement of a "compromise" that in fact entailed almost total capitulation to the military. Clinton described the plan as 85 percent of what he sought, and then acquiesced to further erosion by Senator Nunn.

One Washington gay lobbyist as inclined as any to support the politics of compromise likened Clinton to John F. Kennedy, who "succeeded in getting a solid vote in the African-American community. . . . Then he got in the White House and he didn't want to have to deal with civil rights. . . . It took him three years before he signed the executive order ending the segregation of public housing."[76] Some of Clinton's advisers were supportive of initiatives on sexual orientation only if there were political gains to be made. They were determined to retain his centrist positioning as a "new kind of Democrat" and to distance him from an unpopular "special interest."[77]

Prior to the election and then during the transition, insider Bob Hattoy recalled hardly a single conversation about how to implement the president's policy on the ban: "Did we have heart-rending, soul-searching discussions about this? No. . . . The Christian right and the military were all organizing base by base and pew by pew around America, and we just thought that the president was going to issue an executive order. There was even discussion in the transition that he was going to issue a whole slew of executive orders—lifting the fetal tissue ban, the pro-choice issues, the federal workers' anti-discrimination thing, gays and lesbians in the military."[78] In fact, it was only late in the six-month cooling off process that any single aide was assigned to manage the issue. As Sam Nunn began his hearings, the White House maintained a hands-off stance, apparently more concerned about the need to "work with Nunn on other issues" than with trying to limit the damage inflicted by the one-sided lineup of witnesses. According to one administration official, the president himself did not lobby members of Congress at all on the issue; apparently "it simply wasn't as important as many of his other issues."[79]

Not only did the administration fail to lead, but also, by its constant assurances, it contributed to delays in mobilizing gay/lesbian support for the president's campaign commitment and misled activists about how badly the cause was faring. In late November, key White House aide George Stephanopoulos urged the gay/

lesbian community to stay calm and trust the Clinton team to manage the issue.[80] In the days leading up to the January inauguration, when word was received by activists of the cooling off period, Stephanopoulos followed up the president's own assurances, telling David Mixner: "There is no way that this six-month period should be viewed as a lessening of the president-elect's commitment. David, he is going to sign that executive order. This I promise you. We need your support for the President's strategy."[81]

In face-to-face meetings with gay and lesbian activists, the White House continued to provide assurances. Presidential advisers were privately discussing some version of "don't ask, don't tell," even knowing that it would be regarded by gays and lesbians as a betrayal, but they still offered assurances of Clinton's commitment to lifting the ban at a March 26th meeting with activist leaders.[82] On April 16, Clinton himself met representatives of gay/lesbian organizations in the Oval Office, and declared unequivocally his attention to sign the executive order lifting the ban on July fifteenth as promised.[83] Tim McFeeley, the seasoned director of the Human Rights Campaign Fund, later wrote of that meeting: "I have lobbied hundreds of straight male politicians on gay issues. And they're always twitching. They're always nervous. Bill Clinton was the coolest cucumber for a straight politician. . . . He went out of his way to assure us not to worry. And he went into all these anecdotes about how, at every ceremony, one or another uniformed person would come up to him and say, 'Thank you. You are doing the right thing.' . . . It was clear to us that he felt he was doing the right thing."[84]

In June, the White House was starting to send signals of compromise. But only a few days away from the announcement, aides were still trying to convince activists that they would be pleased with the president's plan—enough to be able to support it.[85] This despite the fact that the policy being drafted clearly fell short, by a wide margin, of what lobbyists had delineated as the absolute minimum acceptable to them.

At every step of their concession on the ban, the White House demanded utter loyalty from gays and lesbians close to the administration. When Mixner threatened to go public with his criticism of Clinton's "segregation" statement in March, presidential aide Rahm Emanuel echoed the plantation mentality that had surfaced during the transition, urging him to be thankful for all the administration had already done for gays and lesbians, and threatening him with banishment from the White House if he criticized the president on television.[86]

Some Washington activists blame Clinton insiders such as David Mixner and Bob Hattoy for not understanding the team-player expectations imposed on them, which are universally known among appointees to any new administration and widely understood within the Washington Beltway. Such criticisms understate the frustration and anger created by the pattern of White House arrogance and deception that was becoming so apparent in March and would intensify in the months to follow.

Activist Weaknesses

By the time of the Clinton election in 1992, national lesbian and gay activist groups were larger and more experienced in the politics of the mainstream than in any other country. The major Washington-based organizations had accumulated some of the resources required to make a difference in American federal politics (see Chapter 9). The Human Rights Campaign now ranks among the top thirty or so political action committees (PACs) in Washington, and the Gay and Lesbian Victory Fund is rapidly gaining influence by channeling donations to selected lesbian and gay electoral candidates. The National Gay and Lesbian Task Force is the longest standing of the three, devoting some of its resources to mainstream lobbying. All three include on their staffs individuals with substantial skill in working Washington's political networks. A number of informed observers believe that the ''insider'' resources of the national groups have been deployed well.

But for playing in the big leagues, and for waging battle on a major national issue, the resources are modest. These groups have had little practice in mobilizing the kinds of political activity that other groups, most obviously the Christian right, have mastered. At the time of the military debate, the national groups had never focused on building a mass base. As one activist put it, ''We don't have any legs in the movement.''[87] Although Barney Frank applies too much weight to this factor as an explanation for the failure to lift the military ban, he does point justifiably to a weakness in the movement:

> The only problem they have is that the troops don't do their job. Lobbying on high-priority issues, high-visibility issues, is a matter of getting people to write and call. The basic problem with the gay and lesbian constituency is that it doesn't have the write-and-call outlook. We're moving away from that some, but people would rather go to a parade or a rally than write to a member of the House or Senate. . . .
>
> We suffer on the political left from a lot of self-fulfilling prophecies—''politicians don't care, they don't listen, it's all big money.'' Money counts on low-priority, low-visibility issues where there is no public opinion. But if there's any significant public opinion on an issue, it will swamp money any day.[88]

The failure to mobilize sufficient grassroots lobbying was therefore in part a function of the priorities of national organizations, but also a function of a political quiescence and skepticism not uncharacteristic of the broader American population.[89] Gays and lesbians have even more reason than the average American for doubting that getting in touch with a member of Congress will make a difference. Writing to an elected politician is an expression of faith in the system which few of them have.

National groups, particularly the Campaign for Military Service (CMS), founded to spearhead political mobilization and lobbying to lift the ban, were also thought to have misjudged some of their strategy. For example, their media stories of lesbian and gay military personnel underrepresented the experience of racial minorities, thus reinforcing the (largely accurate) perception of the gay activist leadership in Washington as overwhelmingly white. This reduced the power of the parallels between homophobic and racist discrimination, and probably diminished the breadth of alliances supporting the campaign.

The most widely heard criticism dealt with the slow buildup of the campaign to lift the ban, though some of that tardiness resulted from White House assurances that the Clinton team would manage the issue. The CMS was formed only after the storm of protest in late January, but even then it seemed slow to organize. It concentrated its early labors on low-key lobbying and on developing media-focused strategies such as the "Tour of Duty" (a cross-country bus tour), some of which was useful and some unproductive. As late as March 22, the head of the CMS was still talking about "revving up" a grassroots campaign.[90] Delay resulted in part from a belief that to be effective, the campaign could not peak until the end of the six-month cooling off period, a belief that persisted despite signs of dramatic slippage in Congress.

Delays were also a product of distrust between the new group and the established Washington-based gay and lesbian organizations. Some of the existing national groups felt that the CMS activists lacked sufficient experience in Washington politics and in lobbying, though others believed that Tom Stoddard, the executive director, was doing the best he could under the circumstances. One said: "It is like mobilizing an army with no vehicles, no gasoline, no money, no resources, and being on the front lines somewhere six months in the future."[91]

The difficulty of organizing a response, including a grassroots response, was exacerbated by the fact that the military ban had not been a high priority for gay activists. In the late 1980s, groups such as the Task Force had taken it on more seriously than in the past. But most activists on the forefront of gay/lesbian politics shared to varying degrees an antipathy toward an institution thought to represent all the hierarchical heterosexual values that their movement abhorred, and believed that the chances for reforming it were slight. The early 1990s saw an important shift in attention, but, as former Task Force head Urvashi Vaid has pointed out, even during the 1992 election, "the antigay ban was not an issue on the minds of most gay and lesbian Americans." Thus, when it became the first issue to be addressed by the new president, many activists were taken aback.[92]

The slowness to mobilize was also a result of the excessive optimism that accompanied Clinton's election. The euphoria and hopefulness were a potent mix, even for experienced activists. Vaid, more skeptical of politicians than most, proclaimed that gays and lesbians "have broken through every barrier that existed in mainstream politics'' and would now be "part of the governing of this country."[93]

The hopes and expectations built up by Clinton's promises, and implicit in the electoral support accorded him, were reinforced in the weeks following the election, with the military ban becoming ever more the focus of attention. Immediately after the election, David Mixner, one of the three gays seen to be most insinuated into the president-elect's networks, was quoted in the *Washington Blade* as saying, "There is not one second of doubt in my mind that Bill Clinton will sign an executive order" lifting the ban.[94] Tim McFeeley of the Human Rights Campaign Fund thought that as president of the United States, Clinton was powerful enough to lift the ban with an executive order if he really wanted to: "With Democratic majorities in both houses of Congress, we didn't think it would be a problem."[95]

Some critics argue that Washington-based activists ought to have known enough about the climate in the capital, and what it takes to get things done in Congress, to have recognized the impediments to removing the ban. But even among some experienced Capitol Hill insiders, there was considerable optimism. As a well-connected Democratic congressional aide recalls of the period right after the election, "The working assumption was that this would not necessarily be an easy thing to do, that it would involve a great deal of delicacy, but ultimately it would happen, and the only question was how quickly and what form it would take."[96] The difficulty facing activists lay partly in their inexperience in dealing with a sympathetic administration and in operating within a political climate that was other than overwhelmingly negative. Unprecedented openings were being created for a kind of "insider" politics that all too easily offered the illusion of power. White House assurances that the ban was to be lifted contributed to the demobilization of activists until it was too late.

The point remains, though, that even if the perceptions of gay and lesbian activists had been more accurate and their connections to a mass of supporters better developed, they could not have matched the volume of mail and phone calls mobilized by the religious right. And even if they had been able to match it, they would not have prevailed against a congressional majority buttressed by the U.S. military. In the words of Bob Hattoy: "All of a sudden the White House . . . and the gay and lesbian community . . . all had to go into high gear to do probably the most difficult task that the community has faced—to lift the ban in the miliary. . . . It was the most difficult because we were up against the military might of the United States of America—we're up against the Pentagon—we're up against the most institutionalized homophobia that you could find in America today."[97]

There were those in the administration and on Capitol Hill who believed that some small progress might emerge from the debacle of 1993, but those hopes were soon dashed. In the years that followed, service personnel were still being asked about their sexual orientation, mental health and medical records were still being pried open, and sweeping investigations were still being instigated on the basis of secondhand reports.[98] There were 597 discharges on the basis of homosexuality in 1994, 722 in 1995, and 850 in 1996—almost up to the same level as before the 1992 election.

Eliminating discrimination against lesbians and gays in the military proved more difficult by far than most proponents of change had believed. Postmortems among activists pitted those who had always believed in accommodating to prevailing American norms of political representation against those who sought a revival of direct action tactics, and between those who attributed failure to the cowardice of politicians and those who blamed the failure of gay organizations to mobilize grassroots support. All but a few shared the peculiarly American optimism that victory would have been attainable but for the failures of individual participants in the process.

Despite the temptation among protagonists to assign blame to one or another single factor, the impediments to success were various, and for the moment insurmountable. And while there was to be sure individual prejudice, weakness, and misjudgment, there were also institutional hurdles that stood in the way of progressive change on a variety of fronts. They do not preclude advances on behalf of gays and lesbians or other marginalized groups, even in the aftermath of defeat, but they make change extraordinarily difficult to attain, especially at the federal level. That was true before the 1994 election, which produced a Republican majority in Congress; it was even more true afterward.

The campaign to lift the ban brought gays, lesbians, and their allies face to face with a military establishment of unusual size and political power. The wholesale resistance of the U.S. military might well have been sufficient to stop even a more determined and skillful president. Although there was real interest in lifting the ban within the new administration, most notably on the part of the president, there were recurrent indications from Clinton himself of a relatively shallow understanding of what real equality in the armed services entailed.

Proponents of lifting the ban also faced a powerful religious right which builds on the high degree of religiosity of Americans, their relative sexual conservativeness, and their anxieties about rapid social change, and which is able to muster precisely the kind of grassroots anger that most intimidates politicians. It is not so much that anti-gay popular sentiment is greater in the United States than elsewhere, but that it can be more readily tapped by political and religious networks that treat gay and lesbian visibility as a symbol for all that is threatening about the modern world.

Gay rights advocates confront a statutory web that discriminates against sexual difference in ways that feed popular stereotypes and reinforce double standards about "private" behavior. They also face the extraordinary challenge of, first, maintaining lobbying contact with hundreds of legislators and officials in an extraordinarily complex political system, and, second, generating enough grassroots pressure to be noticed above the din created by thousands of lobbyists. But even in the American legislative arena, gains are possible. Hate crimes legislation that included sexual orientation was passed in 1990, under a Republican administration. AIDS funding was increased substantially by President Clinton at the same time that his proposal to lift the military ban was turning into a rout. Even in the disheartening aftermath of that debacle, the administration issued a directive (through the Office of Personnel Management) citing existing law as prohibiting discrimination against federal employees on the basis of sexual orientation.

The contradictory messages that can be pulled out of the Clinton presidency illustrate a continuing dilemma for gay/lesbian and other progressive movements. The U.S. system creates inescapable inducements to organize within the political mainstream, but in the process it sows the seeds for separation between, on the one hand, those wrapped up in mainstream political mechanisms and, on the other, the average citizen, or community member and even local activists. The sheer complexity of the system envelops those closest to it in its intricacies and alienates those more distant from it by its incomprehensibility. Activists oriented exclusively to insider politics risk being absorbed into a political culture that exaggerates the impact of legal change and imposes severely judgmental limits on what are thought to be "realistic" goals and acceptable tactics.

Some Washington-based activists have such allegiance to the political order within which they work that they understate the tilt of the playing field against gay rights, and overstate the potential for success. This leads them to believe, for example, that the military ban could have been lifted with more effective gay and lesbian mobilizing. They are not necessarily wrong in the criticisms they level at lobbying groups, but they may overestimate the extent to which the legislative system responds to that kind of pressure.

Engagement with mainstream political institutions is more essential in the American political system than in any other because of the constant need for vigilance. The failure to lift the ban, however, served as a reminder that political activism focusing only on political maneuvering inside the Washington Beltway is insufficient for effecting change. Gays and lesbians of diverse political orientations have all drawn from the defeat on the military ban the lesson that national groups have to build more substantial grassroots foundations.

The failure to lift the ban also constitutes a timely reminder of the place of lesbians and gays on the American political agenda. If they are in the mainstream, they are at best on the fringe, and too often not even there. The claims to equal rights can be framed in traditional liberal language, but they do represent, and are perceived by many to represent for many a challenge to entrenched constructs of gender, sexuality, and family. In a political culture so often riven by anxiety about social change, and in which questions of sexuality have so regularly stood for a broader discomfort with changing social relations, politicians remain loath to speak of homosexuality at all.

Representative Barney Frank, in his Rayburn Building office in Washington (June 1992). Photo: David Rayside

Barney Frank at the 1993 March on Washington. Photo: *Congressional Quarterly*/Jenkins

8

Barney Frank and the
Art of the Possible

There is really no honest way not to be pretty open about

being gay. No human being can get through the day and

give honest answers to questions without telling people what

his sexual orientation is.

Barney Frank, in _The Advocate_ (17 October 1995)

In the summer of 1987, Barney Frank became the second member of the U.S. Congress to reveal that he was gay. Gerry Studds had been first, forced by imminent revelations to disclose his sexual orientation in 1983. Both were Democrats representing districts outside Boston, in the relatively "liberal" state of Massachusetts. Each in his own entirely distinct way had already earned a reputation as an effective legislator and conscientious district representative.

Frank had spoken out on sexual diversity issues before coming out, and in the years following his revelation he developed as high a profile in relation to these issues as any politician in Washington. He earned admiration within activist networks spanning a considerable ideological and strategic range, and among lesbians and gay men who would not normally pay attention to congressional politics. With a short-lived exception, Frank also continued to earn the respect of legislative colleagues as a highly intelligent, forceful participant in Capitol Hill debate.

Frank has performed three quite distinct roles that are difficult to combine in most other political systems—one as a district representative with high local visibility, another as a partisan legislator in Washington, and a third as vocal spokesperson for a national lesbian/gay constituency. In undertaking the last in particular, he has been able to intervene in legislative debate and decision-making with a degree of independence and prominence that is rare for individual politicians in other countries. The fragmentation of power and the absence of strict party discipline in the American political system allow this openly gay legislator to exercise real influence. Barney Frank is an unusual politician, but the electoral support he receives in his home district and the respect he has won among congressional colleagues provide a glimpse of the opportunities available to and constraints imposed on openly gay or lesbian legislators in the U.S. system more generally.

If the potential for policy entrepreneurship in the U.S. Congress has provided room for Barney Frank and others like him to build bridges between party politics and social movement activism, the pressures within the system to maneuver in pragmatic ways inevitably impose strains. The complex balance of power in the American political order makes all but impossible the sort of dramatic political change that social movement activists demand. It is precisely when some change seems attainable that the gap widens between activists with transformative objectives and those who work inside institutions governed by norms of incrementalism. At such times, a legislative role like Frank's is indispensable for both exacting gains and minimizing losses, but it inevitably casts him—fairly or unfairly—as a pragmatist willing to compromise fundamental principles.

African-American, Latino, and feminist legislators have similar conflicts. They too see themselves as representative of cross-country constituencies in addition to their home districts. They too enter legislative politics with high expectations loaded onto their shoulders by a broader social movement.

Barney Frank and "Prudent Liberalism"

Barney Frank was born in 1940 of Roosevelt Democrat parents, and descended from Russian immigrant grandparents—"a born outsider, a left-handed Jewish guy from New Jersey with a lifelong tendency toward overweight and speech tics." Every description of Barney Frank begins with reference to his intelligence and his quickness. As one journalist has commented: "The thoughts crackle across his synapses and into his speech so fast that Frank often leaves his listeners in the dust."[1] His gatling-gun speech, accented with New Jersey and Massachusetts inflections, has none of the set phrases or self-importance often associated with public figures.

Frank can be witty, and news photographs often show him with a glint in his eye, those next to him smiling or laughing in return. But he can be devastating in attack, prompting Democrats to designate him "point man" in their opposition to the Republican congressional majority elected in November 1994—"unofficial House leader of the opposition."[2] Frank's skill and intelligence sometimes translate into an impatience with those who do not understand the intricacies of legislative politics. As one acquaintance has remarked, "If you say something he doesn't like . . . Barney will rip your ideas to shreds and spit it right back at you."[3] He can also be impatient with the social niceties that are usually expected of politicians. One newspaper profile described his brusque style: "In a rumpled blue T-shirt and casual pants, Frank announces himself to guests by walking briskly out to the reception desk and grunting, while gazing in the direction of the window, 'all right, I'm ready.' There were no hellos, no pleasantries, Frank explained later, because 'I do a lot of things at one time and I like to do them fast.' "[4]

Those who work with him refer to his "strong values" and his caring attention to constituency needs. He might impatiently refuse to look at a constituent's photograph of her husband, killed in an airplane crash she wants investigated, but still ensure that her request will be treated seriously. "In the way he'll treat someone face-to-face, the person might think they got nowhere with him; then they get a letter from some agency saying that Barney Frank had been calling and their problems had been solved."[5]

A *New York Times* profile described him as one of the last "old-time liberals" who still believe that "government is good."[6] The ratings given him by lobby groups of the left and right, based on his voting record, consistently show him on the left-liberal side of the congressional Democratic Party.[7] But his own beliefs and sense of strategy pull him back from some positions that would be thought typical of his own party's progressives. In *Frankly Speaking*, a book outlining his political views published in early 1992, Frank argued to the nation's Democrats that they should work harder at striking responsive chords with mainstream American values and worry less about angering their own left wing: "Democrats have come to be perceived as insufficiently pro-American, both internationally and at home; unenthusiastic about free enterprise, especially the principle that one should work for one's keep; unwilling and unprepared to move harshly against criminals; and disrespectful of the way average Americans live their lives."[8] His beliefs are not just about tactics. The author of one 1992 profile described Frank's liberalism as being shaped by patriotism, and then quoted his sister, Democratic activist Ann Lewis: "For us, there was this wonderful, precious, never-to-be-taken-for-granted fact that we were living in a country where we had a right to participate—where if you cared enough, you could make a difference."[9]

Discussing his book, as well as his ideological outlook, in a personal interview, Frank offered this self-analysis: "I would say that I'm more of a free-market believer than most of the book [implies]. I'm very good with wanting to give maximum amounts of money to poor people, and freedom of expression, and combating discrimination. . . . I think we can reduce [spending] militarily. On the other hand, I'm more of a deregulator. I think the profit motive is a good thing. On crime, I believe that, one, bad social conditions cause crime, and two, that they never justify crime. You should try to get rid of bad social conditions and lock up anybody who hurts anybody else."[10]

Frank's outlook was formed more by the pragmatic reformism of the 1950s than by the radical and anti-establishment politics of the 1960s. Although he was liberal enough in his early years to be thought something of an outsider, the prudence echoing through his more recent writing reflects views that have always marked him as a maverick even within the liberal camp. Since his first election to Congress, an observer notes, he has also become "more conscientious about pocketbook issues and unwilling to burden people with taxes."[11]

Election and Re-election

Barney Frank has built a solid electoral foundation in the Fourth Congressional District of Massachusetts by paying careful attention to local needs, and campaigning effectively on the basis of beliefs that appeal to a wide range of his constituents. His eventual coming out as gay did little to tarnish his considerable reputation at home, thus securing him a congressional platform from which to wield legislative influence.

Frank first scored electoral success at the state level in 1972, winning a seat from the Republicans in part on the strength of a progressive left appeal to a Boston constituency that included a large student population. He then won three more elections to the state legislature in 1974, 1976, and 1978, his sexual orientation a secret throughout. Like Chris Smith in Britain and Svend Robinson in Canada, Frank became active in party affairs as a young man, joining the Young Democrats Club as a Harvard undergraduate. Later, as a Ph.D. student in political science, he worked on the campaign of Boston mayoralty candidate Kevin White, becoming executive assistant to the new mayor from 1967 to 1971. He then spent a brief period as a Washington-based aide to one of the state's Democratic members of Congress.

In 1976 Massachusetts State Representative Elaine Noble had come out as lesbian, the first lesbian or gay politician in the country to reveal her sexual orientation publicly. Frank knew Noble, but felt he could not follow her example. He recalled: "When I got involved in politics, I was terribly closeted. I was terribly frightened of anyone finding out. I thought it would just destroy whatever kind of life I wanted to live. In 1972 when I decided to run for State Senate, I made a conscious choice for a political career over a personal life."[12] But that did not prevent him from taking pro-gay positions: "When I ran for the [Massachusetts] legislature in '72, I had to deal with this. A 32-year-old man, unmarried. People begin to speculate and guess. I was not in a position to come out, but I promised myself I would never back away from the issue in a public-policy sense. In 1973, when I cosponsored a gay-rights bill, I was scared to death."[13]

In 1980 he ran for the U.S. House of Representatives, with the endorsement of the retiring Democrat, and won with 52 percent. The Republicans attacked his liberalism, but he narrowly resisted the Reagan-led Republican tide. Redistricting then combined part of his constituency with that of incumbent Republican Margaret Heckler—much more of her district than his. Her campaign played on family themes, jabbing at Frank's "bachelor" status and his support for gay rights. The Democrats countered, in part, with a commercial featuring sixty-nine-year-old Elsie Frank talking about Barney Frank and his support for the elderly: "And how do I know? Well, I'm his mother!"[14] He won that election, with 62 percent of the vote.

In being closeted, Frank by and large avoided the impediments facing candidates for political office who were open about their sexual orientation from the beginning. They were much more dependent on unusually progressive districts with substantial concentrations of gay and lesbian constituents. They were also more vulnerable to claims that they would be interested only in sexual orientation issues. Although Frank's Fourth District certainly had liberal pockets, it also had more traditional areas. At the time, the district ran from upper-middle-class suburbs on the southwestern edge of Boston to a scattering of towns farther south, many suffering from industrial decline and working-class unemployment. The Boston end of the district includes a large Jewish population; other areas include substantial Roman Catholic working-class populations. In contrast to Frank's early local Boston constituency, his congressional district has little in the way of a visible sexual minority presence.

In 1983 Congressman Gerry Studds, representing a neighboring district southeast of Boston, was forced out of the closet by soon-to-be-public allegations of sexual relations with a seventeen-year-old congressional page ten years before. Ultimately the House censured Studds, along with another member of the House of Representatives found guilty of having sex with a seventeen-year-old female page. In subsequent hard-fought elections, Republicans did not hesitate to raise the issue of homosexuality and "family values." The district had sizable conservative pockets, delivering more votes for Ronald Reagan in 1980 and 1984 than any other in Massachusetts. But Studds held on, in part because of his extraordinary devotion to constituency service.[15]

Frank faced less serious opposition from the Republicans than Studds did in 1984, and none in 1986, winning with 74 percent and 89 percent of the vote, respectively. The anti-gay innuendo that had featured in the 1982 campaign was also largely absent. At the same time, Frank's own homosexuality and his support for gay-related causes was becoming more visible in both Washington and Boston. By 1984 he was, as he puts it, "half in and half out" of the closet.[16]

In the spring of 1987, the death from AIDS of a Republican Congressman provoked media speculation about that politician's sexuality. Frank concluded that he never wanted that to happen to him.[17] Then a reference to Frank in the autobiography of ex-Congressman Robert Bauman that same spring provided him an extra nudge. He made known to the supportive *Boston Globe* his readiness to answer questions about his sexuality. And on May 30 the newspaper printed the page one story that gave Massachusetts and the United States their second openly gay Congressman.[18]

Asked why he had not come out earlier, Frank cited a "fear of the consequences" among constituents.[19] Like Chris Smith, Svend Robinson, and other openly gay politicians, he acknowledged that he would "have to work harder to offset the suggestion that all I care about is gay rights."[20] Some years later, in a published article, he persisted in his view of the dangers: "The single most important piece of advice that I can give to openly gay or lesbian candidates is to resist the effort that will almost certainly be made to portray you as someone who will focus almost all of your energies on gay and lesbian issues to the exclusion of all other issues."[21] In the end, Frank had little difficulty with the "one-issue-candidate" charge, since he had already established a track record on a variety of fronts, and had congressional committee assignments that bore no obvious relationship to sexual orientation issues.

In any event, once he did come out, local public reaction suggested to Frank that people were more accepting than was commonly believed. A poll in his district revealed that twice as many people thought he was damaged politically as were themselves upset by his gayness. "In other words," he concluded "there is a greater perception of anti-gay prejudice than actually exists."[22] In a 1995 interview he reflected on the same theme: "A lot of people are not homophobic, but they think they're supposed to be. They think that if they don't express prejudice, people will think there's something the matter with them."[23]

The 1988 election was the first that Frank fought as openly gay, and its results seemed to support his growing impression that the electoral costs would be low or nonexistent. The Republican challenger, Debra Tucker, a supporter of Pat Robertson's presidential campaign, raised the question of "family values," but was swept aside by Frank's 70 percent majority. Frank benefited, of course, from incumbency, in a political system that has long rewarded it to an extraordinary degree.

In August 1989 the roof seemed to cave in, when sometime hustler Steve Gobie publicly revealed a relationship with Frank (between 1985 and 1987). Gobie claimed that he had used the congressman's Washington apartment for prostitution, and that Frank had helped him by fixing parking tickets and securing probation. The news was covered extensively on front pages across the country. Even the otherwise supportive *Boston Globe* called on him to resign. In a late-September cover story, *Newsweek* described the episode as "a scandal that so plainly reflects discredit on the House of Representatives, and on the gay-rights movement, that some of Frank's former allies are quickly and quietly deserting him."[24]

In the early weeks of the scandal, Frank himself was unsure whether his constituents would continue supporting him. He chose to confront the charges directly by admitting to "stupid mistakes," and his fortunes seemed to improve. As one aide put it: "I think people expected him to sort of hedge and hide, and try to deny it. When the story came out . . . he held a press conference immediately and just put it on the table and said, 'I made a mistake.' And I think that is the way he is about everything that he does, and people like that."[25] Then Newt Gingrich, Republican minority whip at the time, tried unsuccessfully to engineer a censure of Frank in the House of Representatives. By an overwhelming majority, the House eventually settled on a much milder "reprimand" that implicitly discounted some of the accusations leveled against him.[26]

Polls taken in the immediate aftermath of the Gobie revelations showed that only 56 percent of constituents believed that Frank deserved reelection.[27] By the time of the reprimand the following summer, some of the local press in his district was predicting a relatively easy election. Even the right-wing *Washington Times*, which had originally broken the story about Gobie, cited a degree of local support, quoting a suburban Republican mayor who described Frank as a "first-class congressman."[28]

The Gobie episode was raised repeatedly by Frank's Republican opponent in the 1990 election. John Soto took an AIDS test and challenged Frank to do the same. But as a local journalist noted: "If a person in Massachusetts is doing constituency service, what they do in their private life, nobody cares."[29] Playing the anti-gay card did not work, and Frank won the election with 66 percent of the vote, down only 4 percent from 1988 (less than the losses suffered by most Massachusetts Democrats).

THE 1992 CAMPAIGN. Frank is a highly effective vote-getter, though he admits to hating the repetitiveness and physical demands of campaigning: "I was not naturally good at campaigning when I started. I was always good at the inside part of life in politics. When I started I was very good at relating to other politicians; but I wasn't very good with the general public, and I've had to work on that. And now I have a sense of pride of craft, that I do this well, but it was not my natural thing."[30] On the hustings, he marshals quick-witted attacks on the Republicans to partisan crowds, liberal defenses of social policy to seniors, and patriotic references to international trade relations to fishing industry workers. All these pitches reflect core beliefs of his, and his audiences are invariably receptive. Frank also highlights his fiscal caution and his opposition to additional taxes. In a radio ad used in the 1992 campaign, Frank spoke of having worked to cut tens of billions from the federal budget. He cited cuts in military spending, federal agricultural subsidies, water projects, and aerospace development: "These savings can build for deficit reduction, and also for health care, education, transportation, and law enforcement. So if people tell you all Democrats are big spenders, you tell them that old saw doesn't cut it any more."[31] To some extent Frank can also play the traditional ward politician, pointing to all the benefits that he has been able to bring a particular part of the district, though his reputation for looking after his constituents comes much more from the attention he and his staff pay to individual requests for assistance than from the traditional pork barrel benefits that members of Congress try to lavish on their districts.

Election campaigning at the local level depends on long-established party networks, and Frank's success in reaching his constituents is built on elaborate party links forged over the years since he first entered politics. In areas newly added to his district, Frank made contact with Democratic Committee chairs and members. He relied on some local contacts from his years in the state legislature to introduce him to key Democrats in New Bedford, and to others connected with the local fishing industry. Forming such networks entails maintaining links to the

Massachusetts Democratic Party, though such connections can create difficulty. In the 1990 gubernatorial race, the Democratic candidate was John Silber, a centrist with conservative views on some social policy matters, including sexual orientation. Frank endorsed him over the victorious Republican William Weld, whose positioning on those issues was substantially more progressive. The support he gave Silbur raised eyebrows among Boston-area gay/lesbian activists. Frank downplayed his involvement, explaining: "Once you're running for a fairly high office in Congress, you make so many demands on people based on party that you really can't turn that on and off. I used to endorse Republicans when I was in the state legislature, because I was more of an entrepreneurial operator— you know, a one-man band. Now I just go to Democrats and ask for help, so I don't endorse Republicans. I was fairly mute [with Silber]; I just had my picture taken with [Democratic candidates]."[32]

ELECTIONS IN 1994 AND 1996. The 1994 election gave the Republicans a majority in both the House of Representatives and the Senate, elevating Newt Gingrich and Bob Dole into leadership positions in the two chambers. The swing had little electoral impact on Frank, who increased his majority to 72 percent, though for the first time he would be entering a new Congress without the kind of access to the House leadership that he had enjoyed under a Democratic majority. Gerry Studds won his race with a relatively comfortable 62 percent of the vote.

Nationwide, there were at least forty-nine openly gay or lesbian candidates for political office.[33] This represented a modest increase over the forty-four in 1992, and a striking contrast to the eighteen who sought electoral office in 1990 and the twelve who ran in 1988. Of the newcomers, two thirds lost their races, some of them citing homophobic attacks. All but one of the twenty-one incumbents won, most arguing that their being gay or lesbian had not harmed them. Some believed that their openness had in fact reinforced constituents' faith in their honesty at a time when cynicism about politicians was widespread.[34] Half of these successful incumbents were women, and one was African-American.

By this time the ranks of openly gay members of Congress had increased to three. Wisconsin Republican Representative Steve Gunderson, edging toward coming out in 1993, was pushed out by anti-gay Republican Bob Dornan in March of the following year.[35] Described in one profile as one of the House of Representatives' brightest, most thoughtful, and most conscientious members, he resigned as chief deputy whip in protest against his party's "growing image of intolerance."[36] He then survived a bruising primary challenge from right-wing forces in his own party and won reelection. He thus became the only Republican among openly gay or lesbian politicians elected to national or state office. In 1996, however, the prospect of another anti-gay challenge from the right-wing of his own party caused him to end his congressional career.[37]

In early August 1996, Republican Jim Kolbe, a veteran representative from Arizona, was nudged out by an impending story in the gay magazine *The Ad-*

vocate.[38] The "outing" was provoked by his having just voted in favor of the anti-gay Defense of Marriage Act (DOMA), although he had a moderately progressive voting record on other gay- and AIDS-related issues. He announced his homosexuality before the story appeared, and made clear his intention to seek reelection. By this time Gerry Studds had indicated that he would not run again, leaving only Kolbe and Frank as openly gay congressional incumbents facing the November polls. In the fall election Frank easily won, his 72 percent vote the same as in the 1994 election despite some anti-gay campaigning by his opponent. Kolbe also won reelection with a slightly increased majority of 69 percent.

THE ROLE OF SEXUAL ORIENTATION. Frank maintains a very high profile in his work on behalf of gay causes, and speaks regularly about them to gay and lesbian audiences, as well as to the national press. He is open to being interviewed by reporters about such issues, in both the gay/lesbian and mainstream press. On a Boston-area radio call-in program taped on election day 1992, most of the callers' questions were on gay-related themes, and Frank never once hesitated to provide full responses. In an article addressing issues facing openly-gay politicians, he declared that "it is neither politically sensible nor morally acceptable for a gay or lesbian candidate to weaken his or her positions on substantive issues involving gay men and lesbians."[39]

But Frank's positions on issues of race, gender, and sexual orientation got almost no play in the 1992 campaign. Neither the Gobie scandal nor other issues connected with Frank's sexual orientation were raised by his Republican opponent, though personal attacks were prominent in the Republican campaign against Gerry Studds. Frank's own campaigning since his coming out in 1987 made little reference to sexual orientation, except at specific times when he had to confront his opponents on the issue. Even detailed summaries of his positions in the 1992 campaign—including, for example, a woman's right to choose—made no reference to sexual orientation. Frank himself sees this as unsurprising: "Let me put it this way: What do you think the purpose of a campaign is? I think the purpose of a campaign is to win votes. . . . There's a lot of things I care about that I don't talk about. I don't talk about race relations; I don't talk much about women; I don't talk very much about free speech. I talk about the issues [with which] I can reach people the most."[40]

The Democratic voters of Bridgewater, and even of relatively liberal Newton, are content to see their congressman's homosexuality only in terms of his personal life, much like constituents of Chris Smith and even of Svend Robinson. As one staffer put it: "I think they keep it as a separate issue. His personal life is his personal life, and what he does in office is completely different. Which is one of the things he talked a lot about after the [Gobie] scandal broke—that 'this is my private life and that has nothing to do with the job I do in office.' Whether they agree with the way Barney lives his life or not, they accept him as a good congressman, and I think they sort of overlook that."[41] The voters, not surprisingly, focus on the work that their congressman accomplishes for the district as a whole, and for individual constituents in particular. Whatever else Frank does in Washington, or in Masschusetts for that matter, is either unknown to them or irrelevant. For example, when asked privately about Frank's gayness, one young Maritime Union organizer acknowledged that all the membership knew about Frank and Studds being gay, but did not care. They cared about jobs, and Studds, their former congressman, had done a lot for them. The Republicans, he said, talk about family values, but families are as much damaged by unemployment as by anything else. He and his fellow union members took pride in the fact that their new member of Congress, Barney Frank, was widely thought to be one of the smartest, if not *the* smartest, in the House of Representatives.

In the period immediately following his coming out, Frank himself seemed to be arguing that his sexuality was a private matter, although he has since acknowledged that homosexuality is not strictly about private life. In an interview published in 1992 he observed: "When you're in the public eye, you're either in or you're out. . . . For instance, I'm invited to the White House, as we all are once a year to the Christmas party, which is a pretty high visibility event with a lot of members and cabinet officers. You bring a date, so do I bring my lover, or do I pretend otherwise and bring some woman? There are no options."[42] Two years later he told another interviewer: "I defy any human being to get through a week in which you honestly answer every question to you and not give away your sexuality. 'What'd you do last night?' 'Are you married?' 'Are you seeing anybody?' Unless you're a total hermit, you're going to give away your sexual orientation."[43] But constituents in Massachesetts see little of this, and they can with relative ease retain their view that Frank's homosexuality is a private affair. He was forthright in addressing the issues raised by the Gobie scandal in a letter he sent to his constituents and is assertive in defense of gay rights when asked about them by constituents or opponents; but outside of that he does not believe that his electors are interested in his being gay, or much interested in sexual orientation issues. In his self-presentation in the district, he does little to flag the matter.

Frank has been reelected regularly since disclosing his homosexuality, and though he would be the last to deny the persistence of homophobia, his wide margins of victory have contributed to his view that gays and lesbians and their issues have entered the mainstream, and that being open about his gayness has not affected his electability in the slightest. Frank can point to his own district to illustrate the ineffectuality of the kinds of attacks featured in the Republicans' 1992 convention and the homophobic campaigning against him in 1996. In his book as well as in interviews, Frank has persisted in the view that he developed shortly after coming out, that electors are less antipathetic to gay candidacies than they think others are:

This, I think, is part of a larger social phenomenon in which race and sexual orientation are mirror opposites. Officially—legally and philosophically—America considers itself a nation opposed to racism. In fact, racism continues to be a serious problem in our society, and thus in our politics. The reverse is true with homosexuality. We have no national policies opposing discrimination against gays and lesbians. On the contrary, a presidential order banning gay men and lesbians from serving in the armed forces—a clear example of official bigotry—is still in effect. But as more and more gay men and lesbians make their sexual orientation clear, prejudice in our day-to-day lives, while still present, is diminishing. In short, I believe that America is both more racist and less homophobic in fact than it is in theory.[44]

Other openly gay candidates for office have had varied experience of anti-gay campaigning, and have divided opinions over its impact. Reports from gay and lesbian candidates at the state and local levels include frequent reference to explicitly homophobic campaigns. Gail Shibly, running for the Oregon House of Representatives in 1992, encountered anti-gay attacks targeted at her by the Oregon Citizens' Alliance, an organization spearheading an anti-gay referendum in the same election. In Seattle, Sherry Harris became the first openly lesbian African American to be elected to office when she won a city council seat in 1991, but only after enduring an anti-gay campaign waged by a Democratic primary opponent.[45]

In the 1996 election there were at least sixty-nine openly gay or lesbian candidates for electoral office. Kathleen DeBold, of the Gay and Lesbian Victory Fund (which supports such candidacies), did not think that gay-baiting by opponents was declining. She acknowledged that the issue was not raised in some races, "but in a lot of them it does matter, and the opponents will use it when they can."[46] New York State Assembly Representative Deborah Glick was accused of being "anti-child"; California gay candidate Ken Yeager was said to be putting "his own agenda first and our families last."[47] In some cases, opponents would simply point to the sexual orientation of a candidate to ensure that voters knew about it.

The issue of gay and lesbian marriage had been forced onto the national political agenda by a Hawaii court ruling in favor of recognizing such marriages. In the few months prior to the election, Congress had passed the Defense of Marriage Act, allowing states to refuse to recognize same-sex unions, and prohibiting recognition of gay marriage by the federal government. President Clinton willingly signed the bill, and his campaign even touted his support of it in an ad aired on religious radio stations. That did not prevent Republicans from using anti-gay rhetoric to attack Democrats. Their presidential campaign aired ads on Christain radio denouncing Clinton's attempt to lift the ban on gays in the military. And in response to a question put during one of the televised presidential debates, Republican candidate Bob Dole referred to a gay civil rights bill as conferring "special rights." At the local level, Republicans were more than prepared to use the marriage issue against Democrats who voted against DOMA, as they did in Barney Frank's district.[48]

The impact of such campaigning was reduced by the fact that those who contested elections for the first time as openly gay or lesbian tended to run in relatively progressive urban districts or areas with concentrations of gay and lesbian residents. Those who had won before were able to rely on the continuing advantages of incumbency, pointing to constituency service and to legislative records on a range of issues beyond sexual orientation. With increasing frequency, newcomers as well as veterans assessed their electoral fortunes as unaffected by their sexuality. San Giego councillor Christine Kehoe argues that voters are more concerned about candidates' taxation orientation than their sexual orientation.[49] Despite the anti-gay campaigning of Republicans, all twenty-four of the incumbent lesbian and gay candidates up for reelection won, as did just under half of the new candidates. The 1996 election boosted the overall total of openly gay politicians in the United States from 115 to 127.[50] For those thought to have a realistic shot at victory, other factors were often at play. When Karen Burstein lost a hard-fought 1994 race for New York State attorney general, early reactions pointed to homophobia as a factor. But a retrospective analysis by Burstein herself showed other factors to be more important, including the popularity of the law-and-order politics of her opponent.[51]

Deborah Glick has had a few years to reflect on the impact of her lesbianism on her electoral fate. She was first elected to the New York State Assembly in 1990, and has won without significant challenge since then.[52] She represents lower Manhattan, an example of both a progressive district and one with a substantial gay/lesbian population. At first, Glick and her campaign team were unsure how prominently to feature her sexual orientation. They prepared a campaign flyer announcing, "She's gay, an MBA, and a city administrator—and simply the best Democrat for the job," and then tested it in focus groups. According to Glick: "One [voter] said, 'I'm not gay myself, but if somebody's got the guts to say this, that's who I want fighting for me.' Somebody else said, 'Oh, this is what they think is most important?! That's terrible; never vote for them.' We had gay people saying, 'I'm horrified that they're trying to appeal on the basis of their sexual orientation.' Then we had people saying, 'YES! Great!' We spent a lot of money and got no answer."[53] In the end she decided to proceed, in part to ensure some control over an aspect of her candidacy that her opponents would be prepared to use against her: "We wanted voters to know that I was upfront about it, and we wanted every gay person in that district to know that there was an out lesbian running." Glick believes that this strategy did not reduce her electoral appeal. Neither does she believe that her candidacy was more difficult than it would have been for a gay man: "I think that men are, to some extent, less threatened by lesbians than gay men. They are titillated more often than not. I think there are women who are more comfortable with and not threatened by gay men—there is a history of straight women feeling comfortable with gay men because there's no threat of sexual harassment—so they are likely to be a little more paranoid about lesbians in their midst, or they just don't quite know. I think it might be a wash electorally."[54]

Barney Frank in Congress

The importance of Barney Frank in the broader movement for change on gay/lesbian/bisexual issues lies much more in his effectiveness in Congress than in the degree to which he challenges his own constituents. In fact, the solidity of his support in Massachusetts provides him with considerable independence in Washington, both to take on a legislative agenda reflecting his own ideological preoccupations, and to take up the concerns of gays and lesbians as a second constituency.[55] Like feminist, African-American, and other minority politicians, he has more legislative freedom than counterparts in his parliamentary systems to do so, and to have an impact.

THE DIFFERENCE MADE BY GENDER AND RACE. Frank has often characterized himself as an outsider on the basis of his class origins and his Jewishness, quite apart from his sexual orientation. But if those characteristics lessened his "fit" with congressional culture, there were others that helped him acquire standing and maintain it. He is of course white, in a legislature that drastically underrepresents African Americans and other visible minorities. He is also a man in an environment that is almost as heavily male dominated as any legislature in the industrialized world. His cigar-smoking bluntness and aggressive legislative style do not evoke stereotypes of gay male behavior, and dovetail perfectly with the masculine culture of national legislative politics.

Those women and African Americans who have gained electoral office have had to do so with their distinctiveness visible from the outset, in contrast to Frank and other gay members of Congress who were first elected with their sexual orientation largely invisible. The barriers to women gaining legislative office in the United States are similar to those in other political systems, exacerbated by the high cost of campaigning in the American system and the very high incumbency rates.[56] Once elected, women often experience some of the role conflict associated with operating within an institutional environment that privileges masculine behavior but punishes women who do not act in "feminine" ways. Most adapt by playing according to the rules, the pressure to do so applying to women and some other groups more forcibly than to white men. This does not prevent those women in Congress who have been influenced by feminism from cooperating with other women on legislative agendas. Congressional norms allow significant room for representatives to speak on behalf of constituencies other than their home districts, even if many "women's" issues are thought of marginal significance.

The difference that race makes for the standing of a member of Congress is difficult to assess, in part because in a public environment such as Congress, racial prejudice is concealed or heavily coded. Racial minority candidates are rarely elected from districts with heavily white majorities, suggesting that barriers to entry into legislative arenas persist. Perhaps because of the character of their home districts, they may be given more freedom to fill a distinctively African-American representional role. American legislative norms allow for "group" representation more than British parliamentary norms, and the long decades of mobilizing by African Americans have given the representation of race issues a certain legitimacy. In the early years after its formation in 1971, the Congressional Black Caucus resisted the usual politics of compromise and collegiality which so shapes the legislative style of elected politicians in Washington. Its members engaged in a number of highly visibile actions to raise the profile of race issues in Congress and increase their political weight.

In more recent years, the Black Caucus's membership has become more diversified ideologically, and less obviously dissenting from congressional norms. Several members have risen to influential positions, at least within the Democratic leadership, and in some estimations have become more effective legislators.[57] But the movement of caucus members toward an accommodation with institutional norms can work to the detriment of their relations with activist networks.[58] Some members have accused the African-American press of "declaring war" on them, and there are certainly women in Congress who could make analogous remarks about at least a portion of the feminist press.

The differences between sexual minority politicians on the one hand, and women and visible minority politicians on the other, is partly a question of numbers. There are rarely more than one or two openly gay or lesbian politicians in any single legislative arena, if any. They do not represent much of a caucus, then, and as a result may experience exaggerated pressure to behave according to prevailing expectations. The issues they speak to are newer to the political agenda than those associated with race and gender, and are more likely to provoke avoidance, even if many of them can also be framed in liberal democratic terms of equality. In short, white male sexual minority politicians are more likely than women and racial minority representatives to be seen as fitting in, while their issues remain marginalized.

The difficulties facing women and visible minorities in getting elected, especially at the national level, largely explain why the openly gay members of Congress, as well as of the British and Canadian national parliaments, have all been white men. As a result, the extent to which women or people of color would be accepted (and influential) remains unclear. About 40 percent of the openly gay politicians elected to American state legislatures have been women, and their experience suggests that disadvantages on more than one dimension do not compound in a predictable manner. Deborah Glick acknowledges the difficulties women have faced in gaining leadership positions in New York State politics, but is less certain that being a lesbian creates additional difficulties.[59]

Like Barney Frank, Deborah Glick stands out from most legislators with her skill and diligence, her widely recognized expertise on legislative matters and deftness working inside legislative politics. The fact that the Democratic speaker of the New York State Assembly was relatively progressive during Glick's early years helped ensure a culture of acceptance, and has provided her with substantial opportunities to speak on the floor of the legislature. Glick herself also argues that the egregiousness of the stereotypes about lesbians are such that they are easy to break. Those who remain obviously prejudiced actually help in some respects, because their bigotry makes others reluctant to associate with them. To some extent, too, acceptance has come from the way the Assembly constitutes a club, geographically removed from the districts of all but a few members.

What about the lesbians and gays of color in legislative politics? Only a few have won office at either the state or local level. One reason is that they are less likely to be out than white lesbians, and especially white gay men. That is partly a function of differences in economic security and job status, and lesser access to role models and gay-dominated commercial spaces. Those who are visible are less likely to have the requisite connections for the massive fundraising needed to contest electoral office in America.

STANDING AMONG COLLEAGUES. Making an impact for an openly gay or lesbian politician means establishing a visible presence in the legislative arena, creating a human face for sexual orientation issues. Impact also derives from gaining a "seat at the table" where bargains are negotiated and decisions made. Both kinds of impact require stature among colleagues in a highly rule-bound institution. Barney Frank is acknowledged throughout the House as possibly the brightest representative. Inside and outside Congress, he is thought an effective legislator. According to a 1995 article in the *New York Times*, he has earned a reputation as "a sharp-tongued and quick-witted debater, an astute deal-maker and one of the most colorful and quotable figures in the Congress."[60] Another profile characterized him as "one of the intellectual and political leaders of the Democratic Party in the House, political theorist and pit bull all at the same time."[61]

When Frank publicly revealed his gayness in 1987, some thought his career was over. Then-Speaker Tip O'Neill, who himself had more than a little difficulty accepting Frank's homosexuality, believed that the announcement had eliminated his chances of one day becoming Speaker of the House.[62] Others suggested that he had cut off any possibility of appointment or election to higher office. But there is a nonjudgmental clubbiness in Congress, as in any other legislative body, which increases the toleration of differences, at least among its members. Colleagues knew Frank, of course, and many had worked with him on committees or in the complex coalition-building process for which he had already established a reputation. Just after coming out, Frank himself talked of the reactions of his colleagues as largely positive: "Most of my colleagues are frankly happy for me that I've been able to do it [be out], because obviously, I'm a much happier, better adjusted individual. I mean, trying to live in two camps like that is a very tough thing to do. . . . [The] reaction has been overwhelmingly supportive. There are a couple of members who have reacted negatively, the sort of fools and bigots I wouldn't want to have anything to do with anyway."[63] More than once, he cited the case of Senator Alan Simpson, "the acerbic and very conservative Republican whip, who told Mr. Frank he admired his courage and wished him well."[64]

Frank is a consummate insider, as the writer of a 1992 article in a gay magazine noted: "Barney Frank is leaning against a rail, schmoozing with representatives after a vote on the House floor, clearly very much at home. At this moment, the House looks more like a cocktail party than a gathering of elected officials, and Frank is working it. He cuts through the sea of blue in his gray suit, smiling, nodding, and if any of them is thinking 'fag,' they do not let it show."[65] Frank's ability to maintain his standing in the House was also influenced by the uncontroversial circumstances in which he came out. The obvious contrast was Gerry Studds, whose sexual relationship with a congressional page years before had cast a permanent shadow over his reputation among colleagues. He was seen as occasionally aloof or patrician, too, unlike the popular, down-to-earth, and quick-witted Frank. Despite seniority that would eventually give Studds the chair of a House committee and a position in the Democratic leadership, he had less than the tremendous respect accorded Frank.

The Gobie affair of 1989 certainly damaged Frank's reputation among colleagues. One of the House's most right wing members at the time, Robert Dornan, was reported to be talking gleefully of Frank as so "radioactive" that "nobody will come near him."[66] The forthrightness that had helped win him the support of constituents, though, helped him confront the integrity issue in the House head-on.

SKILL IN THE POLITICS OF COMPROMISE. Frank's willingness to compromise is critical to his acceptability as a member of the congressional club, a club of 435 semi-autonomous lawmakers constantly in need of one another's cooperation. Capitol Hill insiders marvel at his skill in political bargaining and legislative maneuvering. According to one Democratic congressional aide: "Barney is as adept a politician as we have around here. He is able to think on his feet, and he is able to achieve his ends as well as anyone. . . . [In one committee deliberation] Barney just stepped in without having spent time with us plotting strategy or learning the issues, and was able to essentially secure the passage of this series of amendments by outwitting the chairman of the committee and the rest of the Democrats. He is a good vote counter; he understands the pulse of this group of people really well."[67]

Frank's "prudent" form of American liberalism also makes him a coalition builder thought to be reasonable, without ideological hangups. He is prepared to work with House members of widely divergent views—white southern Democrats as well as northern liberals. His party's leadership has often used him to broaden support on difficult issues. In discussing his role in the 1993 debate over lifting the ban on lesbians and gays in the military, in which Frank offered a compromise proposal that shocked many gay/lesbian activists (see Chapter 7), he talked about the ethos of Congress: "Being able to effect a compromise—that's a basic rule with this place. I can say, 'By the way, my position is, only a total lifting of the ban is acceptable; now let me negotiate a compromise.' Nobody around here is stupid enough to let you do that. It's like poker: if you haven't got the stakes, stay out of the game. I saw a compromise coming, and I saw that compromise being negotiated without any of us. You can't be part of the compromise if you are not willing to compromise."[68]

One gay Capitol Hill Democratic aide agreed that the compromise fit the ethos of Congress: "It may not be what we are entitled to; it may not be what should happen; but [Frank] believes that it is as good as we'll get. . . . That is politics, and that is where Barney is approaching this. The way he thinks about it is, "My goal is to get rid of this blatantly discriminatory practice, period. If that isn't possible, then I want to improve the quality of life for lesbians and gays as much as I possibly can, even if it is on the surface hypocritical and unfair and contradictory.' "[69]

Frank's readiness to work within the constraints of what is possible is accompanied by strong beliefs about timing. As was demonstrated in the military debate, his view on the opportune moment to shift positions or suggest a compromise was not the view of most activists engaged in the issue. He argues that on controversial issues in particular, waiting too long to adjust one's bargaining position risks backing other politicians into declaring their opposition publicly, substantially reducing their room for maneuver.[70]

Generally, then, Frank is well suited for a legislative system in which progressive change almost always proceeds by small increments. It is also an arena in which the ideological range within the Democratic Party, even if narrower than in the past, is such as to require compromise to secure the passage of bills even when the party holds a majority of congressional seats. He enters legislative politics with principles, but is prepared not only to play by the rules of compromise but also to believe in the appropriateness of those rules. In this he contrasts with some of the progressives who have served in Congress, who have bridled under the restraints.[71]

PARTY LOYALTY. Barney Frank is more independent-minded than most members of Congress, ready to deviate from or criticize his colleagues. In Massachusetts state politics during the 1970s, as a critic on the left he created enemies among some Democrats. He feels more constrained now, but is capable of criticizing both left and right within his congressional Democratic ranks. In a published interview Frank characterized Senator Sam Nunn, who had led the opposition to lifting the military ban, as "an outstanding bigot," and expressed delight when Nunn decided not to seek re-election in 1996.[72] But even in the U.S. system, with its relatively lax party discipline, partisan loyalty is a central tenet of the legislative code. And Frank is a loyal Democrat. His designation as one of two "point men" to confront the new Republican majority on the floor of the House following the 1994 election was a mark of the party leadership's overall respect for and faith in his partisan credentials (even if a few conservative Democrats grumbled).

When Frank offered his compromise on the military ban, he was to some extent providing cover for a Democratic president willing to abandon principles. To Frank, constantly having to negotiate gains on an array of issues, and in need of allies in the White House as well as on Capitol Hill, helping the president was a normal part of the job. To fail in that, or even more obviously to criticize the president too strongly, would have risked burning bridges he would need on the road ahead. In both the long run and the short run, his loyalty was strategically important. The same calculus seemed evident in the face of the administration's capitulation on the ban. Though critical of the president's "compromise," Frank set about convincing gays and lesbians that Clinton had expended as much political capital as he could on the issue, and that his failure to lift the ban was due to factors beyond the White House. In any event, he argued, whatever the opposition to gay rights in the Democratic Party, the support for them was almost nonexistent among Republicans.

LEGISLATIVE IMPACT. Does the presence of Frank and other openly gay members of Congress change the hearts and minds of colleagues? There are a number of indicators that it does not. David Mixner, recalling a 1987 fund-raising dinner honoring Frank and Studds, was struck by the absence of their colleagues: "Sixteen hundred gays and lesbians had come together from all over the country to honor our two openly gay congresspersons, Barney Frank and Gerry Studds. It struck me how very few straight politicians were in the ballroom. Most elected officials would normally kill to be in a room with a crowd like this, each of whom had paid $250 for their tickets. Even those who had received large checks from HRCF [Human Rights Campaign Fund] to push for our concerns were somehow unable to join us."[73]

In a collegial environment like a legislature, the friendliness of other politicians is an unreliable gauge of impact. Right-wing representatives have shown a form of courtesy to Frank, for example, even while continuing to support anti-gay measures. In 1990, Republican Dana Rohrabacher of California telephoned both Frank and Studds "to assure them personally that nothing that I was doing was an attack on them or their lifestyle. . . . We believe in individual freedom in this country!" He then stood on the House floor and launched an attack against the National Endowment for the Arts for sponsoring "drawings of homosexual orgies, bestiality and a Statue of Liberty turned into a transvestite, complete with male sex organs."[74]

A similar point was illustrated soon after the Republican gains in the 1994 election, when the new House majority leader, Dick Armey, referred to Frank as "Barney Fag." After widespread condemnation of the remark, he apologized for what he described as a "slip of the tongue." A number of observers counted the apology as a sign of a shift in political culture, away from a climate in which such remarks would be commonplace and unchallenged. As one Republican aide put it put it: "Here he was, the second-ranking Republican in the whole House

Republican caucus, apologizing for using a homophobic slur on national television. So obviously it's [thought to be] a disgrace that it's happened. It sort of shows where these guys are coming from. They know the Republican Party can't be the Pat Buchanan Party.''[75] But the apology does not appear to have altered Armey's stance on the issues. What it did was help avoid the tarring brush of extremism, while at the same time reassuring a popular constituency opposed to recognition of sexual diversity.

Nevertheless, the presence of openly gay politicians has had an impact on some legislative colleagues and on some policy outcomes related to sexual orientation. They have been prominent, first, for their willingness even to speak in pro-gay ways, in a legislative environment in which outspoken advocates of gay/lesbian rights are few.[76] Republican Steve Gunderson's impact while in Congress was less clear than Frank or Studds's. After the 1994 election, he led a ''moderate'' group of about forty Republicans called the ''Tuesday Group.'' He was said to be highly respected in those circles, as well as in the House leadership. But the voting patterns of his party's congressional membership indicated only the slightest support for gay-positive initiatives. He was alone in voting against the anti-gay Defense of Marriage Act in 1996. Though clearly a partisan observer, Frank was critical: ''On the Republican side it seems to me he's tolerated but not really listened to on the issues. . . . I think he's more of an apologist than he should be, and in fact he's not able to deliver that much. He doesn't even vote with us all the time. . . . On some of the procedural issues, which can be the key issues, he votes with the Republicans.''[77]

An important part of Frank's contribution to the policy process lies in his staff's day-to-day vigilance over the minutiae of congressional activity. Whether the Democrats are in the majority or the minority, Frank's staff in the Rayburn Building (and, while he was in Congress, Studds's staff in the Cannon Building) keeps track of bills to ensure that opponents do not try to attach unfavorable amendments to bills before Congress. According to an aide: ''Things come up every week you don't know about. So-and-so is contemplating an amendment to strike any funding to the Department of Transportation as long as they [commemorate] Gay Pride Day, which they did for the first time this year [1993]. And for three days, four or five of us on the Hill are furiously working the issue.''[78] An illustration of the need for vigilance was provided in March 1994 during consideration of an education reauthorization bill. In the House, Republican Mel Hancock proposed an amendment banning federally assisted schools from presenting homosexuality in a positive light. A secondary amendment was then proposed to neutralize this move by ensuring that local school boards retained the right to decide what was taught in schools. The secondary amendment passed narrowly, but had to survive a conference committee bringing together House and Senate members to reconcile differences in wording. Congressional staffers and gay/lesbian lobbyists were kept furiously busy tracking the bill in all of its steps through the legislative process. Such detailed attention is necessary in Washington to a far greater extent than in other parliamentary settings, where the agenda is controlled by the government, and individual legislators have far fewer resources for intervening in the decision-making process.

In an arena such as the U.S. Congress, an energetic and knowledgeable politician like Barney Frank was able to make legislative progress even during the years of Republican presidents. In 1990 Frank spearheaded a successful campaign to remove the ban against gay/lesbian immigration, and paved the way for lifting the exclusion of HIV-positive immigrants. In 1992, as chair of the House Judiciary Committee's Subcommittee on Administrative Law and Governmental Relations, Frank pursued the Federal Emergency Management Agency for its retention of a list of gay employees extorted from an employee under questioning for a security clearance, and effectively stopped the practice.

There were other legislative gains in which he engaged in a less central role but was still a participant. In 1987 the Ryan White Act secured considerable new funding for AIDS-related programs. In 1990 the Hate Crimes Statistics Act became the first congressional measure to include lesbians and gays in a positive way, and in the same year the Americans with Disabilities Act outlawed discrimination against people with HIV and AIDS. On these and other legislative matters, in the words of one gay lobbyist speaking in 1992, "both Frank and Studds, to a large extent, are our eyes and ears. And on a host of sensitive issues, it is they who can determine what strategy to take and what would have the most effect. They have the ability to speak with most of their colleagues on the floor, and find out exactly what their concerns are. . . . I cannot think of a recent example where we made an effort without having a go-ahead from them."[79]

Frank's capacity to use his reputation as an effective legislator and loyal Democrat was illustrated in the final stages of the military debate. A meeting with Gerry Studds and gay/lesbian groups resolved that an amendment ought to be presented that would clearly seek to remove language encoding the Sam Nunn version of the ban, thereby leaving the matter to presidential discretion (see Chapter 7). The amendment, moved by Representative Martin Meehan, was certain to lose, but would force supporters and opponents on the record and demonstrate that there was in fact considerable support in Congress for lifting the ban. There were Democrats who did not want such a vote, including some of the supporters of lifting the ban. As one Democratic aide explains: "It makes little sense, legislatively, to force members to walk the plank when the vote itself will have no real-life consequences—when you know it's a losing vote. The general wisdom is, 'Don't put your friends through that; don't put them in a situation where they have to prove their loyalty to you in a manner which will put them in jeopardy back home.' "[80]

But Frank was insistent. When asked what kind of pressure he applied to get his way, he answered: "I'm an active Democrat who helps my leadership on a lot of issues, and I'm useful to them, and I made this kind of a personal vote of confidence. . . . And so, yeah, I was in a position to say, 'This is very, very important to me. I need it, I have helped raise money among gays and lesbians for the Democratic presidential campaign committee, and more importantly, I have campaigned for colleagues to some extent and have made the argument that there are some very real differences between the parties on this issue.' . . . They would have risked alienating me and losing my support on a whole range of other matters, and I made that very explicit.''[81] Frank never claims that the slow pace of change and the paucity of pro-gay measures are satisfactory. His preoccupation is with the attainable, and with convincing those who might be dismissive of Congress or the Democrats that some change is occurring. He sees openings in congressional politics, holding to the view that the prospects are significantly more favorable to gays and lesbians than when he first entered the House.

Even in the aftermath of defeat on the military ban, Frank pointed to signs of progress. Looking back in early 1995, he acknowledged that there had been a setback when Congress effectively blocked the District of Columbia's attempt to legalize domestic partnerships. But apart from that, he says: ''We had a pretty good year. The District of Columbia repealed its sodomy law in 1981 and Congress stepped in. In 1993 . . . it didn't even come up. And part of our argument in keeping it from coming up was to say to them, 'Hey, during gays in the military you kept saying this was special because this was the military—you didn't favor discrimination in general.' And that helped us.''[82]

He also cited the failure of the Hancock amendment on schools and the Helms amendment seeking retaliation against antidiscrimination measures taken by the transportation secretary. Both passed in the Senate but failed to gain enough support in the House, in part because of widespread reluctance of members of Congress to engage gay-related issues at all. As Frank argues, such patterns of avoidance represent a favorable shift from an earlier time, a shift from a ''no way!'' response to gay rights to an ''oh, shit!'' reaction. ''That's good for us, because the role of Congress has always been to be negative, not positive. . . . When I first got here, there was no sense that they wanted to be rid of this issue: many of them looked forward to it; it was an easy way to go. The fact that they feel conflicted by it now is a sign of progress. Obviously it's not nearly enough, but it also works in our favor. And our threat to make everything a roll call is part of that issue.''[83]

As was evident in the case of the military ban, Frank is inclined to explain defeat as a product of forces largely external to Congress and the administration, for example, the failure of gays and lesbians to marshal themselves in sufficient numbers to counter the forces mobilized by the right. This is a view that naturally arises out of the position that Frank occupies. Not surprisingly, he is a loyalist both to his party and to the institution in which he serves. It would be highly unusual for an elected politician to think otherwise, except in an expedient way to curry favor among cynical voters. But because his analysis of success and failure deflects criticism away from Democrats in Congress and the White House and toward activist groups, it opens up a breach with a social movement with which he has had close links—a breach that was all too evident during the debate over gays in the military.

Relations with the Lesbian and Gay Movement

For most of the time since he was first elected, Barney Frank has maintained links with social movement activists working on sexual orientation issues and has treated lesbians and gays as a second constituency. The role that Frank plays within party and legislative institutions makes him an effective agent in policy making and an important front line representative of that movement, but just as inevitably creates tensions, especially evident during the debate over the military ban.

Whether openly gay politicians face national constituencies that are more or less demanding than those faced by African Americans and women is hard to judge. When members of such groups first attempt to gain a degree of political access, there can be a certain "halo" effect for those who succeed. Their voices constitute a dramatic break from patterns of political silence, enough to be credited even by those activists most cynical about electoral politics. After the first few years and the first few representatives, people become willing to discriminate between those who represent social movement ideals well and those who do not.

Sexual minority representation is not yet at that point, and generalizations are hazardous. Even in the early stages of the community's entry into legislative politics, expectations imposed on the few openly lesbian or gay politicians were high. After her 1974 election to the Massachusetts State House, Elaine Noble found herself caught between the demands of a legislative role and the expectations of impatient activists. In 1978, at a point when she had decided not to seek reelection, she talked of that pressure: "Because I was considered the gay politician, I had not only more work, but got more flack, more criticism, more heartache from the gay community than from the people who elected me. . . . I really tried the best I could and it wasn't good enough for the gay community. To be honest, I don't know what 'good enough' is. . . . If I were straight they probably would have thought that half of what I did was so terrific."[84]

Sherry Harris, who served as a city councilor in Seattle from 1991 to 1994, is one of a handful of openly lesbian or gay African-American elected officials. Once in office, Harris too found that the expectations of the communities she was seen to represent were sometimes difficult to satisfy.

Minority people who are in public office are held to a higher standard of performance on behalf of minority groups than white people are. Some of my white colleagues might get away with going to one gay community event a year, and the gay community will acknowledge that—they're supportive because they showed up at this one important event. Whereas I have to show up at everything. And the same is true for the black community. Minority communities will also expect higher results. My white colleagues might get away with just voting in favor of something that they perceive the minority communities want, and I have to lead on these issues. I have to demonstrate that I've made some things happen, that I'm proactive, as opposed to being supportive when something comes up. So you're held to a higher standard, in both the black community and the gay community.[85]

New York State Assembly member Deborah Glick may not share Frank's judgment about when and how much to compromise, but she does acknowledge the potential for tension between her inside role as legislator and the activist politics on the outside: "There are times when there is a certain frustration and antagonism because I haven't been able to make it all better in a particular area. You try not to be defensive, but sometimes people really yell and scream at you. . . . There are times when I have said to groups, 'If you want me to negotiate, I will do that, but understand that if I negotiate, I may have twelve items. I may only get six. If I get six, I'm still going to have to support it, because that's what negotiation is.' " Some groups want it both ways—they want to be both inside players and outside players, wanting access but refusing to compromise. Glick, like most politicians, knows that "you can't be both."[86]

Whatever the differences between them, the experience of Glick and Harris and Frank illustrates the distance that can open up between the day-to-day demands of the legislator's role and the world of group activism. Each of the three has a different relationship to community activism from the others, and a different perspective on the art of the possible, but all acknowledge that the expectations of activists and community members exceed the possibilities of delivering.

RESPECT FROM GAYS AND LESBIANS. For most of his career, Barney Frank has maintained a close relationship with a wide range of groups in the gay and lesbian movement, without significant tension. This was in part a product of his long years of outspokenness. Since the beginning of his political career, and long before he was open about his sexual orientation, Barney Frank was active on gay issues, and in part for that reason garnered respect even from activists whose tactics he sometimes judged imprudent. In 1973 he introduced a gay rights bill in the Massachusetts House, and he signed on as a co-sponsor of the congressional gay rights bill from his first term. He has always been ready to offer advice about influencing politicians, and he maintains contacts with a wide range of activist groups, and in that sense has never sought to distance himself from the broader movement for social and political change.

In that broader movement the standing of politicians such as Frank and Studds (and to some extent Gunderson) is based in part on their visibility, and on their willingness to recognize the importance of that visibility in the highly symbolic environs of the nation's capital. Frank and Studds both attended functions at the White House with their partners, and activist admirers routinely cite that as part of the contribution they have made. Even though Studds made it very clear that he did not want to be seen as "the gay congressman" in the years immediately following his coming out and censure, he was still described in the press as "the focus for the political hopes and aspirations of the gay community."[87]

Support for Frank comes most obviously from those who work in organizations with congressional lobbying as part of their mandate. According to one activist in the National Gay and Lesbian Task Force, "He's an integral part of each and every gay-related vote we have on Capitol Hill." Speaking in 1992, another activist in the same organization spoke of checking with Frank on every lobbying step the group took.[88]

Respect comes from gays and lesbians working on other fronts. When activists agreed to the formation of the Victory Fund to help openly lesbian and gay candidates run for public office, Frank was "overwhelmingly supportive," willing to appear at and sponsor fund-raisers and offer advice.[89] In planning for the 1987 March on Washington, Frank was also helpful, as this National Gay and Lesbian Task Force activist recalls: "When we put together the lobby days for the 1987 March on Washington, for gay rights, Barney came down to help us do our training of activists. He came down and sat on a table—he didn't stand or sit on a chair—he just sat himself right on the table, put his foot on the table, and talked to people. I think they liked that."[90] In early 1992 Frank appeared with his partner, Herb Moses, at a demonstration against anti-gay discriminatory practices of the Cracker Barrel restaurant chain, and represented gays and lesbians in Atlanta's annual March of Celebration to mark the Martin Luther King, Jr., Holiday.

For some years Frank maintained a productive working relationship with direct action groups, despite publicly voicing criticism of some tactics, and a general distaste for the all-or-nothing purism he sees as widespread in them. "He maintains a certain distance from direct-action groups," one ACT UP member argued in 1992, "but there aren't many people in the halls of Congress who call ACT UP and Queer Nation on a regular basis and ask what they're up to."[91] Frank's support for outing hypocritical politicians (those who are gay themselves but behave politically in anti-gay ways) also draws the approval of the radical strand of lesbians and gays who favor aggressive politics.

Approval of Frank has been as pronounced among lesbians as among gay men. A Boston-based lesbian activist admitted to having "a hard time saying that Frank and Studds represent the lesbian community," but noted that they were attuned to issues that affect women.[92] Another lesbian, based in Washington, and entirely critical of "compromise politics," was even more positive: "He is one of those people that when it comes to lesbian and gay issues, but also when it comes to a number of issues that are important to women, you can depend on him."[93]

AFTERMATH OF THE MILITARY DEBATE. Strains in the relationship between elected politicians and the most attentive portions of the identity-based constituency they are seen to represent are especially likely to appear when those politicians belong to a party that incorporates that constituency's demands in its electoral platform and then wins government office. A lone figure standing against the tide remains a tribune for a marginalized cause; a member of a party holding power risks becoming the focus of high expectations destined for disappointment. What may be distinctive about the sexual minority constituency is that it has had less experience than the civil rights movement or the women's movement with the heartbreak that can come with having friends in government.

Frank's part in the debate over the military ban reflected his preoccupation with taking what steps one can even at the expense of compromise, and illustrates the tensions between his legislative role and his links to the broader social movement. In May 1993, as he saw slippage toward San Nunn's version of "don't ask, don't tell," Frank suggested a compromise that would avoid restricting off-base or off-duty activity. Frank clearly believed that this compromise represented a significant advance, even if not to a degree acceptable to those most engaged by the issue. He argued that under his plan the lives of individual lesbians and gays in the military would be substantially improved by virtue of a major reduction in the likelihood of discharge. Furthermore, he believed that the compromise would increase familiarity with gay men and lesbians in the military, and that greater toleration would result. Tied to this was his view that a significant shift had occurred in the military's own framing of this issue, away from the position that gays and lesbians are in and of themselves bad for the military (for example, because they represent a security risk) to the reasoning that because heterosexual personnel are so prejudiced, military discipline and morale will be adversely affected.

Frank believed, too, that the compromise was inherently unstable in ways that were favorable to an eventual lifting of the ban. He seemed to agree with a view developing in certain activist circles that some or all of the restrictions being discussed, including his own compromise, could be successfully challenged in court as unreasonable limitations on free speech. (Frank also believed that the strength of the military's opposition to lifting the ban was enormously increased by the prestige and popularity of Colin Powell, chair of the Joint Chiefs of Staff, and that the possibility of further change would be improved when he was no longer in that position.)

Frank argues that he had to move when he did because the ground was slipping fast. He believed that activists were using a campaign model more suitable for an election than for lobbying—one that imagined the campaign peaking just before the president's decision deadline of July 15. "Members of Congress don't wait until the week before a vote to lock in their positions. They had to figure out their positions right away to answer the hundreds of letters they were getting. A majority had locked in against us in January. You can't turn that around later. . . . [The]voters can think one thing in May and change in July. But members of Congress can't."[94]

In late 1992, after the Clinton victory, there was serious talk among activists about the possibility of passing a gay civil rights bill (however unlikely that seemed to Capitol Hill veterans), but little discussion among activists about the need to shore up ground to ensure an end to the military ban. The confidence was disturbing enough to elicit a late December warning from Frank directed at the two major gay/lesbian lobby groups: "I begged them to get a letter-writing campaign going. . . . The groups were making a fundamental error. They thought that having a president on your side means you've won. Having the president on your side is a necessary condition, but it's not a sufficient condition. I told the groups, 'You're deciding what to have for dessert when we haven't even killed the chickens for dinner yet.' "[95]

When the Campaign for Military Service and other gay/lesbian organizations eventually did start mobilizing popular support for lifting the ban, Frank was critical of some of their tactics. In one meeting with activists he was shown stacks of petitions signed by thousands in support of the president's commitment. Frank dismissed the petitions as ineffective lobbying instruments, and said that they might as well be trashed. His unease intensified in April, during and immediately after the huge March on Washington:

> It's not that the people in the gay and lesbian community are not energetic. They are very energetic; they just wasted all their energy. When they came to Washington they surrounded the Capitol and turned their backs and held hands. That had zero impact on public policy—zero. But it took a lot of energy, and they thought it would have an impact. The debate about whether or not we are 300,000 people or a million people [at the March on Washington] is irrelevant. The point is that nobody in Congress cares. Literally, nobody cares. What they care about is how many of those people they heard from. And if there were a million people but nobody heard from them, that is not as good as 10,000 people everybody heard from. . . . The March was an important cultural event; it was an important self-actualizing event; but it had no short-term political impact for us. . . . So by May I was very discouraged about our inability to make the transition from a marginal to a mainstream political group. And that is the problem when people have the preference for the tactics of the margins—sit-ins, demonstrations. When is the last time the NRA had a sit-in, or a demonstration, or a shoot-in? They don't do that. Who is more influential?[96]

Some gay/lesbian lobbyists, like this one, acknowledged at the time that Frank was dealing with a difficult situation: "In the military issue, he saw things moving in a certain way and felt like he needed to throw the gauntlet down to stop it from moving any farther in that direction. And while that may have been controversial for folks outside the Beltway, for folks inside the Beltway that's what politics is—lots of different people doing what they see fit, given a particular circumstance."[97] The dominant reaction, though, was critical. A number of lobbyists pointed to his failure to consult others active on the issue. For many, too, Frank's compromise represented little or no gain, since it encoded the closet and fed public stereotypes that same-sex orientation is strictly a private matter. The principles at issue in the debate were starkly simple, and there was no halfway position in ending discrimination. One gay lobbyist stated this view: "The dilemma that comes from what Barney did, in my opinion, is that it gives the administration cover for a less-than-100 percent response to this particular issue. . . . Once you have a precedent, it can be layered onto other examples. Let's assume that you accept the Barney proposal that you can be in the closet at work and out of the closet at home. And let's just say that the military codifies that. And then someone says, 'Let's apply the same rule to the House of Representatives.' Do you think Barney would accept that?"[98]

From May 1993 onward, activists began to talk more openly of the contrast and tension between Frank's role and theirs. Tanya Domi of the National Gay and Lesbian Task Force had told an interviewer: "Barney Frank is performing his role as a member of Congress who perceives himself as a reasonable politician. The National Gay and Lesbian Task Force has a different role from Barney Frank. We advocate for civil rights for Lesbian and Gay Americans. There can be no compromise on that." Sue Hyde of the Task Force told the same reporter: "For Barney, for any member of Congress, a compromise is better than a loss. It doesn't mean that the community, that those of us who've worked on this for years, have to say OK."[99]

Some both inside and outside the Washington Beltway saw in Frank's compromise a degree of partisanship that went beyond what they considered acceptable for a representative of a broader movement. The overwhelming majority of activists recognized that a Republican victory would represent a setback. But Frank's provision of cover for the president went too far. Queer Nation members called him "Uncle Barney—a happy homosexual househand on the Democratic Party plantation." Urvashi Vaid, former director of the National Gay and Lesbian Task Force, publicly denounced "the debacle of Democratic weasels in the Senate pandering to homophobia as well as the painful sight of Barney Frank defending a sellout on the military ban."[100] The view that a partisan concern to help the president was prominent in Frank's calculus is evident even in this assessment by an openly gay Democratic politician at the state level: "I believe it was the responsibility of our representatives to stand up to this wave, this onslaught of homophobia and hate, and call it as it was. For a gay man who had been jostled out of the closet to stand up and say, 'Well, maybe people can live this half-assed kind of existence'—it doesn't work for people, and we needed somebody to say it stunk. . . . What I saw Frank doing was throwing a life preserver to Bill Clinton, not to lesbians and gay men. This was face-saving for the administration, and while I think there's some value in that, I think there were other Democrats who could have done it."[101]

Frank's tendency to assign blame for defeat on the military ban primarily to activists' shortcomings widened the gap. To some extent, criticism of excessive optimism and insufficient marshaling of troops was fair, but it ignored the role of Democratic insiders in sustaining the expectations that accompanied Clinton's election in 1992. Frank's own campaigning on behalf of Clinton among gays and lesbians helped generate that optimism. On a 1992 election day phone-in show in his district, he responded to one questioner criticizing Clinton's record in Arkansas: "By the way he ran the Democratic convention, by his own remarks, by his involvement with some openly gay people, he's already done a great deal. By his comments on AIDS he has done a great deal. And I don't have any doubt that if he wins, he will abolish the ban on gays and lesbians serving in the military.''[102] He told another caller that he had been assured by Clinton himself that lifting the ban was as good as done. Long before the election Frank was in a position to advise the president and his circle that the ban was a more explosive issue than they seemed to believe. The fact that his advice on gay-related issues was worth hearing was evidenced in his being called on to brief candidate Clinton immediately prior to an early April meeting with New York AIDS group leaders.[103]

Frank has criticized groups for not mobilizing earlier than they did; but this ignores the White House advice to them throughout the transition period to lie low. He has also criticized activists for not supporting a suggestion that the chair of the House Armed Services Committee, a pro-gay African-American ex-marine, launch hearings early enough to counter the propaganda of the Senate committee headed by Sam Nunn.[104] Resistance to that idea, however, was also coming from the White House and at least some elements of the congressional Democratic leadership, who feared that hearings would be a vehicle for House Republicans to mobilize against lifting the ban.

At the end of the day, Frank was prepared to criticize Clinton's compromise— in itself an unusual step for a loyalist insider. But he was also prepared to excuse Clinton's statement about avoiding the promotion of a ''gay lifestyle'': ''Well, that one is what all of the pollsters point to—that people don't like discrimination but they don't want to encourage people to be gay. It seems a rather dumb notion, and he shouldn't have used the word 'gay lifestyle.' . . . But I think that was just an inept statement of what everybody said strategically, including the gay groups—that you promote anti-discrimination, that you don't promote or encourage [homosexuality].''[105]

Frank has repeatedly pointed to Clinton's provided unprecedented support for gay- and AIDS-related initiatives. (In his first term as president, Climton opened up innumerable channels of access to government agencies, ensured protection from discrimination in almost all federal employment, increased AIDS funding, and endorsed an Employment Non-Discrimination Act that would have prohibited discrimination on the basis of sexual orientation.) He has also pointed justifiably to the fact that a Democratic Party divided on gay and lesbian equality still represents a stark contrast to a national Republican Party that is almost entirely opposed to it. But in the aftermath of the military ban debate, Frank's playing the role of the partisan loyalist widened the gap with social movement activists skeptical of the president's commitment to lifting the ban. Clinton's endorsement of the Defense of Marriage Act at the end of his first term also dismayed activists, and their doubts about congressional Democrats were increased when a majority of them supported DOMA as well.[106]

At the core of Barney Frank's admonitions to gays and lesbians in the aftermath of the military defeat lies a belief ''that America works in the textbook sense,'' a belief that he sees as more widely shared on the right than the left: ''People on the left are more likely to say: 'Well, wait a minute, writing letters is nothing. We need a demonstration.' That is absolutely backward. . . . In fact, direct action, as a political tactic, is second choice. The first choice is to exercise political power, to scare them into voting the right way. Direct action is what you do when you have no power.''[107] If mass action is called for, it ought to be shaped by pragmatic considerations of what will gain leverage in Washington. Frank has on more than one occasion juxtaposed the March on Washington with demonstrations arising from civil rights mobilization of the 1960s: "When blacks marched on Washington in 1963, it was a disciplined political performance, not cultural self-expression. In 1993, a comedian, Lea Delaria, said how she would like to have sex with Hillary Clinton. . . . If Redd Foxx had gotten up during the black march and speculated about having sex with Jacqueline Kennedy, he would have been thrown into the Reflecting Pool, *after* the water was drained. The gay community has tended to fuse cultural self-expression with political tactics. For us, our right to offend people is a political statement. Too much of our energy has gone into cultural expression, and not enough into conventional politics.''[108]

There had always been a certain distance between Frank's own biography and the confrontational and outrageous side of ''liberationist'' politics, and it was becoming more obvious in the aftermath of the military debate. Frank had fully come out only when he was already in Congress, precluding direct engagement with the gay/lesbian activism of the 1970s and early 1980s, so often driven by anger and impatience. His strategic views were formed by his own shrewd judgments about what tactics were effective in building popular support for a cause. As he saw gay and lesbian issues coming closer to mainstream legitimacy, he became more vocal in his critique of certain aspects of the confrontational politics of the left: "ACT UP has some positive aspects, some negative. Interrupting Catholic Mass was wrong and politically stupid. It backfired on them. Demonstrating requires a lot of thought and discipline. ACT UP and Queer Nation sometimes forget about that. . . . Bullying is not a bad idea if it stays within bounds. When used against corporations bullying works, but not against politicians and priests.''[109] In 1992 he told an interviewer: "I want to give people on the left less rhetorical satisfaction in return for more policy progress. . . . Now I don't deny rhetorical satisfaction. I think gay people are entitled to hear members of Congress say Jesse Helms is a vicious bigot and Bill Dannemeyer is an irrational fool. That's important, but we've paid a high price for that degree of rhetorical satisfaction in policy. I want to shift the balance.''[110] Increasingly, his public attacks on direct action groups and on the left of the movement were opening up a divide that he had previously managed to straddle.

At the core of the view adopted by Frank and some of Washington's gay/lesbian lobbyists lies a belief that the national political system creates a playing field that is level enough for gays and lesbians to effect significant change. Ultimately, anyone believing in the essential fairness of the game will argue that failure to make gains is largely a result of not knowing the rules well enough. The disagreements with Frank over his introduction of the compromise came in part from people who were less optimistic. Many activists have seen a recurrent pattern of promises broken or only half-kept, more often by Republicans but often enough by Democrats. There may have been uncritical enthusiasm and optimism in the period between Clinton's election and inauguration, but that was a temporary exception in a long tradition of political wariness. Interestingly, there were large numbers of activists who in late 1992 were more optimistic about Clinton than seasoned Capitol Hill politicos such as Barney Frank, but who are now more pessimistic than Frank.

The division between Barney Frank and many social movement activists was probably inevitable, reflecting a long-standing gap between inside and outside activism that is sometimes papered over. Frank's leverage in Congress depends on his willingness to accept that politics is the art of the possible. In the case of the military ban, he was drawn to formulate what he believed was the most favorable compromise possible under the circumstances, but it was one that did not meet the minimum requirements of activists. In the aftermath of defeat, Frank risked sharpening tensions with them by explaining the defeat primarily in terms of their failure to mobilize. In so doing, he implicitly downplayed the weakness of support for lifting the ban inside the Democratic congressional majority and the administration. He was also implicitly overstating the chances of winning the day with more social movement pressure, since even the ideal level of organization could never have matched the forces of the right or overcome military opposition.

The very traits that have allowed Barney Frank to work on the inside have created the potential for rifts with the larger social movement—rifts that are particularly evident when the Democrats are in power. There is an obvious parallel with the difficult position of gay rights supporters in the Ontario provincial New Democratic government formed in 1990 (see Chapter 5), and in the position in which Chris Smith finds himself as a front bench member of Britain's Labour government. It is no surprise that Frank's standing among activists rose in the period following the Republican gains of late 1994. The new Congress saw Democrats in a minority, no longer able to manage the business of the House and Senate. Frank's designation as point man for the House Democrats spotlighted his role as a tribune for groups and causes marginalized by the Republican revolution, and backgrounded his role as a skillful legislative bargainer. In the congressional sessions that began in 1995 and 1997, he was regularly cited in the gay/lesbian press as a critic of Republican action or inaction, and a sponsor of equality measures such as the Employment Non-Discrimination Act.[111]

Important as the role of his openly gay counterparts in Britain and Canada is, the peculiar characteristics of the American political system make Frank's role more significant. The entry of gay/lesbian issues onto the national political agenda, no matter how limited and distorted a form they assume, increasingly requires representatives in Congress who are prepared to engage wholeheartedly in the day-to-day work required to eke out gains or minimize disaster. Gay politicians are not the only ones able to do that work, but in a political climate in which fears persist about being over identified with these issues, openly gay politicians willing to take them on are invaluable.

Barney Frank, then, has more continuous opportunity to exercise influence, and more opportunity to play a diversity of roles in the quite separate milieux of the Fourth Congressional District of Massachusetts, Capitol Hill, and lesbian/gay meeting places. Of the three politicians, he operates in the most complex political system, and juggles a more complicated array of roles. It took the military debate to illustrate how difficult it is to sustain such roles without their conflicting with one another. And yet even some of those who remain very critical of Frank's role in the military debate acknowledge his indispensability. According to an openly gay local politician much more unambiguously affiliated with radical and confrontational politics than Frank: "People were very angry with Barney because he proposed a compromise that was not acceptable to people who were working on the issue. I completely understand his point that we needed to do that to get ahead, to get that issue behind us, to be supportive of the president—I really do see that. I don't agree with it. I think you have to fight out a little bit further and save your support for another time. We do need people like him, absolutely. Do I respect him? Absolutely. And if he were ever in trouble, would I be there and send him money? You bet I would."[112]

President Bill Clinton meeting representatives of lesbian and gay organizations (April 1993). Photo: White House

March on Washington for Lesbian, Gay, Bisexual Rights and Liberation (April 1993). Photo: Wayne Shimabukuro

9

The Inescapable Allure of
the American Mainstream

We are definitely part of the mainstream, but we are on the

fringe of the mainstream. Our issues are on the table, but the

problem is the other people in the dining hall have no desire

to smell this meal.

Human Rights Campaign Fund lobbyist, July 1993

The American gay/lesbian/bisexual movement is as visible as any in the world, with an impact on activist agendas and strategies beyond United States borders. Cultural and social networks have proliferated both within and outside the mainstream. Political activists have developed permanent organizations to intervene in all aspects of governmental, partisan, electoral, and legal processes, though recurrent waves of protest draw many activists into confrontations with those processes.

The exceptionalism of United States politics is apparent in the scale and energy of social movement activism in general, and lesbian and gay activism in particular. The United States is also unusual in the extent to which political mobilization has generated an institutionalized presence and ongoing visibility within the political mainstream. That is particularly evident in the development of national organizations lobbying or litigating for gay rights. To some extent, this activity reflects the growth of lesbian and gay communities in cities across the country, and to some extent also the urgency of the challenge to equal rights posed by the emergence of the religious right as a political force.

But the effectiveness of the movement depends on more than resources. Impact on policy outcomes depends on the permeability of the institutional settings in which activists work, the constellation of partisan forces, the political leanings of governing parties, the receptivity of the media, the range of allies, and the beliefs of the general public. The case studies presented in previous chapters demonstrate that lobby groups with ample resources and skill sometimes lose (as in the British age of consent debate in Britain), while those with few resources sometimes win (as in the Canadian Human Rights Act amendment). The case of the United States military ban may well have exposed some movement weaknesses, but it also revealed an opposition to change that no organized movement could have surmounted.

The development of resources, however, is critical to longer-term success, especially in the highly volatile American environment. The persistent power of the moralistic right guarantees that secure gains will not be won without large-scale effort. Much has been accomplished in establishing an activist presence in national political and legal institutions, particularly since the late 1980s. The growth of national gay/lesbian organizations attests to that, as does the development of networks in each of the two national parties. But there are weaknesses in national activism that have been exposed at precisely the time when opportunities for dramatic change were opening up. Major fissures exist in the national movement, and between its activists and groups focusing on state and local affairs, this despite only moderate ideological differences in comparison to social movements in other countries. These disabilities impair the capacity of national groups to shape legislative outcomes and public opinion.

The Development of Movement Strength

The United States was not home to the earliest organized protests against sexual oppression. In the first third of the twentieth century, Germany was the center of a reform movement that acquired national and international prominence in its campaign against laws criminalizing homosexual activity.[1] In the United States, major cultural, and political networks did not form until the postwar period. Then, in the growth of mainstream reformism in the mid-1960s and the protest wave of the late 1960s, lesbian and gay activism in the United States was more widespread than anywhere else. That decade opened with a new administration in Washington, imbued with the imagery of optimistic reformism (even if exaggerated). By the middle of the decade, the civil rights and student movements were engendering a sense of discontent, soon augmented by women's movement challenges to traditional gender roles.

Such a social and political climate greatly expanded the availability of meeting places for homosexuals and created the potential for developing political networks. Growing cities, the already striking geographic mobility of Americans, the sexual revolution: all these made it easier for gays and lesbians to discover one another there than in other parts of the world (though easier for men than women, and easier for whites than minorities). Political reformism and the loosening of heterosexual mores did not diminish institutionalized discrimination and homophobia. But if police attacks were as common as in Britain, Canada, and other countries, nowhere else were such assaults butting up against such rapidly proliferating institutions and a spreading sense of political entitlement.

THE FORMATION OF A PECULIARLY AMERICAN MOVEMENT. Radical movements emerged with great forcefulness in western Europe during the 1960s and 1970s. But what is distinctive about the United States is the extent to which minimal class consciousness and relatively weak political parties permitted the development of autonomous political movements and groups. Such a setting nurtured new forms of identity politics, based on race, culture, gender, disability, and sexual orientation. Moreover, the unusually fragmented character of the American political order, and the multiplicity of access points, allowed activists to engage with established political and legal institutions from the beginning.

That said, the American movement has always maintained a subculture distinct from the mainstream, marked by a current of confrontationalism. United States activists are less likely to be radically critical of existing economic and political structures than their European counterparts. Radicalism in Europe, and to some extent in Canada, dovetails with largely socialist critiques of these foundations, whereas in the United States, it tends to focus on individuals and groups.

The struggle to come to terms with a disparaged sexual orientation, and to discover others of like bent, produces in many lesbians and gays a determination to assert a distinct identity in uncompromising terms. Although attacks on the expression of sexual difference drive some into various forms of respectability and discretion, at the same time they propel many toward outrageous expressions of that sexuality. Such is the basis for the visual imagery of gay, lesbian, bisexual, and transgendered pride days celebrated in large cities across the United States and around the world.

The tendency, especially pronounced in North America, for gays and lesbians to gravitate to particular residential areas, where gay businesses then develop around them, reinforces the creation of a cultural and social life with a distinctive character in some respects opposed to the dominant culture. A strong community identity therefore produces a continuing potential for confrontational politics. It is this sentiment that fuels activism of groups such as ACT UP, Queer Nation, and Lesbian Avengers.

THE LURE OF THE MAINSTREAM. One of the paradoxes of American gay and lesbian political mobilization, even in its most radical and oppositionist forms, is that its agenda always included crucial demands frameable in the classic political language of rights to equal protection and privacy. Civil rights are an established element of American political discourse. The power of the courts to recognize the rights of individuals and groups created openings from the beginning of the modern movement, even when it was shut out of legislative and governmental channels.

The 1970s were a period of scattered legislative, administrative, and judicial successes. In a few isolated cases, the growth of gay communities spawned candidacies of openly gay men and lesbians, and the first organized entry into local party networks. San Francisco provided early examples in work of the Society for Individual Rights in the late 1960s, the formation of the Alice B. Toklas Democratic Club in the early 1970s, and the 1977 election of city supervisor Harvey Milk. If optimism was fading from the politics on the streets, there was increasing hope about what was possible within established political institutions.

In the late 1970s and 1980s, the ascendancy of the New Right, and in particular its moral authoritarianism, heightened activist interest in using mainstream politics either to defend those small gains already made or to go on the offensive where change seemed within reach. For example, the 1978 Briggs Initiative in California, seeking the dismissal of openly gay teachers from public schools, produced an extraordinary mobilization to persuade people to vote no, and contributed significantly to the politicization of gays and lesbians across the state.[2] Right-wing attacks on the most basic of civil rights for gays and lesbians in other parts of the country forced even those activists with radical agendas to acknowledge the urgent need to work in mainstream politics.

The AIDS epidemic mobilized extraordinary political energy and muscle. The number of activists in paid staff positions in New York City gay/lesbian organizations provides an illustration, rising from less than a dozen in 1981 to close to two hundred in 1990.[3] The tardiness of governmental response to AIDS, particulary at the national level, created a gap in expertise that provided some political openings for community-based activists. Whereas earlier gay activists had challenged governmental, judicial, and police intrusion into sexual matters, AIDS mobilization called for an increase in state resources and changes in health policy. This necessarily required activists to insinuate themselves into mainstream political networks previously thought inaccessible or irrelevant.

Shifts in public opinion, largely a result of longer-term challenges to traditional sexual and gender morality, have provided yet another impetus for activists to engage with electoral politics. There can be no doubt that public attitudes to homosexuality are volatile, as in reactions to the question of gays in the military. Nevertheless, support for gay and lesbian equality rights grew during the 1980s, and this increased the forcefulness of arguments within the Democratic Party that gay and lesbian issues could be taken on without electoral damage. It also increased the lure for openly gay men and lesbians to seek public office. To some extent, the development of strategies for working inside parties and legislatures was a conscious decision based on the expansion of available resources; it also marked a recognition of new opportunities for "inside" activism and the costs of ignoring them.[4]

National Activist Resources

It was in the 1980s that the presence of lesbian and gay activists in mainstream politics increased most dramatically at the national level. Prior to that, the prospects for influence in any branch of the federal government seemed slim enough to discourage devoting substantial resources to the enterprise. Sexual minority politics had always been intensely local, and the widespread American distrust of political authority, as well as pessimism on the left about state policy, were most intensely felt in relation to higher levels of government. Not coincidentally, the focus on Washington increased during a twelve-year period of Republican ascendancy in the executive branch, which threatened what few gains had been made to that point. The spread of the AIDS epidemic also drew more and more gays and lesbians to the view that federal intervention on gay-related issues was essential.

The late 1980s and early 1990s were a period of especially dramatic growth in the size and visibility of mainstream gay organizations operating at the national level. The six largest groups went from a combined budget of $3.2 million in 1987 to $8.8 million in early 1991, reflecting both the development of resources within gay and lesbian communities and the opening up of opportunities for activist entry into national politics. To some extent, organizational growth was accompanied by specialization in each of the primary channels of mainstream activism: the instigation of legal challenges through the courts; the lobbying of legislators and officials; the promotion of lesbian and gay electoral candidates; and the participation in partisan networks.

MULTIPURPOSE GROUPS. In 1972 New Yorkers associated with the Gay Activists' Alliance established the National Gay Task Force "to bring gay liberation into the mainstream of American civil rights." The Task Force acted in part as a clearinghouse for information and a source of advice for local groups in its early years, but it was also in other respects a "self-consciously elite organization," narrow in its demographic base and cautious in its strategic choices.[5] The group remained small for several years, experiencing organizational and debt problems in the late 1970s and early 1980s (the annual budget for 1980 was only $260,000). It moved to Washington in 1986 and changed its name to the National Gay and Lesbian Task Force. The large National March on Washington for Lesbian and Gay Rights in October 1987 provided an impetus for growth, amplified by the surge of confrontational activism resulting from governmental inaction on AIDS.

At the end of the 1980s, the Task Force moved beyond its work on issues of violence, privacy, and AIDS by developing projects on the military ban and family issues—the latter taking up questions of relationship recognition, adoption, foster care, and reproductive rights. Its development of a commitment on military and family issues was accompanied by a substantial increase in the involvement of lesbians in the group's leadership. The 1980s also saw increased attention to the racial composition of the organization's staff and the racial dimensions of its focus. In late summer 1996, it had forty thousand members, an annual budget of $2.4 million, and twenty-two full-time staff.

The Task Force has shown ambivalence about engaging with mainstream pro-

cesses. Through the 1990s it has been prepared to distance itself from the traditional rules of lobbying, perhaps more so than at the end of the 1980s. Most of
the staff had experience in direct action and supported its use. Starting in 1988,
the Task Force held an annual "Creating Change" conference for local activists
and devoted considerable staff resources to contacts with activists "on the
ground." But the grassroots organizing envisaged in the 1990s was different from
the radical politics of the early 1970s. It was aimed at effecting change by gaining
visibility and influence within the political mainstream. As one staff member put
it in 1995, the task force "loved crisis." But now, "more political sophistication
in lobbying is required—a deeper level of it, where enough people are ready to
really work though an issue."[6]

The National Coalition of Black Lesbians and Gays was formed in 1978, and
in 1979 it organized a conference of "third world" lesbians and gays held in
conjunction with the first National March on Washington for Lesbian and Gay
Rights. It tried to support a national office in the mid-1980s, but failed. It was
succeeded, after the 1987 March on Washington, by the National Black Gay and
Lesbian Leadership Forum, a group long based in Los Angeles. It established a
permanent organizational presence in Washington in 1996, with a total organizational budget of over half a million dollars and with a staff of eight.[7] It has
only recently taken up legislative lobbying, with a particular emphasis on the
Congressional Black Caucus.

Other groups have formed in recent years, including the Latino/a Lesbian and
Gay Organization (established in 1987), National Gay Asian and Pacific Islander
Network, Asian Lesbians of the East Coast, and the South Asian Lesbian and
Gay Association, although each has difficulty raising the funds required for vis-
ibility either within or beyond gay and lesbian communities themselves.

LITIGATION GROUPS. Seeking equity through the courts has been an especially
important aspect of American activism. The individualism embedded in United
States political culture, the early constitutional entrenchment of a Bill of Rights,
the complexity of the legislative process, and the assertiveness of the courts in
striking down legislative and executive action have all contributed to the lure of
litigation. Cases pursued by African Americans and women in the postwar period
became prototypes for other groups seeking change. In this context it is not
surprising that two of the three largest national gay and lesbian groups in the
early 1990s were devoted to litigation strategies.

The first group formed for the instigation of gay-related court challenges was
the New York–based Lambda Legal Defense and Education Fund, founded in
1973. By 1996 it had a budget of over $3 million, a staff of eleven attorneys,
and two regional offices.[8] The second oldest group is the National Center for
Lesbian Rights, with offices in San Francisco and New York. The ACLU's Lesbian and Gay Rights Project was the third. And the fourth was the Servicemembers Legal Defense Network, formed in 1993 specifically to help gay and lesbian
armed forces personnel fight military discharge.

286   **UNITED STATES**

HUMAN RIGHTS CAMPAIGN. The Human Rights Campaign Fund, was formed in 1980 as a PAC (political action committee), and from the beginning staked out its ground fully within the mainstream. The organization grew out of the pioneering work of the Gay Rights National Lobby, which had been established in 1978 to lobby Congress and build a national network of lobbyists at the local level.

In early 1991 HRCF had a budget of $4.5 million, having experienced a five-fold increase in budget and a threefold increase in staff since the 1987 March on Washington. By mid-1992 it was among the fifty largest PACs in Washington. In the lead-up to the 1996 elections, the Human Rights Campaign (dropping "Fund" from its name) had a $10 million budget, sixty full-time staff members, and a membership of 175,000. A significant portion of the money sustaining the organization is raised by highly publicized dinners in over twenty cities across the country, some of them able to attract over a thousand people, each prepared to pay at least $150.

The bulk of HRC's energies go into building connections to supportive politicians, in part by donating to their election campaigns. The linkage to party politics has inevitably tilted the organization in a Democratic direction, simply as a result of the positioning of the two major parties on issues of sexual orientation, though it does establish ties to as many Republicans as it can, and in 1995 donated $5,000 to the National Republican Congressional Committee.

GAY AND LESBIAN VICTORY FUND. The formation of the Gay and Lesbian Victory Fund in 1991 was supported from the outset by activists associated with the Human Rights Campaign Fund. Modeled on organizations such as EMILY's List and the WISH list, designed to support the candidacy of women for electoral office, the Victory Fund sought to raise money for openly gay and lesbian candidates at all levels of government. Because it bundles donations from members and supporters, it can essentially circumvent the limits on donations that can go to a single candidate from a PAC.

The Victory Fund is a peculiarly American formation, one that illustrates the prominence of money in United States elections and the need for candidates to raise funds outside party channels. The United States has a vast number of elected offices, almost 500,000 at all levels. Even if only a minuscule proportion of contests provide much encouragement for openly gay or lesbian candidates, there are still enough to warrant the formation of an organization like the Victory Fund.

The group entered its first major election campaign in 1992. Apart from being openly lesbian or gay, candidates seeking support by the Victory Fund had to endorse the federal gay/lesbian civil rights bill, have "aggressive positions" on AIDS funding and other nondiscrimination issues, have viable candidacies, and be pro-choice.[9] In its first election, about seventy openly lesbian or gay candidates contacted the Victory Fund for assistance. It recommended twelve, and channeled half a million dollars in contributions to them. In 1994 it backed twenty-seven candidates with $800,000 in contributions, fourteen of whom won. In 1996, it backed thirty-two, of whom twenty-two won.

The American gay/lesbian movement, like the American women's movement, has attached more importance to entering electoral contests than movements in other countries. Even among those most likely to be disdainful of and alienated from mainstream politics, the importance of "out" public figures has given such politicians very high profiles. The novelty of the role, and the unusual qualities of the earliest incumbents, added to the enthusiasm with which they were greeted. In circumstances in which engagement with the state seemed necessary and inevitable, in a political system sufficiently complex that insider contacts were indispensable, the gay politician seemed to play a crucial role.

The fact that over 125 gay men and lesbians have now won elected office in the United States makes them a visible phenomenon for the social movement as a whole, the national constituency of sexual minority members, and the mainstream press. Such politicians still constitute a tiny proportion of the total number of elected officials, but they are now spread across a large number of localities and regions. The last decade or so has been notable for the number of candidates who were open about their sexuality from the outset. Such candidates have not, and cannot realistically, run in all parts of the country. They have tended to gravitate toward progressive areas and those with substantial gay and lesbian concentrations. Once in office, they generally retain their seats, even when running against partisan tides.

PARTY ACTIVISM. The growth of national organizations autonomous of the party system has been paralleled by the development of gay and lesbian activism within the Democratic and Republican parties, with visibility at the national level becoming particularly pronounced in the 1990s. Despite the weakness of party organizations in American politics, especially at the national level, party politics infuses most social movements. Most local elections are contested on a partisan basis, as they are in Europe, though not in Canada. Since local party groups can form with relative ease, social movement activists can gain entry into party politics while at the same time operating in virtual autonomy from other party organs. The permeability and localism of American party politics makes shifting in and out of partisan and electoral politics easier than in most other countries, where influence tends to require engagement over a long period.

The stark contrasts between Democrats and Republicans on issues of sexual orientation, gender, and race, particularly since the 1980s, have provided an incentive for social movement activists on the left and the right to do battle within party ranks. The religious right has entered the local and state levels of the Republican Party over the last decade, and activists associated with a variety of progressive movements have entered Democratic Party networks over a longer period than that. Gay and lesbian groups, like many other organized interests, have become more entwined with partisan and electoral politics as they have come to realize that access to policy makers and impact on outcomes depends in part on the outcome of elections.[10]

In 1972 Jim Foster and Madeleine Davis addressed the Democratic convention as openly gay and lesbian delegates, though to a small audience at 3:00 A.M. Prior to that, party politics was so closed to gays that, according to one activist, "the whole notion of getting involved with it didn't seriously cross people's minds."[11] Two years later, *The Advocate* was reporting a proliferation of local Democratic clubs being formed by gays and lesbians.[12] The development of gay "ghettos" in major American cities also facilitated the development of local partisan clubs and allowed them to construct themselves as political brokers or pressure groups analogous to other groups defined by geographic concentration or ethnic identity.

The prospect of access to and influence over presidential politics seemed to increase slightly under Jimmy Carter in the late 1970s. The 1980 Democratic convention in New York represented an additional opening to national party politics. Gay activists were visible on the campaign team of Senator Edward Kennedy, contesting Carter's renomination. The Carter camp recognized the significance of gay forces within the party and the need to woo them, though Carter later distanced himself from sexual orientation commitments when running against the Republican candidate, Ronald Reagan. The 1980 convention passed the national party's first pro-gay resolution (opposing anti-gay discrimination and specifying the ban on homosexual visitors and immigrants), and enough signatures were garnered to place the name of an openly gay African-American delegate, Mel Boozer, in nomination for vice president, providing a vehicle for nomination speeches taking up gay rights issues.[13]

At the 1984 Democratic convention in the San Francisco, Jesse Jackson's candidacy was assertively pro-gay. In the streets outside the convention hall, 100,000 gays and lesbians demonstrated for their rights. Walter Mondale won the nomination, and the Democratic election campaign kept gay issues at arm's length (especially with the Republicans using the phrase "San Francisco Democrat" as a coded attack on gay visibility within the party). After Reagan's reelection, gay influence was reduced by the Democratic leadership's increasing centrism and its concern with the "special interest" label. The 1988 nominee for president, Michael Dukakis, combined electoralist caution with personal unease around such issues.

The 1992 election year represented an enormous breakthrough, with gay and lesbian support actively wooed by the five leading contenders for the Democratic nomination, especially Paul Tsongas and Bill Clinton. Gay involvement in campaign fund-raising was thought to be making a difference in a number of state and local races. Clinton's communications director, George Stephanopoulos, admitted that the appeal of this new constituency was based on more than principle: "This is a group with money and a group that votes."[14] The attitude of the Democratic candidates, and Clinton in particular, contrasted dramatically with the Republicans' blatant pandering to right-wing anti-gay sentiment.

Gay visibility at the convention itself was on an unprecedented scale. It was reflected, of course, in the increase in the gay and lesbian caucus from fewer than eighty members. But beyond sheer numbers, it was reflected in access to influential organizing committees, and in featured speakers such as Roberta Achtenberg and Bob Hattoy. As one delegate remembers: "In New York it was phenomenal; at one point you looked out and there was literally a sea of rainbow flags on the convention floor."[15] There was more gender balance than ever, too. According to Liz Hendrickson of the National Center for Lesbian Rights, there were lesbians "all over at the Democratic convention," perhaps more numerous than gay men.[16] The gay and lesbian caucus was welcomed with open arms by Democratic officials, and was influential in helping run the convention. As one report put it at the time, "After years of being shunted into the shadows, Gay and AIDS issues took an extraordinary step forward into the limelight at the Democratic National Convention this week."[17]

The platform adopted by the convention embraced a substantially pro-gay agenda at a moment when the party was eager to distance itself from other progressive constituencies to which it had long been obligated. As one gay Democrat who attended the convention recalled: "In the past . . . discrimination on the basis of sexual orientation [had been] slipped in on a long list of things. This time there was a clear, forthright statement in support of lesbian, gay, and bisexual rights."[18] During debates on the platform, the gay/lesbian and AIDS-related positions were passed with virtually no opposition.

The national media provided substantial coverage of the gay and lesbian presence at the convention. In 1988 the coordinators of gay and lesbian media operations had to "cajole and beg and push and shmooze and pray" to get press coverage of gay issues. In 1992 the operation coordinated by representatives from the Task Force and the Campaign Fund had reporters coming to them, often already familiar with the issues. As Robert Bray, the coordinator, said at the time: "It is difficult to turn on the TV or read a newspaper and not see something about Gays in this convention. The effect of this is to tell politicians they need to take Gay and Lesbian voters and our issues seriously."[19] With the election nearing its climax, a *New York Times Magazine* article announced that gay politics was going mainstream: "Out of the closet and into the voting booth, gay men and lesbians are becoming major players for the first time in a presidential election."[20]

The 1996 convention was a reminder of the limits of gay and lesbian influence in the Democratic Party. There were short speeches by gay member of Congress Barney Frank and activist Phill Wilson, and a brief mention of gay rights from former New York governor Mario Cuomo, but little else. Even an openly gay candidate for the House of Representatives, Rick Zbur, avoided reference to gays and lesbians during his turn at the podium, explaining afterward that "if we talk about gays, we court controversy."[21] In three days of seminars sponsored during the convention by the centrist Democratic Leadership Council, once led by Bill Clinton, the issue of gay rights never came up. This prompted one San Francisco

Democrat to enter a successful caucus motion reminding party officials that gays are "part of the American family" and later to comment that "we are the relatives who have disappeared."[22] Most gay and lesbian Democrats seemed ready to acquiesce in the pragmatism that dictated gay issues on the hustings. They agreed that, given the Republicans' hostility, it was more important to return Clinton to the White House and a Democratic majority to Congress than to highlight sexual diversity in the convention or the election. According to one of the openly gay party members who served on the platform committee: "It's a hard pill to swallow, but you have to realize that Bill Clinton is not running for West Hollywood City Council. He's running for president. That means he's also running for president of Nebraska—and a lot of those constituents don't like us."[23]

During the Reagan-Bush years, Republican inhospitability drove gay/lesbian activists out of the party and kept loyal party members in the closet. In 1984, a reception was held for gay delegates or alternates, but gays at the convention were otherwise almost entirely invisible. A small number of local groups of gay Republicans had existed for a few years; the earliest formed in California at the time of the 1978 Briggs initiative. The 1987 March on Washington occasioned a get-together, out of which came United Republicans for Equality and Privacy, a national coordinating group. At the 1988 convention there was much more visibility. A gay reception at the convention attracted about eighty participants and some media attention, though there were still almost no openly gay or lesbian delegates, and virtually no impact on party policy.

In 1990 all the clubs agreed to join together as the Log Cabin Federation. During the next two years, veteran organizer Marvin Liebman and Rich Tafel, the new head of the Federation, began to gain media attention. At the 1992 convention in Houston, the Federation's third annual meeting brought together fifteen clubs from ten states, but Log Cabin activists were still essentially outsiders in a party now heavily influenced by the religious right, and the platform agreed to by the convention opposed what were claimed to be efforts by the Democratic Party "to include sexual preference as a protected minority receiving preferential status under civil rights statutes."[24] Not surprisingly, the group unanimously approved a motion not to endorse the Bush-Quayle candidacy. The anti-gay temper of the convention helped to propel Log Cabin Republicans into the spotlight and attracted growing numbers of adherents. By late 1993, there were thirty-two clubs in twenty-one states.

Earlier in 1993, a somewhat distinct group was formed in Washington to act as a lobby group as well as a clearinghouse for information about legislation and legislators—merging two years later with the Log Cabin Federation. By late 1996, Log Cabin Republicans had a $700,000 budget and six employees, and claimed a membership of ten thousand. Although there were only a handful of openly gay delegates at the 1996 convention, they and their Log Cabin colleagues gained significant visibility in the media and on the convention floor. This time, in contrast to 1992, the party leadership managed to curtail anti-gay vitriol, recognizing the electoral damage inflicted on George Bush's candidacy by the hateful rhetoric of that convention. The platform agreed to by the convention, however, explicitly rejected the inclusion of sexual orientation in anti-discrimination legislation, endorsed the anti-gay Defense of Marriage Act, and criticized Bill Clinton's "assault on the culture and traditions of the Armed Forces," affirming that homosexuality was incompatible with military service.[25] A survey of delegates revealed that 82 percent disagreed that it was necessary to have laws to protect homosexuals from discrimination (as distinct from 55 percent in the general population).

Fissures within National Mainstream Activism

The lesbian and gay movement has developed visibility in all the major institutional domains of the political mainstream, at the national as well as the local level. The 1990s witnessed particularly strong growth in gay/lesbian resources devoted to such arenas. However impressive the activist presence in the mainstream compared to only a decade before, or in comparison to the resources mobilized by many other social movements, it pales by contrast to those marshaled in opposition to gay and lesbian equality. It is the scale of such opposition, whipped up at every level of government, that so distinguishes the challenges faced by the American movement from those in most other liberal democratic countries.

U. S. movement groups also face internal challenges, some of them of a distinctively American cast. National organizations are isolated to some extent from one another, and much more seriously from activist networks at state and local levels. National activism is marked by deep divisions over partisan loyalty. There are also differences in ideological and strategic orientation between national groups, ranging from Log Cabin Republicans on one side to the Task Force and the National Leadership Forum on the other. To some extent this simply reflects the divisions that come inevitably with the growth in size and strength of a social movement, though difficulties also arise from competition over status and membership within the broader gay and lesbian constituency.

PARTISANSHIP. The formation of local party clubs and the visible presence at national conventions were tentative steps toward inclusion in party politics, often taken by skeptics. But as inside access increased, so did expectations of loyalty, sharpening the divide not only between those who opted for one party or another, but also between those who threw their lot in with party politics generally and those who chose to remain at arm's length. The deeper "inside" that gay activists are, the more likely they are to overestimate the party's support for their cause, leaving themselves open to attack from rivals or outsiders.

The high profile of the Log Cabin Republicans has made partisan rivalry within gay and lesbian networks obvious. With the Republican Party so heavily influenced by the religious and secular right, most activists in the lesbian and gay social movement are suspicious of any identification with the national party. Many admire in the abstract those who try to challenge the party from within but wonder how the party could attract that kind of loyalty. Barney Frank was more outspoken than most, but hardly alone, in calling Log Cabin "Uncle Tom's Cabin Club."[26]

The leaders of the Log Cabin Republicans have been just as eager to attack gay Democrats. Like many in the British gay Conservative group TORCHE, they have as strong a commitment to combating anti-Republican and anti-right sentiment in the gay movement as they have to fighting anti-gay sentiment in their own party. The distrust with which they have been regarded within their party seems to intensify their need to demonstrate their loyalty—as a means of establishing their credentials and securing what access they have gained. They seem at times more focused on attacking Democrats than homophobes within their own party. Log Cabin loyalists defend their party in part by overstating the supportiveness of Republican legislators. An illustration was provided by one Log Cabin activist, who described Senator Bob Dole as a moderate on the basis of the relative absence of explicitly anti-gay rhetoric in his opposition to lifting the military ban in early 1993.[27] It is a style of party loyalty that has provoked even some Republicans. One admits: "I have a philosophical problem with Log Cabin. It's one thing to want to change the Republican Party to be receptive to gay issues, and it's another thing to be really blind to a whole host of instances of intolerance. It's like this mentality of, 'As long as I'm treated okay we'll let everything else go'—trying to convince yourself that if you just look right, and talk right and toe the line on all the issues, then the Republicans will accept you and you can be the Republican you always wanted to be."[28]

Partisan antagonism intensified in the aftermath of the debate over lifting the military ban. Democratic politicians and activists were quick to defend the administration and the congressional majority against activist critics, reminding them of gains on other fronts. With varying degrees of subtlety, they also sought to shift the blame over to groups such as the Campaign for Military Service. Gay Republicans answered with charges of sellout by President Clinton and Representative Barney Frank, downplaying the roles of Republicans such as Dole.

Partisanship exerts an unrelenting push and pull on national gay activism. The inescapability of partisan considerations inside legislative, presidential, and electoral politics, coupled with the lack of party discipline, constantly embroils social movement activists. As in other aspects of the American political system, activists are drawn into party channels in large numbers, at the same time as many in their constituency and grassroots activists are wary of letting loyalty to party exceed loyalty to the movement. The establishment of an ongoing presence within each of the national parties is crucial to the movement, but building influence requires a degree of partisan loyalty that inevitably creates tensions inside the movement.

ISOLATION. Even inside the Washington Beltway, growing access to the political mainstream has opened up divisions between insiders and others. The tendency toward isolation—between those favoring different types of activist engagement with the mainstream and those with different degrees of insider con-tact—increases with that access. Human Rights Campaign activists tend to see their organization as the most politically savvy of the Washington groups, ad-mitted to the centers of power because they know the rules of the game. Of course they do have to know these rules, since the group is wholly focused on lobbying the executive and legislative branches of government. Such preoccu-pations, however, can perpetuate a professionalized structure that encourages stra-tegic caution, and that credits only the HRC with doing important work.[29] The risk of insiders' being isolated from other parts of the movement may have in-creased with gay entry into presidential politics. As activist Urvashi Vaid points out, during the 1992 election cycle and its aftermath, major gay donors and fund-raisers enjoyed a kind of access to Democratic presidential candidates completely unavailable to others who had spent years in national activist organizing.

Litigation can also produce isolation, in part because of the specialized exper-tise required and the tendency for legal work to operate almost entirely inside the legal system itself. Vaid acknowledges that gay/lesbian rights lawyers gather reg-ularly in conferences to discuss strategy and specific cases: ''On an operational, day-to-day level, however, cooperation between legal groups and national politi-cal organizations remains minimal. Legal groups pursue litigation, speak before legal and legislative bodies, and speak out in the media in a parallel world to the political groups. Political organizations, too, rarely involve the legal groups in drafting legislation or in debating the merits of various approaches they are con-sidering.''[30]

This isolation is risky, in part because the constitutional grounds for court challenges can highlight arguments that are at odds with the longer-term goals and strategies of other parts of the movement. For example, there is frequent reference to the right to privacy in establishing gay rights claims in court, despite the risks inherent in reinforcing popular perceptions of gay and lesbian sexuality as ''private'' matters. The jurisprudence of equality rights protections in the Con-stitution has often induced lawyers to portray gays and lesbians as members of a discrete and politically powerless minority defined by an ''immutable'' char-acteristic. The construction of sexual diversity implied in that characterization is contested among gays and lesbians themselves, and can contribute to a victim mentality that is ultimately debilitating.

The relationship between HRC and the Victory Fund, generally seen as closely allied, is another example of different parts of the movement potentially working at cross-purposes. HRC sponsorship is granted potentially to any politician with at least a moderately good record on gay issues, whereas the Victory Fund sup-ports only openly gay or lesbian candidates. These distinct strategies, one based on ''identity'' and the other on political performance, can easily collide. An illustration of the risk is provided by the 1990 election for the Massachusetts state legislature, before the Victory Fund began sponsoring candidates. Openly gay Republican Michael Duffy ran for the Massachusetts State House against Byron Rushing, an incumbent African-American Democrat with one of the most progressive records in state politics. In 1994 openly gay Tony Miller challenged progressive pro-gay incumbent Michael Woo for the Democratic nomination in the race for California secretary of state.

Relationships to Local and State Activism

If the fissures that occur within Washington gay networks threaten to hamper the movement, those that have opened between Washington groups and local activists are even more dangerous. The events of the 1990s demonstrated that access inside national political institutions needs to be backed up by grassroots mobilization. The impediments to forging such links, however, remain imposing.

IDEOLOGICAL AND STRATEGIC DIFFERENCES. Urvashi Vaid, former Task Force director, talks of a gulf between national and local activism that was particularly pronounced during the period when national groups were being established: "It was grassroots, direct-action, feminist, and progressive queers who took the New Right most seriously. Mainstream gay and lesbian organizations tended to disregard it or treat it as an aberration. The two camps also disagreed on strategy; grassroots activists favored education and direct confrontation, and mainstream activists believed legislation and straight support were paramount. As a result, a chasm formed between the local political movement and its national counterpart. This break in ideology, strategy, communication, and vision polarized the gay and lesbian movement in the late 1970s and early 1980s."[31]

This assessment overstates somewhat the contrast between local and national activism at the time, but it does capture some of the elements that contributed to a persistent pattern of isolation. The 1980s saw both greater variation among Washington-based groups than there had been at first and less strategic caution. Local activism is also highly variable across both ideological and strategic alternatives. In cities of all sizes, activist groups can be found that perform the roles played by the major national groups. The entry into party politics is in fact more a local than a national phenomenon, and electoral campaigns by openly gay and lesbian candidates are more likely to occur at the local level than at any other, and are usually built on a substantial activist base.

Nevertheless, one of the differences between local and national politics is that local engagement with mainstream institutions tends to be balanced by more confrontational activism. The spontaneous, outrageous, and often angry street politics that emerged in the form of ACT UP and Queer Nation is entirely local. Such activism may have waned by the mid-1990s, but that strand of confrontationalism sometimes recurs, demonstrating a continuing impatience with the gradualism of the political mainstream.

At the national level there is little of the kind of transformative politics prominent in the early years of gay liberation. Even if some activists in the Task Force and the Human Rights Campaign did come to Washington with a set of radical objectives, the work itself inevitably focuses their attention on more incremental change. National political groups that are closest to the inside (like HRC) tend to be nervous about the outspokenness and outrageousness that are widespread in local gay communities. This does not necessarily mean that they have been absorbed into the politics of respectability (though that is true of some), but only shows that they work in an environment in which confrontational images undermine the claim for rights. The very fact that gay and lesbian activism in Washington is as new a phenomenon as it is, and that its demands are so little understood and so virulently opposed, makes the pressure on lobbyists to conform to mainstream political norms enormous.

Contrasting assessments of the 1993 March on Washington illustrate the differences of perspective between those from different activist locations. Congressman Barney Frank expressed disappointment that so few marchers attempted to lobby their congressional representatives, and was critical of organizers for including outrageous performers onstage. Gay and lesbian lobbyists whose work focused on Capitol Hill agreed that the march did nothing to help lift the military ban. And yet many of those who had contributed to the sheer magnitude of the march came from activist circles that resisted setting boundaries around the acceptable. For many of them, tailoring a march on the nation's capital to a particular legislative agenda would have been unthinkable.

A gap of a different sort opened up for a time between national and local groups on the issue of gay/lesbian marriage. For some years there had been a rapid increase in the number of couples arranging commitment ceremonies. Local groups had been organizing around the issue, and in Hawaii won their first court cases, before national groups even became involved. The delay in reaction was sometimes rooted in strategic caution on the part of those who believed that the battle was unwinnable. But there were activists at all levels who simply did not believe that significant movement energies should be devoted to a demand they saw as a conservative one—a demand for inclusion in an essentially patriarchal institution. By 1996 there was a much more widespread community consensus that gays and lesbians should have the option of marriage available to them, and the victories in Hawaii demonstrated that in some locations the fight could be won. At the same time, the Republican majority on Capitol Hill was pushing the Defense of Marriage Act through Congress, forcing national group engagement just to contain the damage.

THE NEED FOR COMPROMISE. Activists on the front lines often would rather, as feminist academic Jane Mansbridge has suggested, ''lose fighting for a cause they believe in than win fighting for a cause they feel is morally compromised.''[32] Some insist on all or nothing; many more draw ''lines in the sand'' that permit movement on some fronts but not others. As national groups have begun to gain access to Congress and the White House, however, the pressures to play according to these established norms of compromise increase, especially because these groups are newcomers with relatively fragile positioning on the political agenda.

The fact that there are occasional opportunities for legislative gain, and for success in stopping legislative retreat, intensifies those pressures. Urvashi Vaid observes: "Among the truisms of American politics is that you have to give to get, pay to play, lose some to win some. The legislative process is about this kind of interplay between power and compromise. . . . If one is not willing to compromise, one is considered stupid, naive, unaware of how the 'game' is played."[33] She recounts an episode that occurred during the legislative debate over the Hate Crimes Statistics Bill:

> Senators Edward Kennedy, Orrin Hatch, and Paul Simon had hammered out an agreement on how to thwart [an anti-gay] amendment; their suggestion was an amendment that read something to the effect that "traditional family values are the backbone of American society. . . ." They wanted our sign-off on the wording. . . . I argued that the compromise was unacceptable, since it effectively legislated language that everyone from judges to the common person would interpret as excluding gay people and would seriously damage our movement's family agenda. . . . [W]e struck on the words *American family values* to replace *traditional family values*. The compromise was acceptable to us, to the Senate staff, and to our coalition partners. We went with it—and the Hate Crimes Statistics Act passed with that bizarre clause.[34]

The legislative arena is more constrained even than party conventions or local party clubs. The internal life of the national parties is filled with caucuses and factions standing firm on principle, pulling back from full engagement in the face of defeat. Legislative politics is quite different, for the short-term consequences of a failure to negotiate or a refusal to compromise can be damaging.[35]

Those immersed in the norms of legislative politics (the Human Rights Campaign is the most obvious case) are prone to measuring gains in small steps taken very slowly. Their own self-esteem and their organization's worth depend on their seeing themselves as effective players within the mainstream. The issue of campaign donations to national legislators illustrates the pressures on gay lobbyists to set their sights low. Lobbyists argue that encouragement ought to be provided to those who are generally supportive, even if not unswervingly or invariably so. That entails compromises that make sense in legislative terms, if not to gays and lesbians outside Washington. HRC is regularly subject to criticism that the politicians it supports in both parties are unreliable. Many would point to the small number of House and Senate members voting against the Defense of Marriage Act as an example. About half of the elected officials endorsed by HRC voted anti-gay on DOMA, including President Clinton himself. HRC sets its standards of acceptability even lower for Republicans than Democrats, to try to broaden its alliances among Republican moderates and reinforce its claims to bipartisanship.

Openly gay legislators are under particular pressure both to compromise and to demonstrate party loyalty, not least because they must continue working within a system of constantly shifting alliances. This is true of gay politicians at all levels, although those operating at the state and local level have more of an opportunity to negotiate regularly with local activists, and explain in detail the complexities of legislative coalition building. National politicians have opportunities to work with the national groups, but they do not have the same ties to local gay communities.

SUSPICION OF WASHINGTON. The fact that Washington, D.C., is a government city, almost exclusively so, deepens the divide with direct action groups and cultural networks outside it. Few countries can match the extent to which Washington and those who work in it are viewed as absorbed in their own machinations. The metaphoric use of the "Beltway," the expressway that circles the Washington area, is a powerful one. Americans, whether social movement activists or not, are both in awe of Washington and distrustful of it. They visit the national monuments that are so inextricably linked with the federal government, and look upon them with deep respect. But they joke about politicians and bureaucrats in a way that reflects profound cynicism about the state itself. Gay and lesbian access to national political institutions may enjoy an aura of novelty, but such access cannot sweep away the distrust of government that is so deeply embedded in American history and popular culture.

The disconnection from Washington that local and regional activist networks feel is not necessarily a result of different political agendas. Donald Rosenthal's research on cities in New York state points to a degree of activist pragmatism that would suit national political networks. But he also points to the "fragile nature of the articulation" between activism at the local level and at either the state or the national level.[36] Lobbying Congress, supporting electoral candidates, and serving as an activist clearinghouse in a country as large and politically complex as the United States all generate demands for resources on a scale to which most social movements are unaccustomed. The need to develop lobbying skill and expertise requires a permanent paid staff, often an issue among local activists who do their work on a volunteer basis. According to one Washington activist: "When you go out to Des Moines, Iowa, and talk about that, people deplore that their money is being spent to sustain a bureaucracy. Well, it has to happen that way. You can't just walk in and talk to a senator about military policy without having a history about what that policy has been doing. . . . Consequently, the industry careerists have a fear of the street activists because the street activists are not interested in structure; they're not interested in hierarchy; they're not interested in being nice; they're just interested in formative change."[37] Local activists sometimes remark that the most visible sign of the Human Rights Campaign's existence are the large dinners it hosts in cities across the country, raising more money than local groups could ever raise, among people who often make little contribution to local activism.

POLITICAL CYNICISM AND APATHY. In 1981 Dennis Altman watched the huge annual Freedom Day Parade in San Francisco, and overheard a group of gay men groaning when political groups went by, "Why do they have to bring politics into everything?"[38] What this reveals is a widespread rejection of "politics" that seems more pronounced in the United States than elsewhere. Many local gay activists are cynical about mainstream processes. Some are so on ideological grounds, seeing the political order as structurally tilted in favor of prevailing economic interests. Others see politicians as individuals corrupted by "the system." That skepticism does not preclude their involvement in campaigns to prevent the passage of an anti-gay referendum, or to support the passage of anti-discrimination legislation. But it does inhibit longer-term involvement in mainstream politics.

There are countless men and women who are prepared to see themselves as part of a gay and lesbian community, but who, like most Americans, are politically apathetic. There are data purportedly showing an electoral turnout of gays and lesbians in excess of 90 percent, but this is a dangerous illusion. Just like data that show gays with a substantially higher-than-average income, figures represent only those who are secure enough in their sexuality to be out or to be on one or another gay-related mailing list. No doubt the participation of gay and lesbians in mainstream politics increases when decisions are being made on their rights, but in the longer term their participation has no obvious reason to rise above the low levels typical of the American population as a whole.

One openly gay politician at the state level, speaking at the time of the 1994 election, remarked:

> I would say there is a big portion of the [gay] community out there that is so apolitical. They may have heard my name; they don't know my face. . . . Last week I went down to a gay bar with the Democratic candidate for governor and introduced him. Later, a young man who just moved to town, who was with our group, said just as we left, "I can't believe it. There was the Democratic candidate for governor standing right there, and there were people who were just walking by, not paying any attention whatsoever. I thought that was a really big event, that one of the major party candidates was campaigning in a gay bar." . . . My partner, who knows more bar people and more non-political people than I do, will sometimes say to me, "You know, most gay people don't care about your bills, they don't care about what you're doing—they're not going to care about it until somebody comes to cart them off to a concentration camp or something."[39]

LEADERSHIP. Ambivalence about Washington is entwined with contradictory attitudes toward leadership. As in the United States at large, leadership is at one and the same time yearned for and distrusted. Activist groups engaging with the political mainstream, particularly those operating at the national level, are inevitably institutionalized and hierarchical. Lines of responsibility must be clear, and those with a right to speak for a particular group must be unambiguously identifiable. The leaders of such organizations acquire a national profile, and in many circumstances are seen as representing the entire social movement. In their search for "responsible" voices, the media will often focus on national groups or politicians, while their more questionable desire for confrontational images will draw on local events. This increases the contrast perceived to exist between activists at the two levels.

The American cultural fixation on "stars," reflected in the highly individualistic and personalized media coverage of politics, creates high profiles for individual activists who have political access. David Mixner rose to national prominence largely because of his perceived closeness to a newly elected president. His profile was then boosted by frequent quotes from him in the national media, gay and straight. Openly gay politicians, particularly at the national level, also acquire the aura of leadership (bolstered in the case of figures such as Barney Frank and Gerry Studds by their skills as legislators and public tribunes, and their willingness to identify themselves publicly with the movement).

There are many gays and lesbians who believe that such leadership profiles are important. Throughout American society there is an extraordinary and unabashed preoccupation with leadership training. Many proponents of confrontational strategies will call for strong leadership rather than challenging the principle of hierarchy. Yet the individualism of Americans in general, and social movement activists in particular, also breeds wariness. There is a strong temptation in American political and activist life to attribute success or assign failure to the personal qualities of individuals. In social movements, the distrust of leadership among at least some activists is wrapped up in a critique of the privilege accorded those perceived as experts. It is also tied to the wariness of bureaucratic forms of organization that so often accompanies the elevation of expertise inside a movement. Direct action groups are the source of some of the harshest critiques. Larry Kramer, widely and justifiably respected for his challenges to complacency on AIDS, issued the denunciation: "[O]ur own forces—our openly gay elected officials, our advocacy groups in Washington, our political organizations around the country, ACT UP and other AIDS advocacy associations—are demoralized, exhausted, burned-out, bureaucratized beyond effectiveness, second-rate, inadequate, useless, hateful, and/or dead. Every executive director has lost touch with reality, and every member of every board of directors should be brought up in a court of law for raping us."[40]

The leaders of national groups make particularly easy targets for criticism, but accounts of local activism in cities as politically distinct as New York and San Francisco regularly report attacks on leaders and other forms of backbiting. One gay journalist has written: "Activist after activist has walked away from a national or local group—or from gay and lesbian community work altogether—claiming that she or he was no longer able to tolerate the intense scrutiny and cutting criticism directed at the more visible members of our community."[41] Torie Osborn, on retiring from the executive directorship of the Los Angeles Gay and Lesbian Center, spoke of "this amorphous and often cannibalistic creature that loves to put you on a pedestal and knock you down."[42] Urvashi Vaid, who preceded Osborn as head of the Task Force, has written in a similar vein: "I was called a 'traitor' for withdrawing my involvement in an ACT UP action in which I had mistakenly agreed to participate. . . . I've been called an Uncle Tom, anti-male, antiwhite, too radical because I engaged in direct action, a sell-out because I met with a GOP leader, too assimilationist because I worked in a traditional political organization, a Stalinist, an anarcho-syndicalist, someone who destroyed NGLTF, un-American, utopian, authoritarian, self-appointed, self-elected, a 'so-called leader,' stupid, naive, not sufficiently hard-working, too narrowly focused, and much more.''[43] The tendency to aim fire inward crosses gender and race lines. Some might imagine it a phenomenon born of male assertiveness or competitiveness, but the commentaries provided by lesbians suggests that it is at least as pronounced among women.[44]

The gay and lesbian movement has never had leaders of the stature or legitimacy of a Martin Luther King, Jr., or even with the same name recognition as a Betty Friedan or Cesar Chavez. This is due in part to the media indifference to the movement that persisted until the 1990s. But it also results from the fact that gay and lesbian activism is relatively new to the political mainstream, where media visibility is most likely. Nor is the lesbian and gay movement unique among contemporary movements in having no uncontested leadership figures.

THE LACK OF REPRESENTIVENESS. The task of forging links between national political groups and the grass roots of the social movement is made more difficult by the fact that many of those who engage in mainstream politics are not representative of the "average person." They tend to be largely male and overwhelmingly white. In most cases they are highly educated, and occupationally secure. Describing a party given by the gay and lesbian caucus at the 1980 Democratic convention in New York, Dennis Altman recorded observations that still resonate today: "The women and men who gathered in UN Plaza . . . were a new brand of gay politicians, smart, affluent, at ease lobbying with members of Congress or being interviewed by *The New York Times*. The two biggest delegations came from California and Florida, where political battles in the last few years . . . had mobilized middle class gays and turned them into political activists. . . . The gay caucus included fewer women than men, had an underrepresentation of blacks and Hispanics, and exuded a general air of quiet competence that would give way during the week to the sort of frenetic activity that marks such events.''[45]

Those who are most involved in lobbying and campaign fund-raising inevitably replicate some of the inequalities embedded in the political institutions they are seeking to enter or challenge. Given the importance of those who have money and connections, the Victory Fund's most influential players are bound to be atypical in in terms of class, race, and gender terms. Board members themselves are expected to donate and raise money, in addition to covering their own expenses to attend quarterly meetings. HRC fund-raising dinners, at $150 or $175 a plate, produce an entirely predictable demographic: mostly men, mostly white, most wearing tuxedos. Even those ticketholders who break the gender and race lines are usually of similar educational level and occupational standing.

That said, gay and lesbian groups engaging the political mainstream at the national level have taken considerable strides to diversify their leadership and membership. The boards of all the national organizations reflect diversity of gender and race. The Victory Fund has consciously sought a diverse candidate pool, and offered its first endorsement to Sherry Harris, an African-American lesbian running for the Seattle City Council. Lesbian involvement has increased considerably in the Human Rights Campaign, and in 1995 the organization appointed former Task Force board member Elizabeth Birch as executive director. The National Gay and Lesbian Task Force has stood out in the extent to which it attracted and nurtured lesbian leadership, with women holding the position of executive director continuously from 1989. It has also reached out to people of color. Its senior staffers in the late 1980s included two women of color, including executive director Urvashi Vaid. Its board of directors in the early 1990s had gender parity, and a quarter were people of color.[46]

None of this really alters the upper-middle-class, professional character of the national groups, most especially the Victory Fund and HRC, and the networks operating inside the Democratic and especially the Republican Party. The complex demands imposed on all of the national groups, including the Task Force, require expertise and often professional training. The acquisition of that training, along with the communication skill and self-confidence required for high-level political activism, is itself influenced by social class. This increases the difficulty for social movement activists in general, and members of the broader lesbian and gay community, to see themselves reflected in the leadership of the national organizations representing them in Washington.

Comparison with Other Movements

Almost all movements are marked by a multitude of ideological and strategic orientations; the balance between such alternatives varies from one place to another and one time period to another. Some are transformative in their vision, others reformist, some hierarchical in their organizational style, others egalitarian, some confrontational in their tactics, others respectable and prepared to compromise. Identity-based movements frequently take in cultural and social modes of self-expression in addition to activism intended to effect specifically political change. Most are based primarily in local networks, but have also established national institutions to press for political reform or defend against political setback. Like the lesbian and gay movement, they have over time moved toward more thoroughgoing engagement with national political institutions. Likewise, the relationship between national political groups and local networks is either underdeveloped or conflictual, particularly when differences exist between those in the mainstream and those outside it.

THE AMERICAN WOMEN'S MOVEMENT. Lesbian and gay engagement with mainstream politics echoes the earlier women's movement.[47] In the 1960s, a reformist women's movement grew in the wake of the Presidential Commission on the Status of Women, committed to forging links with government offices wherever openings appeared. The radicalism that surged at the end of the decade never completely displaced that interest in mainstream politics, though a profoundly important generational shift did reduce its prominence. But in the early 1970s, political opportunities opened up for more substantial engagement with party politics, and a variety of feminist groups took advantage of them.

By the early 1980s, feminist activism had led to the creation of numerous political action committees, litigation groups, and organizations aiming to increase the number of women elected to office. The attraction to Washington and the move toward institutionalization was felt earlier and more powerfully for feminists than gays and lesbians. Political opportunities made mainstream engagement tempting in the 1970s, and inevitable in the 1980s.

Feminist attraction to partisan politics was amplified by the sheer size of the electorate for which they claimed to speak. The opening up of a gap between women's and men's party preferences and issue stances piqued the interest of party strategists in the 1970s, creating the potential for women to exercise influence in both the Democratic and Republican camps. The rise of both neoliberalism and neoconservatism in the Republican Party at the end of the 1970s closed down the potential for substantial linkage between women in that party and the women's activist movement, but the interest of national feminist groups in partisan and electoral politics as a whole continued to grow. The policy gains made in the 1970s, often with only modest resources, encouraged women to believe that mainstream engagement could effect change.[48] The struggle over ratification of the Equal Rights Amendment, and the growth of right-wing threats to gains already made, further intensified interest in the political mainstream.

The National Organization for Women (NOW) was the group most committed in theory to balancing the politics of protest and those of the inside. NOW included electoral politics in its repertoire throughout the period of high-profile radicalism in the broader movement, and during the 1980s it tilted more toward mainstream political action. But its membership was regularly rent by debate over that priority.[49] In the 1990s, under the presidency of Patricia Ireland, the commitment to protest and mass action increased, though without substantial decline of interest in electoral politics.

The difficulty of building and maintaining links between national-level activism and local groups is evident in the history of NOW and other Washington-based groups, compounded by the tension between the mainstream impulses of national groups and the more varied attitudes toward governmental and legal authority at the local level. NOW's openness to strategic diversity has not saved it from grassroots perceptions that it is too closely identified with cooptation. The unsuccessful attempt to secure support in state legislatures for the Equal Rights Amendment was seen by some analysts as illustrating the isolation of national groups.

NEW AND OLD SOCIAL MOVEMENTS. It is tempting but inaccurate to draw a stark contrast between late twentieth-century social movements and more established ones. Many academic observers overstate the separation of "new" movements both from activist politics of the past and from conventional political life today. Such movements are variously described as strategically oriented to direct action, and ideologically oriented to the radical overturning of established social norms, without the kind of resources suitable for traditional lobbying.

In fact, even social movements with strong currents of opposition to mainstream politics are inevitably drawn into a relationship with the state, and have been from their earliest years. The gay and lesbian movement, like the feminist and African-American movements, has always included a diversity of strategies and objectives. There are variations in emphasis on transformation and reform, cooperation and confrontation, in part a function of larger-scale waves of radicalism and protest. But the balance also varies according to the availability of resources and political opportunities. New social movements, just like older ones, are "fields of action," with individual activists, networks, and groups sometimes working cooperatively and sometimes in conflict.[50]

The phrase "new social movement" usually includes movements taking up issues of peace, environmentalism, feminism, ethnic identity, regional autonomy, race, nuclear energy, animal rights, disability, and sexual diversity. Some of these are based on group identity; some are based on what are thought to be the excesses of advanced industrialization; some include issues of material deprivation in their agendas; others focus on quality of life; some include strategies that are distinct from those of more established social movements; most include tactics drawn from well-practiced repertoires.

The labor movement's long history in the United States and elsewhere illustrates the hazards of too clearly demarcating new and old movements, or too easily imagining a single trajectory from radical spontaneity to reformist institutionalization, and of construing a social movement in unitary terms. The labor movement in the United States, and even more so in other countries, has experienced periods of militancy following periods of quiescence, sometimes in response to economic hardship, sometimes in response to relative prosperity. The unions have engaged with legislative and partisan processes, but without following a path from opposition to full absorption. Here too we find a multiplicity of strategies coexisting in the same period, sometimes even within a single organization.

Comparisons with Other Countries

The pattern of gay and lesbian activist engagement with the political mainstream in other political systems illustrates the uniqueness of American social movements, and the unusual challenges they face in matching the capacity for mobilization demonstrated by their opponents on the religious right. Gay and lesbian engagement with state institutions is much greater in the United States than in Britain, Canada, and most other liberal democracies. It is that difference which has led to the establishment of national organizations on an unparalleled scale. As we have seen, the difference lies in the prominence of gay and lesbian communities, the opportunities available to them for entering into mainstream political institutions, the traditions of group organizing, and the threat from a politically organized right. The necessity of engagement with mainstream processes has not eliminated fractionalism, but as befits a country in which liberal individualism has so long dominated the political culture, divisions within the movement are less over ideology than over strategic and organizational issues. There are ideological differences to be sure, represented in the writings of academics and of prominent figures such as Andrew Sullivan and Urvashi Vaid, but they are neither widespread nor deep by European standards.

BRITAIN. The British lesbian and gay movement has always had currents of mainstream activism. The lobbying in favor of decriminalizing homosexuality in the early 1960s included many liberal allies as well as gays. Since that time, one or another lobbying organization has always existed, though at times in a weakened state. In recent years this activist current has been revived in the growth of the Stonewall Group, with an emphasis on respectability and expertise reminiscent of the Campaign for Homosexual Equality before it, and the Homosexual Law Reform Society before that. But the forces drawing resources into such campaigning have not been as strong or continuous as in the United States.

There is more ideological division at the national level in Britain than in the United States. Socialist sentiment has been particularly strong in social movement politics. Since London is overwhelmingly the largest city in the United Kingdom as well as the capital, the radicalism that is by its very nature an essentially local phenomenon can more easily acquire a national profile. In that sense the group OutRage operates at a national level in a way that ACT UP in the United States does not. It differs from Stonewall on strategy more than ideology, but activist networks in the capital do include many voices that radically dissent from the mainstream and are critical of groups that are focused on it.

There has been campaigning within all three of the major parties since the late 1970s, undertaken by individuals and groups that recognize the centrality of parties in the British political order. As in the United States Democratic Party, gay and lesbian activism in the Liberal and Labour Parties, and eventually in the Conservative Party, grew at times when there seemed to be openings to reformism, or in the case of early-1980s Labour, to radicalism. In contrast to the United States, though, where entry into parties was aided by the permeability of local partisan structures, party politics in Britain attracted activists simply because of parties' dominance over the country's political life. British parties are not permeable, and activism within them entails very long marches through complex policy processes, requiring knowledge of rules and norms. In part because of that very impermeability, the gulf separating British gay activists who work inside the parties from those outside is wide. In the United States there certainly is a gap between partisans and non-partisans, especially at the local level, but the opportunities for access create more movement across that gap than would occur in Britain. In a number of localities and states as well, anti-gay referendum initiatives have led to the large-scale recruitment of gays and lesbians into electoral politics.

The fissures that characterize British gay and lesbian politics conflate ideological and strategic dimensions. Unity is therefore harder to maintain in Britain than in the United States, where it is difficult enough. The age of consent debate witnessed significant cooperation across such lines, but the immediate aftermath demonstrated its fragility. The rarity of opportunities for legislative change exacerbates the difficulty of crossing such lines. Many more British than American activists and groups question the value of any engagement with mainstream politics whatsoever and insist that mass action offers the only hope for change.

The capacity of British mainstream groups to tap into grassroots energy compensates to some extent for their fissiparousness. The country is, of course, much smaller than either the United States or Canada, with more centralized, nationally integrated political and media institutions. Gays and lesbians across Britain, whether activists or not, are simply more reachable from London than their counterparts in the various cities and towns across North America. Even modest-sized gay and lesbian groups are thus poised to take advantage of those few openings to reform that do occur in such a centralized and political system.

British gays and lesbians also seem less apathetic and cynical than their American counterparts. Voter turnout is much higher in Britain (and just about everywhere else) than in the United States, no doubt including gays and lesbians as well as the rest of the population. The political system is simpler in some respects, making political intervention easier to direct. In addition, openings to legislative reform are so rare that people are moved to act at those moments when they are asked to write or visit their MPs.

The resources mobilizable by groups operating in the mainstream count for more in Britain than they would in the United States because of the relative weakness of organized extraparliamentary opposition to gay and lesbian rights. Counterparts to the American religious right are marginal, and few elements of the secular right are driven to oppose law reform on issues of sexuality and gender. At times, the moderation of opposition may produce a degree of complacency, but energies can be activated in the face of blatant legal discrimination when political opportunities arise.

CANADA. Gay and lesbian political activism in Canada has always been more sporadic than in either Britain or the United States. In the late 1960s and early 1970s, no Canadian city witnessed the surge of gay liberationist activism that was sweeping across New York, San Francisco, and London. In later years there were short periods of large-scale activism, during the early 1980s in response to police raids in Toronto, Ottawa, and Montreal, and later in reaction to opportunities for legal reform that appeared at the provincial level in Ontario and to some extent Quebec. Outside of that, the kind of membership numbers that critics of United States national groups lament as inadequate would be unimaginable in Canada, even adjusted for population base.

The development of engagement with mainstream politics has never been as thoroughgoing as in the United States. The small size and impermanence of activist groups derives in part from a political system that does not offer the continuous inducement to mainstream activism that its American counterpart does. It is also the result of a legal environment that has helped impel change, at times with little activist intervention. The weakness of the religious right, at least as compared to its counterpart south of the border, further reduces the urgency of activist mobilization in most periods. Unlike in Britain, and especially the United States, neither the federal nor most provincial governments have been in the hands of political parties committed to a right-wing moral agenda.

The small scale of ongoing gay and lesbian organizing at the federal level is explainable by the extraordinary decentralization of the federation, the relatively small and isolated national capital, and the difficulty of maintaining cross-national representation from a population spread thinly across vast distances and divided by language. As in the British system, too, there are only occasional openings for significant change, limiting the rationale for a large institutional presence in Ottawa, and reducing the capacity to raise community money for such ends. The disincentives for institution building provided by the parliamentary system operate at the provincial level as well, though provincial capitals located in major regional cities can benefit from local gay and lesbian networks. To some extent, this reduces the degree of division that exists between American mainstream groups and other activist networks, for in Canada there are simply fewer groups and activists whose work focuses entirely on inside politics. In dramatic contrast to the United States, and modest contrast to Britain, Canadian mainstream gay activism employs almost no paid staff outside of AIDS groups.[51]

Although Canadian gay and lesbian activists have probably had the least sustained links to mainstream politics, they are also the least divided over the principle of such engagement. In comparison to Britain, the ideological range is not as great, not as likely to coincide with social class differences, and not as regularly translated into particular strategic preferences. In Canada, though a socialist current is evident in social movement activism as in the country's party politics, it offers a softer critique of strategic reformism than in Britain. There is also less bitterness in the debate over engagement with mainstream processes than in the United States, the latter characterized by widespread anti-statist distrust of authority.[52] Relatively small population size reduces the potential for activist groups to divide infinitely along ideological fissure lines. The party system in Canada extends less through political and social movement life than in other countries. Parties are less permeable than in the United States, doubly so because most local elections in Canada are not contested along party lines, a pattern that also reduces the relevance of party affiliations for local activists.[53] In Canada only a small minority of social movement activists are tempted into the fold even of parties that create openings for their issues.

In Canada, then, the activist resources available for linking the movement to established political processes are relatively modest, and in any event spread across three jurisdictional levels. The opposition that gays and lesbians face from right-wing forces is much better financed, though weaker than its United States counterparts and more likely to be characterized as extremist. Campaigns for gay and lesbian equality also have stronger support in the country's legal framework than in either Britain or America, and are therefore more able to circumvent legislative stumbling blocks.

Impact of Gay/Lesbian Engagement with Mainstream Politics

The impact of social movement presence on mainstream United States politics clearly must be measured not only in the statutory, administrative, and judicial advances of recent years, but also in longer-term shifts in institutional response and public opinion outside government and law. Account must also be taken of the effect of mainstream engagement on the movement itself, for that will shape the gay and lesbian agenda in future years, as well as the impact of the movement on future public policy and institutional practice.

INTERNAL IMPACT. Analyses of social movements, often using "life cycle" metaphors, point to the tendency toward mainstream assimilation as movements come to use more traditional methods of applying political pressure and set more tempered goals. If such metaphors imply a "short wave" internal dynamic affecting movements at a particular stage in their development, other analysts would also suggest a "long wave" transformation of social movement politics over substantial historical periods, for example, away from the radicalism of the 1960s and early 1970s and toward the more accommodationist approaches of the 1980s and 1990s.[54]

Some accounts of gay and lesbian politics echo these views, speaking of institutionalized, centralizing, professionally led organizations replacing the radical grassroots politics of the 1970s.[55] This is seen not only as a change in tactics, but also as a shift away from a potentially transformative challenges to gender roles and the very construction of homosexuality, in favor of a much narrower agenda focused on rights—on "letting us in." Activists engaging legal issues and equal rights are, according to such observers, inevitably drawn into a liberal framework that implicitly reinforces the legitimacy of the existing political structure.

In fact, social movement groups working inside the American political mainstream have no choice but to institutionalize in response to the need for specialized expertise, historical continuity, clear lines of responsibility, and recognizable leadership. Long-term engagement in both lobbying and litigation ties activists more and more firmly into political networks that are inevitably removed from grassroots activism. As we have seen, the value attached to compromise, incrementalism, "responsible" leadership, and loyalty to the process itself in such networks potentially isolates insiders from much of their movement.

When doors to executive and legislative offices are opened to gays and lesbian as officeholders and lobbyists, access can be confused with influence. The mystique of access is particularly pronounced in United States presidential politics; activists as well as lawmakers in Washington talk of the White House with a sense of awe and fascination. The assimilative pressures on mainstreaming activists may well be greater on gays and lesbians than on those in other social movements because they do not yet marshal the kinds of resources that can force politicians and administrators to listen. Activists are expected to play by rules that groups with real power can selectively ignore.

On such fragile terrain, lobbyists will sometimes emphasize the limited nature of the measures they press for. When such measures are enacted, their proponents will then be tempted to do the opposite and overstate their impact. Mainstream lobbyists will also tend to keep their distance from members of their communities who are deviant and outrageous. Many will publicly claim that activists who confront politicians and the media with radical demands actually help lobbyists look like the responsible alternative. Some among them more frankly argue that radicals, especially the sexually explicit paraders on gay/lesbian/bisexual pride days, hamper the prospect of advancing in the slow, pragmatic progress toward gay rights. Sexuality itself tends to be downplayed in the political mainstream, just as it is highlighted in significant portions of the movement and the community beyond. All too easily tensions can grow between values developed in gay culture and those that are ascendant in the political movement defending it.[56]

But the very fact that a social movement is much bigger than the individual groups representing it in the political mainstream serves as a check on assimilation to the norms of legislative and electoral politics. Although the tendency for Washington to isolate itself from developments outside the capital is strong, the recent experience of having friends in high office has also taught American activists that existing national organizations do not command the kinds of resources needed for significant progress. That may well induce even the most mainstream of Washington groups to ensure that their staffs include individuals with grassroots experience alongside those whose principal strength lies in lobbying know-how.

EXTERNAL IMPACT. The impact of a social movement has to be measured over the long term. Much of the change it provokes depends on the often isolated effort of thousands of individuals and groups, some working inside the political process, others in workplaces, still others in convincing friends and family members of the worthiness of their cause. This localized and varied activity creates changes in social and political climates, which then enable particular groups to make more specific inroads into public policy and institutional practice.

As is evident in the experience of gay and lesbian groups in the United States as well as Britain and Canada, achieving policy gains depends at least as much on the structure of political opportunities as on the resources available to movement groups. In some circumstances, victory relies on the skillful mobilization of a wide range of resources, including grassroots pressure. In cases where partisan alignments are particularly favorable and political receptivity unusually high, success may hinge on only modest nudges. The American movement is less likely than its Canadian or British counterparts to score victories with slight nudges, given the scale of anti-gay forces. But gains do depend on very particular opportunities.[57]

An assessment of the legislative record in Washington reveals a mixture of gains, losses, and stalemates. The inclusion of sexual orientation in the 1990 Hate Crimes Bill, the lifting of anti-gay restrictions in the 1991 Immigration Act, and the significant increase in AIDS funding during the first Clinton administration all mark important gains. The continuing resistance to granting even formal protections against discrimination, and the passage of explicitly anti-gay measures, continue to position the United States Congress as more resistant to equality than most legislatures in Canada and northern Europe. AIDS appropriations pass only with amendments prohibiting the "promotion" of homosexuality. The legislative outcome of the 1993 military debacle came close to encoding the status quo ante. The 1996 passage of the Defense of Marriage Act, signed willingly by President Clinton, played to fears of the social disruptiveness of gay and lesbian rights. In the fall of 1996, the Employment Non-Discrimination Act (ENDA) failed in Congress, despite highly restrictive provisions limiting its application to workplace discrimination against individuals and exempting small businesses, the military, and religious organizations. Nevertheless, ENDA failed in the Senate by only one vote, although as recently as 1993 this measure was seen by congressional insiders as having no foreseeable chance of passage.

The Clinton presidency has provided mixed results as well. More gains than setbacks were registered, particularly in securing protections against discrimination for federal employees. In the end, Clinton did provide strong support for ENDA, though applauding the bill's restrictions—for example, praising the fact that it did not require employers to provide "special benefits."[58] The Clinton administration's determination to keep a low profile on sexual orientation issues during the 1996 Democratic convention and election campaign served as a reminder that gay issues are still not considered mainstream or safe.

Looking at political outcomes beyond Washington, we see a similarly mixed ledger. The number of states and localities that have enacted measures prohibiting discrimination on the basis of sexual orientation has increased notably.[59] By the mid-1990s, fifteen states included sexual orientation in hate crimes legislation. The same period has also witnessed some erosion in the numbers of states with sodomy laws criminalizing homosexual acts, with courts in Michigan and Kentucky, and the legislatures in Nevada and the District of Columbia effecting reform. More than a fifth of United States citizens reside in local jurisdictions with anti-discrimination measures that include sexual orientation.[60] But vast tracts of the country are without such protections, and more are regularly threatened by right-wing attempts to dismantle them. In 1984, five anti-gay measures were introduced at the state level across the country; in 1994, there were twenty-four.[61] Between 1991 and 1995, close to forty anti-gay referenda passed. By mid-1997, there were already twenty-three states with bans on same-sex marriage, with many more in prospect.

The courts, too, have provided mixed results in sexual orientation cases. Challenges to the military ban were victorious in some instances, but less so in higher courts. Court judgments at all levels indicated uncertain coverage for gays and lesbians by the constitutional provisions on equal protection. A significant victory was won in May 1996, when the Supreme Court threw out a Colorado constitutional provision forbidding laws barring discrimination on the basis of sexual orientation. In the words of Justice Anthony M. Kennedy, "A state cannot so deem a class of persons a stranger to its laws." The *Romer v. Evans* decision was an especially important win in light of the number of similar provisions being fought for by the religious right in other states. But it did not signal so wholesale a shift of judicial attitudes to prevent Justice Antonin Scalia from defending the Colorado amendment as "designed to prevent piecemeal deterioration of the sexual morality favored by a majority of Coloradans." Legal experts also did not hold out hope that this judgment implied that the Court was prepared to rule favorably in cases of relationship recognition.[62]

Through the 1990s, the number of openly gay politicians at the state and local level grew steadily, the new wave consisting largely of those who were entering their first elections as open about their sexual orientation. The degree of acceptance by voters and fellow legislators has attested to a shift in view among both. The high rate of reelection of such candidates also suggests that otherwise cynical voters take their openness about homosexuality as evidence of their honesty on other fronts. And yet the repeated suspicions that these will be one-issue politicians also reminds us how the "special interest" label is used to suggest a preoccupation with narrow group concerns.

There has been a shift in the balance of wins to losses. The anti-gay mobilizing of the religious right tipped the scale toward setback during the late 1970s and early 1980s. But then gay and lesbian wins began matching losses. By the mid-1990s, more politicians than ever had begun to realize that pro-gay positions would not automatically lose votes and that anti-gay positions would not necessarily win them. As is so often true in the complex institutional environment of United States politics, gains are more likely to be incremental than sweeping, and more common at the state and local level. Still, the gay/lesbian and mainstream press now regularly report victories in courts, executive offices, and legislatures across the country.

Such a shift is even more evident outside legislative and partisan politics. Corporations and other institutions are extending recognition to gay and lesbian community issues, and in some cases to same-sex relationships.[63] In growing numbers, companies are becoming anxious about offending sexual minorities, and some are eagerly advertising themselves as gay-friendly.[64] Cultural institutions are paying more attention to sexual orientation themes, and providing visibility for openly lesbian/gay artists. The mass media are offering more vehicles for positive portrayals of sexual minorities in both news and drama.

Public acceptance of sexual diversity has been slow to increase, but recent signs are hopeful. Moral disapproval, however, remains strong, over half of the population persisting in the belief that homosexuality is wrong. Questions tapping stereotypes about gays and lesbians preying on children also elicit unfavorable responses. But on most indicators, the period from 1988 to 1992 revealed noticeable improvements. Support for the principle that gays should have equal rights in terms of job opportunities now consistently exceeds 70 percent, and the majority favoring laws to prevent discrimination has increased. Even moral disapproval, long stuck at over 70 percent, has declined somewhat to a range of 50 to 66 percent.[65]

COMPARATIVE IMPACT. Though less rabidly than in the United States, rightist parties in Canada and Britain are still willing to play on anti-gay sentiment, but are learning to temper the *sounds* of extremism within their ranks. Their opposition is based in part on the prejudices and stereotypes of their own legislators, and in part on fear of the reactions of conservative constituents and extraparliamentary party members. In both countries, as well as the United States, parties of the left and center are much more supportive of equality for sexual minorities. But while they often have formal platform commitments opposing discrimination, their parliamentary parties are usually more equivocal when faced with the moment of legislative decision. This leads to a pattern of delay and compromise when such parties win government office.

The Canadian lesbian/gay movement has few resources committed to mainstream intervention, and little of the sort of institutionalization that is so obvious in Washington. And yet more gains have been made in Canada than in the United States, in relation to both individual rights and relationship recognition. The extension of rights has of course been eased by the Charter of Rights and Freedoms. Although politicians in all three countries have yielded to the temptation to defer to courts on sexual orientation issues, in Canada the jurisprudential record has been largely positive for both individual and relational rights. The pattern of public opinion is similar to that in the United States, but with perhaps stronger support for the principle of equal rights protections for gays and lesbians. More important is the weaker force of anti-gay campaigning that plays on uncertainty and disapproval.

In Britain, the entry into mainstream politics has led to more institutionalization of gay activism than in Canada, not least because of the concentration of political power and sexual minority visibility in London. But despite the considerable skill of activists and their success in forging links with a countrywide constituency, statutory, administrative, and judicial gains have been harder to effect until now.

That was in part a function of the relative impermeability of a highly centralized political order, and in part of the long tenure of a hostile Conservative government. In Britain, too, there may be an even stronger pattern of avoidance of sexual diversity issues within and beyond the political class.

Nonetheless, the growth of gay and lesbian visibility has had an enormous effect on British media and culture. Theater, literature, and film are replete with gay themes and characters, many of them forthrightly confronting traditional British repressiveness. The same is true of both dramatic and documentary productions aired on British television, which is especially provocative on sexual diversity themes in contrast to the still cautious style of U.S. television.

In all three countries, change has resulted from the movement as a whole, not from any one part of it. Progress has been no more the unique contribution of those who have worked the respectable channels of the political and social mainstream than it has been of those who made enemies by making an outrageous nuisance of themselves. The work in the mainstream at the national level has provided public pressure and private nudges on both the big issues and the week-to-week small issues that arise in legislative and administrative politics. In the American case particularly, institutionalization has created ongoing expertise that has allowed movement groups to intervene regularly and skillfully in the political process. National groups in all three countries, and most indispensably in the United States, have provided spokespeople for the national media.

The still slender ranks of openly gay and lesbian politicians have often found themselves in an awkward position, trying to represent both a local district and a regional or national sexual minority constituency, all the while operating in an institutional setting that demands compromise and party loyalty. But they have been the movement's eyes and ears inside government, and in some cases the source of invaluable strategic advice about operating within a complex rule-bound environment. They have sometimes stood alone in legislatures permeated by fear of speaking forthrightly in favor of gay and lesbian equality.

But the ranks of confrontational street activists are just as crucial. They are inevitably more spontaneous, more likely to make strategic mistakes, less knowledgeable about the political system, and perhaps less aware of the difficulty of achieving gains within that system. Above all, they remind sexual minorities of our anger and our impatience, and they point out the extent to which the appearance of progress exceeds the reality.

Gay and lesbian movements in all three countries illustrate how difficult it is to retain links between political insiders and the streets, between accommodation and confrontation, between the national and the local. The American and British movements in particular also illustrate the tendency of activists to aim their fire at other activists rather than at the enemy without. Urvashi Vaid speaks for many participants in the lesbian and gay social movement beyond her own country when she says: "We are a people hungry for simple answers and we often place each other in simplistic categories. Whatever ideology we espouse is what we insist others subscribe to. We say we care about political diversity, but we conduct our political fights like jihads. The slash-and-burn style of political argumentation leaves us little room for growth: one must be for direct action or against it, either a sell-out or a hold-out, either Republican or Democrat, either a conservative or a progressive.''[66] Activists are widely prone, in public as well as in private, to blame one another for their defeats, even though the reasons for defeat are rarely due to the failures of social movement groups working specifically on those measures.

Those who criticize gay and lesbian groups for failing to develop a grassroots network make a valuable point. But to claim that such a network would have made the difference in a case such as the U.S. military ban, or to argue that a grassroots base comparable to the religious right could be constructed, is unfair and misleading. Such claims reflect a strand of American social movement politics which maintains that if only one plays well enough by the rules of the game, one will win. The field of mainstream political action is still tilted against gay and lesbian activists, and if the outcome rests on counting letters and faxes to legislators, they face insurmountable odds.

Playing on such a tilted field requires insiders and outsiders, those with limited agendas and those with transformative agendas. No one is totally right; no one is totally wrong. Gays, lesbians, bisexuals, and the transgendered carry within themselves both ''the yearning for acceptance and the determination to dissent.''[67] The conflict within us is carried into the movement that we want to be representative of our aspirations. The result is a diverse movement, filled with spontaneity and outrageousness and untempered anger, impossible to coordinate and moderate. If in some short-term political struggles its messiness and lack of focus seem detrimental to its purposes, in the longer term its uncontrollable diversity will propel it forward.

NOTES

Introduction

1. For useful comparative overviews, see Dennis Altman, *Power and Community: Organizational and Cultural Responses to AIDS* (London: Taylor and Francis, 1994); and Barry D. Adam, *The Rise of a Gay and Lesbian Movement*, rev. ed. (New York: Twayne, 1995), chap. 7.
2. Margaret Cruikshank talks about the particular benchmark that 1990 itself constituted in the United States: "The year 1990 brought so many victories and signs of encouraging developments for gay liberation that it seemed to mark a turning point for the movement. Gay rights bills passed in communities where they would not have had a chance of being enacted ten years earlier, in San Diego and Pittsburgh, for example. The Hate Crimes Statistics Act included lesbians and gay men, an official recognition of their minority status. Congress revoked anti-gay immigration laws." Margaret Cruikshank, *The Gay and Lesbian Liberation Movement* (New York: Routledge, 1992), p. 192.
3. I have written on this (with Scott Bowler) in "Public Opinion and Gay Rights," *Canadian Review of Sociology and Anthropology* 25 (1988): 649–60.
4. This is commonly argued in the literature on social movements. See, for example, Hanspeter Kriesi et al., *New Social Movements in Western Europe: A Comparative Analysis* (Minneapolis: University of Minnesota Press, 1995).
5. William Gamson, "Framing Political Opportunity," paper presented at the conference on European/American Perspectives on Social Movements, Washington, D.C., 1992, p. 15.
6. This is true of some of the contributors to Russell J. Dalton and Manfred Kuechler, eds., *Challenging the Political Order: New Social and Political Movements in Western Democracies* (Cambridge: Polity Press, 1990), most notably Claus Offe.
7. See Robin Murray, "Fordism and Post-Fordism," pp. 38–53; Stuart Hall and David Held, "Citizens and Citizenship," pp. 173–88; and other contributions in *New Times: The Changing Face of Politics in the 1990s*, ed. Stuart Hall and Martin Jacques (London: Lawrence & Wishart, 1989).
8. Among the writers criticizing the concept of "new social movement" are Kay Leman Schlozman and John T. Tierney, *Organized Interests and American Democracy* (New York: Harper & Row, 1986), p. 198; Lorna Weir, "Limitations of New Social Movement Analysis," *Studies in Political Economy* 40 (Spring 1993): 73–102; and David Plotke, "What's So New about New Social Movements?" *Socialist Review* 20, no. 1 (1990): 80–102.
9. Life cycles and protest waves are discussed in Karl-Werner Brand, "Cyclical Aspects of New Social Movements: Waves of Cultural Criticism and Mobilization Cycles of New Middle-Class Radicalism," and Claus Offe, "Reflections on the Institutional Self-Transformation of Movement Politics: A Tentative Stage Model," in Dalton and Kuechler, *Challenging the Social Order*, pp. 23–42, 232–50.
10. The tendency toward institutionalization is discussed in Sidney Tarrow, *Power in Movement: Social Movements, Collective Action, and Politics* (Cambridge: Cambridge University Press

1994); and in A. Paul Pross, *Group Politics and Public Policy*, 2d ed. (Toronto: Oxford University Press, 1992), chap. 7. Cycles of protest are also discussed in Kriesi et al., *New Social Movements in Western Europe*, chap. 5.

11. This is a point made in an excellent analysis of the relationship between the women's movements and party systems in Canada and the United States by J. Lisa Young, "Can Feminists Transform Party Politics? Women's Movements and Political Parties in Canada and the United States, 1970–1993," (Ph.D. diss., University of Toronto, 1996).

12. Urvashi Vaid, *Virtual Equality: The Mainstreaming of Gay and Lesbian Liberation* (New York: Anchor Books, 1995), chap. 2.

13. Both urban concentrations and "identity" politics are more pronounced in North America than in Continental Europe but present to some degree in Britain.

14. The first two are predominantly American, although they do or did exist in parts of Canada and Europe. AIDS Action Now is a Toronto-based group, and OutRage is London-based.

15. On the tensions between those seeking to influence governments and those focused on the development of identity and community, see Altman, *Power and Community*

16. As Jack Walker points out, too, limits on available resources can shape a movement's strategic choices. See his *Mobilizing Interest Groups in America: Patrons, Professions, and Social Movements* (Ann Arbor: University of Michigan Press, 1991), chap. 1.

17. The political opportunity structure is discussed by many writers on social movements, including Tarrow, *Power in Movement*, chap. 5; and Kriesi et al., *New Social Movements in Western Europe*, esp. chap. 3.

18. Anne Costain provides an illustration of impact with few resources in 1970s United States feminist activism, in *Inviting Women's Rebellion: A Political Process Interpretation of the Women's Movement* (Baltimore: Johns Hopkins University Press, 1992). A diagnosis of failure with quite a different message about resources can be found in Jane J. Mansbridge, *Why We Lost the ERA* (Chicago: University of Chicago Press, 1986).

19. See Altman, *Power and Community*; and Adam, *The Rise of a Gay and Lesbian Movement*. British activists have begun using European Tribunals, though still with less frequency and impact than North American activists.

20. For a comparative treatment of European, Canadian, and American jurisprudence on sexual orientation, see Robert Wintemute, *Sexual Orientation and Human Rights: The United States Constitution, the European Convention, and the Canadian Charter* (Oxford: Clarendon Press, 1995).

21. For Canadian-U.S. comparisons on this point, see Seymour Martin Lipset, *Continental Divide: The Values and Institutions of the United States and Canada* (New York: Routledge, 1990), chap. 5.

22. This is an important theme in Young, "Can Feminists Transform Party Politics?"

1. Promoting Heterosexuality in the Thatcher Years

1. The final wording of Section 28 reads: "A local authority shall not: (a) intentionally promote homosexuality or publish material for the promotion of homosexuality; (b) promote the teaching in any maintained school of the acceptability of homosexuality as a pretend family relationship by the publication of such material or otherwise; (c) give financial assistance to any person for either of the purposes in paragraphs (a) or (b) above." Until the Local Government Bill was passed into law as the Local Government Act, this section was referred to as Clause 28. For the sake of simplicity, I refer to it as Section 28 throughout.

2. See Davina Cooper and Didi Herman, "Getting 'The Family Right': Legislating Heterosexuality in Britain, 1986–1991," *Canadian Journal of Family Law* 10 (1991): 51.

3. John Pratt, "The Place of Sexuality in New Right Discourse," *Canadian Criminology Forum* 3 (Spring 1981): 87.

4. David Willetts, "The Family," in *The Thatcher Effect: A Decade of Change*, ed. Dennis Kavanagh and Anthony Seldon (Oxford: Oxford University Press, 1989), p. 265. In Willetts's view, the Conservatives' family policy agenda generally avoids issues of sexuality and reproduction. This is

largely but not wholly true. There are some leading party members who are clearly interested in such issues, and willing to use the issue of homosexuality for opportunistic reasons at least.

5. See Martin Durham, *Sex and Politics: The Family and Morality in the Thatcher Years* (London: Macmillan, 1991), pp. 125–26, 155–56. Not to be outdone, the Federation of Conservative Students at about the same time was talking of "sexually insecure" men being sucked into a homosexual "vortex of criminality and vice, indisputably demonic in its destructive power" (p. 153).

6. From chap. 2 of the Wolfenden Report. See also Jeffrey Weeks, *Sexuality* (Chichester and London: Ellis Horwood and Tavistock, 1986), p. 102; Charles Berg, *Fear, Punishment, Anxiety, and the Wolfenden Report* (London: George Allen & Unwin, 1959), pp. 23, 32. The age of consent was chosen to coincide with the age of majority at the time, although the age of consent for heterosexual acts was sixteen. (Two years later, in 1969, the voting age was reduced to eighteen, though without any lowering of the age of consent for homosexual acts.)

7. At the same time, they attacked the "promiscuous, diseased, angry, flaunting, self-promoting and militant homosexual." Anna Marie Smith, *New Right Discourse on Race and Sexuality: Britain, 1968–1990* (Cambridge: Cambridge University Press, 1994), p. 18. See also Cooper and Herman, "Getting 'The Family Right.' "

8. Durham, *Sex and Politics*, pp. 78, 85.

9. Quoted in David Smith, "The Anatomy of a Campaign," in *A Simple Matter of Justice?*, ed. Angelia R. Wilson (London: Cassell, 1995), p. 11.

10. Quoted in Stuart Wavell, "How Sir Ian's Gay Crusaders Put Britain in the Pink," *Sunday Times Review*, 30 January 1994.

11. Stephen Jeffery-Poulter, *Peers, Queers, and Commons: The Struggle for Gay Law Reform from 1950 to the Present* (London: Routledge, 1991), p. 254.

12. Pratt, "The Place of Sexuality in New Right Discourse," pp. 94–95.

13. John Dearlove and Peter Saunders, *Introduction to British Politics: Analyzing a Capitalist Democracy* (Cambridge: Polity Press, 1984), p. 374.

14. Simon Watney, *Policing Desire: Pornography, AIDS, and the Media* (London: Methuen, 1987), p. 23.

15. Patricia Day and Rudolph Klein, "Interpreting the Unexpected: The Case of AIDS Policy Making in Britain," *Journal of Public Policy* 9 (July-September 1989): 346–49.

16. For example, see Jeffrey Weeks, *Against Nature: Essays on History, Sexuality, and Identity* (London: Rivers Oram Press, 1991), p. 127.

17. *New Statesmen*, 8 January 1988, p. 3.

18. Jeffery-Poulter, *Peers, Queers, and Commons*, p. 201.

19. Reported in the *Guardian*, 9 April 1986: cited ibid., p. 202.

20. *Gay Times* (October 1986): 17

21. See Smith, *New Right Discourse on Race and Sexuality*, intro.

22. I discuss this in more detail in "Homophobia, Class, and Party in England," *Canadian Journal of Political Science* 25 (March 1992): 121–49.

23. Jeffrey Weeks, *Sex, Politics and Society: The Regulation of Sexuality Since 1800* (London: Longman, 1981), p. 109.

24. See Jeffrey Weeks, *Coming Out: Homosexual Politics in Britain, from the Nineteenth Century to the Present* (London: Quartet, 1977), pp. 158–60.

25. Durham, *Sex and Politics*, p. 6.

26. Interview, 18 June 1992.

27. See Eric Hobsbawm, *Workers: Worlds of Labour* (New York: Pantheon, 1984), chap. 10; and E. P. Thompson, *The Making of the English Working Class* (Harmondsworth: Penguin, 1968), chap. 12, although they differ with each other in dating the foundations of working-class culture.

28. Louis Crompton, *Byron and Greek Love: Homophobia in Nineteenth-Century England* (Berkeley: University of California Press, 1985), p. 307.

29. Allan Horsfall, "Battling for Wolfenden," in *Radical Records: Thirty Years of Lesbian and Gay History, 1957–1987*, ed. Bob Cant and Susan Hemmings (London: Routledge, 1988), p. 21. Peter Wildeblood recognized the power of the stereotype of homosexuality as "a kind of fashionable vice restricted to decadent intellectuals and degenerate clergymen," in *Against the Law* (Harmondsworth: Penguin, 1955): p. 29.

30. Ann Tobin, "Somewhere Over the Rainbow," in Cant and Hemmings, *Radical Records*, pp. 255–56.
31. Anna Coote and Polly Pattullo, *Power and Prejudice: Women and Politics* (London: Weidenfeld & Nicholson, 1990), p. 184.
32. This defection was symbolized by a policy commitment on the age of consent. Rather than calling for complete equality, the 1982 Labour program called for an age of consent for homosexuals of eighteen. Jeffery-Poulter, *Peers, Queers, and Commons*, pp. 165–66.
33. Interview, 25 June 1992.
34. See Peter Tatchell, *The Battle for Bermondsey* (London: Heretic Books, 1983).
35. Jamie Gough and Mike Macnair, *Gay Liberation in the Eighties* (London: Pluto, 1985), p. 120.
36. Interview, 10 May 1995.
37. Interview, 25 June 1992.
38. The party hierarchy tried unsuccessfully to have the issue referred back to the National Executive Committee. Jeffery-Poulter, *Peers, Queers, and Commons*, p. 204.
39. On Labour reticence on the issue, see Sarah Roelofs, "Labour and the Natural Order," in *High Risk Lives: Lesbian and Gay Politics after the Clause*, ed. Hara Kaufman and Paul Lincoln (Bridport: Prism Press, 1991), p. 180.
40. Interview with Labour MP, 25 June 1992.
41. This is the assessment of Coote and Pattullo, *Power and Prejudice*, p. 186.
42. Policy Directorate, Home Policy Committee, "Lesbian and Gay Rights: A Procedural Note" (September 1987).
43. Coote and Pattullo, *Power and Prejudice*, pp. 174–75.
44. See Lynne Segal, "Lynne Segal Interviews Diane Abbot," *Feminist Review* 27 (1987); quoted in Joni Lovenduski and Vicky Randall, *Contemporary Feminist Politics: Women and Power in Britain* (Oxford: Oxford University Press, 1993), p. 145.
45. Roelofs, "Labour and the Natural Order," p. 181.
46. Ibid., p. 182.
47. Interview, 25 June 1992.
48. "Speech by the Rt. Hon. Neil Kinnock MP, Leader of the Labour Party, at the Opening Session of the Labour Local Government Conference, 29th January 1988, Edinburgh" (London: Labour Party, 1988).
49. Quoted in Jeffery-Poulter, *Peers, Queers, and Commons*, p. 244.
50. Ibid., pp. 252–53.
51. Interview, 22 June 1992.
52. Survey reported in the *Guardian*, 6 March 1990.
53. Jeffery-Poulter, *Peers, Queers, and Commons*, p 254. Some 82 percent favored legislation outlawing discrimination in employment; 75 percent favored repeal of Section 28.
54. Interview with Liberal activist, 28 March 1992. Jeremy Thorpe was likely the proposer of that motion.
55. Interview with Liberal activist, 26 March 1992.
56. See Simon Edge, "Out on the Doorstep," *Gay Times* (March 1997): 32.
57. According to a Liberal account of the period: "Out of the undemocratic and squalid horse-trading that produced the Alliance Manifesto came a ruthless purging of gay rights from every public policy document and statement in that election." Bruce Galloway and Bernard Greaves, "Out from the Closet: A Liberal Focus on Gay Rights," Association of Liberal Councillors, Grass Roots Series, no. 2 (1983): 18.
58. The party's founding convention had deleted sexual orientation from its human rights commitment, helping to earn its media characterization as "the heterosexual wing of the Liberal Party."
59. Jeffery-Poulter, *Peers, Queers, and Commons*, pp. 211–12.
60. Maggie Clay, "Negotiating in the Alliance," *What Next? A Radical Quarterly Pamphlet* (1987): 10.
61. Interview, 22 June 1992.
62. Interview, 18 June 1992.
63. Richard Davenport-Hines, *Sex, Death and Punishment: Attitudes to Sex and Sexuality in Britain since the Renaissance* (London: Collins, 1990), p. 145.

64. Paul Crane, *Gays and the Law* (London: Pluto, 1983).
65. Gough and Macnair, *Gay Liberation in the Eighties*, p. 11. On earlier judicial treatment, see H. Montgomery Hyde, *The Other Love: An Historical and Contemporary Survey of Homosexuality in Britain* (London: Heinemann, 1970), chap. 5.
66. Jeffrey-Poulter, *Peers, Queers, and Commons*, p. 260. See also Simon Watney, *Policing Desire: Pornography, AIDS, & the Media*, 2d ed. (Minneapolis: University of Minnesota Press, 1989).
67. Tatchell, *The Battle for Bermondsey*, pp. 102–4.
68. *Sun*, 16 May 1990.
69. *Sun*, 4 November 1988.
70. Wildeblood, *Against the Law*, pp. 36–37.
71. Horsfall, "Battling for Wolfenden," p. 26.
72. The *Independent*, 2 February 1988. At the time the paper leaned toward a centrist Social Democratic Party position. Since then it has become much more pro-gay.
73. See Weeks, *Against Nature*, p. 139; and David Rayside and Scott Bowler, "Public Opinion and Gay Rights," *Canadian Review of Sociology and Anthropology* 25 (November 1988): 649–60.
74. Crompton, *Byron and Greek Love*, p. 245.
75. Hyde, *The Other Love*, p. 151.
76. See John Lauritsen and David Thorstad, *The Early Homosexual Rights Movement (1864–1935)* (New York: Times Change Press, 1974).
77. This included early 1890s amendments modeled after the 1885 Labouchere amendment in England. On this and related questions, see Gary Kinsman, *The Regulation of Desire: Homo and Hetero Sexualities,* 2d ed. (Montreal: Black Rose, 1996), chaps. 5–6.
78. See, for example, Sylvia Bashevkin, "Tough Times in Review: The British Women's Movement during the Thatcher Years," *Comparative Political Studies* 28 (January 1996): 525–52.
79. John D'Emilio and Estelle B. Freedman, *Intimate Matters: A History of Sexuality in America* (New York: Harper and Row, 1988), pp. 40, 123. D'Emilio and Freedman are inclined to emphasize the similarity between England and the United States; I am claiming here that there were differences in degree. The Progressive era, late in the century, was witness to a certain amount of vice crusading, but it never had the focus on homosexuality that some of the English moral panics had. Crompton agrees that during Byron's time, English homophobia was more virulent than American (*Byron and Greek Love*, p. 253).
80. D'Emilio and Freedman, *Intimate Matters*, p. 234.
81. John Costello, *Love, Sex, and War: Changing Values, 1939–45* (London: Collins, 1985), p. 357.

2. Activist Openings on the Age of Consent

1. These included Lisa Power, Jenny Wilson, and Peter Ashman. See John Marshall, "Sticks and Stones," *Gay Times* (December 1989): 13.
2. The group was described in one account as having its genesis in a meeting of three journalist-activists—Chris Woods, Keith Alcorn, and Simon Watney—resulting in a draft call to other activists and a meeting held at the London Lesbian and Gay Centre which thirty-five people attended. Simon Garfield, "The Age of Consent," *Independent on Sunday*, 10 November 1991, p. 4.
3. Stephen Jeffery-Poulter, *Peers, Queers, and Commons: The Struggle for Gay Law Reform from 1950 to the Present* (London: Routledge, 1991), p. 254.
4. John Marshall and Colin Richardson, "PM Meets Ian McKellen at Downing Street," *Gay Times* (October 1991): 5.
5. This according to Conservative columnist Matthew Parris, "The Red, the Blue, and the Pink," The *Times*, 26 March 1992.
6. Smith, for example, was not pro-choice, though Kinnock was liberal on reproductive rights as well as on a number of other feminist issues (perhaps in part a reflection of the influence of his wife).
7. *Capital Gay*, 23 July 1993.

8. Early in the new year, Major himself tried to argue that his campaign was not about personal morality. But that jarred with statements about the campaign by some of his senior ministers, and his own talk of the campaign seeking "no-nonsense distinctions between right and wrong" seemed to confirm MPs' readings. Patricia Wynn Davies and Steve Boggan, "Major Says Basics Not a Moral Crusade," The *Independent*, 7 January 1994; "Stick to Basics," *Daily Telegraph*, 7 January 1994; and "Tory Values Right Hollow," *Daily Mirror*, 3 January 1994. On Major's pandering to the moralistic right, see also Andrew Marr, "Thunder That Drowned the Liberal Voice," *Independent*, 25 February 1994; and Hugo Young, "When a Love Child Makes a Black Sheep," *Guardian*, 4 January 1994.

9. There had been talk in some quarters of extending beyond the age of consent to take in other discriminatory features of the 1967 Homosexual Offenses Act, but a decision was made to put those other issues off as unlikely to be acceptable to the government. Donald Macintyre, "Gay Groups Consider Extra Changes to Law," *Independent*, 19 January 1994. The other issues included offenses of "gross indecency" and "buggery," as well as the restrictive conceptions of privacy imposed on gay men and the continuing criminalization of homosexual acts in the armed forces and merchant navy. Northern Ireland was also excluded from the amendment, to the annoyance of gay rights activists in Ulster, not least because its heterosexual age of consent was seventeen. Louise Jury, "Gay Age Change Omits Ulster," *Guardian*, 7 February 1994.

10. The news of the bill's impending appearance was reported in a *Sunday Times* article on December 22 (Philip Webster and Edward Gorman, "MPs to Vote on Allowing Gay Sex at 18"). There were other Conservative MPs who might have been called on to lead the charge, but a few of the most prominent among them were promoted to the front benches after the 1992 election and were thereby ineligible to sponsor a cross-party amendment.

11. Stonewall's estimates come from a letter from Angela Mason to *Times*, 31 December 1993. Those estimates were still in use as the vote approached in late January, broken down as 200 Labour, 20 Liberal Democrat, and 30 Conservative. "Thousands Descend on Parliament," *The Pink Paper*, 21 January 1994. The Labour poll result was revealed in a letter to *Guardian*, 13 January 1994. See also "Consent to Gay Sex at 16 'To be Rejected,' " *Independent*, 23 December 1993.

12. One conservative commentator suggested that the prime minister had the whips spread the word about his favoring eighteen in January, and solicited backbench volunteers to put a motion to that effect. Paul Johnson, "From Children to Rent Boys in One Parliamentary Vote," *Spectator*, 12 February 1994, p. 12.

13. Interview, 11 May 1995. One Conservative MP reportedly told lobbyists, "There's just no way at the moment, with what's going on with my constituents, that I can vote for sixteen—no way."

14. Donald Macintyre, "Survey Says That MPs Will Vote for Change," *Independent*, 24 January 1994. A week later 270 MPs were reported by Stonewall to favor sixteen, including about 30 Conservatives but not including 35 Labourites opposed. Patricia Wynn Davies, "European Court's Gay Sex Ruling Could Embarrass Tories," *Independent*, 3 February 1994. Even polling in mid-February, just a week before the vote, confirmed only about 210 votes for sixteen among Labour's 267 MPs. "Hopes High for Equality at 16," *The Pink Paper*, 18 February 1994.

15. Interview with Conservative, 9 May 1995.

16. There was a 90 percent turnout, in contrast with the usual low turnout for free votes. Philip Norton, "Analysis of a Free Vote," revised text of an article published in *Parliamentary Brief* 2 (April–May 1994): 88–89.

17. House of Commons, *Hansard*, 21 February 1994, p. 75.

18. Ibid., p. 100.

19. Ibid., p. 112. He also pointed out, quite reasonably, that the amendment for sixteen was based on consent.

20. Interview, 23 June 1995.

21. Seven Labour MPs, one Liberal Democrat, and one Conservative who had supported sixteen refused to vote for the compromise. The division lists showed that 425 voted yes on sixteen, even though the voting figure was announced as 427. Norton, "Analysis of a Free Vote," p. 5.

22. The opposition of Ann Taylor, the shadow education secretary, was a surprise to many. Anya Palmer, "Lesbian and Gay Rights Campaigning: A Report from the Coalface," in *A Simple*

Matter of Justice? ed. Angelia R. Wilson (London: Cassell, 1995), p. 39. David Blunkett (shadow health minister) was less of a surprise, despite his priding himself as being on the left of the party. A number of activists called for the resignation of Taylor and Blunkett. Patricia Wynn Davies and Colin Brown, "Vote to Lower Age of Consent Met with Fury," *Independent*, 22 February 1994; Philip Webster et al., "Police to Enforce New Law on Gay Age of Consent," *Times*, 23 February 1994.

23. Keith Alcorn, "An Insult to Us All," *Capital Gay*, 25 February 1994.
24. "Inequality at 18 Is No Answer," *Independent*, 23 February 1994.
25. Jeffrey Weeks, *Against Nature: Essays on History, Sexuality, and Identity* (London: Rivers Oram, 1991), p. 137.
26. Palmer, "Lesbian and Gay Rights Campaigning," p. 35.
27. Lisa Power and Tim Barnett, "Gathering Strength and Gaining Power: How Lesbians and Gay Men Began to Change Their Fortunes in Britain in the Nineties," in *The Third Pink Book: A Global View of Lesbian and Gay Liberation and Oppression*, ed. Aart Hendriks et al. (Buffalo, N.Y.: Prometheus Books, 1993), pp. 173–74.
28. The Labour Campaign had launched preparations by drafting a bill for lesbian and gay rights in 1986 and calling for such a conference. See "Legislation for Lesbian and Gay Rights: A Manifesto," Labour Campaign for Lesbian and Gay Rights, August 1986.
29. Quoted in David Smith, "The Betrayal of the Gay Community," *Gay Times* (June 1987), p. 11. The "pig's ear" comment is from an interview, 23 June 1992.
30. Interview, 23 June 1992. This view is reflected in the group's own description of itself (Stonewall General Information Note," 1992, p. 1) as an organization concerned "solely with issues of direct relevance to lesbians and gay men on the basis of their sexuality"; working with supporters of every political background and creed; and operating in the sort of "professional and authoritative" manner designed to appeal to "people and organisations in positions of influence and power."
31. Interview, 26 March 1992.
32. Interview, 28 March 1992. Keith Alcorn, Chris Woods, and Simon Watney are credited with having formed the group originally; Peter Tatchell joined it soon afterwards.
33. Interviews, 28 March 1992, 18 June 1992.
34. Power and Barnett, "Gathering Strength and Gaining Power" (discussing the campaign to amend or remove a discriminatory clause of the 1991 Criminal Justice Bill).
35. Interview, 25 June 1992.
36. Interview, 27 March 1992.
37. "The Age of Consent," *Gay Times* (February 1994): p. 18.
38. Interview with OutRage activist, 10 May 1996. On sixteen as the age of consent, see Peter Tatchell, "Equality Is Not Enough," *Capital Gay*, 14 October 1994.
39. "Consent to Gay Sex at 16 'To Be Rejected,' " *Independent*, 23 December 1993.
40. Useful coverage of the mobilizing campaigns can be found in David Smith, "The Anatomy of a Campaign," and Palmer, "Lesbian and Gay Rights Campaigning" pp. 10–31 and 32–50 in Wilson, *A Simple Matter of Justice?*; and Richard Dunphy, "The Effect of Parliamentary Lobbying on Scottish MPs in the Age of Consent Debate," (Department of Political Science and Social Policy, University of Dundee, n.d.).
41. OutRage, "Research Reveals Anti-Gay Bias," press releases, n.d.; and David Smith, "Waiting in the Rain," *Gay Times* (November 1991): 24.
42. Chris Smith, "A Consent Sadly Withheld," *Guardian Weekend*, 26 February 1994.
43. Interview, 11 May 1995.
44. Interview with gay journalist, 9 May 1995.
45. Palmer, "Lesbian and Gay Rights Campaigning," p. 38.
46. Interview, 9 May 1995.
47. At least a couple of unions contacted their MPs in the Labour Party. See Celia Hall, "Doctors Defend Homosexual Boys," *Independent*, 14 January 1994; "Thousands Descend on Parliament," *The Pink Paper*, 21 January 1994.
48. Before lunch on January 11, Proops had favored an age of eighteen; after lunch with Sir Ian McKellen, she immediately printed a column favoring sixteen, headlined "How Sir Ian Won My

Vote on Gay Sex at 16.'' David Smith, ''Anatomy of a Campaign,'' *Gay Times* (February 1994): 11).

49. Interview, 10 May 1995.
50. In 1990 the Press Council ruled against the notorious *Sun*'s use of offensive terms for gays such as ''poof.'' Jeffery-Poulter, *Peers, Queers, and Commons*, pp. 261–62.
51. The view of a new temperateness in the tabloids is shared by Simon Fanshawe, ''Gay Old Times in Fleet Street,'' *Evening Standard*, 26 January 1994. The references to *Sun* writer Richard Littlejohn are from the same article, and from ''Terry's Sanderson's Media Watch,'' *Gay Times* (February 1994): 15.
52. Quoted in ''Terry Sanderson's Media Watch,'' *Gay Times* (March 1994): 22.
53. Interview, 10 May 1995.
54. Interview with Conservative activist, 25 June 1992.
55. Interview with Conservative MP, 9 May 1995.
56. Interview with Conservative MP, 9 May 1995.
57. Interview, 28 March 1992.
58. Interview, 18 June 1992. This Conservative also pointed out the disarray into which Major's own marriage had fallen, which but for his elevation would almost certainly have led to separation. His apparent openness on such issues may have been in part a product of his representing an area of South London with a substantial gay/lesbian presence. Later events were to indicate that Major's belief in equality was highly compromised.
59. Simon Garfield, ''The Age of Consent,'' *Independent on Sunday*, 10 November 1991. See also Marshall and Richardson, ''PM Meets Ian McKellen at Downing Street,'' pp. 5–8.
60. Quoted in Vicky Powell, ''Publicity Session,'' *Gay Times* (May 1996): 54. See also Edwina Currie et al., *What Women Want* (London: Sidgwick & Jackson, 1990).
61. See, for example, the *Times* editorial of 6 January 1994.
62. Chris Blackhurst, ''Suspected Gay MPs Face Pressure to Marry,'' *Independent*, 15 February 1994. The whips reportedly told at least a few MPs that ''if you are found out the week after and you voted for twenty-one, we can't save you; if you are found out the week after and you voted for sixteen, you are in a much stronger position.'' Interview, 9 May 1995. The urgings do not appear to have been altogether effective; according to Peter Tatchell, a dozen MPs ''known for [their] covert gay lives'' voted against equality. Lesley White, ''Indecent Exposure,'' *Sunday Times Magazine*, 25 April 1995, p. 23.
63. Dr. Adrian Rogers, quoted in *Sunday Telegraph*, 1 September 1991; cited in Simon Watney, ''Rights and Responsibilities,'' *Gay Times* (October 1991): 12.
64. Letter from Stephen Green, dated 5 January 1994. This kind of language, along with pronouncements such as ''Allowing homosexual men to bugger teenagers [is] not consistent with 'core Conservatism' '' contributed to the defection of at least five MPs previously supportive of the group, one of whom described the whole CFC as ''cracked.'' Jerry Hayes, quoted in ''Put Family First,'' *Times*, 16 February 1994. See also Stuart Wavell, ''How Sir Ian's Gay Crusaders Put Britain in the Pink,'' *Sunday Times Review*, 30 January 1994.
65. Matthew Parris, quoted in Maggie Scammell, ''Gay Tories Claim New Party Mood,'' *Capital Gay*, 18 October 1991.
66. As late as February 1991, CGHE print material suggested considerable membership reluctance to embrace the principle of domestic partnership and a strong minority preference for eighteen as the age of consent. Peter Campbell, ''Homosexual Equality Bill,'' CGHE, 17 February 1994.
67. Interview, 24 June 1992.
68. Interview, 11 May 1995.
69. In his early years as leader, Kinnock had more than once betrayed his ''Welsh rugby-playing type of background, where real men are real men'' in remarks about homosexuality (quoted from interview with a journalist, 24 June 1992). His slow shift from that stance seems to have accelerated during the debate over Section 28. He had come around to agreeing to sixteen as the age of consent by 1994, though his House of Commons speech on the subject was still qualified by a traditional framework: ''Let us tell young people that a heterosexual life, in the sense that it is what most of us live and want to live, is the norm: that it is and will remain the basic human relationship upon which the family is founded. But let us also tell young homosexuals that we

still have regard for them and want them to live in a society that accepts their nature and will give them the same chance as others for personal happiness." House of Commons, *Hansard*, 21 February 1994, pp. 82–86.

70. David Smith, "Kinnock Approves Commitment to Reform of Sex Offenses Law," *Gay Times* (October 1991): 8

71. Labour Party Policy Directorate, *Policy Briefing Handbook*, §§ 39.1 and 39.3 outline Labour policies; §39.4 criticizes the Conservative record; and §39.2 provides sample questions and answers.

72. Interviews, 28 March 1992 and 25 June 1992.

73. Mark Lawson, "Left Behind?" *Independent Magazine*, 13 June 1992, p. 28.

74. Interview with activist, 11 May 1995.

75. This was evident to some extent in his speech at a lesbian/gay fringe meeting at the 1993 Labour Party conference. See "Modernising Our Culture," *Gay Times* (November 1993): 13; "Shadow Home Secretary to Address Fringe Meetings," *Capital Gay*, 24 September 1993; and Andrew Saxton, "Labour's Tony Blair Backs 16," *The Pink Paper*, 1 October 1993.

76. Interview with Labour activist, 11 May 1995.

77. Interview with Liberal Democratic activist, 26 March 1992.

78. *The Pink Paper*, quoted in DELGA, "Councillor Information Pack, Issue 1," n.d., p. 14.

79. Ibid., p. 14. It also pledged to repeal Section 28, and to challenge police entrapment in securing arrests.

80. Paraphrased by a BBC journalist, interview, 24 June 1992.

81. Quoted in Andrew Brown, "Hume Advises against Strict Moral Line," *Independent*, 3 February 1994.

82. Gerry Berminham, MP for St. Helens South, quoted in "Committee to Decide on Consent Debate," *Capital Gay*, 30 April 1993.

83. Interview, 11 May 1995.

84. A 1984 report recommending a variety of rights measures, including specific mention of the age of consent, was accepted by the European Parliament, though without follow-up by the more powerful bodies of the European Community. In 1989 a British Labour MP successfully added an equality rights provision including sexual orientation to Parliament's version of the European Community Social Charter.

85. In 1981 the European Court delivered its first pro-gay judgment in a case brought to force the British government to extend the 1967 Wolfenden reforms to Northern Ireland. In 1988 the court ruled against Ireland in a case challenging that country's criminalization of all homosexual activity. The Isle of Man, Jersey and Guernsey, and Gibraltar were dependencies that still criminalized homosexual activity. Smith, "The Anatomy of a Campaign," in *A Simple Matter of Justice*, p. 13. A useful review of European developments can be found in Jeffery-Poulter, *Peers, Queers, and Commons*, chap. 12; Kees Waaldijk and Andrew Clapham, eds., *Homosexuality: A European Community Issue: Essays on Lesbian and Gay Rights in European Law and Policy* (Dordrecht: Martinus Nijhoff, 1993); and Peter Tatchell, *Europe in the Pink: Lesbian and Gay Equality in the New Europe* (London: GMP, 1992).

86. See, for example, an article calling for volunteers, "Young Man Wanted for Court Battle," *Capital Gay*, 16 October 1992.

87. Interview with activist, 10 May 1995.

88. Interview, 18 June 1992.

89. Interview, 27 March 1992.

90. Interview, 10 May 1995. Yet, the same MP acknowledged that in the aftermath of the vote, supporters of sixteen had managed to sway a few more of their colleagues to their side by doing precisely the sort of persuading that was thought to have been unnecessary beforehand.

91. The first statement is from Chris Smith, "The Age of Consent," *Gay Times* (September 1993): 9. (The actual Labour vote for sixteen was closer to 80 percent, with over three quarters of opponents casting their votes rather than staying away.) The second is from an interview, 25 June 1995.

92. Of respondents to a 1992 Harris Poll commissioned by Stonewall and TORCHE, 74 percent favored an equal age of consent (Stonewall, "The Case for Change," 1993). But a 1991 Harris

Poll that asked about specific ages arrived at significantly different results, with only 15 percent favoring sixteen, and a full 53 percent favoring twenty-one. These details are taken from reports by Harris to Stonewall, July 1991 and February 1992. One National Opinion Polls survey commissioned in February 1994 by the *Sunday Times* on lowering the age of consent for homosexual acts alone found that 48 percent favored lowering the age and 44 percent opposed it. Of that 48 percent, 35 percent favored eighteen, and only 13 percent sixteen, with 42 percent of the total favoring a rise in the heterosexual age of consent. See Peter Kellner and Tim Rayment, "Majority Oppose Cut in Homosexual Age of Consent to 16," the *Sunday Times*, 20 February 1994. See also Norton, "Analysis of a Free Vote," p. 8.

93. *Times*, editorial, 21 February 1994.

94. "Danger of Consenting to Predator's Charter for Gays," *Daily Express*, 3 June 1992; *News of the World*, 16 January 1992, quoted in "Terry Sanderson's Media Watch," *Gay Times* (February 1994): 15.

95. Alcorn, "An Insult to Us All."

96. Stonewall's Michael Cashman was once quoted as describing OutRage as "a metropolitan phenomenon of media queens." Melanie Phillips, "Politics of the New Queer," *Guardian*, 23 June 1992.

97. Ibid. Phillips quotes gay journalist Neil McKenna describing Stonewall as "a self-perpetuating oligarchy," and filmmaker Derek Jarman saying, "Stonewall have set themselves up as the voice of the gay community yet they are in no way representative or democratic." See also Chris Woods, *State of the Queer Nation: A Critique of Gay and Lesbian Politics in 1990s Britain* (London: Cassell, 1995).

98. Interview, 30 March 1992.

99. "Divisions Grow over Way Forward for Campaign," *Capital Gay*, 25 February 1994. Relations between the various groups involved in the campaign were not eased by what some saw as a Stonewall snub after the Commons vote: a meeting rescheduled unilaterally by Stonewall and then not attended by some of its key leaders. Interviews with activists in OutRage and DELGA, 10 May 1995.

100. Tatchell raised the age issue in an article more broadly critical of Stonewall strategy, "Up Against the Stonewall," *Gay Times* (October 1994): 34, and discussed it more fully in "Sweet Fourteen," *New Statesman & Society*, 23 June 1995, p. 25.

101. See, for example, Trish Leslie, "Dry, Wet, and Blue," *The Pink Paper*, 13 May 1994.

102. Simon Edge, "Out on the Doorstep," *Gay Times* (March 1997): 32.

103. Interview with Conservative activist, 11 May 1995.

104. Quoted in Stonewall, "Vote for Equality! A Gay Guide to the General Election" September 1996.

105. See David Smith et al., "The Cold Light of Labour's New Dawn," *Gay Times* (June 1997): 44–45; and David Smith and Vicky Powell, "A Vision of a New Society," *Gay Times* (July 1997): 8.

106. *Washington Blade*, 14 June 1996.

107. Simon Edge, "Proudly, Openly, Equally Gay," *New Statesman* (18 July 1997): 23.

3. The Parliamentary Ascent of Chris Smith

1. Chris Smith, "A Consent Sadly Withheld," *Guardian Weekend*, 26 February 1994, p. 15.

2. In an article appearing in the 12 November 1993 issue of *New Statesman and Society*, Smith named Tawney, Keynes, Orwell, Dickens, Yeats, Wordsworth, and Keats among the authors most influential on him.

3. Kris Kirk, "The Politics of Obscenity," *Gay Times* (June 1986): 29; and "My Name's Chris Smith, I'm the Labour MP for Islington South and Finsbury and I'm Gay," *New Socialist* (January 1985): 31.

4. Interview, 24 June 1992.

5. According to one detailed calculation, the vote for Cunningham was almost 16 percent higher than what would have been expected for such a riding. Interview, 26 March 1992.

6. See Bruce Cain, et al., *The Personal Vote: Constituency Service and Electoral Independence* (Cambridge.: Harvard University Press, 1987).

7. Interview, 24 June 1992.

8. This was in part a reference to Smith's claim that England had already had at least one gay monarch, and would no doubt have more. *London Standard*, 29 November 1985: 14.

9. Quoted in John Marshall, "MP's Fury after Gutter Press Report," *Gay Times* (July 1986): 12.

10. *Sun*, 24 November 1987.

11. Andrew Lumsden, "Breaking the Silence," *Gay Times* (January 1985): 6.

12. Chris Smith, "The Politics of Pride," *The Pink Paper*, 24 June 1994, p. 17.

13. *Islington Gazette*, 23 November 1984, p. 1.

14. Kirk, "The Politics of Obscenity," p. 31. See also "My Name's Chris Smith," p. 31.

15. "A Courageous Man," *New Society*, 5 June 1987, p. 10.

16. Ibid.

17. Stephen Jeffery-Poulter, *Peers, Queers, and Commons: The Struggle for Gay Law Reform from 1950 to the Present* (London: Routledge, 1991), pp. 206–8.

18. "Chris Smith Predicts 'Grim Future' Under Tories," *Gay Times* (July 1987): 7, and interview, 24 June 1992.

19. Interviews with gay politicians, June 1992.

20. Interview with Labour campaigner, 25 June 1992.

21. Interview, 24 June 1992.

22. Jeffery-Poulter, *Peers, Queers, and Commons*, p. 220.

23. House of Commons, *Debates*, 9 March 1988; quoted ibid., p. 218.

24. Interview, 25 March 1992.

25. Comments from two activists, 25 March 1992 and 23 June 1992.

26. Interview, 23 June 1992.

27. "My Name's Chris Smith," p. 30.

28. Interview with local Labour activist, 25 June 1992.

29. Simon Edge, "Out on the Doorstep," *Gay Times* (March 1997): 30–32.

30. Ivor Crewe, quoted in A. Adonis, *Parliament Today*, 2d ed. (Manchester: Manchester University Press, 1993), p. 72.

31. Edmund Burke, quoted ibid., p. 58.

32. Interview, 24 June 1992.

33. Interview, 18 June 1992.

34. Interview, 24 June 1992.

35. See Heather Mills and Lucy Johnston, "Sisterhood Signals End to Macho Politics," *Observer*, 4 May 1997; and Mark Henderson, "Minorities Join Record Number of Women MPs," *Times*, 3 May 1997.

36. Interview, 10 May 1995.

37. Interview, 25 June 1992.

38. One observer of parliamentary politics counted four MPs who had been arrested on homosexual offenses in the decade prior to 1992. Interview, 26 March 1992.

39. See Simon Edge, "Stoned Love," *Gay Times* (March 1997): 20.

40. See Edge, "Out on the Doorstep," p. 32.

41. James Hopegood, "Party Animal," *Money Marketing*, 17 October 1991, p. 29.

42. Interview, 24 June 1992.

43. "My Name's Chris Smith," p. 30.

44. Interview, 18 June 1992.

45. Interview, 11 May 1995.

46. Interviews, 9 May 1995, and 18 June 1992.

47. Interview, 10 May 1995.

48. In 1992 Smith recieved 135 votes from fellow MPs (four others received more votes); in 1993, 124 votes, placing ninth of eighteen; in 1994, 125 votes, placing ninth; in 1995–96, 148 votes, placing seventh; and in 1996–97, 188 votes, placing fifteenth.

49. David Hencke and Michael White, "Rebels Eye Shadow Cabinet," *Guardian*, 20 July 1996.

50. Steve Richards and Kirsty Milne, "Interview: Chris Smith," *New Statesman*, 14 February 1997, p. 26.
51. Colin Richardson, "Smith May Lose Health Job after Election," *Gay Times* (April 1997): 43.
52. Quoted in David Smith et al., "The Cold Light of Labour's New Dawn," *Gay Times* (June 1997): 45.
53. Interview, 11 May 1995.
54. Interview, 10 May 1995.
55. Interview, 24 June 1992.
56. Interview, 23 June 1995. On Blair's speech to the party conference, see David Smith, "Labour Leader Voices Support for Lesbian and Gay Equality," *Gay Times* (November 1994): 31.
57. Colin Richardson, "Blair at Heart," *Gay Times* (March 1997): 24.
58. Quoted in Simon Edge, "Proudly, Openly, Equally Gay," *New Statesman*, 18 July 1997, p. 22.
59. Ibid.
60. Interview, 23 June 1995. The question posed was, "Do you think he is equally comfortable with issues like relationship recognition and same-sex parental adoption?" to which the response was: "I have no idea—I have never talked to him about this."
61. Interview, 23 June 1995.
62. "What a Shower," *Gay Times* (May 1996): 9.
63. Quoted in Simon Edge, "Can New Labour Come Out?" *New Statesman*, 21 June 1996, p. 20.
64. See "Armed Forces Ban: Prejudice Prevails," *Stonewall Newsletter* (June 1996): 5. See also "Blair to Consult Generals over Ban," and David Smith et al., "A House Divided—MPs Vote to Maintain Forces Ban," *Gay Times* (June 1996): 43, 49.
65. Edge, "Can New Labour Come Out?" p. 20. Even Angela Mason, executive director of the Stonewall Group, admitted with apparent resignation, "But we all appreciate that some of the normal rules no longer apply in the period up to the election." (ibid.).
66. Only John Prescott failed "to exude gay-friendliness" among the most influential Labour front benchers. Ibid., p. 20.
67. Interview, 10 May 1995.
68. Interview, 27 March 1992.
69. Smith et al., "The Cold Light of Labour's New Dawn," p. 44.
70. Interview, 24 June 1992.
71. "Chris Smith Banned from Labour Fringe Meeting," *Gay Times* (November 1987): 7. See also letter to editor, *Gay Times* (December 1987): 23.
72. Interview, 24 June 1992.
73. Interview, 9 May 1995.
74. Interview, 28 March 1992.
75. Quoted in Smith at al., "The Cold Light of Labour's New Dawn," p. 45.

4. The Canadian Human Rights Act and Liberal Party Pragmatism

1. Provincial government expenditures began exceeding federal spending in the early 1990s. The fact that the federal government has traditionally had greater tax-raising leeway has given it some leverage over the provinces even when they had formal jurisdictional control, but that leverage too is declining.
2. Joseph Wearing points out that dissent occurs on about 30 percent of recorded votes, a higher figure than is generally believed, yet it is usually confined to a single MP or a small handful, most often on votes of modest significance. Personal correspondence, August 1996.
3. Peter Aucoin, "Prime Ministerial Leadership," in *Leaders and Leadership in Canada*, ed. Maureen Mancuso, Richard G. Price, and Ronald Wagenberg (Toronto: Oxford University Press, 1994), p. 115.
4. Ian Stewart, "Scaling the Matterhorn: Parliamentary Leadership in Canada," in Mancuso, Price, and Wagenberg, *Leaders and Leadership in Canada*, pp. 156–57. Well into the 1980s, the local

candidate's influence on the vote was modest. See Lawrence LeDuc, "Leaders and Voters: The Public Images of Canadian Political Leaders" ibid., p. 56.

5. The British law reform of 1967 seems to have provided the model, decriminalizing homosexual activity in private between consenting adults (twenty-one years of age). For a historical and theoretically critical treatment of sexual regulation in Canada, see Gary Kinsman, *The Regulation of Desire: Homo and Hetero Sexualities*, 2d ed. (Montreal: Black Rose Books, 1996).

6. Chrétien did so partly on the grounds that it was socially "a very difficult area," and partly because of what he claimed were definitional problems. See Special Joint Committee of the Senate and House of Commons on the Constitution of Canada, 29 January 1981, 48:31. A portion of this testimony was quoted by Reform MPs in the House during the debate over the Human Rights Act amendment. In 1978 a Liberal Party national convention approved a resolution urging that anticipated revisions to the Canadian Constitution should prohibit discrimination on the grounds of, among other things, sexual orientation.

7. An important qualification was introduced as Section 1: "The Canadian Charter of Rights and Freedoms guarantees the rights and freedoms set out in it subject only to such reasonable limits prescribed by law as can be demonstrably justified in a free and democratic society."

8. See Janet Hiebert, "Debating Policy: The Effects of Rights Talk," in *Equity and Community: The Charter, Interest Advocacy, and Representation*, ed. F. Leslie Seidle (Toronto: Institute for Research on Public Policy, 1993), pp. 31–60.

9. Quoted in Mary C. Hurley and James R. Robertson, "Sexual Orientation and Legal Rights," Library of Parliament, Research Branch, Current Issue Review 92–1E, p. 5.

10. I have written in detail on Bill 7 in David M. Rayside, "Gay Rights and Family Values: The Passage of Bill 7 in Ontario," *Studies in Political Economy*, no. 26 (Summer 1988): 109–47.

11. Reported in "Liberal MP Says Gays Are 'Unnatural,'" *Toronto Star*, 21 September 1994.

12. Prime ministerial aides were more dismissive, suggesting that dissidents numbered only about a dozen.

13. See, for example, the editorial "Sexual Orientation," *Toronto Star*, 10 April 1995.

14. David Vienneau and Tim Harper, "Fall in Line—or Else PM Warns Rebel MPs," *Toronto Star*, 14 June 1995. See also Tu Thanh Ha and Susan Delacourt, "PM Threatens to Block Rebels' Candidacy," *Globe and Mail*, 15 June 1996.

15. Memorandum to Members of Reform Caucus Task Force on the Family, 16 August 1994. The chair was MP Sharon Hayes, from the fundamentalist right portion of the caucus, who was "dogged in terms of getting the family agenda onto the agenda of the caucus." Interview with Reform Party member, 2 November 1996.

16. Quoted in Tu Thanh Ha, "Reform to Debate Spreading Its Wings," *Globe and Mail*, 14 October 1994; and see survey, ibid.

17. He then added, "I have never in my experience, inside or outside of this House, heard anyone call for active discrimination against individual homosexuals." House of Commons, *Debates*, 1 June 1995, pp. 13157–58.

18. Susan Delacourt, "Liberals Could Renege on Promise to Homosexuals," *Globe and Mail*, 21 February 1996.

19. For example, see the front-page story by Ann McIlroy, "Yalden Flunks Liberals on Gay Rights," *Globe and Mail*, 20 March 1996.

20. Interview with Liberal activist, 29 April 1996.

21. As one Liberal activist in Ottawa noted, this resolution was not very charitable toward single mothers as well as gays and lesbians. Interview, 29 April 1996.

22. The booklet's response to the question "Won't this mean the government will have to amend 40 or 50 other statutes?" was: "No. This amendment does not deal with benefits for same-sex partners. No other changes to federal legislation are planned or necessary as a result of this amendment." "Working against Discrimination: The Amendment to the Canadian Human Rights Act—The Facts." As one journalist observed, "Rock attempted to head off opposition with careful wording in the bill itself and a government brochure stating the legislation will have little practical effect other than to bring the federal human rights act in line with court rulings and human rights codes in seven provinces." Joan Bryden, "Gay Rights Legislation Introduced," *Ottawa Citizen* 30 April 1996.

23. Headline story in *Toronto Star*, 30 April 1996. Ringma is quoted in Peter O'Neil, "Gay Would Be Fired If Business Hurt: MP"; Chrétien is quoted in Anne McIlroy and Susan Delacourt, "Chrétien on Attack Over Rights for Gays," *Globe and Mail*, 1 May 1996.

24. One of the first media reports of the interview appeared in "Reformer Quits as Party Whip," *Toronto Sun*, 2 May 1996. In a subsequent interview with the *Sun*, Chatters qualified his statement by arguing that firing would be justified only if an employee were openly promoting homosexuality. Reform deputy leader cited in Anne McIlroy, "Ringma Responds as Whip after 'Unequivocal Apology,'" *Globe and Mail*, 2 May 1996.

25. The estimate of ten is cited from Bloc Québécois MP Real Ménard, in Gilles Gauthier, "Le 'Vote Libre' Evite une Crise aux Communes," *La Presse*, 2 May 1996.

26. Sean Durkan, "Gay Bill on Fast Track," *Toronto Sun*, 2 May 1996. Committee deliberations were accompanied with instructions from the Liberal front bench to have it ready for final approval in a week.

27. See House of Commons, *Debates*, 30 April 1996, p. 2106. The Income Tax Act has this effect because of tax deductions for pension contributions and income.

28. He was questioned on this by Reform MP Sharon Hayes, Bloc Québécois MP Real Ménard, and Svend Robinson of the NDP. House of Commons, Standing Committee on Human Rights and the Status of Persons with Disabilities, *Evidence*, 1 May 1996.

29. House of Commons, *Debates*, 7 May 1996, pp. 2453–54.

30. Quoted in David Vienneau, "Gay Rights Law to Pass Today," *Toronto Star*, 9 May 1996.

31. Derek Ferguson, "Manning Rejects Action against MP," *Toronto Star*, 9 May 1996; and Chantal Hébert, "Le Vote sur l'Orientation Sexuelle Met à l'Epreuve la Solidarité des Partis," *La Presse*, 10 May 1996.

32. Anne McIlroy, "Bill Protecting Gays Moves on to Senate," *Globe and Mail*, 10 May 1996.

33. Gays of Ottawa, a local group formed in 1970, had included some such work in its mandate but was not preoccupied by it.

34. See, for example, "Gay-Rights Group Releases Letter," *Globe and Mail*, 19 April 1996.

35. Interview, 26 June 1996.

36. Apart from a small group in Toronto established after the defeat of Ontario's Bill 167, gays and lesbians have no institutionalized groups providing funding for court cases. The Canadian Civil Liberties Association and at times the Legal Education and Action Fund (a Toronto-based feminist litigation group) have been notable for their lack of support on sexual orientation cases.

37. Toward the end of the long saga leading up to the passage of Bill C-33, the Canadian Human Rights Campaign emerged as a second gay lobby group. It presented a brief on the bill and was thought to have met the justice minister before that. The group's approach seems an echo of the cautious and accommodating approach once characteristic of EGALE, and likely to isolate it from most gay/lesbian activist networks outside Parliament Hill. It certainly played nothing like EGALE's role in applying pressure to the government and developing credibility with the media. It is too early to tell whether the Canadian Human Rights Campaign will endure.

38. House of Commons, *Debates*, 7 May 1996, p. 2444.

39. Reform MP Jim Abbott, in House of Commons, *Debates*, 14 June 1995, p. 13817.

40. House of Commons, *Debates*, 14 June 1995, pp. 13825, 13831. Stan Dromisky was another MP who talked of being frightened by the language in a few of the letters. House of Commons, *Debates*, 7 May 1996, p. 2425.

41. Interview, 1 July 1996.

42. Interview, 26 June 1996.

43. "Another Step," editorial, *Toronto Sun*, 1 May 1996.

44. David Taras, "Political Parties as Media Organizations: The Art of Getting Elected," in *Canadian Parties in Transition*, 2d ed., ed. A. Brian Tanguay and Alain-G. Gagnon (Scarborough, Ont.: Nelson, 1996), p. 425.

45. "The Right to Be Wrong," *Globe and Mail*, 29 September 1994.

46. "Justice Delayed for Homosexuals," *Globe and Mail*, 22 February 1996.

47. Editorial, *The Province*, 22 March 1996.

48. Interview, 29 April 1996.

49. Interview, 29 April 1996.

50. Robert Miller, "The Meaning of Party," *Parliamentary Government* 6 (1987): 6–7.
51. Interview, 13 October 1995.
52. See Jenefer Curtis, "Good as Goldenberg," *Saturday Night* (February 1997): 47.
53. Interview with Liberal aide, 13 October 1995.
54. Interview, 29 April 1996. Alain Dubuc, in "Le Beau Geste Raté," *La Presse*, 3 May 1996, speculated in print about the role of the tax promise in moving the government to act on human rights.
55. "The Liberals and Gay Rights," editorial, *Globe and Mail*, 11 May 1996.
56. Murray Dobbin, quoted in Derek Ferguson, "Has Manning Got the 'Right Stuff?' " *Toronto Star*, 4 June 1996.
57. Quoted in "The EGALE Election Project," August 1993, p. 6.
58. Dalton Camp, "Reform's Circled Wagons Look Strangely Like Walls," *Toronto Star*, 19 October 1994.
59. Editorial, *Globe and Mail*, 2 May 1996. The editorial then went on to comment on Jean Chretien's silence over past comments by his own backbenchers and his early lack of leadership on the issue.
60. Ross Howard, "Reform's Grassroots Dig in on Tough Ground," *Globe and Mail*, 8 June 1996. See also Susan Delacourt, "Reformers Adopt Equality Policy," *Globe and Mail*, 7 June 1996.
61. In September 1995, eight voted against a private member's bill proposing recognition of same-sex relationships (including justice critic Pierrette Venne), and additional opponents may have stayed out of the House. House of Commons, *Debates*, 18 September 1995, pp. 14507–80.
62. House of Commons, *Debates*, 30 April 1996, pp. 2117–18.
63. The responses of NDP MPs to an EGALE survey conducted before the 1993 election were notable for their strong support of gay and lesbian equality, including relationship recognition.
64. On court judgments, see Hurley and Robertson, "Sexual Orientation and Legal Rights"; Douglas Sanders, "Constructing Lesbian and Gay Rights," *Canadian Journal of Law and Society* 9:2 (1994): 99–143. There was one court decision, in the Alberta Court of Appeal in February 1996, that contradicted the trend. In *Vriend v. Alberta*, the court ruled that human rights statutes did not have to conform to judicial reading of the Charter in every respect. This may well have contributed to a change of heart on Rock's part about the urgency of legislative action.
65. Canadians, however, are somewhat less likely than Americans to support equal rights for homosexual teachers. See Paul M. Sniderman et al., *Clash of Rights: Liberty, Equality, and Legitimacy in Pluralist Democracy* (New Haven: Yale University Press, 1996), pp. 105–07.
66. One 1990 survey found that while 81 percent of Canadians approved of extending civil rights to include gays and lesbians, 60 percent had difficulty accepting homosexuality as normal. Study conducted by Reginald Bibby, reported in Michael Valpy, "Canadians' Ideas on Sex Stabilizing, Survey Finds," *Globe and Mail*, 1 April 1991. REAL Women of Canada cited a May 1992 Gallup Poll showing 61 percent opposing legal recognition of same-sex relationships, and a 1994 Angus Reid poll showing 67 percent opposing the introduction of "special benefits" to same-sex couples. House of Commons, Standing Committee on Human Rights and the Status of Persons with Disabilities, *Evidence*, 2 May 1996, 17:55.
67. Reported in Andrew Duffy, "Gay Marriages Gain Acceptance," *Vancouver Sun*, 7 June 1996.
68. On the 1995 poll, see C. M. Donald, "The Spousal Collection," Coalition for Lesbian and Gay Rights in Ontario, 1997, p. 48. On the earlier poll, see David Rayside and Scott Bowler, "Public Opinion and Gay Rights," *Canadian Review of Sociology and Anthropology* 25 (November 1988): 649–60.
69. Cited in Anne McIlroy, "Adoption Cited for No Vote on Gay Bill," *Globe and Mail*, 3 May 1996.
70. See "How We Differ: Maclean's/CTV Poll," *Maclean's*, 3 January 1994, p. 12.
71. Interview, 3 June 1993.
72. Interview, 2 November 1994.
73. Sniderman et al., *Clash of Rights*, p. 105. Ninety-one percent of New Democratic parliamentarians were supportive, as were 84 percent of those attached to the Parti Québécois (the provincial counterpart to the Bloc Québécois.)
74. Interview, 31 October 1994.

75. Interview with Liberal aide, 13 October 1995.

76. *INFOEGALE* (Fall-Winter 1996): 3.

77. David Gamble, "Rock Knocks Same-Sex Bill," *Toronto Sun*, 27 May 1994.

78. Reported in Tu Thanh Ha, "Idea of Extending Benefits Revived by Justice Minister," *Globe and Mail*, 31 May 1995.

79. Half of the Liberals supporting the bill were women, including Deputy Prime Minister Sheila Copps. See House of Commons, *Debates*, 18 September 1995, pp. 14507–8.

80. According to one constitutional law expert, the preamble to Bill C-33 and the explanatory booklet accompanying the legislation could well reinforce the reluctance of courts to recognize those relationships fully (John Whyte, "Clouding Equality: The Rights Bill Comes with a Subtext," *Globe and Mail*, 9 May 1996). Gary Kinsman talks about the limitedness of change on a number of fronts, and its restriction to narrow rights implicitly aimed at "normal" and "responsible" individuals (*The Regulation of Desire*, esp. chap. 10).

81. EGALE's John Fisher indicated a preference for a preamble that would acknowledge that there are many different family forms in Canadian society. House of Commons, Standing Committee on Human Rights and the Status of Persons with Disabilities, *Evidence*, 1 May 1996.

82. Interview with parliamentary aide, 26 June 1996. Rock had promised a future move to delete the specific list of grounds in the section in additional amendments to the Human Rights Act. Follow through on such a commitment seemed unlikely, given the near-certainty of controversy.

83. Interview, 31 October 1994.

84. I was one such activist, formally responsible for coordinating the campaign to support the amendment. Didi Herman has useful observations on that campaign, although at times she imagines that those in the campaign were more absorbed in prioritizing legal reformism than they were. See Didi Herman, *Rights of Passage: Struggles for Lesbian and Gay Equality* (Toronto: University of Toronto Press, 1994), chaps. 3–4. See also Rayside, "Gay Rights and Family Values."

5. The Fight for Relationship Recognition in Ontario

1. The statement read: "All people, regardless of sexual orientation, have the right to determine for themselves their primary personal relationships and to have those relationships supported and recognized in law and by social institutions. CLGRO believes that, whereas our preference would be that benefits be available on an individual basis (with allowances for the dependence of children, the aged and the disabled), whenever benefits are available to heterosexuals living in couples, these same benefits also must be made available to same-sex couples on the same footing." "The CLGRO Relationship Recognition Lobbying Kit," 1993.

2. The benefits package made an exception of survivor pension benefits, since the provincial government's policy was constrained by federally regulated income tax law.

3. Nancy Jackman campaign literature, cited by Thomas Walkom, "Liberals Most Subtle of Political Players on Gay Rights Issue," *Toronto Star*, 26 May 1994.

4. Eleanor Brown, "Whose Side Are You On?" *Xtra!* 10 June 1994, p. 12. On March 9 McLeod wrote to Rae, "I am writing to urge your government to act on the issue of the extension of family and survivor benefits to same-sex couples and the CLGRO brief." She referred to an earlier letter to the attorney general, "asking for action on the government's review of all provincial policies and laws that contain a definition of 'spouse,' with a view to possible reform."

5. Interview with Liberal activist, 22 June 1994.

6. Interview, 22 June 1994.

7. The proposed human rights code amendments were initially thought to leave unaffected the other statutes in need of change, though some legal opinion later on suggested that they could have more sweeping repercussions.

8. Attorney General Howard Hampton and his supporters claimed to have been more active with the file when he was running for the NDP leadership in 1996. If so, few others seem to have been aware of it. Glenn Wheeler, "Bitter Gays Find an NDP Fall Guy," *Now*, 25 April–1 May 1996, p. 25.

9. Alex Munter, "Fighting for Our Families: The Challenge of Mobilizing Ontario's Lesbian, Gay and Bisexual Communities," unpublished ms., April 1994, p. 3.
10. Some proponents of this strategy seemed to favor an eventual broadening of the Murphy bill through amendment; others anticipated that the government would introduce its own much broader bill after public hearings on Bill 45. Boyd was thought to favor the latter. Interview with NDP activist, 25 September 1994.
11. This was Bill 55, introduced by Conservative Don Cousens and withdrawn in the face of protest.
12. Thomas Walkom, "Same-Sex Struggle Mismanaged from the Start," *Toronto Star*, 11 June 1994.
13. Glen Cooly, "Rae vs. Rae," *Now*, 7–13 April 1994, p. 13; Thomas Walkom, "NDP Skittish over Same-Sex Spousal Rights," *Toronto Star*, 21 April 1994.
14. William Walker, "Rae Eyes Free Vote on Gay Benefits," *Toronto Star*, 29 April 1994.
15. Joseph Couture, "Attorney-General Appeals to Armchair Activists," *Xtra!* 27 May 1994, p. 11.
16. Interview, 21 July 1994. In the end, the bill sought the amendment of the human rights code and fifty-six other statutes.
17. Craig McInnes, "Vote on Same-Sex Issue Test of NDP Solidarity," *Globe and Mail*, 12 May 1994.
18. *LGBC News* (Newsletter of the Ontario NDP Lesbian, Gay, and Bisexual Committee), no. 9, 10 August 1994, p. 3. Mammolitti was quoted in William Walker, "Gay Rights Bill May Die Tomorrow," *Toronto Star*, 18 May 1994.
19. Paper, pens, and tips for writing MPPs were also made available. Nicholas van Rijn, "Catholics Told: Fight Same-Sex Benefits," *Toronto Star*, 29 May 1994.
20. George Smitherman, quoted in Martin Mittelstaedt, "Same-Sex Bill Called Model of Tolerance," *Globe and Mail*, 2 June 1994.
21. Common law relationships are entitled to almost all the benefits and responsibilities of marriage in Canada. The divisiveness of the marriage issue, and the unwillingness (for a time) of gay/lesbian activists to wage battle on that front, has been evident in the United States. In striking contrast, a consultative process spearheaded by EGALE in 1995 led to the termination of a court case by a gay male couple in Ottawa who claimed the right to a marriage license. Marriage was kept off the agenda at the provincial level, in any event, because its definition in law lay within federal jurisdiction.
22. Environics, *Focus Ontario*, no. 2, (1994): 38.
23. On the Canadian union movement's relationship to sexual orientation issues, see Gerald Hunt, "Sexual Orientation and the Canadian Labour Movement," *Rélations Industrielles/Industrial Relations*, vol. 52, no. 4 (Fall 1997).
24. Interview with gay activist, 21 July 1994.
25. See, for example, Sheryl Smolkin, "Who Is a Spouse?" *Benefits Canada* (January 1992): 15–16.
26. Interview, 29 September 1994.
27. Interview, 22 September 1994.
28. Interview, 22 June 1994.
29. The Legal Education and Action Fund (nongovernmental litigation group) and the Ontario Women's Directorate were thought to oppose the campaign for benefits. Interview, 23 June 1994.
30. Interview, 20 June 1994.
31. Interview, 29 September 1994.
32. Interview, 23 June 1994.
33. See, for example, William Walker, "50% of Ontarians Want New Same-Sex Bill: Poll," *Toronto Star*, 15 August 1994.
34. See David Rayside, "Gay Rights and Family Values." *Studies in Political Economy*, no. 26 (Summer 1988): 109–47.
35. See Tim McCaskell, "The Bigots Grab for Power," *Xtra!* 3 September 1994, p. 15. The organizing handbook for the principal lobbying group against changes in the school system advises members to avoid sitting together as a group, making religious arguments, or identifying themselves as linked to the organization doing the mobilizing.
36. Interview, 20 June 1993.
37. Interview, 21 June 1994.

38. Interview, 27 June 1994.
39. Interview, 23 June 1994.
40. Interview, 21 June 1994.
41. Interview, 22 June 1994. One journalist differed in characterizing McLeod as having some sympathy with more progressive ideas, including those linked to feminism, but shifting to the right as a response to public opinion polling. Interview, 20 June 1994.
42. Interview, 27 June 1994.
43. Interview, 6 October 1994.
44. Interview, 23 September 1994.
45. Interview, 20 June 1994.
46. Interview, 22 June 1994.
47. Interview, 30 November 1995.
48. Interview, 22 September 1994.
49. See, for example, Walkom, "Same-Sex Struggle Mismanaged from the Start."
50. Interview, 22 September 1994.
51. Interview, 19 April 1995.
52. Interview, 30 November 1995.
53. Interview, 22 September 1994.
54. Interview, 30 November 1995.
55. Interview, 22 September 1994.
56. Interview, 23 September 1994.
57. Walkom, "Same-Sex Struggle Mismanaged from the Start." The "kamikaze" comment appeared in earlier column, "The Real Aim of Same-Sex Campaign," *Toronto Star*, 4 June 1994.
58. Interview, 22 September 1994.
59. Interview with legislative aide, 21 June 1994.
60. Interview, 23 September 1994.
61. Interview with legislative aide, 21 June 1994.
62. John Argue makes the point that NDP ministers such as Marion Boyd and Evelyn Gigantes had always stressed the importance of maintaining pressure on the government to achieve what the gay/lesbian communities wanted. Private correspondence, 15 February 1995. Still, coupling such admonitions with assurances of intentions to proceed sent at best an ambiguous message.
63. Chuck Rachlis and David Wolfe, "An Insider's View of the NDP Government in Ontario: The Politics of Permanent Opposition Meets the Economics of Permanent Recession," in *The Government and Politics of Ontario*, 5th ed., ed. Graham White (Toronto: University of Toronto Press, 1997), pp. 331–64.
64. Interview, 30 November 1995.
65. Interview, 27 June 1994.
66. See Ed Jackson and Stan Persky, eds., *Flaunting It!* (Vancouver and Toronto: New Star and Pink Triangle Press, 1982); Gary Kinsman, *The Regulation of Desire: Homo and Hetero Sexualities*, 2d ed. (Montreal: Black Rose, 1996); Tim McCaskell, "The Bath Raids and Gay Politics," in *Social Movements/Social Change: The Politics and Practice of Organizing*, ed. Frank Cunningham et al. (Toronto: Between the Lines, 1988), pp. 169–88.
67. See David Rayside and Evert Lindquist, "Canada: Community Activism, Federalism, and the New Politics of Disease," in *AIDS in the Industrialized Democracies: Passions, Politics and Policies*, ed. David Kirp and Ronald Bayer (New Brunswick, N.J.: Rutgers University Press, 1992); pp. 49–98; and "AIDS Activism and the State in Canada, *Studies in Political Economy*, no. 26 (Summer 1988): 37–76.
68. This is a point given particular emphasis by sociologist Barry Adam from his vantage point in Windsor. Personal correspondence, 8 February 1995.
69. Interview, 22 June 1994.
70. Interview, 20 June 1994.
71. Interview, 20 June 1994.
72. Tom Warner, a longtime CLGRO leader, has argued that unity over the issue became more tenuous over time, and has raised important questions about the consequences of pursuing a strategy based wholly on incorporating same-sex relationships into existing law. He himself felt

that the campaign increasingly attracted supporters preoccupied with short-term legislative reform, creating unease in those like him who sought broader social change, and were worried about privileging same-sex relationships that mirrored heterosexual marriage. Nonetheless, the pursuit of relationship recognition, short of marriage, did enjoy widespread community support at the time of the Bill 167 debate, and still does. See Tom Warner, "Story of a Same-Sex Spousal Rights Strategy," *Xtra!*, 5 June 1997, p. 28.

73. Interview, 27 June 1994.
74. Munter, "Fighting for Our Families," p. 3.
75. Interview, 27 June 1994.
76. Quoted in Munter, "Fighting for our Families," p. 5. Barry Adam observes about the campaign: "It is very difficult to mobilize the grassroots when it is not clear who the enemy is. Gay/lesbian people outside the inner circles were tired of being told to write another letter to their MPP year after year. If the government had let the party and the movement know what was going on (and if they had had a strategy at all!), then it would have been possible to inspire local people to lobby Liberals, recalcitrant NDP MPPs, etc." Personal correspondence, 8 February 1995.
77. Munter, "Fighting for our Families,", p. 6.
78. Interview, 22 June 1994.
79. Interview, 23 September 1994.
80. Interview, 23 June 1994.
81. Interview, 21 July 1994.
82. Interview, 27 June 1994.
83. Interview, 22 September 1994.
84. Derek Leebosh has written about the lessons of the election along these lines in *Xtra!* 23 June 1995, p. 41. He was told by the NDP MP for Cochrane South (a mining area in northern Ontario) that when planted questions challenged his strong support for Bill 167, audience members roundly booed the questioner. Personal correspondence, 12 October 1995.
85. Some socially conservative MPPs were unhappy with the neglect of such issues, but they seemed largely on the margins, and likely to remain so at least as long as the party retained popularity on the basis of spending cuts and tax reductions. See Scott Anderson, "Tory Tempest," *Now Magazine*, 13–19 March 1997, pp. 18, 19, 26.
86. For a detailed chronicle of court cases and related events, see C. M. Donald, "The Spousal Collection," CLRGO, Toronto, 1997.
87. See Margot Gibb-Clark, "Same-Sex Health Benefits Ordered," *Globe and Mail*, 14 June 1996. Justice Minister Rock indicated that it would abide by the ruling on the provision of benefits but challenge the requirement to review all existing legislation. Anne McIlroy, "Ottawa Extends Benefits for Gays," *Globe and Mail*, 16 July 1996.
88. The case involved two women known as "M" and "H." See Margot Gibb-Clark and Thomas Claridge, "Same-Sex Couples Win in Appeal Court," *Globe and Mail*, 19 December 1996.
89. By the end of 1996, the Canadian Automobile Workers had negotiated same-sex benefits in thirty collective agreements, including those with General Motors of Canada. See Donald, "The Spousal Collection," p. 57.
90. Robert Matas, "Religous Leaders Out to Scuttle B.C. Spousal Law," and Craig McInnes, "B.C. Passes Legislation Redefining Term 'Spouse,' " *Globe and Mail*, 11 July and 23 July 1997. The coalition of opponents included Vancouver's Roman Catholic archbishop, and representatives of Sikh, Orthodox Jewish, Muslim, and Mennonite organizations.

6. The Activist Roles of MP Svend Robinson

1. David Spaner, "From 'Mouthy Kid' to High Profile MP," *Burnaby Now*, 5 February 1986.
2. Interview with gay activist, 22 March 1992.
3. Interview, 22 October 1993.
4. Interview, 22 October 1993.

5. Quote in John Lownsbrough, "Svend Robinson: An MP Who Happens to be Gay," *Saturday Night* (May 1989): p. 38.

6. Reported by Robinson in a 1981 talk at the University of British Columbia. Nancy Campbell, "Let Them Make Love, Not War," *Ubyssey*, 17 February 1981.

7. Shelley Banks, "Robinson: Portrait of the MP as a Young Man," *Vancouver Sun*, 5 February 1981.

8. Interview, 23 October 1993.

9. Interview, 24 October 1993.

10. Interview, 23 October 1993.

11. Interview, 24 October 1993.

12. Devine was quoted as saying, "I don't want my children thinking that this is a normal, reasonable thing to do." "Homosexual Revelations," *Maclean's Magazine*, 14 March 1988, p. 13.

13. Joanne MacDonald, "Gay Candidate Sparks Muted Debate," *Vancouver Sun*, 6 October 1988.

14. Mulroney's comment and other incidents are cited in Lownsbrough, "Svend Robinson," p. 41.

15. Interview with campaign worker, 1 June 1993.

16. Interview, 23 October 1993.

17. E. Kaye Fulton, "Gay and Proud," *Maclean's Magazine*, 16 May 1994, p. 39.

18. Interview, 24 October 1993.

19. Interview, 21 October 1993.

20. *Vancouver Sun*, 28 April 1995.

21. Interview, 2 June 1993.

22. Interview, 2 June 1993.

23. Bill Siksay, quoted in Guido Marziali, "Peck Smears Secure Robinson Victory," *Burnaby News*, 27 October 1993.

24. Presentation to Annual Meeting of Canadian Lesbian and Gay Studies Association, Calgary, June 1994.

25. Robinson confided to the writer of one profile that for years he had been able to raise more money nationally than any other New Democratic Party MP. David Beers, "Political Prisoner," *Vancouver* (September 1994): 40.

26. Quoted in Tom Yeung, "Svend under Siege," *Xtra! West*, 1 May 1997, p. 13. See also Robert Sheppard, "The Battle for Burnaby," *Globe and Mail*, 22 May 1997.

27. Conversation with Karen Murray, reported in correspondence, 5 July 1997.

28. This is a view that is framed by Maurice Duverger's classic distinction between mass and cadre parties. Such categories no longer have the utility that they did when Duverger first wrote, but there remain differences in the seriousness with which parties take membership, and in the importance attached by party leadership to policy convention debates. See Maurice Duverger, *Political Parties* (New York: Wiley, 1954). For overviews of the NDP, see Alan Whitehorn, "The CCF-NDP: Fifty Years After"; and M. Janine Brodie, "From Waffles to Grits: A Decade in the Life of the New Democratic Party," in *Party Politics in Canada*, 5th ed., ed. Hugh G. Thorburn (Scarborough, Ont.: Prentice-Hall, 1985), pp. 192–204 and 205–17.

29. Sue Thomas, *How Women Legislate* (New York: Oxford University Press, 1994), esp. chap. 4.

30. Interview, 3 June 1993.

31. Interview, 8 December 1993.

32. After the 1997 election, 21 percent of the 301 seats were held by women, up from 18 percent in 1993. Forty percent of the NDP's twenty-one MPs were women.

33. This topic is taken up in much of the literature on women and politics, for example, in Sylvia Bashevkin, *Toeing the Lines: Women and Party Politics in English Canada*, 2d ed. (Toronto: Oxford University Press, 1993); and Thomas, *How Women Legislate*.

34. Interview, 3 June 1993.

35. Interview, 3 June 1993.

36. Interview, 28 April 1996.

37. Interview, 28 April 1996.

38. Criminal lawyer Clayton Ruby took the case for legal aid fees, along with Harriet Sachs, well known in civil litigation.

39. Interview, 28 April 1996.
40. Interview, 1 June 1993.
41. Interview, 1 November 1994.
42. Interview, 1 June 1993.
43. Interview, 1 June 1993.
44. These incidents are repeated in Fulton, "Gay and Proud," p. 37.
45. Quoted in Daniel Gawthrop, "Svend the Survivor Beats the Odds," *Georgia Straight*, 26 August–2 September 1994, p. 9. Another staffer comments, "When we send out a notice that he's having a press conference, they show up; they don't call and say, 'Is it important? What's he going to say?' They just show up." Interview, 8 August 1995.
46. Interview, 2 June 1993.
47. Interview, 1 November 1994.
48. Interview, 6 August 1995.
49. Interview, 1 November 1994.
50. Interview, 28 April 1996.
51. Interview, 2 June 1992.
52. Interview, 2 June 1993.
53. Interview, 3 June 1993.
54. Interview 1 June 1993.
55. Kevin Orr, "Svend Robinson: Speaking Out on Capital Hill," *The Body Politic* 91 (March 1983): 15.
56. This was the "notwithstanding" clause, Section 33, allowing federal or provincial governments to legislate in contravention of the charter.
57. Interview, 23 October 1993.
58. Interview, 28 April 1996.
59. Interviews with gay activists, 1 June 1993 and 22 March 1994.
60. Kevin Orr, "Svend Robinson." Since then, Robinson has consistently received ample and favorable coverage in the gay/lesbian press.
61. Interview, 25 October 1993.
62. Interviews with two activists, 24 October 1993.
63. Interview, 20 October 1993.
64. Beers, "Political Prisoner," p. 43.
65. Interviews with activists, 1 June 1993, 21 October 1993. A number of progressive groups, especially feminist, had mobilized against what they saw as a step backward in the accord on constitutional change, particularly in its decentralizing thrust. Robinson's convictions about Quebec'saspirations were part of what drove him to accept the accord despite its weaknesses, and the disapproval he encountered was troubling for him.
66. Interview, 22 October 1993.
67. Ross Howard, "Robinson Seeks to Lead NDP Back to Page 1," *Globe and Mail*, 28 April 1995.
68. Interview, 8 August 1995.
69. There were primaries for party members in each of five regions (Atlantic, Quebec, Ontario, Prairies, and British Columbia combined with the North), and one for labor affiliates. To move on to the October convention, a candidate had to win at least one primary or 15 percent of the total primary vote. The choice of leader would still be left to convention delegates chosen in the traditional manner, with union affiliates assigned 25 percent of the convention's seats. Representation from each region is shaped not only by overall population but also by party membership, so that the Prairie region is allocated 479 delegates as compared to the more populous Ontario with 396.
70. See Gerald Hunt "Sexual Orientation and the Canadian Labour Movement," *Rélations Industrielles/Industrial Relations*, vol. 57, no. 4 (Fall 1997).
71. "It All Comes Down to Svend," *Globe and Mail*, 12 October 1995.
72. Interview, 15 October 1995.
73. Interview, 14 October 1995. This observer also reported that one well-connected McDonough supporter complained that Robinson made few overtures toward others in that camp worried

about electoral survival—about being "painted off the edge"—and speculated that on a second ballot with Nystrom and Robinson, 60 to 75 percent of McDonough supporters would have gone to the former.

74. Interview, 28 April 1996.
75. Glenn Wheeler, "Radical Overthrow of the NDP," *Now*, 19–25 October 1995, p. 16.
76. Interview, 14 October 1995.
77. Interview, 14 October 1995.
78. Interview, 28 April 1996.
79. Interview, 15 October 1995.
80. Interview, 28 April 1994.
81. Cited in interview with Robinson campaign team member, 14 October 1995.
82. Interview, 15 October 1995.
83. Paul Gessell, "Robinson's Homosexuality Is Unspoken Issue at NDP Convention," *Ottawa Citizen*, 13 October 1995.
84. Interview, 2 June 1993.

7. The Military Ban and the Perils of Congressional Politics

1. R. Kent Weaver and Bert A. Rockman point out that the same pattern of fragmentation can slow change and at the same time create openings for innovation. See their introduction to their co-edited volume *Do Institutions Matter? Government Capabilities in the United States and Abroad* (Washington, D.C.: Brookings, 1993), pp. 1–41.
2. Some might claim that in the early 1990s the Republican Party achieved discipline and control analogous to that in parliamentary parties, an analysis mirrored by claims that discipline in British parliamentary parties is declining. The gap between the American and parliamentary systems, however, is still formidable.
3. On the increase of negative campaigning, see, for example, Morris Fiorina, *Congress: Keystone of the Washington Establishment*, 2d ed. (New Haven, Conn.: Yale University Press, 1989), pt. 2; David Price, *The Congressional Experience: A View From the Hill* (Boulder, Colo.: Westview Press, 1992), pp. 155–56; and Roger H. Davidson and Walter J. Olesjek, *Congress and Its Members*, 4th ed. (Washington, D.C.: Congressional Quarterly Press, 1994). The separation of powers also makes it easy to shift blame or evade responsibility for taking a stand.
4. In 1962 veteran Washington activist Frank Kameny issued a press release calling for the lifting of the ban.
5. One report estimated the rate of discharge for women at 8.1/10,000, and for men 3.4/10,000. See Jeffrey Schmalz, "Homosexuals Wake to See a Referendum: It's on Them," *New York Times*, 31 January 1993.
6. Elizabeth Drew, *On the Edge: The Clinton Presidency* (New York: Simon and Schuster, 1994), p. 42; David Mixner, *Stranger among Friends* (New York: Bantam, 1996), pp. 210–11; and Craig A. Rimmerman, "Promise Unfulfilled: Clinton's Failure to Overturn the Military Ban on Lesbians and Gays," in *Gay Rights, Military Wrongs: Political Perspectives on Lesbians and Gays in the Military*, ed. Craig Rimmerman (New York: Garland, 1996), pp. 111–126.
7. See Chris Bull and John Gallagher, *Perfect Enemies: The Religious Right, the Gay Movement, and the Politics of the 1990s* (New York: Crown, 1996), p. 129.
8. Lisa Keen, "Clinton Stands Firm on Vow to Repeal Military's Gay Ban," *Washington Blade*, 13 November 1992, pp. 1, 15.
9. Lisa Keen, "Clinton to Act on Ban," *Washington Blade*, 22 January 1993, p. 1.
10. The Senate, for example, does not require that amendments be substantively related to the bill under deliberation.
11. Interview with administration official, 2 September 1993.
12. White House officials freely admitted that they had no plans to lobby Congress during the six-month cooling-off period announced at the end of January, and gay activists have confirmed that

there was no one in the administration "managing" the issue until June. Clifford Krauss, "Agreement Is Setback for Republican Amendment," *New York Times*, 31 January 1993; and interviews with activists, 30 June and 2 September 1993.

13. Of the 31 senators who had signed on as co-sponsors of the Employment Non-Discrimination Act by the end of the 103rd Congress, only three were Republicans, and of the 136 House members co-sponsoring it, only 6 were Republicans (Human Rights Campaign Fund, "Highlights of the 103rd Congress" [Washington, D.C.: HRCF, 1995]). In the final votes on the ban, one of the Republican co-sponsors in the Senate and two in the House failed to support the pro-gay positions.

14. Interview, 7 February 1995.

15. Interview, 7 February 1995.

16. Interview, 13 February 1995.

17. The Human Rights Campaign Fund counted him as voting favorably on only two out of five votes in their overview of the entire 103rd Congress ("Highlights of the 103rd Congress"). On pro-gay votes listed by the National Gay and Lesbian Task Force, Nunn's support was 46 percent in the 1987–88 session, 70 percent in 1989–90, and 36 percent in 1991–92. Freiberg, "Nunn Vows Hearings on Gay Ban Will Be Unbiased," *Washington Blade*, 5 February 1993, p 17.

18. Nunn's willingness to confront the president on the the gay ban was thought by some observers to be partially motivated by pique at not having been appointed to the cabinet, or resentment at having had his own longer-term presidential ambitions undercut by the success of a fellow southern Democrat. Even if such suspicions are true, other factors seemed more significant.

19. Bill Gertz, "Nunn: No OK for Gays," *Washington Times*, 31 May 1993.

20. Interview with gay activist, 7 February 1995; and Drew, *On the Edge*, p. 43.

21. Thirty votes was, significantly, fewer than the one third required to prevent overturning a presidential veto. Later events were to show that this estimate may have been low by a few crucial votes, though in January there seemed little interest in pushing the issue to the extent of threatening a veto on any legislation to which a restoration of the ban was attached.

22. Lisa Keen, "Clinton Stands Firm on Vow to Repeal Military's Gay Ban," *Washington Blade*, 13 November 1992, p. 15. As the president was finalizing the plan for a six-month delay, he told a reporter: "I agree that any sort of improper conduct should result in severance. . . . The narrow issue on which there is disagreement is whether people should be able to say that they are homosexual . . . and do nothing else, without being severed." Lisa Keen, "Clinton 'Pretty Close' to Plan on Ban," *Washington Blade*, 29 January 1993, p. 1.

23. Senator Nunn and committee Republicans at first seemed dubious about distinguishing between status and conduct, clearly concerned that removing bars against status would allow open declaration of homosexuality. Their nervousness may have been allayed somewhat by one "expert" social anthropologist who testified at the hearings that speaking was a form of behavior. Carrol J. Doherty, "Heated Issue Is Off to a Cool Start as Hearings on Gay Ban Begin," *Congressional Quarterly Weekly*, 3 April 1993, p. 852.

24. Armed Services Committee member Charles Robb was quoted as saying, "That's where the dividing line is now." Pat Towell, "Nunn Offers a Compromise: 'Don't Ask/Don't Tell,' " *Congressional Quarterly Weekly*, 15 May 1993, p. 1240.

25. Interview with Democratic congressional aide, 10 June 1993.

26. See Towell, "Nunn Offers a Compromise," p. 1240; and John Gallagher, "Feds Appeal Meinhold Ruling," *The Advocate*, 6 April 1993, p. 19. Congressman Barney Frank himself believed that early House hearings would have been useful. Interview, 9 February 1995.

27. For a useful account of the reasoning behind and reactions to the Frank compromise, see Chris Bull, "No Frankness," *The Advocate*, 29 June 1993, pp. 24-26.

28. Studds criticized Frank for "prematurely raising the white flag." Eric Schmitt, "Gay Congressman Offers a Plan on Homosexuals in the Military," *New York Times*, 19 May 1993. Frank himself acknowledges that Studds was annoyed at him, though only temporarily. Interview, 30 June 1993.

29. Interview, 2 September 1993.

30. See Peter Freiberg, "Many Wonder What Military Compromise Will Emerge," *Washington Blade*, 11 June 1993, p. 21.

31. Gertz, "Nunn: No OK for Gays"; Pat Towell, "Clinton Calls Compromise Close, but Nunn Won't Deal on Gays," *Congressional Quarterly Weekly*, 29 May 1993, p. 1380.
32. This was being claimed even as late as July 14th. Lisa Keen, "Gays 'Bracing for the Crash,' " *Washington Blade,* 16 July 1993, pp. 1, 13.
33. Lisa Keen, "Was Memo a Smokescreen by Pentagon?" *Washington Blade*, 25 June 1993, p. 27.
34. Tom Sheridan of the Campaign for Military Service asserted that if Clinton took a principled stand on lifting the ban, 45 Senators and 172 House members would support it, with 15 Senators and 101 House members undecided. Pat Towell, "Aspin Seeks a Deal on Gays That the Brass Will Bless," *Congressional Quarterly Weekly*, 26 June 1993, pp. 1670–71.
35. Interview with Democratic congressional aide, 1 July 1993.
36. John Lancaster and Ann Devroy, "Aspin Backs a 'Don't Ask, Don't Tell' Policy on Gays," *Washington Post*, 23 June 1993.
37. Senator Sam Nunn, floor remarks as prepared for delivery, 16 July 1993.
38. Quoted in Pat Towell, "As Clinton Ponders Ban Details, Both Sides Go on Offensive," *Congressional Quarterly Weekly*, 17 July 1993, p. 1889.
39. A July 19 memo to Clinton from Attorney General Janet Reno confirmed that some of the adjustments made even in Clinton's own policy improved its immunity to constitutional challenge over the old policy.
40. Even conservative extremists such as Senator Jesse Helms and Representative Robert Dornan seemed satisfied with the Nunn amendment. See Kitty Cunningham, "The Senate's Last Word on Gays," *Congressional Quarterly Weekly*, 11 September 1993, p. 2401; "Victory over Homosexual Lobby," *Free Americans* (July–August 1993): p. 9; "Two Cheers for Nunn's Legislative Maneuver," *Human Events*, 7 August 1993, p. 5; and William P. Hoar, "Mr. Clinton Loses Again," *The New American*, 6 September 1993, pp. 13–14.
41. Democrats voted 140 to 121, Republicans 12 to 161.
42. Southern black Democrats voted 88 percent with Meehan, and 87 percent of the Congressional Black Caucus as a whole voted yes. See David A. Bositis, *The Congressional Black Caucus in the 103rd Congress* (Washington, D.C.: Joint Center for Political and Economic Studies, 1994), pp. 134, 150.
43. A lower court judgment rendered in March 1995 ruled the new ban unconstitutional, but there is no indication that this and other court decisions on the pre-Clinton ban will survive appeals up the judicial ladder.
44. See Kathy Marks and George Jones, "Fight to Keep Homosexual Forces Ban," and Peter Almond, "Homosexuals Will Hurt Forces Morale," *Daily Telegraph*, 8 June 1995.
45. The contrast with Canada, with a longer tradition of positive regard for political authority, is analyzed in Seymour Martin Lipset, *Continental Divide: The Values and Institutions of the United States and Canada* (New York: Routledge, 1990).
46. See Rimmerman, "Promise Unfulfilled"; also Sean C. Ford, "A Pentadic Analysis of the Controversy Surrounding the Military's Ban on Lesbians and Gays" (M.A. Thesis, University of New Mexico, 1994).
47. Lawrence Korb, "Evolving Perspectives on the Military's Policy on Homosexuals: A Personal Note," in *Gays and Lesbians in the Military: Issues, Concerns, and Contrasts*, ed. Wilbur J. Scott and Sandra Carson Stanley (New York: Aldine de Gruyter, 1994), p. 225; quoted in Alan S. Yang, "Mass Opinion Change with and without Elites: Examining a 'Top-Down' Approach to Public Opinion about Homosexuality," paper presented to the Annual Meeting of the American Political Science Association, San Francisco, 1996.
48. For example, Powell rejected the parallel between discrimination based on sexual orientation to that based on race, invoking the language of the religious right in describing the former as "benign." On the vehemence of his views, see Drew, *On the Edge*, pp. 45–46.
49. Quoted in Art Pine, "Issue Explodes into an All-Out Lobbying War," *Los Angeles Times*, 28 January 1993.
50. Jeffrey Schmalz, "Gay Groups Regrouping for War on Military Ban," *New York Times*, 7 February 1993. David Mixner describes gay leaders as "exultant" at Aspin's appointment, in part because it meant that Sam Nunn was not going to be named to the position, in part because he was seen as a supporter of lifting the ban. Mixner, *Stranger among Friends*, p. 285.

51. Quoted by Peter Applebome, "Gay Issue Mobilizes Conservatives against Clinton," *New York Times*, 1 February, 1993.

52. From 1992 to 1993, the Christian Coalition reported a 20 percent increase in budget and membership, much of the increase arising from its high-profile opposition to the Clinton administration, and much of that based on its stance on the ban. Bull and Gallagher, *Perfect Enemies*, p. 150.

53. Michael Weisskopf, " 'Gospel Grapevine' Displays Strength in Controversy over Military Gay Ban," *Washington Post*, 1 February 1993.

54. Ibid.

55. Kevin Merida and Helen Dewar, "In Boom of Phone and Fax Activism, Citizens Give Government an Earful," *Washington Post*, 1 February 1993. A similar sentiment was voiced by a Republican congressman quoted in Schmalz, "Homosexuals Wake to See a Referendum."

56. Interview, 13 February 1995.

57. Cited in Jeffrey Schmalz, "Gay Politics Goes Mainstream," *New York Times Magazine*, 11 October 1992, p. 41.

58. "Straight Talk about Gays," *U.S. News and World Report*, 5 July 1993, p. 44. Opposition to adoption seems higher than among Canadians, though lower than among Britons.

59. "Feeling thermometers" give respondents a scale from 0 to 100 degrees in order to register their feelings. Average response to gays and lesbians was 29, to environmental activists 77, illegal aliens 39, blacks 60. Cited in Kenneth Sherrill, "On Gay People as a Politically Powerless Group," in *Gays and the Military: Joseph Steffan versus the United States*, ed. Marc Wolinsky and Kenneth Sherrill (Princeton: Princeton University Press, 1993), p. 98.

60. Kenneth Sherrill, "The Political Power of Lesbians, Gays, and Bisexuals," *PS: Political Science and Politics* (September 1996): 470.

61. See Mary Fainsod Katzenstein, "The Spectacle as Political Resistance: Feminist and Gay/Lesbian Politics in the Military," *Minerva: Quarterly Report on Women and the Military* 11 (Spring 1993): 5; and *USA Today*, 22 September 1992 and 12 November 1992.

62. The first was a *Washington Post*/ABC News poll (*Washington Post*, 27 January 1993); the second, showing 41 percent approval, was a *Wall Street Journal*/ABC News poll, phrasing the question in terms of "Bill Clinton's goal of allowing gays and lesbians to serve in the U.S. military" (*Wall Street Journal*, 28 January 1993); the third was a more generally phrased question in a *New York Times*/CBS poll conducted just a few days later, showing 42 percent support (*New York Times*, 1 February 1993); and the fourth a *Los Angeles Times* poll two weeks later, showing 40 percent in favor (28 February 1993). The *New York Times* poll showed a considerable gender gap, with 52 percent of women favoring removal of the ban but only 31 percent of men. Some decline had already been registered by the time of the 1992 election; a *Newsweek* poll showed 59 percent support, and a Gallup Poll 57 percent (both cited in *USA Today*, 12 November 1992). Alan Yang examines these and other data, pointing out the sudden drop in support for lifting the ban and a subsequent revival of pre-debate levels, in "Mass Opinion Change with and without Elites." National election studies in the fall of 1992 and '93 showed relative stability or even a slight increase in support for allowing gays and lesbians to serve, this also suggesting some bounce back from the impact of anti-gay campaigning in early 1993. See Clyde Wilcox and Robin M. Wolpert, "President Clinton, Public Opinion, and Gays in the Military," in Rimmerman, *Gay Rights, Military Wrongs*, p. 131.

63. One poll showed 56 percent agreeing that he was giving the issue too much time and only 29 percent saying that he was spending about the right amount of time. "Straight Talk about Gays," p. 44.

64. Interview, 18 October 1993.

65. Interview, 18 October 1993. One congressional staffer had a similar view of public attitudes: "I've seen the polls where people say, 'Let people live their own lifestyle, we don't care.' But it is very easy when you scratch beneath the surface for people's prejudices, biases, and their uncomfortableness—it is very easy to bring that out." Interview, 29 June 1993.

66. Interview, 9 February 1995.

67. Interview, 9 February 1995.

68. As far back as 1986, he was arguing that a gay rights bill would be approved two to one in a

secret ballot, even though only 70 members of the House were prepared to identify themselves with it publicly. See Rex Wockner, "Congress's One-Man Caucus," *The Body Politic* (July 1986): 21.

69. Interview conducted by Jean Schroedel, reported in "Out of the Closet and into the Mainstream: The Changing Civic Status of Gays and Lesbians," paper presented to the Annual Meeting of the American Political Science Association, San Francisco, 1996, p. 22.
70. Interview, 10 June 1992.
71. See Debra Dodson et al., *Voices, Views, Votes: The Impact of Women in the 103rd Congress* (New Brunswick, N.J.: Center for the American Woman and Politics, Rutgers University, 1995), p. 9.
72. Schroedel, "Out of the Closet and into the Mainstream," p. 25.
73. Bull and Gallagher, *Perfect Enemies*, pp. 73–74, 87.
74. Jeffrey Schmalz, "Difficult First Steps," *New York Times*, 15 November 1992, p. 22.
75. The following morning the White House confirmed that the president was not ruling out duty restrictions. On this, see Mixner, *Stranger among Friends*, pp. 301–3.
76. Interview, 1 July 1993.
77. See Rimmerman, "Promise Unfulfilled," p. 118.
78. Panel discussion on the military, Annual Meeting of the American Political Science Association, Washington, D.C., 3 September 1993.
79. Interview, 1 July 1993.
80. Craig Rimmerman, "Promise Unfulfilled," reports such assurances from White House advisers such as David Lindsey even at the end of January. See also Mixner, *Stranger among Friends*, p. 270.
81. Mixner, *Stranger among Friends*, pp. 275–76.
82. Interview with administrative official, 2 September 1993.
83. Quoted in Mixner, *Stranger among Friends*, p. 314.
84. Quoted in Urvashi Vaid, *Virtual Equality: The Mainstreaming of Gay and Lesbian Liberation* (New York: Anchor Books, 1995), p. 184.
85. Stephanopoulos told Mixner on July 15, "We are still drafting the policy, and I feel that you will be pleasantly surprised. The President and I hope you will know that he did his best and that you will support the policy." Mixner, *Stranger among Friends*, p. 325.
86. Ibid., p. 305.
87. Interview with National Gay and Lesbian Task Force activist, 29 June 1993.
88. Interview, 9 February 1995.
89. There is a great deal of political science literature on the persistence of apathy and disengagement. For a critical view, see John C. Berg, *Unequal Struggle: Class, Gender, Race, and Power in the U.S. Congress* (Boulder, Colo.: Westview Press, 1994).
90. Eric Schmitt, "Months after Order on Gay Ban, Military Is Still Resisting Clinton," *New York Times*, 23 March 1993.
91. Interview, 1 June 1993. Stoddard had been executive director of the New York–based Lambda Legal Defense Fund.
92. Vaid, *Virtual Equality*, pp. 161–62.
93. Quoted in Peter Freiberg, "Gays Now 'Part of the Governing Coalition,' " *Washington Blade*, 6 November 1992, pp. 21, 14. Vaid expressed the same sentiment in Jeffrey Schmalz, "Gay Areas Are Jubilant," *New York Times*, 5 November 1992.
94. Freiberg, "Gays Now 'Part of the Governing Coalition,' " p. 14.
95 Chris Bull, "D-day," *The Advocate*, 10 August 1993, p. 34. Clinton aides were also inclined to the same sort of optimism. See, for example, Eric Schmitt, "Challenging the Military," *New York Times*, 12 November 1992.
96. Interview, 8 February 1995.
97. Both made their remarks at a panel on gays in the military, Annual Meeting of the American Political Science Association, Washington, D.C., 2 September 1993. Similar points were made by political scientists Larry Sabato and Craig Rimmerman, quoted in Bull, "D-day," p. 32.
98. One report has indicated that in 1995 there were 363 violations of the new policy, and in 1996, 443 violations. See Wendy Johnson, "Military Discharges Jump in 1996 by 15 Percent," and

"Secretary of Defense Asks for Probe of Policy Abuse," *Washington Blade*, 28 February 1997 and 1 March 1996. In 1996 there were reports of witch hunts against lesbians in the navy and gay men in the air force. See, for example, Lisa Keen, " 'Witch Hunt' under Way in Air Force, Activists Charge," *Washington Blade*, 26 July 1996, pp. 1, 25; and J. Jennings Moss, "Losing Its War," *The Advocate*, 15 April 1997, pp. 22–30.

8. Barney Frank and the Art of the Possible

1. Both comments are from John Mulligan, "Suited for the House," *Sunday Journal Magazine* (Providence), 26 May 1991, p. 8.
2. Claudia Dreifus, "Being Frank," *Mother Jones* (May/June 1995): 70.
3. Interview, 4 November 1992.
4. Dana Kennedy, "Back Home, Few Warnings for Congressman Barney Frank," *Herald News* (Fall River), 7 July 1990.
5. Interview with constituent, 4 November 1992.
6. Claudia Dreifus, "And Then There Was Frank," *New York Times Magazine*, 4 February 1996, p. 23.
7. Frank is regularly given ratings of 100 or close to that by groups representing organized labor, the American Civil Liberties Union, and other progressive organizations. He is given zero ratings by right-wing groups such as the American Conservative Union and the Christian Coalition.
8. Barney Frank, *Speaking Frankly: What's Wrong with the Democrats and How to Fix It* (New York: Random House, 1992), pp. 17, 21.
9. Joshua David, "Barney Frank: Un-censured," *NYQ*, 8 March 1992, pp. 27–28.
10. Interview, 4 November 1992.
11. Interview with a Boston journalist, 4 November 1992.
12. Dreifus, "Being Frank," p. 72.
13. " 'I Was Emotionally Vulnerable,' " *Newsweek*, 25 September 1989, p. 17.
14. Paraphrased by Barney Frank in Dreifus, "And Then There Was Frank," p. 25. After that, Mrs. Frank became active in seniors' work, eventually becoming president of the Massachusetts Association of Older Americans.
15. After the scandal broke in 1983, he nervously returned for his usual appearance at a Roman Catholic celebration in the working-class town of New Bedford: "Instead of meeting with hatred and anger and ridicule, however, Studds was treated to a four-mile concert of cheers and hurrahs from these Portuguese Roman Catholics." Rex Wockner, "Congress's One-Man Caucus," *The Body Politic* (July 1986): 21. See also Michael D. Green, "Gerry Studds," *Washington Blade*, 19 August 1983.
16. Dreifus, "And Then There Was Frank," p. 24.
17. See Linda Greenhouse, "Why a Congressman Told of His Homosexuality," *New York Times*, 3 June 1987.
18. By then there were about twenty openly gay/lesbian public officials in the United States, at state and local levels in addition to the national level.
19. Kay Longcope, "Why a Gay Politician Came Out," *Boston Globe*, 31 May 1987.
20. Greenhouse, "Why a Congressman Told of His Homosexuality."
21. Barney Frank, "Reaching a Broader Audience," in *Out for Office: Campaigning in the Gay '90s*, ed. Kathleen DeBold (Washington, D.C.: Gay and Lesbian Victory Fund, 1994), p. 147. There are similar tendencies, perhaps not quite as strong, in media coverage and public perceptions of women politicians and candidates from other marginalized populations. See, for example, Susan J. Carroll and Ronnee Schreiber, "Media Coverage of Women in the 103rd Congress," paper presented to the Annual Meeting of the American Political Science Association, San Francisco, 1996.
22. " 'I Was Emotionally Vulnerable,' " p. 17.
23. Jim Schroeder, "The Boys in the Band," *The Advocate*, 17 October 1995, p. 40.
24. *Newsweek*, 25 September 1989. For an analysis of press coverage and constituent response, see

Lisa Keen, "Poll Shows Frank's Constituents Still 'Real Supportive,'" *Washington Blade*, 15 September 1989, p. 7.

25. Interview, 4 November 1992.
26. The panel found that he had acted improperly in trying to fix Gobie's parking tickets, and that he had been misleading in a 1986 memo that might have been perceived as trying to influence a probation hearing for Gobie.
27. *Boston Globe* poll, reported in Keen, "Poll Shows Frank's Constituents Still 'Real Supportive,'" p. 7.
28. Jay Mailin, "Back Home, Conservatives Upset," *Washington Times*, 23 July 1990. In the *Sun Chronicle* (Attleboro) of 30 July, the district commander of a local veterans' organizations was quoted as saying, "We rely on Barney because he's done a good job for vets. His personal preference is his personal preference. He never let that interfere with his job as far as I'm concerned."
29. Interview, 4 November 1992.
30. Interview, 4 November 1992.
31. Transcribed from a tape made available by Barney Frank's district office.
32. Interview, 4 November 1992.
33. Peter Freiberg, "Burstein's Heart-Breaking Loss," *Washington Blade*, 11 November 1996.
34. This was a widely held impression among openly gay officials gathered in convention in Seattle in November 1994.
35. See Chris Bull, "Outward Bound," *Advocate*, 4 October 1994, pp. 40–46.
36. See Schroeder, "The Boys in the Band."
37. He is reported to have been advised by House Speaker Newt Gingrich that right-wing activists were mounting a campaign to unseat him, one that could include innuendo that he was HIV-positive. See Colleen Marzec, "Gunderson Bows Out after Warning from Gingrich," *Washington Blade*, 2 August 1996.
38. Lou Chibbaro, "Kolbe Lauded for Decision to Come Out," *Washington Blade*, 9 August 1996; J. Jennings Moss, "On the Record," *The Advocate*, 3 September 1996, pp. 20–24.
39. Frank, "Reaching a Broader Audience," p. 147.
40. Interview, 4 November 1992.
41. Interview, 4 November 1992.
42. Joanne Peters, "The Clout of Being Out: An Interview with Congressperson Barney Frank," *Etcetera*, 17–23 January 1992, p. 18.
43. Dreifus, "And Then There Was Frank," p. 24.
44. Frank, *Speaking Frankly*, pp. 158–9.
45. "Seattle's Sherry Harris Wins City Council Seat with Victory Fund Support," *Victory: The Newsletter of the Gay and Lesbian Victory Fund*, no. 1 (November 1991): 1.
46. Peter Freiberg, "Dozens of Gays Are Running for Office," *Washington Blade*, 25 October 1996.
47. J. Jennings Moss, "Rude Awakenings," *The Advocate*, 29 October 1996, p. 37.
48. See Hastings Wyman, "Politicians across the Land Quibble over Gays," *Washington Blade*, 18 October 1996; John Gallagher, "Our Way at the Races," *The Advocate*, 29 October 1996, pp. 31–36.
49. J. Jennings Moss, "No Limits," *The Advocate*, 24 June 1997, p. 56.
50. The numbers of candidates varies by report. See J. Jennings Moss, "The Winning Ticket," "Same as It Ever Was," and "No Limits," *The Advocate*, 21 January 1997, pp. 38–39, 10 December 1996, pp. 34–35, and 24 June 1997, pp. 50–60.
51. Workshop at "Identity/Space/Power: Lesbian, Gay, Bisexual, and Transgender Politics," conference organized by the Center for Lesbian and Gay Studies at the City University of New York, February 1996.
52. See Peter Freiberg, "Deborah Glick's Political Courage," *Washington Blade*, 24 December 1993.
53. Interview, 19 November 1994.
54. Interview, 19 November 1994.
55. This is a point made, for example, by Robert P. Weber, "Home Style and Committee Behavior: The Case of Richard Nolan," in *Home Style and Washington Work*, ed. Morris P. Fiorina and David W. Rohde (Ann Arbor: University of Michigan Press, 1989); pp. 71–94. See also Morris

P. Fiorina, *Congress: Keystone of the Washington Establishment*, 2d ed. (New Haven: Yale University Press, 1989); and Bruce Cain et al., *The Personal Vote: Constituency Service and Electoral Independence* (Cambridge: Harvard University Press, 1987).

56. See Sue Thomas, *How Women Legislate* (New York: Oxford University Press, 1994). In the 104th Congress, there were eight women senators (8 percent), up from two in 1990, and 47 representatives (11 percent). In the 105th, there were two more women in the House and one more in the Senate. Among Western industrialized countries, only Australia and Britain fared worse.

57. This is the judgment of Carol Swain, *Black Faces, Black Interests* (Cambridge: Harvard University Press, 1993).

58. See John Berg,"Representation of the Oppressed in the United States Congress," paper presented to the Annual Meeting of the American Political Science Association, Chicago, 1992; idem, *Unequal Struggle: Class, Gender, Race, and Power in the U.S. Congress* (Boulder, Colo.: Westview Press, 1994).

59. Interview, 19 November 1994. The legislative career success of two lesbian members of the California State Assembly, Speaker Pro Tem Sheila Kuehl and Appropriations Chair Carole Migden, would suggest a similar conclusion. See Jonathan Curiel, "Lesbian Legislators," *The Advocate*, 22 July 1997, pp. 37–38.

60. Jerry Gray, "A Witty Debater Emerges as Point Man," *New York Times*, 6 January 1995.

61. Michael Barone and Grant Ujifusa, *The Almanac of American Politics, 1996* (Washington, D.C.: National Journal, 1995), p. 647.

62. Mulligan, "Suited for the House," p. 6.

63. Jeanne Peters, "The Clout of Being Out," p. 18.

64. Greenhouse, "Why a Congressman Told of His Homosexuality."

65. David, "Barney Frank," p. 29.

66. Mulligan, "Suited for the House," p. 16.

67. Interview, 29 June 1993. On legislative norms, see Richard Fenno, Jr., *Learning to Legislate: The Senate Education of Arlen Specter* (Washington, D.C.: Congressional Quarterly Press, 1991).

68. Interview, 30 June 1993.

69. Interview, 29 June 1993.

70. An openly gay state legislator makes the same point: "If you start out with this very hard-line position, you're going to have people that will turn off at the beginning. . . . And then you never get them back." Interview, 18 November 1994.

71. The difficult of working contrary to the norms of compromise is illustrated by Minnesota Representative Richard Nolan, who resigned after six years, frustrated at the difficulties in working within an institution as incrementalist as the Congress. See Robert P. Weber, "Home Style and Committee Behavior: The Case of Richard Nolan," in Fiorina and Rohde, *Home Style and Washington Work*, pp. 71–94.

72. Dreifus, "And Then There Was Frank," p. 23.

73. David Mixner, *Stranger among Friends* (New York: Bantam Books, 1996), p. 186.

74. Phil McCombs, "Out of the Cloakroom: The Anti-Gay Crusade," *Washington Post*, 25 January 1990.

75. Interview, 8 February 1995. On this subject, see Anna Marie Smith, "Why Did Armey Apologize? Hegemony, Homophobia, and the Religious Right," paper presented to the Annual Meeting of the American Political Science Association, Chicago, 1995.

76. This is reflected in the testimony of lesbian and gay legislators across the United States. See, for example, Curiel, "Lesbian Legislators," and Moss, "No Limits." In the latter, Buffalo city councillor Barbara Kavanaugh talks of "advocacy by presence" (p. 52).

77. Interview, 9 February 1995. Gunderson announced his intention to end his congressional career prior to the 1996 election.

78. Interview, 3 September 1993.

79. Interview, 11 June 1992.

80. Interview with congressional aide, 8 February 1995.

81. Interview, 9 February 1995.

82. Interview, 9 February 1995.

83. Interview, 9 February 1995.

84. Interview with Sasha Gregory-Lewis for the *Advocate*, reprinted in *Long Road to Freedom: The Advocate History of the Gay and Lesbian Movement*, ed. Mark Thompson (New York: St. Martin's Press, 1994), pp. 168–69.

85. Interview, 20 November 1994.

86. This demand is not particularly characteristic of lesbian and gay groups. Glick was talking of the feminist organization NOW. Interview, 19 November 1994.

87. Michael D. Green, "Gerry Studds," *Washington Blade*, 19 August 1983.

88. The first quote is from David, "Barney Frank," p. 27; the second from an interview, 11 June 1992.

89. Interview with activist, 9 June 1992.

90. Interview, 11 June 1992.

91. David, "Barney Frank," p. 28.

92. Interview, 2 November 1992.

93. Interview, 8 June 1992.

94. Chris Bull, "D-Day," *The Advocate*, 10 August 1993, p. 35.

95. Ibid., p. 34.

96. Interview, 30 June 1993.

97. Interview, 7 February 1995.

98. Interview, 1 July 1993.

99. Carrie Wofford, "Frank's Compromise Denounced," *Washington Blade*, 21 May 1993, p. 14.

100. Urvashi Vaid, "Compromising Positions," *The Advocate* (June 1993): 96.

101. Interview, 19 November 1994.

102. Comments on "One in Ten," phone-in show on gay/lesbian issues broadcast on WFNX Radio (Boston), 26 October 1992.

103. Mixner, *Stranger among Friends*, p. 231.

104. Interview, 30 June 1993.

105. Interview, 30 June 1993.

106. When it came to a vote in the House, 65 Democrats voted against DOMA, 118 for it. In the Senate, only 14 Democrats voted against the bill.

107. Dreifus, "And Then There Was Frank," p. 2.

108. Dreifus, "Being Frank," p. 73.

109. "Barney Frank," *Monk* (1993): 22.

110. David, "Barney Frank," p. 28.

111. Gay and lesbian movement views of Frank were also influenced by the overall decline of confrontational activism in the U.S. and elsewhere, reflected in the virtual disappearance of Queer Nation and the reduced size and visibility of ACT UP.

112. Interview, 19 November 1994.

9. The Inescapable Allure of the American Mainstream

1. Magnus Hirschfeld's Scientific Humanitarian Committee mounted a campaign in Germany itself that was supported by newspapers, politicians, and thousands of signatories of petitions across the country. Hirschfeld traveled to other countries, including the United States, but political organizing elsewhere was short-lived, small in scale, or nonexistent. See John Lauritsen and David Thorstad, *The Early Homosexual Rights Movement (1864–1935)* (New York: Times Change Press, 1974).

2. See Dennis Altman, *The Homosexualization of America* (New York: Beacon Press, 1982), pp. 126–27. See also Urvashi Vaid, *Virtual Equality: The Mainstreaming of Gay and Lesbian Liberation* (New York: Anchor Books, 1995), pp. 67, 113, 137.

3. John D'Emilio, "After Stonewall," in *Making Trouble: Essays on Gay History, Politics, and the University* (New York: Routledge, 1992); pp. 234–74.

4. Strategic options are influenced by a complex array of factors, perhaps even more than is evident

in the analysis of Jack L. Walker, *Mobilizing Interest Groups in America: Patrons, Professions, and Social Movements* (Ann Arbor: University of Michigan Press, 1991).

5. Both quotes are from Mark Thompson, ed., *Long Road to Freedom: The Advocate History of the Gay and Lesbian Movement* (New York: St. Martin's, 1994), p. 82. See also Altman, *The Homosexualization of America*, p. 123; and Darice Clark, "Building a Movement from the Grass-roots, *Washington Blade*, 17 December 1993.
6. Interview, 8 February 1995.
7. See Sidney Brinkley, "Black Gay History in the Making," *Washington Blade*, 7 February 1997.
8. See Peter Freiberg, "Courting Gay Civil Rights," *Washington Blade*, 3 January 1997.
9. For this and more on the Victory Fund, see Craig A. Rimmerman, "New Kids on the Block: The WISH List and the Gay and Lesbian Victory Fund in the 1992 Elections," in *Risky Business? PAC Decisionmaking in Congressional Elections*, ed. Robert Biersack, Paul S. Herrnson, and Clyde Wilcox (Armonk, N.Y.: M. E. Sharpe, 1994), pp. 214–23. See also Rick Harding, "New National Group Seeks to Raise Funds for Regional Races," *The Advocate*, 18 June 1991, p. 20.
10. See Walker, *Mobilizing Interests*, p. 10.
11. Interview, 9 September 1993.
12. Thompson, *Long Road to Freedom*, p. 98.
13. See Lou Chibbaro, "Open Gays Have Been Visible at Conventions since 1972," *Washington Blade*, 17 July 1992.
14. Quoted in Colin MacKenzie, "Clinton Courting Gay Vote," *Globe and Mail*, 16 July 1992.
15. Interview, 1 July 1996.
16. Quoted in Achy Obejas, "Capitol Hill or Bust," *The Advocate*, 3 November 1992, p. 47.
17. Peter Freiberg, "Gays Bask in Convention Limelight," *Washington Blade*, 17 July 1992; see also Lou Chibbaro, "Caucus Wooed by Candidates, Press," *Washington Balde*, 17 July 1992.
18. Interview, 1 July 1993.
19. Quotes on 1988 and 1992 are from Freiberg, "Gays Bask in Convention Limelight," p. 16.
20. Jeffrey Schmalz, "Gay Politics Goes Mainstream," *New York Times Magazine*, 11 October 1992, p. 18.
21. Quoted in J. Jennings Moss, "Off Camera," *The Advocate*, 1 October 1996, p. 27.
22. Dennis Conkin, "Gay Dems Argue over Visibility," *Bay Area Reporter*, 29 August 1996, p. 18; and Lou Chibbaro, "At DNC, Gay Delegates Showered with Attention," *Washington Blade*, 30 August 1996. Openly gay Texas state representative Glen Maxey agreed that his party had courted gay and lesbian votes in the previous presidential election but now was taking them for granted. Moss, "Off Camera," p.22.
23. Moss, "Off Camera," p. 30.
24. Peter Freiberg, "GOP Convention Packed with Anti-Gay Rhetoric," *Washington Blade*, 21 August, 1992, p.17. On the Log Cabin Federation's formal mandate and structure, see Rich Tafel, "The Log Cabin Federation," in *Out for Office: Campaigning in the Gay Nineties*, ed. Kathleen DeBold (Washington, D.C.: Gay and Lesbian Victory Fund, 1994), pp. 51–52. See also J. Jennings Moss, "The Outsiders," *The Advocate*, 29 October 1996, pp. 22–31.
25. Peter Freiberg, "Convention Curtails Onstage Gay Bashing," *Washington Blade*, 16 August 1996, p. 22.
26. See Matthew Rees, "Homocons," *New Republic*, 8 June 1992, pp. 30–31.
27. Interview, 4 September 1993.
28. Interview, 8 February 1995.
29. Former Task Force head Urvashi Vaid has talked about the resulting sense of political caution, illustrated in HRC's reluctance to devote resources to the Hate Crimes Statistics Act until very late. The leadership of Tim McFeeley led to more principled positions in the 1990s, but there was still a difference in style and in constituency base between the Human Rights Campaign and the Task Force. Vaid is of course not a disinterested observer, but the difference in style and staff makeup is obvious to even a casual visitor. Vaid, *Virtual Equality*, pp. 91–93.
30. Ibid., p. 133. More recently, there have been some attempts to increase contact; see Peter Freiberg, "Legal Knights of the Roundtable," *Washington Blade*, 10 January 1997.
31. Vaid, *Virtual Equality*, pp. 112-13.
32. Jane J. Mansbridge, *Why We Lost the ERA* (Chicago: University of Chicago Press, 1986), p. 3.

33. Vaid, *Virtual Equality*, p. 138. The literature on pressure group politics makes an analogous point, that groups seeking access to "policy communities" are expected to demonstrate a degree of autonomy from or control over their constituency.
34. Vaid, *Virtual Equality*, p. 145.
35. For a critical examination of the compromise issue, see Mary Bernstein, "Countermovements and the Fate of Two Morality Policies: Consensual Sex Statutes and Lesbian and Gay Rights Ordinances," paper presented at the Annual Meeting of the American Political Science Association, Chicago, 1995.
36. This is ongoing work that has produced a number of papers, among them Donald Rosenthal, "Gay and Lesbian Political Incorporation and Agenda Setting in Four New York Cities," paper presented at the Annual Meeting of the American Political Science Association, San Francisco, 1996.
37. Interview, 9 June 1992.
38. Altman, *The Homosexualization of America*, p. 108.
39. Interview, 18 November 1994.
40. Larry Kramer, "Why We Are Failing," *The Advocate*, 13 August 1992, p. 39. See also Vaid, *Virtual Equality*, pp. 352–53.
41. Robin Stevens, "Eating Our Own," *The Advocate*, 13 August 1992, p. 33.
42. "Torie Osborn: 'We Have a Righteous Scepticism,' " *The Advocate*, 13 August 1992, p. 37.
43. Vaid, *Virtual Equality*, p. 366.
44. One Washington-based activist found herself the object of attacks from fellow lesbians, the intensity of which she sees as heightened by their unease with more institutionalized and rule-bound groups. Interview, 11 June 1992. See also Vaid, *Virtual Equality*, pp. 277–78.
45. Altman, *The Homosexualization of America*, p. 116–17.
46. The HRCF board at the time was about one third women, though only two of a total of twenty-nine members were people of color.
47. Useful sources include contributions to Mary Fainsod Katzenstein and Carol McClurg Mueller, eds., *The Women's Movements of the United States and Western Europe: Consciousness, Political Opportunity, and Public Policy* (Philadelphia: Temple University Press, 1987); Anne N. Costain, *Inviting Women's Rebellion: A Political Process Interpretation of the Women's Movement* (Baltimore: Johns Hopkins University Press, 1992); Joyce Gelb, *Feminism and Politics: A Comparative Perspective* (Berkeley: University of California Press, 1989); Lisa Young, "Women's Movements and Political Parties: A Canadian-American Comparison," *Party Politics* 2 (1996): 229–50.
48. This is Costain's point in *Inviting Women's Rebellion*.
49. This is a point made artfully by Maryann Barakso, "Playing with Fire? Social Movements and Electoral Politics: The Case of the National Organization for Women," paper presented to the Annual Meeting of the American Political Science Association, San Francisco, 1996.
50. The description of social movements as fields of action is William Gamson's in "Framing Political Opportunity," paper presented at the conference on European/American Perspectives on Social Movements, Washington, D.C., 1992, p. 15.
51. The federal group EGALE is one of the few exceptions, paying its only staff member, the executive director.
52. Jill Vickers has made this point in relation to the women's movement. See "The Intellectual Origins of the Women's Movement in Canada," in *Challenging Times: The Women's Movement in Canada and the United States*, ed. Constance Backhouse and David H. Flaherty (Montreal: McGill-Queen's University Press, 1992), pp. 39–60.
53. Gay and lesbian involvement in local electoral politics does take place, both in support of openly gay candidates in cities such as Vancouver, Toronto, and Ottawa, and in alliance with other social movement activists in quasi-formations such as Vancouver's Coalition of Progressive Electors. But the links between these activist engagements and the provincial and national party systems are indirect and frail.
54. For a discussion of cycles of protest, and for some of the other trends in social movement literature, see Sidney Tarrow, "National Politics and Collective Action: Recent Theory and Research in Western Europe and the United States," *American Review of Sociology* 14 (1988):

421–40. There are analyses informed by either a class analytical framework or a Weberian one which emphasize the absorptive and assimilationist capacity of the state and its organizational routines. There is also a growing critical literature on law and legal change that points to the ways in which social movement demands are narrowed and distorted as they enter legal, legislative, and administrative processes. For class analytical versions, see, for example, William Carroll, ed., *Organizing Dissent: Contemporary Social Movements in Theory and Practice* (Toronto: Garamond, 1992); and Roxanna Ng et al., eds., *Community Organization and the Canadian State* (Toronto: Garamond, 1990).

55. This is language used by Mary Bernstein in her thoughtful analysis in "Countermovements and the Fate of Two Morality Policies," paper presented to the annual meeting of the American Political Science Association, August 1995, p. 22.

56. This is a point made by Urvashi Vaid in *Virtual Equality*, p 30.

57. Anne Costain's analysis of the impact of the women's movement on American public policy in the 1970s points to the considerable effectiveness of feminists who were haphazardly organized and armed with only limited resources; see *Inviting Women's Rebellion*.

58. By mid-1977, eleven states had banned such discrimination. Lisa Keen, "Clinton Announces Support for ENDA," *Washington Blade*, 20 October 1995; and Chris Bull, "A Clean Sweep," *The Advocate*, 22 July 1997, p. 35.

59. See Sue Fox, "State of the States," *Washington Blade*, 3 January 1997.

60. This and other details of anti-discrimination measures, as well as analysis of why they occur where they do, is provided by Kenneth D. Wald et al., "The Politics of Gay Rights in American Communities: Explaining Antidiscrimination Ordinances and Policies," paper presented to the Annual Meeting of the American Political Science Association, Chicago, 1995; and Steven H. Haeberle, "Gay Men and Lesbians at City Hall, *Social Science Quarterly* 77 (March 1996): 190–98.

61. Vaid, *Virtual Equality*, pp. 139–40.

62. See Lisa Keen, "Gay Legal Activists Still Wary of Supreme Court," *Washington Blade*, 2 August 1996.

63. See Karin Wadsack and Sue Fox, "More Than Half of Fortune 500 Protect Gays," *Washington Blade*, 19 July 1996.

64. Some of these observations are made forcibly by Andrew Kopkind, "The Gay Moment," *The Nation*, 3 May 1993, pp. 590–602.

65. Reported in Vaid, *Virtual Equality*, pp. 18–27.

66. Ibid., p. 235.

67. Ibid., p. 205, quoting *Village Voice* writer Richard Goldstein.

Index

Brown, Jan, 114, 116, 129
Brown, Lord Justice, 232
Brown, Michael, 73, 87, 91–92, 96, 100
Burgess, Guy, 25
Burnaby, 181–89, 193, 199
Burstein, Karen, 260
Bush, George, 220–22, 227, 234, 291
Byron, Lord, 39

Campaign for Equal Families, 148, 165, 167–68, 169, 172
Campaign for Homosexual Equality (CHE), 33, 53, 55, 81, 83, 305
Campaign for Military Service (CMS), 225, 242–43, 274, 293
Campbell, Kim, 110–11, 114
Canadian AIDS Society, 118
Canadian Association for Community Living, 121
Canadian Automobile Workers, 151, 204
Canadian Conference of Catholic Bishops, 123
Canadian Human Rights Act. *See* Human Rights Act (Canada)
Canadian Jewish Congress, 121
Canadian Labour Congress (CLC), 151
Canadian Union of Public Employees, 151
Carter, Jimmy, 289
Cashman, Michael, 18, 47, 87
Catholics/Catholic church
    in Britain, 26, 31, 35, 39, 68, 101
    in Canada, 123, 133, 148, 155–56
    in U.S., 234, 253, 277
censorship, 23, 35, 43
Charter of Rights (Quebec), 109
Charter of Rights and Freedoms (Canada), 11, 13, 41, 106–7, 109, 120, 131, 143, 149–50, 175, 192, 197–98, 200, 232
Chatters, David, 116
Children's Aid Societies of Ontario, 151
Chrétien, Jean, 109, 111, 113, 117, 119–20, 124–27, 133–36
Christian fundamentalism/Christian right. *See* religious right/religious fundamentalism
Church of England, 26, 68
class/social class differences
    as analytic category, xiii, 14
    in electoral politics, xvi, 14, 20–32, 34–35, 39, 43, 65, 90, 180, 189, 195, 253, 261
    in social movements, 5, 7, 12, 180–182, 283, 301–2, 307
Clinton, Bill, 13, 259, 273–76, 278, 289–91, 297, 310
    and military ban, 96–97, 215, 219–22, 224–33, 235–36, 239–41, 243–46, 266, 275–76, 279, 292–93

Coalition for Lesbian and Gay Rights in Ontario (CLGRO), 143–44, 146–48, 165, 167, 169–72, 200
Coalition to Maintain Military Readiness, 233
coming out
    and Barney Frank/U.S. politics, 253–54, 257–58, 263–64, 271, 277
    and Svend Robinson/Canadian politics, 130, 182, 184–87, 195, 197, 211
    and Chris Smith/British politics, 81–83, 90–93, 97, 100
Concerned Citizens for the Family, 185
Congressional Black Caucus, 239, 262, 286
Conservative Family Campaign (CFC), 21, 62, 73
Conservative Group for Homosexual Equality (CGHE), 63
Conservative Party (Britain), 81, 87, 96–97, 99–100, 108, 217, 305, 313
    and age of consent debate, 46–52, 55, 58, 60–64, 67, 70, 72–74, 80
    historical development of, 11, 19–43
    openly gay members of, 91–93
Conservative Party (Canada, Ontario). *See* Progressive Conservative Party
Copps, Sheila, 126, 188
Council of Canadians with Disabilities, 121
Council of Europe, 69
Council of the British Medical Association, 58
court(s), 6, 8–9
    in Britain, 22, 35–36, 38, 43, 48, 95
    in Canada, 13, 41, 106–7, 109–10, 117, 120, 131, 133, 136–37, 194, 312
    in Ontario, 142, 149–50, 153–54, 175
    in U.S. 219, 232, 273, 285–86, 294, 311–12
    See also European courts; judiciary
Cracker Barrel restaurant chain, 272
Criminal Justice Bill, 48–50, 57, 67
criminal law/criminalization, 21–22, 24, 27, 35, 38, 41, 46, 68, 107, 305
Crosbie, John, 110, 193
Cunningham, George, 81
Cunningham, Jack, 30
Currie, Edwina, 22, 44, 49–51, 61–62, 73, 80, 96

Davis, Madeleine, 289
DeBold, Kathleen, 259
Defense of Marriage Act (DOMA), 276, 296–97, 310
DELGA. *See* Liberal Democrats for Lesbian and Gay Action
Dellums, Ron, 227–28, 231
Democratic Leadership Council, 290

mainstream politics/mainstreaming (*cont.*)
 in U.S., 234, 242, 244, 246, 258, 274, 277, 281–314
Major, John, 21, 45, 47–48, 61, 63, 70, 73, 101, 217
Mammolitti, George, 148
Manning, Preston, 104, 116, 128–30, 194
March on Washington (1987, 1993), 272, 274, 277, 280, 285–86, 291, 296
Mason, Angela, 44, 55, 101
Matlovich, Leonard, 219
McDonough, Alexa, 203–10
McFeely, Tim, 241, 244
McKellan, Ian (Sir), 44, 47, 57, 61
McLaughlin, Audrey, 189, 194, 196
McLeod, Lyn, 112, 119, 125, 144, 146, 148–49, 151, 158, 163, 174
media/press, 2, 5, 9–10
 and age of consent, 46–48, 55–57, 59–60, 62, 71
 in Britain, 19, 22, 25, 28, 34, 35–38, 42
 in Canada, 106, 111–12, 114, 118, 120–25, 132, 138
 and Svend Robinson, 184–85, 194–96, 199, 201, 207–8
 and same-sex relationship recognition, 141, 148, 150–51, 155, 164, 166–68, 170, 172
 and Chris Smith, 82–83, 86, 91–92, 94, 100
 in U.S., 257, 281, 288, 290, 300–301, 309, 311–13
 and U.S. military ban, 219, 221, 225–26, 234
 See also tabloid press
Meehan, Martin, 231, 268
Menard, Real, 113, 130, 136, 195
Methodist/Methodism, 34
military, ban on gays and lesbians in
 in Britain, 38, 52, 63, 74, 90, 95–97, 101, 232
 in Canada, 110, 131, 192–93, 232
 in U.S. xiv, xv, xvi, 165, 176, 215–47, 259, 265–66, 268–70, 272–79, 282, 284–86, 292–293, 296, 310, 314
Military Freedom Project, 219
Milk, Harvey, 284
Miller, Tony, 295
Mixner, David, 241, 244, 266, 300
Mondale, Walter, 289
moral conservatism/moralism, xiv, 2
 in Britain, 24, 26, 31, 35, 40–41, 43, 48, 60, 62, 91, 101
 in Canada, 108, 159
 in U.S., 284
 See also religious right/religious fundamentalism

Moses, Herb, 272
Mowlam, Marjorie, 44, 65–66
Mulroney, Brian, 110, 125–26, 185, 195
Munter, Alex, 171
Murphy, Tim, 144–46, 158, 165

National Action Committee on the Status of Women (NAC), 126
National Association of Citizens Advice Bureaux, 58
National Association of Women and the Law, 121
National Black Gay and Lesbian Leadership Forum, 286, 292
National Center for Lesbian Rights, 286, 290
National Coalition of Black Lesbian and Gays, 286
National Endowment for the Arts, 266
National Gay and Lesbian Task Force (NGLTF), 285–86, 290, 292, 295, 300–302
 and Barney Frank, 272, 275
 and military ban, 219, 225, 242–43
National Gay Asian and Pacific Islander Network, 286
National Organization for Women (NOW), 303
National Viewers' and Listeners' Association, 25, 48
New Democratic Party (NDP)
 in British Columbia, 175
 in Canada, 12, 108, 110–12, 116–17, 126, 130, 134, 179–211
 leadership convention (NDP), 205–11
 in Ontario, 141–77, 278
Noble, Elaine, 252, 270
Nunn, Sam, 214, 220–31, 240, 265, 268, 273, 276
Nystrom Lorne, 203–10

O'Neill, Tip, 263
Ontario Association of Professional Social Workers, 151
Ontario Conference of Catholic Bishops, 148
Ontario Federation of Labour, 151
Ontario Public Service Employees Union, 151
Oregon Citizens' Alliance, 259
Organization of Lesbian and Gay Action (OLGA), 18, 54
Osborn, Torie, 300
outing, 72, 92, 257, 272
OutRage, 7, 47, 54–60, 71, 79, 305
Outright Scotland, 58
Owne, David, 33–34

same-sex relationship recognition, xv, xvi, 2, 8
  in Britain, 38, 63, 74, 95, 101
  in Canada, 109, 111–12, 115, 117–18, 130–38
  in Ontario, 141–77
  in U.S., 194, 259, 269, 285, 296, 311–12
Scalia, Antonin, 311
scandal, 33–34, 36, 39, 42, 48, 50, 62, 82, 91–93, 254–55, 257–58, 264
Scargill, Arthur, 28
Schroeder, Patricia, 227–28
Scott, Ian, 158
separation of powers, 217
Section 28, Local Government Bill (Britain), 19–20, 22, 23, 30, 32, 34, 36–38, 43, 45–75, 86, 101. See also age of consent campaign
Servicemembers Legal Defense Network, 286
sex education, 22–23, 51, 63, 267
Shibley, Gail, 259
Siksay, Bill, 195, 201
Silber, John, 256
Simon, Paul, 297
Simpson, Alan, 263
Skelton, Ike, 227, 230
Skoke, Roseanne, 112, 117, 122, 124, 127, 135, 137, 194
Smith, Chris, xiv, 18, 77–101, 179, 184, 188–89, 194, 199, 202, 210, 252–53, 257, 278
  and age of consent, 50–52, 57, 64–66, 70
  constituency issues, 80–87
  standing among lesbians, gays, and activists, 97–101
  stature in parliament and party, 88–97
Smith, John, 48–49, 65, 93
Social Contract (Ontario), 160–61
Social Democratic Party (Britain), 32–34, 81, 85–86
Society for Individual Rights, 284
Soto, John, 255
South Asian Lesbian and Gay Association, 286
St. George–St. David, 144–45, 173, 202
Steele, David, 33
Stephanopoulos, George, 240, 289
Stoddard, Tom, 225, 243
Stonewall (The Stonewall Group), 44, 79, 87, 95–97, 99–100, 305
  and age of consent, 47–49, 52, 54–60, 63, 66, 71–72
strategy/tactics, xiv, xv, 3, 5–8, 12, 14
  in Britain, 53, 56–57, 71, 99
  in Canada, 153, 159, 163–66, 168–70, 176
  in U.S., 243, 251, 260, 266, 276, 285, 292, 294–96, 302–4, 306–8, 313

Studds, Gerry, xiv, 184, 249, 253, 256–58, 264, 266, 268, 271–72, 300
  and military ban, 219–20, 227–28, 235, 238

tabloid press, 23, 28, 33, 35–38, 42, 123–24
  and age of consent, 50, 59–60
  and Chris Smith, 78, 82–83, 84–85, 87, 91–92
Tafel, Rich, 291. See also Log Cabin Republicans
Tatchell, Peter, 18, 27–28, 33, 36, 53, 59, 61, 71–72, 84. See also Bermondsey; OutRage
Tebbit, Norman, 19, 23
Terrence Higgins Trust, 54, 73
Thatcher, Margaret, 11–12, 19–26, 31, 41, 43, 46–47, 59, 61, 63, 81
Thatcherism/Thatcherite politics, 23–24, 30, 36, 38, 45, 70, 77, 101
Thompson, Myron, 114
Thorpe, Jeremy, 32–33, 92
Tocqueville, Alexis de, 13
Tory Campaign for Homosexual Equality (TORCHE), 63–64, 72–73, 92, 293
trade unions. See labor movement
Trudeau, Pierre Elliott, 108–9, 125, 196
Tsongas, Paul, 219, 289
Tucker, Debra, 254
Tuesday Group, 267
Twigg, Stephen, 87, 97, 100

Uniform Code of Military Justice (UCMJ), 220–21, 240
unions. See labor movement
United Church of Canada, 121
United Food and Commercial Workers (UFCW), 205–6

Vaid, Urvashi, 1, 215, 243, 294–95, 297, 300, 302, 305, 313
Victoria-Haliburton, 146, 158
Victory Fund. See Gay and Lesbian Victory Fund
voting, legislative
  in Britain, 31, 45–46, 49–52, 74, 96
  in Canada, 96, 116–18, 120, 126–27, 136, 147–49, 160, 162–63
  free votes, 31, 49, 96, 116, 120, 126–27, 147–49, 160, 162–63, 218

Walkom, Thomas, 141, 163
Wappel, Tom, 112, 117, 127
Warner, Tom, 168, 171
Watney, Simon, 57

Weeks, Jeffrey, 31, 53, 56, 64, 101
welfare state, 4, 9, 170
Wheeler, Glenn, 207
Wheeler, Sir John, 47–48, 61
Wilde, Oscar, 24, 39
Wildeblood, Peter, 37
Wilson, Harold, 27
Wilson, Phill, 290
Wolfeden Report, 21, 32, 37, 40, 43, 68, 80
women. *See* gender

women's movement. *See* feminism/feminists
Woo, Michael, 295
World War II, 25, 26, 40, 42

Yalden, Max, 115
Yeager, Ken, 259
Youths for Social Justice, 203
YWCA, 121

Zbur, Rick, 290